CROSS-BORDER PROTOCOLS IN INSOLVENCIES OF MULTINATIONAL ENTERPRISE GROUPS

ELGAR CORPORATE AND INSOLVENCY LAW AND PRACTICE

Series Editors: Andrew Keay, *Professor of Corporate and Commercial Law, University of Leeds, UK* and *Chief Insolvency and Companies Court Judge* Nicholas Briggs

The Elgar Corporate and Insolvency Law and Practice series is a library of works by leading practitioners and scholars covering discrete areas of law in the field. Each title will be analytical in approach, highlighting and unpicking the legal issues that are most critical and relevant to practice. Designed to be detailed, focused reference works, the books in this series aim to offer an authoritative statement on the law and practice in key topics within the fields of company law, corporate governance, corporate insolvency and personal insolvency.

Presented in a format that allows for ease of navigation to a particular point of law, each title in the series is written by specialists in their respective fields, often with insight either from private practice or from an academic perspective.

Titles in the series include:

Creditor Treatment in Corporate Insolvency Law
Kayode Akintola

Insolvency Practitioners
Appointment, Duties, Powers and Liability
Hugh Sims QC, Rachel Lai, Neil Levy, Stefan Ramel, Holly Doyle, James Hannant and Samuel Parsons

Cross-Border Protocols in Insolvencies of Multinational Enterprise Groups
Ilya Kokorin and Bob Wessels

CROSS-BORDER PROTOCOLS IN INSOLVENCIES OF MULTINATIONAL ENTERPRISE GROUPS

ILYA KOKORIN

PhD Researcher, Department of Financial Law, Leiden University, the Netherlands

BOB WESSELS

Professor Emeritus of International Insolvency Law, Leiden University, the Netherlands and Expert Advisor on Insolvency and Restructuring Law of the European Commission

ELGAR CORPORATE AND INSOLVENCY LAW AND PRACTICE

Edward Elgar PUBLISHING

Cheltenham, UK • Northampton, MA, USA

Published by
Edward Elgar Publishing Limited
The Lypiatts
15 Lansdown Road
Cheltenham
Glos GL50 2JA
UK

Edward Elgar Publishing, Inc.
William Pratt House
9 Dewey Court
Northampton
Massachusetts 01060
USA

A catalogue record for this book
is available from the British Library

Library of Congress Control Number: 2021932443

This book is available electronically in the **Elgar**online
Law subject collection
http://dx.doi.org/10.4337/9781800880542

Printed on elemental chlorine free (ECF)
recycled paper containing 30% Post-Consumer Waste

ISBN 978 1 80088 053 5 (cased)
ISBN 978 1 80088 054 2 (eBook)

Typeset by Columns Design XML Ltd, Reading

Printed and bound in the USA

CONTENTS

About the authors ix
Preface xi
List of abbreviations xiv
List of insolvency protocols xviii
Table of cases xx
Table of legislation xxiii

1. Introduction to *Cross-border Protocols in Insolvencies of Multinational Enterprise Groups* 1
2. The phenomenon of multinational enterprise groups 9
3. Insolvency of multinational enterprise groups 17
4. Cross-border insolvency protocols and agreements: Introduction and evolution 29
5. UNCITRAL and facilitation of cross-border insolvency cooperation: From entity to enterprise 53
6. European Insolvency Regulation (Recast) and group insolvencies 71
7. Legal nature of cross-border insolvency protocols 84
8. General features and limitations of insolvency protocols 101
9. Cross-border insolvency protocols and national law 122
10. Recommendations for use of insolvency protocols in group insolvencies 135
11. Bank insolvencies and cooperation agreements between resolution authorities 172
12. Recommendations for protocols in group insolvencies 186
13. Group insolvency protocol design 194
14. Annex 200

Bibliography 311
Index 323

EXTENDED TABLE OF CONTENTS

About the authors ix
Preface xi
List of abbreviations xiv
List of insolvency protocols xviii
Table of cases xx
Table of legislation xxiii

1. INTRODUCTION TO *CROSS-BORDER PROTOCOLS IN INSOLVENCIES OF MULTINATIONAL ENTERPRISE GROUPS*

2. THE PHENOMENON OF MULTINATIONAL ENTERPRISE GROUPS
   A. The rise of multinational enterprise groups 2.01
   B. Definition of an enterprise group 2.08
   C. Typology of enterprise groups 2.12

3. INSOLVENCY OF MULTINATIONAL ENTERPRISE GROUPS
   A. Entity-by-entity approach in insolvency law 3.01
   B. Corporate group insolvency and 'group insolvency solution' 3.08
      1. Recognition of a corporate group in insolvency 3.08
      2. The rise of 'group insolvency solution' 3.14
      3. The limits of 'group insolvency solution' 3.19

4. CROSS-BORDER INSOLVENCY PROTOCOLS AND AGREEMENTS: INTRODUCTION AND EVOLUTION
   A. Purpose and goals of cross-border insolvency protocols and agreements 4.01
   B. Early cases of cross-border insolvency protocols: Targeted crisis response 4.09
      1. Macfadyen Protocol 4.09
      2. Maxwell Protocol 4.13
      3. Commodore Protocol 4.18
   C. Cross-border Insolvency Concordat and early harmonization process 4.23
      1. Principles of Cross-border Insolvency Concordat 4.23
      2. Application of Concordat Principles in insolvency protocols 4.30
   D. Loewen as a new model insolvency protocol 4.36
   E. Evolution of cross-border insolvency protocols: Initial observations 4.42

5. UNCITRAL AND FACILITATION OF CROSS-BORDER INSOLVENCY COOPERATION: FROM ENTITY TO ENTERPRISE
   A. Model Law on cross-border insolvency 1997 5.01
   B. Practice Guide on Cross-border Insolvency Cooperation 2009 5.11
   C. Legislative Guide on Insolvency Law, Part III 2010 5.17
   D. Model Law on Enterprise Group Insolvency 2019 5.25
      1. Purpose and goals of Model Law 2019 5.25
      2. Scope and tools of Model Law 2019 5.29
      3. Model Law 2019 and insolvency agreements 5.34

6. EUROPEAN INSOLVENCY REGULATION (RECAST) AND GROUP INSOLVENCIES
   A. Background of EIR Recast and treatment of corporate groups in insolvency 6.01
   B. EIR Recast and coordinated solution to group insolvencies 6.07

1. Cooperation and communication in group insolvencies 6.09
2. Group coordination proceeding 6.16

C. Cross-border insolvency protocols under EIR Recast 6.21

7. LEGAL NATURE OF CROSS-BORDER INSOLVENCY PROTOCOLS

A. What are insolvency protocols? 7.01
1. Insolvency protocols and issue of jurisdiction 7.12
2. Insolvency protocols and issue of applicable law 7.19

B. Legal effect of insolvency protocols 7.31

8. GENERAL FEATURES AND LIMITATIONS OF INSOLVENCY PROTOCOLS

A. Procedural principles and insolvency protocols 8.01
1. Procedural efficiency 8.03
2. Fair trial and procedural justice 8.07
3. Transparency and access to information 8.16

B. Compatibility with national law and EIR Recast Framework 8.30
1. Agreement on jurisdiction for claims against debtors 8.32
2. Agreement on COMI and jurisdiction for related actions 8.37
3. Agreement on law applicable to claims 8.41

C. Information exchange and conflicts of interest 8.45

9. CROSS-BORDER INSOLVENCY PROTOCOLS AND NATIONAL LAW

A. Model Law 1997 and common law jurisdictions 9.01

B. Insolvency protocols and civil law jurisdictions 9.09
1. The Netherlands 9.09
2. Germany 9.13
3. Other jurisdictions 9.19

10. RECOMMENDATIONS FOR USE OF INSOLVENCY PROTOCOLS IN GROUP INSOLVENCIES

A. Circumstances supporting conclusion of protocols 10.01

B. Securing protection or best realization of valuable assets 10.05

C. Participation rights and facilitation of group reorganization plans 10.13
1. Right to appear and be heard in group insolvency 10.13
2. Negotiation and implementation of group reorganization plans 10.17

D. Treatment of claims 10.23
1. Resolution of intra-group claims 10.23
2. Agreement concerning common set of financial accounting records 10.28
3. Special intercompany claim resolution mechanism 10.30
4. Agreements addressing coordination of claims and transactions 10.36

E. Supplementing existing cooperation frameworks 10.54
1. Group centralization and group governance in insolvency 10.57
2. Structuring of court-to-court communication 10.71

11. BANK INSOLVENCIES AND COOPERATION AGREEMENTS BETWEEN RESOLUTION AUTHORITIES

A. From self-interest to close cooperation 11.01

B. Cooperation within resolution colleges and crisis management groups 11.05

C. Cooperation agreements between resolution authorities 11.10

12. RECOMMENDATIONS FOR PROTOCOLS IN GROUP INSOLVENCIES

13. GROUP INSOLVENCY PROTOCOL DESIGN

14. ANNEX

A. Maxwell Protocol 200

B. Commodore Protocol 208

C. Everfresh Protocol 217

D. Loewen Protocol 228

E. Inverworld Protocol 241

F. Pioneer Protocol 258

G. Sendo Protocol 268
H. Lehman Brothers Protocol 278
I. Madoff Protocol 291
J. Jet Airways Protocol 298

Bibliography 311
Index 323

ABOUT THE AUTHORS

ILYA KOKORIN

Ilya Kokorin is a PhD researcher at the Department of Financial Law at Leiden University (The Netherlands). In 2017–2019 he was a lecturer in international insolvency and comparative corporate law at Leiden Law School.

His areas of research and scholarship include enterprise group insolvency and the role of intra-group financial arrangements (e.g. cross-guarantees, cross-entity ipso facto clauses and intra-group loans) in rescue and restructuring of distressed multinational enterprise groups, including banking groups. He also explores how new technologies, such as AI and blockchain affect and transform financial practices, as well as rules of financial, corporate and insolvency law. His articles have appeared in the *Singapore Journal of Legal Studies*, *International Insolvency Review*, *European Company and Financial Law Review*, *Norton Journal of Bankruptcy Law and Practice*, and the *Journal of International Banking Law and Regulation*.

Prior to joining the Leiden faculty, he studied in Russia, Hungary and the Netherlands and worked as a lawyer in Saint Petersburg (Russia), where he advised insolvency practitioners and assisted corporate debtors and creditors in restructuring and insolvency proceedings.

He is a member of INSOL Europe's Young Academics' Network in Insolvency Law (YANIL), and Insolvency Tech & Digital Assets Wing, III NextGen IX class and a Committee member of INSOL International's Early Researcher Academics (ERA). He also acts as a coach of Leiden University teams in Ian Fletcher International Insolvency Law Moot.

BOB WESSELS

Bob Wessels has been Professor Emeritus of International Insolvency Law at Leiden University (The Netherlands) from 2007–2014. Prior to this position, he was Professor of Commercial Law at Vrije University (Amsterdam, The Netherlands) (1988–2008). Since 1995 his professorship was only part-time (one day a week). He retired from academia in 2014. He has 45 years of business law experience, including 13 years as a partner of (law firm successors of the corporate legal arm of) EY (Ernst & Young), in Amsterdam and London, including a global managerial function. Since 2005 he has had his own independent (international) legal practice, acting as expert witness for over ten non-Dutch courts and as (international) arbitrator.

He is the Chair of the Conference of European Restructuring and Insolvency Law (CERIL), fellow of the American College of Bankruptcy, member of the American Law Institute (ALI), Honorary Member of INSOL Europe, for which he chaired its Academic Forum, and Honorary Member of the Netherlands Association of Comparative and International Insolvency Law (NACIIL), which he founded.

Since 2010 he has been Expert adviser to the European Commission regarding matters of bank and (international) corporate restructuring and insolvency. His past functions include

Member of the Joint Board of Appeal of the three European Supervisory Authorities (ESAs; ESMA, EBA and EIOPA respectively) (2013–2019); Deputy Justice at the Court of Appeal in The Hague (1987–2016); Chair of the Netherlands Association for Comparative and International Insolvency Law (NACIIL) (2011–2014); Director of the International Insolvency Institute (III) (2004–2010); Consultant to the International Monetary Fund (1998) and the World Bank (1999).

Since 1999 he has been the sole author of the Dutch series Wessels Insolventierecht (10 Volumes, presently in its 5th edition).

PREFACE

Cross-border insolvency protocols or agreements have proven critical in facilitating efficient resolution of complex insolvencies, including insolvencies of large multinational enterprise groups, such as Lehman Brothers, Nortel Networks and Bernard Madoff Investment Securities. They can promote cooperation and information sharing between insolvency practitioners and courts in different jurisdictions, align the adoption of common strategies and restructuring plans, facilitate insolvency estate value maximization by preserving key assets and encouraging intra-group financial support arrangements, help resolve intercompany claims, ensure procedural fairness, the right to appear and be heard, as well as other participation rights (e.g. right to attend creditors' meetings or meetings of a committee of creditors).

Insolvency protocols originated as an innovation of insolvency practitioners and were initially used predominantly in common law jurisdictions. Unlike the early days of protocols, presently insolvency protocols are prescribed and regulated by the European Insolvency Regulation (recast, 2015) and are approved by the UNCITRAL Model Law on Cross-Border Insolvency (1997) and the UNCITRAL Model Law on Enterprise Group Insolvency (2019). They have also found their way into national legislation (e.g. Germany, Spain, France, Australia, Canada).

In the currently overwhelming volume of soft law instruments references to protocols have also been made. These instruments include IBA Cross-Border Insolvency Concordat (1995), ALI-III Guidelines Applicable to Court-to-Court Communications in Cross-Border Cases (2001), European Cooperation and Communication (CoCo) Guidelines (2007) and ALI-III Global Principles for Court-to-Court Communications in International Insolvency Cases (2012). The latter have formed a solid basis for the EU Cross-Border Insolvency Court-to-Court (JudgeCo) Cooperation Principles and Guidelines (2015), which acknowledge the role of insolvency protocols in coordination of cross-border insolvency proceedings. Judicial Insolvency Network (JIN) Guidelines for Communication and Cooperation between Courts in Cross-Border Insolvency Matters (2016) view insolvency protocols as a tool to promote efficient and timely administration of parallel insolvency proceedings.

These developments underline the importance and utility of cross-border insolvency protocols. Nevertheless, despite the general acceptance of their value and practical relevance, the usage of protocols remains limited, particularly among insolvency practitioners and courts in the European Union (EU) Member States. The reasons for this outcome are manifold and include differences between legal systems and cultures, language obstacles, absence of a solid legislative basis, and a simple lack of knowledge about an insolvency protocol, its potential scope and common provisions, its limitations and benefits, as well as circumstances under which a protocol should be considered for adoption. While bringing legal systems and cultures closer to each other is an overly ambitious task, systemizing and building up the knowledge about insolvency protocols are worth pursuing.

This book serves as a comprehensive introduction to insolvency protocols and focuses on their application in the context of insolvency of cross-border groups of companies. Enterprise group insolvency typically leads to multiple (separate) insolvency proceedings opened with respect to group entities in several jurisdictions. This aggravates the collective action problem. It also makes coordination and cooperation between parallel proceedings difficult, but indispensable for the preservation of group synergies and efficient group reorganization or going-concern business sale. Insolvency protocols as a flexible, adjustable and non-binding (or binding) instrument may be used to establish a framework for the resolution of complex group insolvencies, filling the gaps in applicable insolvency law and/or supplementing and elaborating the existing regional arrangements, such as the EIR Recast.

The book aims at education and information sharing for capacity and knowledge building among insolvency judges, insolvency practitioners, practising lawyers as well as students and representatives of academia all over the world. It starts by laying down the problems caused by the prevailing entity-by-entity approach in insolvency of groups of companies. It then traces the rise of insolvency protocols as a way to address these problems in practice and make insolvency proceedings opened with respect to group entities more efficient. Having outlined the origins of insolvency protocols and their evolution over time, the book discusses the modern instruments in the area of international insolvency law, namely the UNCITRAL Model Laws (1997 and 2019) and the European Insolvency Regulation (recast), both of which provide for the adoption of insolvency protocols. It is acknowledged that one of the major impediments to the conclusion of protocols rests with their legal nature. This is why the book pays particular attention to the discussion of the legal nature and legislative basis of protocols, their effects, major features and limitations, linked to the compatibility with certain national and regulation rules. Based on this analysis, previous experience of entering into cross-border insolvency protocol, the review of their most common and unique provisions, the book offers a number of recommendations and guidelines.

The book would have been incomplete without highlighting the role of cooperation agreements within the framework of bank insolvency and bank resolution. The last chapters of the book provide a concise overview of some cooperation arrangements entered into by resolution authorities and other competent authorities in the context of cross-border resolution of banking groups.

In the Annex, this book contains the text of some of the landmark insolvency protocols. These and other insolvency protocols, as well as arrangements for cooperation in the context of bank resolution, referred to in this book, are available in the International Resource Library, maintained and updated by the International Insolvency Institute (III), available at https://www.iiiglobal.org/international-resource-library.

This book has been written as a part of the grant provided by the International Insolvency Institute 'Cross-border insolvency protocols in the context of insolvency of enterprise groups'. We would like to express our gratitude to the III for their support and their trust in us. The III ever since its establishment twenty years ago has always recognized the importance of protocols for improving international cooperation in the insolvency field. Our views and recommendations could not have been developed without the cumulative effort made by individual insolvency professionals (insolvency practitioners, judges, lawyers) creating and working with insolvency protocols. Our texts are therefore dedicated to all working in the global insolvency practice.

This book could not have been made without the valuable help of our junior colleague and researcher Sara Jain. We also thank Adam Crane and Annie Jain for sharing the texts of some of the most recent insolvency protocols with us. Finally, we would like to express our gratitude to Edward Elgar and its excellent team.

Developments have been taken into account until 12 November 2020. For remarks and commentary, the authors can be contacted via: i.kokorin@law.leidenuniv.nl.

Ilya Kokorin and Bob Wessels
Leiden, The Netherlands, November 2020

ABBREVIATIONS

ABTC	AgriBioTech Canada
ALI	American Law Institute
BCBS	Basel Committee on Banking Supervision
BIS	Bank for International Settlements
BRRD	Bank Recovery and Resolution Directive
CBIR	Cross-Border Insolvency Regulations 2006
CCAA	Companies' Creditors Arrangement Act
CCSBSO	Central American College of Banking Supervisors
CDIC	Canada Deposit Insurance Corporation
CEL	Commodore Electronics Limited
CERIL	Conference of European Restructuring and Insolvency Law
CFTC	Commodity Futures Trading Commission
CGBS	Caribbean Group of Banking Supervisors
CGT	Capital gains tax
CIL	Commodore International Limited
CIWUD	Directive on the reorganisation and winding up of credit institutions
CJEU	Court of Justice of the European Union
CMG	Crisis management group
CoCo Guidelines	European Communication and Cooperation Guidelines for Cross-border Insolvency
COMI	Centre of main interests
D-SIBs	Domestic systemically important bank
DIP	Debtor in possession
DLT	Distributed ledger technology
EBA	European Banking Authority
EC	European Commission
ECB	European Central Bank
ECGI	European Corporate Governance Institute

ECHR	European Convention on Human Rights
ECtHR	European Court of Human Rights
ECOMI	Enterprise centre of main interests
EEA	European Economic Area
EIR 2000	European Insolvency Regulation of 2000
EIR Recast	European Insolvency Regulation of 2015 (recast)
EMEAP	Executives' Meeting of East Asia-Pacific Central Banks
ESMA	European Securities and Markets Authority
EU	European Union
EU JudgeCo Guidelines	EU Cross-Border Insolvency Court-to-Court Communications Guidelines
FDIC	Federal Deposit Insurance Corporation
FinCo	Finance company
FSB	Financial Stability Board
FSI	Financial Stability Institute
G-SIFIs	Global Systemically Important Financial Institutions
GIP	Group Insolvency Protocol
Guide to Model Law 2019	UNCITRAL Enterprise group insolvency: draft guide to enactment
HoldCo	Holding company
IBA	International Bar Association
IFSA	Interim Funding and Settlement Agreement
III	International Insolvency Institute
InsO	Insolvenzordnung
INSOL	International Association of Restructuring, Insolvency and Bankruptcy Professionals
IP	Insolvency practitioner
ISDA	International Swaps and Derivatives Association
JIN	Judicial Insolvency Network
JIN Guidelines	Judicial Insolvency Network Guidelines for Communication and Cooperation between Courts in Cross-Border Insolvency Matters
Key Attributes	Key Attributes of Effective Resolution Regimes for Financial Institutions
KSV	KSV Kofman Inc.
LBHI	Lehman Brothers Holdings Inc.
LBIE	Lehman Brothers International (Europe)
Legislative Guide 2004	UNCITRAL Legislative Guide on Insolvency Law – Parts I and II

Legislative Guide 2010	UNCITRAL Legislative Guide on Insolvency Law – Part III: Treatment of enterprise groups in insolvency
Loewen	Loewen Group Inc.
Macmillan	Macmillan Inc.
Maxwell	Maxwell Communication Corporation plc
MEG	Multinational enterprise group
MNE	Multinational enterprise
MOC	Memorandum of cooperation
Model Law 1997	UNCITRAL Model Law on Cross-Border Insolvency
Model Law 2019	UNCITRAL Model Law on Enterprise Group Insolvency
MOU	Memorandum of understanding
MPOE	Multiple point of entry
NBSG	Nordic-Baltic Stability Group
NCWO	No-creditor-worse-off
NNSA	Nortel Networks SA
OAG	Official Airline Guides, Inc.
OECD	Organisation for Economic Co-operation and Development
OHADA	Organisation for the Harmonization of Business Law in Africa
Olympia & York	Olympia & York Developments Ltd.
OpCo	Operating company
p.	page
para.	paragraph
pp.	pages
RBNZ	Reserve Bank of New Zealand
RP	Resolution Professional
Rome I	Rome I Regulation
SDNY	Southern District of New York
SPOE	Single point of entry
SPV	Special purpose vehicle
SRB	Single Resolution Board
SRMR	Single Resolution Mechanism Regulation
TTBC	Trans-Tasman Council on Banking Supervision
UK	United Kingdom
UNCITRAL	United Nations Commission on International Trade Law
UNCITRAL Practice Guide	UNCITRAL Practice Guide on Cross-Border Insolvency Cooperation, 2009
USA	United States of America

VAT	Value-added tax
World Bank Principles	The World Bank Principles for Effective Insolvency and Creditor/Debtor Regimes, 2015
WTO	World Trade Organization

LIST OF INSOLVENCY PROTOCOLS

Insolvency protocol	*Year*	*Jurisdictions involved*
1. Macfadyen protocol	1908	UK, India
2. Maxwell protocol	1992	USA (NY), UK
3. Olympia & York protocol	1993	Canada (Ontario), USA (NY)
4. Commodore protocol	1994	USA (NY), Bahamas
5. Everfresh protocol	1995	Canada (Ontario), USA (NY)
6. Nakash protocol	1996	USA (NY), Israel
7. AIOC protocol	1998	USA (NY), Switzerland (Zug)
8. Solv-Ex protocol	1998	Canada (Alberta), USA (New Mexico)
9. Philip Services protocol	1999	USA (Delaware), Canada (Ontario)
10. Livent protocol	1999	USA (NY), Canada (Ontario)
11. Loewen protocol	1999	USA (Delaware), Canada (Ontario)
12. InverWorld protocol	1999	USA (Texas), UK, Cayman Islands
13. AgriBioTech Canada protocol	2000	Canada (Ontario), USA (Nevada)
14. 360Networks protocol	2001	Canada (British Columbia), USA (NY)
15. Matlack protocol	2001	Canada (Ontario), USA (Delaware)
16. Pioneer protocol	2001	Canada (Quebec), USA (Texas)
17. PSINet protocol	2001	Canada (Ontario), USA (NY)
18. Financial Asset Management protocol	2001	Canada (British Columbia), USA (California)
19. Laidlaw protocol	2001	Canada (Ontario), USA (NY)
20. Federal-Mogul protocol	2001	USA (Delaware), UK
21. Systech protocol	2003	Canada (Ontario), USA (North Carolina)
22. Mosaic protocol	2003	Canada (Ontario), USA (Texas)
23. Refco Capital protocol	2006	USA (NY), Bermuda
24. Eurodis Electron protocol	2006	UK, Netherlands
25. Sendo protocol	2006	France, UK
26. Pope & Talbot protocol	2007	Canada (British Columbia), US (Delaware)

27. Calpine protocol	2007	Canada (Alberta), USA (NY)
28. THL-PMPL Holding protocol	2008	Canada (Ontario), USA (Delaware)
29. Quebecor protocol	2008	Canada (Quebec), USA (NY)
30. Progressive Moulded protocol	2008	Canada (Ontario), USA (Delaware)
31. Smurfit-Stone Container protocol	2009	USA (Delaware), Canada (Ontario)
32. Lehman Brothers protocol	2009	USA (NY), Netherlands, Germany, Australia, Hong Kong, etc.
33. Masonite protocol	2009	Canada (Ontario), USA (Delaware)
34. Abitibibowater protocol	2009	Canada (Quebec), USA (Delaware)
35. Nortel protocol	2009	Canada (Ontario), USA (Delaware)
36. SemCanada protocol	2009	Canada (Alberta), USA (Delaware)
37. Madoff protocol	2009	USA (NY), UK
38. TLC Vision Corporation protocol	2009	Canada (Ontario), USA (Delaware)
39. Barzel Industries protocol	2009	Canada (Ontario), USA (Delaware)
40. Eddie Bauer protocol	2009	Canada (Ontario), USA (Delaware)
41. Graceway Canada protocol	2011	Canada (Ontario), USA (Delaware)
42. Trident Microsystems protocol	2012	USA (Delaware), Cayman Islands
43. Montreal, Maine & Atlantic protocol	2013	USA (Maine), Canada (Quebec)
44. Soundview Elite protocol	2014	USA (NY), Cayman Islands
45. Urbancorp Group protocol	2016	Canada (Ontario), Israel
46. Aralez protocol	2018	Canada (Ontario), USA (NY)
47. Payless Holdings protocol	2019	Canada (Ontario), USA (Missouri)
48. Jet Airways protocol	2019	India, Netherlands
49. LATAM protocol	2020	USA (NY), Cayman Islands, Chile, Colombia

TABLE OF CASES

INTERNATIONAL

CJEU

Bank Handlowy w Warszawie SA, PPHU 'ADAX'/Ryszard Adamiak, v. Christianapol sp. z o.o., Case C-116/11, ECLI:EU:C:2012:739 .... 7.28

Bryan Andrew Kerr v. Pavlo Postnov, Natalia Postnova, Case C-25/18, ECLI:EU:C:2019:376 .... 7.30

Christopher Seagon v. Deko Marty Belgium NV, Case C-339/07, 12 February 2009, ECLI:EU:C:2009:83 .... 8.39

Comité d'entreprise de Nortel Networks SA and Others v. Cosme Rogeau, and Cosme Rogeau v. Alan Robert Bloom and Others, Case C-649/13, ECLI:EU:C:2015:384 .... 7.12–7.14, 7.18, 7.19

Eurofood IFSC Ltd., Case C-341/04, ECLI:EU:C:2006:281 .... 6.03, 8.07, 8.13

Peter Valach and others v. Waldviertler Sparkasse Bank AG and others, 20 December 2017, Case C-649/16, ECLI:EU:C:2017:986 .... 8.39

Petra Engler v. Janus Versand GmbH, Case C-27/02, ECLI:EU:C:2005:33 .... 7.23

Rastelli Davide e C. Snc v. Jean-Charles Hidoux, Case C-191/10, ECLI:EU:C:2011:838 .... 3.03, 6.05

Simona Kornhaas v. Thomas Dithmar, Case C-594/14, ECLI:EU:C:2015:806 .... 7.30, 8.39

UB v. VA and others, 4 December 2019, Case C-493/18, ECLI:EU:C:2019:1046 .... 8.39

Wiemer & Trachte, 14 November 2018, ECLI:EU:C:2018:902, Case C-296/1 .... 8.39

European Court of Human Rights

Affaire Cipolletta v. Italy, Application no. 38259/09, ECtHR 2018 .... 8.09

Allan Jacobsson v. Sweden (no. 2), Application no. 16970/90, ECtHR 1998 .... 8.26

Bochan v. Ukraine, Application no. 7577/02, ECtHR 2007 .... 8.09

Ramos Nunes de Carvalho e Sá v. Portugal [GC], Applications nos. 55391/13, 57728/13 and 74041/13, ECtHR 2018 .... 8.26

Schuler-Zgraggen v. Switzerland, Application no. 14518/89, ECtHR 1993 .... 8.26

Zavodnik v. Slovenia, Application no. 53723/13, ECtHR 2015 .... 8.09

NATIONAL

Australia

Halifax Investment Services Pty Ltd., In the matter of, (No 5) [2019] FCA 1341 .... 9.08

Parbery; Re Lehman Brothers Australia Ltd. [2011] FCA 1449 .... 9.08

Canada

Calpine Canada Energy Ltd, In re, 2006 A.B.Q.B. 743, 2006 CarswellAlta 1313 .... 4.08
Everfresh Beverages, Inc., Re (1995) 1995 CarswellOnt 2336 .... 9.05
Hunt v. T & N plc., Supreme Court of Canada, 1993 CarswellBC 294 .... 4.43
Nortel Networks Corporation (Re), 2015 ONSC 2987, 12 May 2015 .... 10.35
Olympia & York Developments Ltd. v. Royal Trust Co. (1993), 20 C.B.R. (3d) 165 (Ont. Gen. Div) 4.24, 7.09, 8.40, 9.05
Ontario Court of Justice, Toronto, Case No. B125/92 (26 July 1993) 4.24
Ontario Court of Justice, Toronto, Case No. 32-077978 (20 December 1995) 4.30
Xinergy Ltd., Re, 2015 ONSC 2692, 37 CBR (6th) 331 .... 10.76

Hong Kong

Performance Investment Products Corp. Ltd., Re, 2014 WL 6443 (CFI), [2014] HKEC 465 .... 7.09

India

National Company Law Appellate Tribunal

In the matter of Jet Airways (India) Ltd. v. State Bank of India and Another. Company Appeal (AT) (Insolvency) No. 707 of 2019, 26 September 2019 .... 8.12

The Bahamas

Commodore Electronics Ltd., In the Matter of, and In the Matter of the International Business Companies Act, 1989 (No. 2 of 1990) and In re Commodore International Ltd. and In re the International Business Companies Act, 1989 (No. 2 of 1990), Supreme Court of the Commonwealth of the Bahamans, No. 473, 8 December 1994 .... 4.20, 4.21, 4.22

The Netherlands

Hoge Raad 2 juni 1967, NJ 1968, 16 .... 9.09
Hoge Raad 31 mei 1996, nr. 16007, NJ 1998, 108 .... 9.09
Hoge Raad 19 Dec. 2008, NJ 2009/456 .... 9.09
Hoge Raad 13 Sept. 2013, ECLI:NL:HR:2013:BZ5668; JOR 2014/50 .... 9.11

UK

Barned's Banking Company, In re (1867) 3 LR Ch 10 .... 2.02
Butlers Wharf Ltd., Re, [1995] 2 B.C.L.C. 43, [1995] B.C.C. 717 .... 10.26
Collins & Aikman Europe SA, Re, [2005] EWHC 1754 (Ch.) 10.59
Collins & Aikman Europe SA, Re [2006] EWHC 1343 (Ch); [2007] 1 B.C.L.C. 182 .... 9.11
McFadyen & Co, ex parte Vizianagaram Co Ltd, Re [1908] 1 KB 675 .... 4.05, 4.09–4.12

Nortel Networks SA and other companies, Re, [2009] EWHC 206 (Ch) 10.59
Nortel Networks SA (No. 2), Re, [2010] B.C.C.21 .... 9.21
Sturgeon Central Asia Balanced Fund Ltd. (in liquidation), Re, [2019] EWHC 1215 (Ch) 5.37
Syncreon Group BV, In the Matter of [2019] EWHC 2412 (Ch) 3.11
Tchenguiz v. Grant Thornton UK LLP, [2017] EWCA Civ 83 .... 8.35
Videology Ltd., In the matter of, and In the matter of the Cross-Border Insolvency Regulations [2018] EWHC 2186 (Ch) 8.38

USA

AIOC Corporation and AIOC Resources AG, Re, Case nos. 96 B 41895 and 96 B 41896 (Bankr. S.D.N.Y. 1996) 4.34, 4.45
Casse v. Key Bank Nat'l Ass'n (In re Casse), 198 F.3d 327, 342 (2d Cir. 1999) 9.03
Davis v. Davis (In re Davis), 170 F.3d 475, 492 (5th Cir. 1999) 9.03
Earl, In re 140 B.R. 728, 741 n. 4 (Bankr. N.D. Ind. 1992) 9.03
Everfresh Beverages, Inc., In Re, 238 B.R. 558 (Bankr. S.D.N.Y. 1999) 4.30, 4.45
Federal-Mogul Global Inc., T&N Ltd., et al., In re Case, No. 01-10578 (Bankr. D. Delaware, 2001) 4.30, 4.47
Lehman Brothers Holdings Inc., et al, In re, (Bankr. S.D.N.Y.) No. 08-13555 (JMP) (14 January 2009) 4.08, 9.03, 10.35
Lehman Brothers Holdings Inc., In re, No. 08-13555 (Bankr. S.D.N.Y. May 26, 2009) 10.28
Maxwell Communications Corp, [1992] B.C.L.C. 465; 170 B.R. 800 (Bankr. S.D.N.Y. 1994); Aff'd B.R. 807 (Bankr. S.D.N.Y. 1995); 593 F.3rd 1036 (2nd Cir., 1996) 4.16–4.18, 10.75
Maxwell Communications Corp, 93 F.3d 1042 (2nd Cir., 1996) 4.17
Nortel Networks, Inc., In re, 532 BR 494 (Bankr. D. Del. 2015) 10.03
Securities Investor Protection Corp. v. Bernard L. Madoff Investment Securities LLC (Bankr. S.D.N.Y.) Adv. Pro. No. 08-1789 (BRL) (9 June 2009) 4.08
Stonington Partners v. Lernout & Hauspie Speech, 310 F.3d 118, 133 (3rd Cir. 2002) 9.02
United States Bankruptcy Court for the Southern District of New York, Case Nos. 92-B-42698-42701 (15 July 1993) 4.24
United States Bankruptcy Court for the Southern District of New York, Case No. 95 B 45405 (20 December 1995) 4.30

TABLE OF LEGISLATION

EUROPEAN UNION

BRRD. Directive 2014/59/EU of the European Parliament and of the Council of 15 May 2014 establishing a framework for the recovery and resolution of credit institutions and investment firms and amending Council Directive 82/891/EEC, and Directives 2001/24/EC, 2002/47/EC, 2004/25/EC, 2005/56/EC, 2007/36/EC, 2011/35/EU, 2012/30/EU and 2013/36/EU, and Regulations (EU) No 1093/2010 and (EU) No 648/2012, of the European Parliament and of the Council 2.10, 3.10, 11.03
- Recital 17 .... 11.04
- Recital 45 .... 3.10
- Recital 96 .... 11.04, 11.06
- Recital 98 .... 11.06
- Art 2(24) 11.06
- Art 2(26) 2.10
- Arts 12, 13, 16 .... 11.06
- Art 34(1) 3.23
- Art 84 .... 11.06
- Art 88(1) 11.06
- Art 88(2) 11.06
- Art 89 .... 11.06
- Arts 90, 91, 92 .... 11.06
- Art 98 .... 11.09

Brussels I Recast. Regulation (EU) No 1215/2012 of the European Parliament and of the Council of 12 December 2012 on jurisdiction and the recognition and enforcement of judgments in civil and commercial matters (recast) 6.01, 7.12, 7.15, 7.16
- Arts 25, 29, 35 .... 7.15

Brussels Convention. 1968 Brussels Convention on jurisdiction and the enforcement of judgments in civil and commercial matters 6.01
- Art 5(1) 7.23

Brussels Regulation. Council Regulation (EC) No 44/2001 of 22 December 2000 on jurisdiction and the recognition and enforcement of judgments in civil and commercial matters 7.14, 7.18

Charter of Fundamental Rights of the European Union 8.07

CIWUD. Directive 2001/24/EC of the European Parliament and of the Council of 4 April 2001 on the reorganisation and winding up of credit institutions 3.01, 3.10
- Art 10(2) 8.35

EIR 2000. Council regulation (EC) No 1346/2000 of 29 May 2000 on insolvency proceedings 1.13, 3.01, 3.10, 6.02, 6.04, 6.21, 7.13, 7.14, 7.18, 7.22, 9.09, 13.05
- Art 31 .... 6.02, 9.10
- Art 32(1) 10.52
- Art 32(2) 10.52
- Art 40 .... 8.15
- Art 46 .... 6.06

EIR Recast. Regulation (EU) 2015/848 of the European Parliament and of the Council of 20 May 2015 on insolvency proceedings 1.06, 1.10, 1.13, 1.15, 1.17, 2.10, 3.10, 3.12, 3.14, 3.21, 4.02, 4.03, 4.48, 5.04, 6.06, 6.07, 6.17, 6.21, 7.17, 7.19, 7.21, 7.22, 7.23, 7.28, 7.37, 8.03, 8.31, 8.37, 8.44, 9.11, 9.12, 9.22, 10.01, 10.03, 10.54, 12.01

Recital 3 .... 8.03
Recital 12 .... 8.19
Recital 48 .... 5.04, 6.21
Recital 49 .... 6.21
Recital 51 .... 6.08
Recital 52 .... 3.14, 6.08, 6.09
Recital 53 .... 10.58
Recital 54 .... 6.08, 6.16
Recital 60 .... 10.63
Recital 83 .... 8.07
Art 2(9) 7.20, 8.30
Art 2(13) 2.10
Art 2(14) 2.10
Art 3 .... 8.30
Art 3(1) 8.38
Art 6 .... 8.30, 8.40
Art 6(1) 7.08, 8.39
Art 6(2) 8.39
Art 7 .... 8.30
Art 7(1) 8.42
Art 7(2) 7.20, 8.35, 8.43
Arts 8–18 .... 8.43
Art 10 .... 7.20
Art 14 .... 8.09
Art 24 .... 8.19
Art 25 .... 8.19
Art 31 .... 7.20
Art 33 .... 7.12
Art 36 .... 7.28, 10.50, 10.55
Art 38(2) 7.28
Art 38(3) 7.28
Art 41 .... 9.21
Arts 41–43 .... 6.09
Art 45 .... 8.30, 10.52
Art 45(1) 8.36, 10.52
Art 45(2) 10.52
Art 46 .... 7.28
Art 56–60 .... 6.07
Art 56 .... 4.02, 7.20, 8.06, 8.45, 9.10, 9.17, 9.21
Art 56(1) 3.21, 3.22, 6.11, 6.13
Art 56(2) ... 6.11, 6.15, 6.21, 10.13, 10.63
Art 57 .... 4.02, 7.20, 8.06, 8.45, 9.10, 10.72
Art 57(1) 3.21, 6.12, 6.13, 10.75
Art 57(3) 6.12
Art 58 .. 3.21, 4.02, 6.13, 7.20, 8.06, 8.45, 9.10
Art 60 .... 6.11, 8.30
Art 60(1) 8.11, 10.05, 10.13
Arts 61–77 .... 6.07
Art 70(2) 6.20
Art 71 .... 6.19
Art 71(2) 6.17
Art 72(2) 6.19
Rome I Regulation. Regulation (EC) No 593/2008 of the European Parliament and of the Council of 17 June 2008 on the law applicable to contractual obligations (Rome I) 7.23, 7.24, 7.28
Art 1(2) 7.30
Art 3 .... 7.27
Art 3(1) 7.24
Art 4(1), (2), (4) 7.28
Art 12 .... 7.23
SRMR. Regulation (EU) No 806/2014 of the European Parliament and of the Council of 15 July 2014 establishing uniform rules and a uniform procedure for the resolution of credit institutions and certain investment firms in the framework of a Single Resolution Mechanism and a Single Resolution Fund and amending Regulation (EU) No 1093/2010 .... 2.10, 11.03
Recital 15 .... 11.03
Recitals 38, 47, 54 .... 11.04
Arts 8, 10, 16 .... 11.03
Art 33(3) 11.25
Treaty on European Union (TEU)
Treaty on the Functioning of the European Union (TFEU)
Art 4(3) 6.14

NATIONAL LEGISLATION

Australia

Cross-Border Insolvency Act, 2008
Art 27(d) 9.06

Canada

Companies' Creditors Arrangement Act (R.S.C., 1985, c. C-36)
sec 18(2) 9.05
sec 52(1) 5.06

Estonia

Bankruptcy Act (*Pankrotiseadus*)
s 111 .... 3.04

France

Commercial Code (*Code de commerce*)
Art 621-2 .... 3.03
Art 695-2 .... 9.21

Germany

Stock Corporation Act (*Aktiengesetz*) 2.09
§§ 17, 18 .... 2.09
Insolvency Code (*Insolvenzordnung, InsO*) 9.13–9.18
§ 3e 9.13
§ 60 .... 9.18
§ 131(2) 3.04
§ 160 .... 9.17
§ 254(2) 10.26
§ 269 .... 4.02
§ 269a 9.13, 9.17
§ 269b 9.13
§ 269d 9.14
§ 269h 9.15, 9.17
§ 357 .... 9.17

Greece

Bankruptcy Code (*Πτωχευτικός Κώδικας*)
Art 42(3) 3.04

India

Insolvency and Bankruptcy Code, 2016 .... 4.12

Ireland

Constitution
Art 34(1) 3.20

Italy

Crisis and Insolvency Code (Codice della crisi d'impresa e dell'insolvenza in attuazione della legge 19 ottobre 2017, n. 155)
Art 288 .... 4.02

Netherlands

Civil Code (*Burgerlijk Wetboek*) 2.08
Art 2.2 .... 2.08
Bankruptcy Act (*Faillissementswet*) 9.09
Art 43(1) 3.04
Art 160 .... 10.26

Spain

Insolvency Act 22/2003 of 9 July 2003 (*Ley 22/2003, de 9 de julio, Concursal*)
Art 71 .... 3.04
Art 135(1) 10.26
Law 29/2015, of 30 July 2015, on international cooperation in civil matters 9.22
Art 4 .... 9.22

Sweden

Bankruptcy Act 1987 (*Konkurslagen*) 9.20

United Kingdom

Insolvency Act 1986
s 239 .... 3.04
s 240 .... 3.04
Companies Act 2006
s 354B, 354C 5.06
s 1662 .... 2.09

Cross-Border Insolvency Regulations 2006 (SI 2006/1030) 5.37
Arts 25, 26 .... 5.06

United States

US Bankruptcy Code (11 U.S. Code Title 11) 10.43
§ 105 .... 9.03
§ 509 .... 10.26
§ 1101(1) 4.14
§ 1104(c) 4.14
§ 1107 .... 4.14
§ 1108 .... 4.14
§ 1525 .... 5.06
§ 1526 .... 9.02
§ 1527 .... 9.02

INTERNATIONAL SOFT LAW INSTRUMENTS

ALI-III Global Principles for Cooperation in International Insolvency Cases, 2012 .... 4.06, 4.28, 8.29, 9.07
ALI-III Guidelines Applicable to Court-to-Court Communications in Cross-Border Cases, 2001 .... 4.45, 8.24, 8.25, 8.46, 9.07, 10.72, 10.74
EU Cross-Border Insolvency Court-to-Court Communications Guidelines (JudgeCo Guidelines), 2015 .... 6.21, 8.07, 8.25, 9.11, 10.72
European Communication and Cooperation Guidelines for Cross-border Insolvency (CoCo Guidelines), 2007 ... 4.06, 4.28, 6.21, 13.05
FSB Key Attributes of Effective Resolution Regimes for Financial Institutions, 2014 .... 11.02, 11.09
FSB Principles for Cross-border Effectiveness of Resolution Actions, 2015 .... 11.12
Global Rules on Conflict-of-Laws Matters in International Insolvency Cases, 2012 .... 9.07
Guidelines for Communication and Cooperation between Courts in Cross-Border Insolvency Matters (JIN Guidelines), 2016 .... 6.21, 8.25, 9.07, 9.11, 10.72, 10.79
IBA Cross-Border Insolvency Concordat, 1996 .... 1.11, 4.22, 4.25, 4.26, 4.27, 4.28, 4.30–4.35, 4.45
III Guidelines for Coordination of Multinational Enterprise Group Insolvencies, 2012 .... 4.06, 10.61
Modalities of Court-to-Court Communication (JIN Modalities), 2019 .... 9.07, 10.79
OECD Guidelines for Multinational Enterprises, 2011 .... 2.08
UNCITRAL Enterprise group insolvency: draft guide to enactment, 2019 ..... 4.49
UNCITRAL Legislative Guide on Insolvency Law, Parts one and two, 2004 .... 4.28, 4.49, 5.18
Ch II
para 82 .... 5.18
para 83 .... 5.18
UNCITRAL Legislative Guide on Insolvency Law, Part three: Treatment of enterprise groups in insolvency, 2010 .... 1.08, 2.04, 3.08, 4.49, 5.01, 5.22, 5.24, 7.09
Ch II
para 57 .... 5.23
para 68 .... 8.45
para 144 .... 5.23
para 152 .... 5.37
Ch III
para 7 .... 5.21
para 30 .... 5.23
para 37 .... 5.23
para 48 .... 5.22
para 50 .... 7.09
Recommendations
211–213 .... 10.11
240–245 .... 5.21
250 .... 10.65
253–254 .... 5.22, 5.32
UNCITRAL Model Law on Cross-Border Insolvency, 1997 .... 1.06, 1.12, 3.01,

4.02, 4.03, 4.12, 4.49, 5.01, 5.02, 5.03, 5.04, 5.05, 5.08, 5.09, 5.11, 5.32, 5.33, 6.02, 6.21, 7.28, 8.03, 9.01, 9.02, 9.04, 9.06, 10.03, 10.55, 10.68
Preamble 5.02, 8.03
Art 20 .... 4.28
Art 25 .... 4.02, 5.06, 10.72
Art 26 .... 4.02, 5.06
Art 27 .... 4.02, 5.07
UNCITRAL Model Law on Recognition and Enforcement of Insolvency-Related Judgments with Guide to Enactment, 2018 .... 7.08
UNCITRAL Model Law on Enterprise Group Insolvency, 2019 ...... 1.10, 1.12, 1.17, 2.10, 3.10, 3.12, 3.14, 3.21, 4.48, 5.01, 5.10, 5.25–5.41, 6.17, 6.21, 8.03, 10.03, 10.07, 10.54, 10.55
Preamble 5.27, 8.03
Art 2(b) 2.10
Art 2(e) 5.31
Art 2(f) 5.30
Art 2(g) 3.14
Art 9 .... 5.32, 10.72
Art 9(1) 10.75
Art 10(h) 10.30
Art 11(2) 5.40
Art 13 .... 5.32
Art 14 .... 5.32
Art 15(c) 10.14, 10.73
Art 16 .... 5.32
Art 18(1) 8.11
Art 18(3) 5.32
Art 18(4) 8.11, 10.14
Art 18(5) 10.14
Art 20 .... 4.38
Art 20(1) 10.06
Art 24 .... 5.31
Arts 28, 30 .... 10.50
UNCITRAL Practice Guide on Cross-Border Insolvency Cooperation, 2009 .... 1.08, 4.04, 4.49, 5.01, 5.08, 5.11, 5.12, 5.13, 5.24, 7.09, 9.07, 13.06
Intro
para 13(i) 7.09
Ch III
para 5 .... 7.32
para 11 .... 7.03
para 17 .... 8.18
para 33 .... 7.07
para 41 .... 5.15
para 62 .... 10.38
para 68 .... 10.70
para 72 .... 10.30
para 100 .... 7.24
paras 104, 107 .... 10.70
para 122 .... 5.16
para 130 .... 10.70
para 146 .... 10.72
World Bank Principles for Effective Insolvency and Creditor/Debtor Regimes, 2015 .... 3.09, 5.23, 10.11

1

INTRODUCTION TO *CROSS-BORDER PROTOCOLS IN INSOLVENCIES OF MULTINATIONAL ENTERPRISE GROUPS*

One of the greatest challenges of international insolvency law is to develop a system of rules to enable efficient administration of insolvency proceedings opened with respect to members of an integrated multinational enterprise group. The absence of such a system may result in a group disintegration, loss of group synergies, unnecessary liquidation of economically viable enterprises, loss of substantial value to the detriment of creditors, employees, public revenue authorities and other stakeholders. Nevertheless, throughout history, the prevailing approach in insolvency has always been, and to a large extent still is, an entity-by-entity treatment of legal entities. Thus, in a typical situation involving a financial crisis within a multinational enterprise group, its constituent entities that are insolvent according to national criteria, will end up in separate (autonomous) insolvency proceedings in different jurisdictions and with separate insolvency estates and pools of creditors. This is despite the fact that before the onset of the crisis, the corporate group could have operated as a single economic enterprise. **1.01**

Mervyn King, the former Governor of the Bank of England, once famously said that banks are 'global in life and national in death'[1] (2009), highlighting the problem that 'markets and financial institutions are operating on a global scale, while sovereign power is defined at the national level'.[2] Ultimately, King criticized the failure of governments to provide (binding) rules and incentives for cooperation between national authorities in times of crisis. As we know a decade later and after the financial crisis, this problem is not unique to bank insolvencies and becomes especially relevant in case of a failure of a large transnational group of companies. As a consequence, this formerly integrated enterprise group collapses into a myriad of separate and disconnected proceedings. **1.02**

---

1 Quote from D. Schoenmaker, *Governance of International Banking: The Financial Trilemma* (OUP, 2013), p. 1.

2 Ibid.

1.03 There may be different reasons for the insufficient level of communication and coordination between insolvency practitioners and courts, dealing with separate group entities, which may be spread all over the globe. The first one can be linked to the general considerations of national economic policy, the lack of consensus on the objectives and underlying values of insolvency proceedings (e.g. rescue or liquidation) and greatly divergent rules of insolvency law. As noted by Sir Peter Millett with respect to insolvency law, '[n]o other branch of the law is moulded more by considerations of national economic policy and commercial philosophy'.[3] Consequently, there may be a natural tendency of governments and courts to favour national interests and protect local creditors. The second reason for the entity-by-entity and jurisdiction-by-jurisdiction approach comes from the longstanding doctrine of separate legal personality, under which each of the enterprise group members, including its assets and liabilities, remains separate and distinct. A corporation has its own legal personality separate from that of the individuals it comprises. This doctrine is the cornerstone of modern company law, whose origins may be traced back to Roman times.[4] In insolvency, the application of this doctrine often leads to the atomistic (separate) treatment of group entities. Some may argue that the active cooperation between insolvency practitioners and courts simply does not sit well with such atomistic nature of insolvency proceedings. The third reason relates to various practical and inborn obstacles. Among them, different languages of jurisdictions involved, dissimilar legal cultures, structurally poor or vague legislation and for practitioners, conflicting systems of charging fees.

1.04 Nevertheless, law (and especially restructuring and insolvency law) cannot exist in a vacuum and ignore the economic reality. And such reality is that business is increasingly conducted across borders through networks of interconnected and interdependent corporate groups. Interestingly, the very doctrine of separate legal personality and the related concept of limited liability prompted the growth of large corporate groups during the late 19th and early 20th centuries.[5] The process of globalization, proliferation of foreign direct investment, opening of markets for capital and creation of supply chains and contractual networks further facilitated formation of multinational enterprise

3 P. Millett, 'Cross-Border Insolvency: The Judicial Approach' (1997) 6(2) *International Insolvency Review*, p. 109.

4 There are ongoing debates about the extent to which the Romans recognized the idea that a corporate personality may separate from that of its shareholders. The supporters of such recognition rely on Ulpian's maxim: *Si quid universitati debetur singulis non debetur, nec quod debet universitas singuli debent* ('Where anything is owing to a corporation, it is not due to the individual members of the same, nor do the latter owe what the entire association does'). Quoted from P. Blumberg, 'Limited Liability and Corporate Groups' (1986) 11 *The Journal of Corporate Law*, p. 578.

5 P. Muchlinski, *Multinational Enterprises and the Law* (2nd ed., OUP, 2007), p. 35.

groups. According to the Organisation for Economic Co-operation and Development (OECD), in 1970 there were only around 7,000 multinational enterprises, but by 2008 this number has increased to 82,000 (excluding financial transnational corporations).[6] However, the outbreak of COVID-19 in 2020 and the subsequent drastic governmental measures to curb the contagion have severely affected international trade, investment and travel, bringing the world economy close to a standstill and intensifying 'territorialist' sentiments.[7] This has particularly affected multinational corporations, dependent on global supply chains and uninterrupted liquidity flows.[8] As a result, we may expect an increase in the number of group insolvencies, spanning various jurisdictions and affecting our everyday life. This brings us to the question, even more so than before the economic downturn on how to efficiently deal with corporate groups in financial distress, preserving and reconciling legal separateness of group entities with the needs and individual characteristics of enterprise groups.

Absent internationally approved standards and procedures for coordination of insolvencies in the context of multinational groups of companies, the pragmatic and workable solution seems to have arisen from legal practice and cases where commercially minded insolvency practitioners and courts (perhaps to some extent intuitively) tried to overcome underdeveloped rules of international insolvency law and the lack of special rules on group insolvencies. This solution was a *cross-border insolvency protocol or agreement.* The early examples of such protocols were negotiated and adopted since the 1980s to address failures within multinational enterprise groups (e.g. Maxwell, Olympia and York, Loewen). In the 2000s, insolvency protocols proved indispensable for efficient resolution of large multinational conglomerates, such as Lehman Brothers, Nortel Networks and Madoff Securities. They sought to promote cooperation between and among courts and insolvency practitioners in many different jurisdictions, to coordinate and improve administration of parallel insolvency proceedings, to reduce costs associated therewith and to avoid duplication of effort. These individual protocols created cooperation frameworks and addressed (with different levels of detail and among other things) the issues of information exchange, treatment of claims (including intercompany claims), preservation of material assets, coordination of actions **1.05**

6 OECD, 'Multinational Enterprises in the Global Economy: Heavily Debated but Hardly Measured', May 2018.

7 A. Capri, 'Coronavirus Accelerates Techno-Nationalism And Puts Multinationals In Spotlight', Forbes, 25 March 2020, available at https://www.forbes.com/sites/alexcapri/2020/03/25/coronavirus-accelerates-techno-nationalism-and-piles-new-constraints-on-multinationals/#30cc47d85af8.

8 C. Zhenwei Qiang et al., 'Foreign Direct Investment and Global Value Chains in the Wake of COVID-19', World Bank Blogs, 1 May 2020, available at https://blogs.worldbank.org/psd/foreign-direct-investment-and-global-value-chains-wake-covid-19.

and proceedings, submission and adoption of reorganization and liquidation plans. Thus, protocols represented a mechanism to, on the one hand, promote mutual dialogue and understanding between different insolvency practitioners and courts and, on the other hand, to create a group-wide governance framework, supplementing existing rules of international insolvency law and overcoming the atomistic treatment of group entities in insolvency.

1.06 Insolvency protocols, strikingly, were a product of creative thinking by experienced insolvency practitioners, as well as a judicial innovation rather than a tool imposed 'from above' by a legislator. Nevertheless, gradually, conclusion of insolvency protocols has been institutionalized, first in soft law via the UNCITRAL Model Law on Cross-Border Insolvency (1997) and then in hard law instruments at regional (e.g. European Insolvency Regulation, 2015 (EIR Recast))[9] and national (e.g. Germany, USA, Australia) levels. Despite this progress, insolvency protocols remain relatively underutilized, especially among practitioners and courts in the European Union (EU) Member States. Apart from a few isolated cases, civil law jurisdictions in and outside the EU are rarely engaged in conclusion of cross-border insolvency protocols. At least one of the possible explanations may be the insufficient awareness and lack of knowledge about the benefits of the use of insolvency protocols, circumstances in which their adoption should promote efficient group resolution, provisions that can be included in a protocol to regulate sharing of information, treatment of assets and liabilities, resolution of disputes, allocation of roles between participating parties, etc.

1.07 This book aims at raising awareness about cross-border insolvency protocols, at sharing knowledge and offering a number of recommendations on their application in the context of insolvency of multinational enterprise groups. It draws on the previous research accumulated in this field.

1.08 This includes the valuable work done by UNCITRAL in promoting cooperation in cross-border insolvency cases and the adoption of insolvency protocols to facilitate such cooperation. UNCITRAL's Practice Guide on Cross-Border Insolvency Cooperation (2009) and the Legislative Guide on Insolvency Law, Part III (2010) served as a solid foundation for detailed analysis of protocols undertaken in this book. We should also note the substantial contribution made by other standard-setting organizations, including the International Insolvency Institute (III), the American Law Institute (ALI), INSOL International, INSOL Europe, the World Bank, the Basel

9 Regulation (EU) 2015/848 of the European Parliament and of the Council of 20 May 2015 on insolvency proceedings.

Committee on Banking Supervision (BCBS) and the Financial Stability Board (FSB). Their vast contribution is manifested in a plethora of authoritative soft law instruments, recommendations and guidelines, some rather general and other more specific, recognizing the significance of information exchange, coordinated crisis responses, building of trust and cooperation in insolvency and bank resolution. Against this background, the book is structured as follows.

Chapter 2 describes various definitions of a 'group of companies', as found in the legal texts, and discusses different types and characteristic features of enterprise groups. For example, enterprise groups may differ in terms of their corporate, organizational and financial models, geographical span, level of interdependence and managerial concentration, impacting their position in restructuring and insolvency. **1.09**

The purpose of **Chapter 3** is to show that insolvency law has for a long time overlooked the problems created by failures of corporate groups. In many instances this has led to economic inefficiency, unnecessary loss of value and group disintegration. The underlying rationale was that each enterprise group member is a separate entity and should be addressed separately in insolvency (entity-by-entity approach, mentioned above). However, as the chapter suggests, especially in the 2010s, there seems to have been a reconsideration of this still prevailing approach through the recognition of a 'group of companies' in insolvency and the promotion of a 'group solution' as an alternative to an 'entity solution'. This is evident in the rules of the UNCITRAL Model Law on Enterprise Group Insolvency (2019), the EIR Recast, the modern instruments on resolution of banking groups and some recent reforms of national law. This chapter also identifies the limitations of a group solution, dictated by the need to preserve the essence of entity separateness. **1.10**

While chapters 2 and 3 set the scene and assist the reader in understanding the background against which insolvency protocols are negotiated and do operate, **Chapter 4** introduces the core subject of the book, namely cross-border insolvency protocols and agreements. It discusses their purpose and goals and examines the early examples of insolvency protocols. This chapter traces how protocols have evolved over time, from being an ad hoc response to a particular problem to increasingly standardized and well-structured arrangements (framework protocols). The process of standardization accelerated with the adoption in 1996 of the IBA Cross-Border Insolvency Concordat and a number of other non-binding guidelines, sometimes directly referred to in insolvency protocols. Another important observation is that many early protocols, even those concerning a single debtor with cross-border operations, **1.11** went beyond the interests and affairs of that specific debtor and gave account of the group existence. Some even treated a group as if it was a single entity.

1.12 Having demonstrated positive results, insolvency protocols and, more generally, cross-border insolvency cooperation attracted attention of the United Nations Commission on International Trade Law (UNCITRAL), which is famous for developing some of the key instruments of international insolvency law, including the Model Law on Cross-Border Insolvency (1997). **Chapter 5** examines the role of UNCITRAL in facilitating the use of protocols, or agreements, as it prefers to call them. UNCITRAL has been persistent in encouraging such use, first to address a single-debtor insolvency and cooperation between main and non-main insolvency proceedings, and then to improve fair and efficient administration of insolvencies concerning enterprise group members. The latter culminated in the approval in 2019 of the Model Law on Enterprise Group Insolvency, which provides for the conclusion of protocols in a group setting.

1.13 **Chapter 6** examines the relevant European developments. It highlights that initially European rules on cross-border insolvency (i.e. the original European Insolvency Regulation, EIR 2000[10]) did not address the issue of enterprise group insolvency and did not explicitly authorize the use of protocols. The prevailing approach was liquidation-oriented and with a narrow entity-by-entity focus. Since then a lot has changed with the adoption of the EIR Recast in 2015. It introduced detailed rules on cooperation and coordination in a group insolvency scenario. The practice of insolvency protocols has now been institutionalized at the EU level. This, however, somewhat counterintuitively, did not trigger an increase in the number of protocols involving European jurisdictions. We discuss why this might be the case. One of the likely reasons is the ambiguity of the legal nature of protocols, including their scope, legal effects and limitations.

1.14 **Chapter 7** explores the major approaches to legal characterization of protocols. For this we use findings from international standard-setting organizations, academic literature and the text of protocols themselves. The first approach emphasizes the public law nature of insolvency protocols and the engagement of courts in their approval (i.e. a protocol as an insolvency-related judgment or a mini-treaty). The second approach points out the contractual nature of protocols and classifies them as contracts or agreements freely negotiated and entered into between insolvency practitioners. Depending on the chosen approach, the relevant conflict of law rules, determining the issues

10 Council regulation (EC) No 1346/2000 of 29 May 2000 on insolvency proceedings.

of international jurisdiction, applicable law, cross-border recognition and enforcement may differ.

While parties are generally free to determine the scope and content of an insolvency protocol, there are important limitations to be aware of. **Chapter 8** explores such limitations. Some of them are imposed to ensure compliance with certain procedural (e.g. right to be heard, equality of arms) and substantive rights and principles (e.g. equality of creditors, ranking of claims), others arise from co-existence with mandatory rules of national law (e.g. pervasive *vis attractiva concursus*) and supra-national regulation, such as the EIR Recast (e.g. guaranteeing the right to simultaneously file a claim in both main and secondary proceedings). Yet another category of limitations is specific to a corporate group environment and seeks to secure and safeguard legal separateness in insolvency. **1.15**

Chapter 9 gives an overview of some national laws relating to the adoption of insolvency protocols. It covers both the Model Law jurisdictions, including the USA, Canada and Australia, as well as a few non-Model Law civil law jurisdictions, such as the Netherlands, Germany, Sweden, France and Spain. It shows that the adoption of a developed regulatory framework for insolvency protocols or solely belonging to the common law tradition do not guarantee the use of protocols in practice. **1.16**

Chapter 10 should have particular appeal to insolvency practitioners and practising lawyers involved in or contemplating the negotiation of an insolvency protocol, as well as to judges overseeing this process and tasked with an approval request. In this chapter, we examine the circumstances which could necessitate and bolster the adoption of insolvency protocols and analyse some of their most common and unique provisions. We group them into three categories: (i) those ensuring protection or best possible realization of group material assets; (ii) those establishing or confirming participation rights and framing negotiation, adoption and implementation of group reorganization plans; and (iii) those facilitating resolution of intra-group claims and coordinating future actions and transactions. Our analysis is followed by the recommendations. We conclude this chapter by suggesting how insolvency protocols can supplement or even replicate the existing regulatory frameworks (i.e. the EIR Recast and the Model Law 2019) or some of their instruments that have remained dormant in practice. **1.17**

The practice of concluding cooperation agreements is not unique to insolvency of non-financial enterprises. The global financial crisis of 2008–2009 has demonstrated that communication and cooperation between resolution **1.18** authorities are key to the efficient resolution of financial institutions, including international banking groups. **Chapter 11** studies various cooperation arrangements that have been created in the wake of the global financial crisis to improve cross-border bank resolution, preserve financial stability, minimize systemic risk and safeguard rights of depositors and other stakeholders. Among such cooperation arrangements, we look specifically at 'cooperation forums' (e.g. resolution colleges and crisis-management groups) and special cooperation arrangements between resolution authorities in Europe and beyond. We highlight the key differences between cross-border insolvency protocols, discussed in the previous chapters of this book, and cooperation agreements in the area of bank resolution.

1.19 **Chapter 12** summarizes our Recommendations related to the conclusion of protocols in insolvencies of multinational enterprise groups. These Recommendations are non-binding and seek to address a few general problems attached to the adoption of insolvency protocols as such, as well as to make a number of suggestions for the improvement of group insolvency coordination through protocols. The Recommendations are followed by **Chapter 13**, which builds upon them and offers a Group Insolvency Protocol Design, or GIP Design, a design for an insolvency protocol addressing cooperation and communication in the context of enterprise group insolvency. This GIP Design may be used by insolvency practitioners and other parties having a task of drafting an insolvency protocol.

1.20 The book concludes with **Chapter 14** (Annex), providing the text of some of the landmark insolvency protocols, which can be consulted when reading this book, engaging in cross-border insolvency cooperation or drafting new protocols.

2

THE PHENOMENON OF MULTINATIONAL ENTERPRISE GROUPS

A. THE RISE OF MULTINATIONAL ENTERPRISE GROUPS 2.01
B. DEFINITION OF AN ENTERPRISE GROUP 2.08
C. TYPOLOGY OF ENTERPRISE GROUPS 2.12

A. THE RISE OF MULTINATIONAL ENTERPRISE GROUPS

2.01 It is difficult to determine the exact date when multinational enterprise groups (MEG) may have come into existence. Some authors trace their emergence to European colonial trading companies of the 16th and 17th centuries, including the English and Dutch East India companies, Hudson's Bay Company and Muscovy Company.[1] Nevertheless, the majority of historians and economists consider that multinational enterprises arose in the mid- to late 19th century.[2] This period was characterized by the development of new industrial technologies, improvement of manufacturing and management processes and international division of production. This was also the time of liberalization of corporate laws in the USA, which authorized companies to acquire shares in other companies.[3] Before that, in the USA corporations could not own shares of other corporations. For contemporary lawyers it may seem almost a given that companies may found other companies and own shares in them. However, it was not always the case. Corporate groups constitute a rather recent phenomenon, postdating the invention of limited liability. In the USA, New Jersey is considered to be one of the first states to have amended its corporation laws in 1888–1893 to provide for corporate ownership of shares.

1 A. Carlos and S. Nicholas, '"Giants of an Earlier Capitalism": The Chartered Trading Companies as Modern Multinationals' (1988) 62(3) *The Business History Review*, pp. 398–419.

2 M. Wilkins, 'The History of Multinational Enterprise', in A. Rugman, *The Oxford Handbook of International Business* (2nd edn, OUP, 2009), p. 16, noting that the modern multinational is a 'post-industrial revolution phenomenon' and that '[o]nly with steamships, railroads, and cables was it possible for managers to exercise control over business operations across borders in a meaningful manner.' See also M. Wilkins, *The Emergence of Multinational Enterprise: American Business Abroad from the Colonial Era to 1914* (HUP, 1970). L. Franko, *The European Multinationals: A Renewed Challenge to American and British Big Business* (Harper and Row, 1976).

3 P. Blumberg, 'Limited Liability and Corporate Groups' (1986) 11 *The Journal of Corporate Law*, p. 605.

This gave rise to groups of companies in the USA, where their emergence at first primarily concerned the business of railroads.

2.02 Notably, corporate ownership of shares in another company was a late arrival in the UK as well. There, the power of intercompany stock ownership was attributed to the provisions of companies' memoranda of association, notwithstanding the omission of the express recognition of such possibility in the incorporation statute. English courts held in the 1860s that neither the common law, nor the Companies Act of 1862 prohibited companies from acquiring and owning shares in other companies, should the memorandum of association so prescribe.[4] Prior to the mid-19th century, it was commonly believed to be beyond the legal power (*ultra vires*) of a company to own shares in another company.

2.03 Muchlinski has identified four historical periods in the evolution of multinational enterprises (MNEs).[5] The first period (1850–1914) features the appearance of internationally integrated and privately owned manufacturing firms. Among such firms, Philips (1891), Royal Dutch Shell (1890) and Singer Sewing Machine Company (1851). The first period lasted until the outbreak of the First World War in 1914. The second period (1918–1939) began in the post-war environment and was marked by a slower rate of expansion of MNEs due to the economic and political instability of that time. The third period (1945–1990), according to Muchlinski, was the period of American dominance (until the 1960s), revival of competition from European MNEs and the emergence of MNEs from certain newly industrializing countries. This period has seen the unprecedented growth of MNEs. The fourth period (1990 onwards) witnesses the adoption of truly global production chains by MNEs, a marked shift from manufacturing towards the service economy, liberalization of trade and investment regimes across the globe, alongside the establishment of the World Trade Organization (WTO) in 1995.

2.04 Nowadays, the existence of multinational enterprise groups – corporate nets, conducting commercial operations across national borders is the fact of life.[6] Microsoft, Royal Dutch Shell, General Motors, Amazon, Toyota, Alphabet

---

4 *In re Barned's Banking Company* (1867) 3 LR Ch 105, 112–13. Read further C. Witting, *Liability of Corporate Groups and Networks* (CUP, 2018), pp. 65–6.

5 P. Muchlinski, *Multinational Enterprises and the Law* (2nd edn, OUP, 2007), p. 9.

6 Blumberg, *supra* note 3, p. 575, noting that '[t]oday, multinational corporations [...] conduct most of the world's business'. It highlights presumably a US view, focusing on large groups dependent on supply coming from other countries. Generally, in Europe, business is generated by some 90 percent of middle and small sized companies. However, quite a few of these are corporate groups, sometimes including group companies incorporated in different jurisdictions.

are all groups of companies that operate on a worldwide scale. According to UNCITRAL, individual stand-alone corporations are typical only for small private businesses, as enterprise groups 'are ubiquitous in both emerging and developed markets'.[7] The Reflection Group on the Future of EU Company Law, which was established in 2010 by the European Commission (EC) to address current problems in EU company law, confirmed that the 'international group of companies – not the single company – has become the prevailing form of European large-sized enterprises'.[8]

There may be multiple financial, economic, operational, fiscal and other **2.05**
reasons for enterprises to operate through networks of separate legal entities. Underpinned by a legal regime of entity shielding and limited liability, separation of an enterprise into distinct legal entities can decrease the exposure to risks arising from failures related to a particular geographical market (e.g. when a group is planning to enter a new untested market) or a business segment (e.g. when a certain activity can lead to significant environmental liability or is simply more risky).[9] In other words, entity separation within groups pursues the protective or risk-reduction function. This function is closely related to another function, which can be referred to as the enabling function. A corporate structure may enable maximization of financial returns. For example, a group may establish special entities responsible for raising funds on capital markets, i.e. special purpose financing vehicles, which can give access to foreign investors and secure better terms of financing. The use of a group structure could be driven by the need to meet specific regulatory requirements and is frequently tied to fiscal considerations (e.g. tax allowances, tax exemptions for intra-group dividends, group relief).[10]

Complex legal structures have also developed naturally as a result of acquisi- **2.06**
tions and joint ventures. Such corporate expansions are often facilitated by the quest for monopoly gains, search for synergies, strategies to neutralize potential competitors, pursuit of the economies of size and scale.[11] Particularly noticeable in recent years are takeovers determined by the desire to acquire

7 The UNCITRAL Legislative Guide on Insolvency Law – Part three: Treatment of enterprise groups in insolvency, 2010 (Legislative Guide 2010), Ch. 1, para. 4.

8 Report of the Reflection Group on the Future of EU Company Law, Brussels, 5 April 2011, p. 59.

9 Sometimes this separation is dictated by law. For instance, the UK's banking sector structural reform mandated that core banking services (taking deposits, making payments and providing overdrafts for UK retail customers and small businesses) was made financially, operationally and organizationally separate from investment banking and international banking activities. In other words, retail and investment banking should be provided by distinct legal entities. For criticism of this strategy see T. Wetzer, 'In Two Minds: The Governance of Ring-Fenced Banks' (2019) 19 *Journal of Corporate Law Studies*, pp. 197–249.

10 Legislative Guide 2010, *supra* note 7, Ch. 1, para. 21.

11 O. Williamson, 'The Modern Corporation: Origins, Evolution, Attributes' (1981) 19(4) *Journal of Economic Literature*, p. 1537. R. van Galen, 'Insolvent Groups of Companies in Cross Border Cases and Rescue Plans',

new technologies and customers. Some of the most well-known tech acquisitions include the acquisitions by Microsoft of Skype (2011) and LinkedIn (2016), by Alphabet (parent company of Google) of YouTube (2006) and Motorola (2012), by Facebook of Instagram (2012) and WhatsApp (2014).

2.07 Either as a result of natural growth and expansion or in pursuit of an attempt to compartmentalize risk and acquire additional benefits, modern large and medium-sized enterprises predominantly exist as networks of legal entities. Writing on modern group structures, the former president of INSOL International Neil Cooper provides an example of Carrian Group, a Hong Kong real estate conglomerate, which collapsed in the 1980s. The group's corporate charts ran over several pages and, according to Cooper, required a magnifying glass to identify the names of individual subsidiaries. Another example is the Federal Mogul group, engaged in the development, manufacturing and supply of products for automotive, commercial, aerospace, marine, rail and other sectors. It filed for insolvency in 2002, mainly due to a large number of product liability claims related to the use of asbestos-containing products. According to Cooper, the group chart of the Federal Mogul group 'when magnified to the point where you can read the names of all the subsidiaries, would fill a wall of a small office'.[12] Another well-known example is the Lehman Brothers group, which consisted of 2,985 legal entities that operated in some 50 countries.[13]

B. DEFINITION OF AN ENTERPRISE GROUP

2.08 Despite the proliferation of multinational enterprise groups at the end of the 20th century, there is no universal definition of a corporate group. For instance, the Dutch Civil Code (*Burgerlijk Wetboek*) defines a group as 'an economic unit in which legal persons and commercial partnerships are organizationally interconnected'.[14] The existence of economic unity and organizational interconnectedness are therefore main characteristics of a corporate group. They highlight interdependence of group members, the importance of group synergies and (typically) centralized management.[15]

Report to the Netherlands Association for Comparative and International Insolvency Law (conference of 8 November 2012), pp. 3–4.

12 N. Cooper, Insolvency Proceedings in Case of Groups of Companies: Prospects of Harmonisation at EU Level, Note to European Parliament, 2011, p. 5.

13 BCBS, Report and Recommendations of the Cross-Border Bank Resolution Group, March 2010, para. 49.

14 Dutch Civil Code, Art. 2:24b.

15 The requirement for centralized management is not mentioned in the Dutch Civil Code. However, the parliamentary history considers it essential for qualification as a group. It is assumed that without central

Somewhat similarly, OECD Guidelines, while not offering a definition of multinational enterprises, describe them as 'companies or other entities [...] so linked that they may coordinate their operations in various ways'.[16]

The German Stock Corporation Act (*Aktiengesetz*) establishes that 'where a controlling enterprise and one or several controlled enterprises are combined under the common management of the controlling enterprise, they form a group'.[17] The key element defining a group is thus control – the ability of an entity to 'directly or indirectly exert a controlling influence'.[18] Such control exists if group members have entered into a control agreement and is presumed whenever one enterprise holds the majority ownership stake in another enterprise.[19] The notion of control is also used in English law, which does not provide a comprehensive definition of a corporate group but describes its constituent members. For example, an undertaking is considered a parent undertaking if it holds a majority of the voting rights in another undertaking, or has a participating interest in that undertaking and can appoint or remove a majority of its board of directors, or has the right to exercise a dominant influence over that undertaking.[20] **2.09**

The definition of a group of companies can be found in insolvency-specific rules. For example, according to the European Insolvency Regulation (recast) (EIR Recast), 'group of companies' means a parent undertaking and all its subsidiary undertakings.[21] A 'parent undertaking' is an undertaking which controls, either directly or indirectly, one or more subsidiary undertakings.[22] In a similar vein, the Bank Recovery and Resolution Directive (BRRD) and the Single Resolution Mechanism Regulation (SRMR) define a 'group' as a parent undertaking and its subsidiaries.[23] The UNCITRAL Model Law on Enterprise Group Insolvency (Model Law 2019) provides that an 'enterprise **2.10**

management, organizational connectedness cannot lead to an economic unity. See A.N. Krol, SDU Commentaar – Commentaar Ondernemingsrecht, 1 juni 2019.

16 OECD Guidelines for Multinational Enterprises, 2011 edn, p. 17.

17 Stock Corporation Act of 6 September 1965 (Federal Law Gazette I, p. 1089), Section 18 Group of enterprises and group member companies.

18 Ibid., §17(1) Controlled and controlling enterprises.

19 Ibid., §17(2). See also A. Scheuch, 'Konzernrecht: An Overview of the German Regulation of Corporate Groups and Resulting Liability Issues' (201) 13(5) *European Company Law*, pp. 191–8.

20 Section 1662 Companies Act 2006.

21 EIR Recast, Art. 2(13).

22 Ibid. Art. 2(14).

23 Art. 2(26) of the Directive 2014/59/EU of the European Parliament and of the Council of 15 May 2014 establishing a framework for the recovery and resolution of credit institutions and investment firms and amending Council Directive 82/891/EEC, and Directives 2001/24/EC, 2002/47/EC, 2004/25/EC, 2005/56/EC, 2007/36/EC, 2011/35/EU, 2012/30/EU and 2013/36/EU, and Regulations (EU) No 1093/2010 and (EU) No 648/2012, of the European Parliament and of the Council.

group' is two or more enterprises that are interconnected by control or significant ownership.[24]

2.11 Thus, control and ownership typically determine the existence of a corporate group. However, the degree of autonomy within an enterprise and the strength and significance of a centralized management may vary from one multinational enterprise to another. Limiting the definition to a particular level of control or ownership may be counterproductive, as the tools offered by insolvency law can be advantageous for different types of groups. The next subchapter gives a general introduction to the typology of enterprise groups.

C. TYPOLOGY OF ENTERPRISE GROUPS

2.12 Enterprise groups diverge greatly in terms of corporate and operational structure, ways of group financing, group management and ownership. They may consist of a complex network of wholly or partly owned subsidiaries, sub-subsidiaries, as well as entities not linked by equity ownership, but still closely related to or dependent on the business of an enterprise group (e.g. suppliers, distributors, franchisees).

2.13 Mevorach has developed a comprehensive typology of multinational groups of companies, depending on their level of centralization, organizational integration and interdependence.[25] While some groups are notable for running a single enterprise, others may consist of relatively self-sufficient business units responsible for separate product or industry lines and being capable of surviving on their own. The former are usually characterized by a vertical hierarchical structure, where a parent company owns, controls and directs its subsidiaries. Such pyramid-like groups are typical for European jurisdictions, such as Germany and Italy.[26] In contrast, the latter may lack centralized control and hierarchical patterns and instead operate in a more heterarchical way, distinguished by decentralized and flatter corporate networks with largely autonomous profit centres.[27]

---

24 Model Law 2019, Art. 2(b). The percentage of shareholding is not always a good predictor of actual control. See L. Bebchuk, R. Kraakman and G. Triantis, 'Stock Pyramids, Cross-Ownership, and Dual Class Equity: The Creation and Agency Costs of Separating Control from Cash Flow Rights' (2000) 249 Harvard Law and Economics Discussion Paper, exploring 'controlling minority structure'.

25 I. Mevorach, *Insolvency within Multinational Enterprise Groups* (OUP, 2009), pp. 135–47.

26 K. Hopt, 'Groups of Companies. A Comparative Study on the Economics, Law and Regulation of Corporate Groups', Law Working Paper No. 286/2015, ECGI Working Paper Series in Law, 2015, p. 2.

27 Muchlinski, *supra* note 5, pp. 47–8, arguing that decentralized corporate structures may replace traditional hierarchical models.

The technological progress of the 19th century, including the invention of telegraph and telephone promoted integration and centralization of corporate structures.[28] Skeel notes that America's first large-scale business enterprises, the railroads, brought many units carrying on different types of economic activities under their control and adopted increasingly hierarchical business structures, 'with a class of middle managers between the railroad's workers and its executive officers'.[29] Hadfield describes this economy as the 'economy of consolidation and vertical integration, the absorption of economic activity in entire industries within the walls of a handful of, maybe even a single, corporation'.[30] **2.14**

Interestingly, nowadays the technological progress seems to pull in the opposite direction by advancing decentralization.[31] The ease with which information can be accessed and disseminated simplifies access to corporate decision-making and corporate ownership. Another decentralizing factor arises from the operation of platform-based businesses and their asset base. Think of Uber, a ride-hailing service, which connects drivers (or driver-partners, as Uber prefers to call them) and riders through a smartphone application. Uber portrays itself as a market intermediary and not as a provider of transportation and logistics services.[32] This has an effect on its assets side, as Uber does not own cars.[33] As regards changing asset structures, Baird persuasively points out that, '[f]ew businesses today center around specialised long-lived assets. In a service-oriented economy, the assets walk out the door at 5:00 pm'.[34] Such 'assets-light' platform-based businesses may have less incentives to adopt a hierarchical corporate model. Decentralization is further **2.15**

---

28 Before the 19th century businesses were typically decentralized. Such was, for instance, the case of the East India Company, whose multi-divisional nature (separation of powers between the board of directors and relatively independent overseas managers (factors)) was highlighted in a number of studies. See E. Erikson, *Between Monopoly and Free Trade: The English East India Company* (Princeton University Press, Princeton, 2014). G. Anderson et al., 'The Economic Organization of the English East India Company' (1983) 4(2–3) *Journal of Economic Behavior and Organization*, p. 226.

29 D. Skeel, *Icarus in the Boardroom: The Fundamental Flaws in Corporate America and Where They Came From* (OUP, 2005), p. 25.

30 G. Hadfield, 'Legal Infrastructure and the New Economy' (2012) 8(1) *I/S: A Journal of Law and Policy for the Information Society*, p. 12.

31 M. Roe, 'Three Ages of Bankruptcy' (2017) 7 *Harvard Business Law Review*, p. 215, suggesting that while collective bankruptcy proceedings are needed for industries comprised of big, vertically integrated firms, they may lose appeal in the case of decentralized organizational structures.

32 See Uber's US Terms of Use, last modified 7/15/2020, containing the following clause: 'You acknowledge that your ability to obtain transportation, logistics and/or delivery services through the use of the services does not establish Uber as a provider of transportation, logistics or delivery services or as a transportation carrier.'

33 It does, however, impose requirements on the model, year and capacity of cars used by Uber drivers.

34 D. Baird, 'The New Face of Chapter 11' (2004) 12(1) *American Bankruptcy Institute Law Review*, p. 82.

promoted by the advent and proliferation of distributed ledger technologies (DLT), such as blockchain.[35]

2.16 The diversity of corporate forms and structures complicates adoption of a single approach to their regulation, including regulation in a situation of financial distress and insolvency. This is why this book suggests a flexible and inclusive approach. At the same time, it recognizes that closely integrated groups – groups consisting of separate legal entities but operating as a single economic unit – deserve special attention in insolvency. The reason is that in such groups the failure of a single group member can be contagious and lead to the collapse of all other group members. The absence of a group-wide solution to financial distress may therefore result in a piecemeal liquidation of assets and suboptimal returns to creditors. As a result, the synergy between group members may be lost, should their assets be sold on a separate basis.

2.17 The next chapter introduces major practical and legal problems related to insolvency of multinational enterprise groups.

35 I. Kokorin, 'Contracting Around Insolvency Jurisdiction: Private Ordering in European Insolvency Jurisdiction Rules and Practices', in V. Lazić and S. Stuij (eds), *Recasting the Insolvency Regulation: Improvements and Missed Opportunities. Short Studies in Private International Law* (The Hague: Asser Press, 2020), pp. 35–40.

3

INSOLVENCY OF MULTINATIONAL ENTERPRISE GROUPS

A. ENTITY-BY-ENTITY APPROACH IN INSOLVENCY LAW 3.01
B. CORPORATE GROUP INSOLVENCY AND 'GROUP INSOLVENCY SOLUTION' 3.08
1. Recognition of a corporate group in insolvency 3.08
2. The rise of 'group insolvency solution' 3.14
3. The limits of 'group insolvency solution' 3.19

A. ENTITY-BY-ENTITY APPROACH IN INSOLVENCY LAW

Until recently the problem of insolvency of corporate groups had not been widely recognized or addressed in regulation. Thus, the UNCITRAL Model Law on Cross-Border Insolvency (1997) (Model Law 1997),[1] the Directive on the reorganisation and winding up of credit institutions (CIWUD)[2] and the original European Insolvency Regulation, EIR 2000[3] lack provisions addressing enterprise group insolvency. The explanation given by the UNCITRAL Working Group V responsible for drafting the text of the Model Law 1997, is quite revealing. It stated that '[w]hen the text of what became the UNCITRAL Model Law on Cross-Border Insolvency (the Model Law) was debated, groups were regarded as 'a stage too far'.[4] This explanation itself raises questions. Could the Model Law 1997 introduce the concept of a 'group' in an era where most national states did not have any rules regarding enterprise groups? Was it the soft law nature of the Model Law 1997 that limited its scope and ambition? Or does 'a stage too far' indicate the lack of 3.01

1 The Model Law 1997 seeks to offer 'effective mechanisms for dealing with cases of cross-border insolvency' and has so far been adopted in 48 states and 51 jurisdictions.

2 Directive 2001/24/EC of the European Parliament and of the Council of 4 April 2001 on the reorganisation and winding up of credit institutions.

3 The Virgos-Schmit Report (1996), supplementing the European Insolvency Convention (1995), the predecessor of the original European Insolvency Regulation (i.e. EIR 2000), directly stated that the 'Convention offers no rule for groups of affiliated companies (parent-subsidiary schemes).'

4 UNCITRAL Working Group V, Thirty-eighth session, UNCITRAL Legislative Guide on Insolvency Law, Part three: Treatment of enterprise groups in insolvency, III: Addressing the insolvency of enterprise groups: international issues, 11 February 2010, A/CN.9/WG.V/WP.92/Add.1, para. 3, https://undocs.org/en/A/CN.9/WG.V/WP.92/Add.1.

agreement among the members of the Working Group V (Insolvency Law) about what a 'group' actually is?

3.02 There are, however, several reasons for the chosen approach.

3.03 First, in the past, and in many respects still, insolvency law focuses on the position of a creditor and its ability to 'be satisfied to the maximum with no regard to the destiny of the debtor, as usually the most predictable, certain and therefore best possible satisfaction of the debtor's creditors is accomplished by complete liquidation of the remaining assets of the debtor'.[5] Any solution entailing piercing of a corporate veil and pooling of assets and liabilities of several companies together can be damaging to the interests of creditors of (at least) one of the entities involved.[6] This is why insolvency laws around the world circle around five basic ground rules: 'one insolvent debtor, one estate, one insolvency proceeding, one court and one insolvency office holder'.[7] The entity-by-entity approach to the treatment of group entities in insolvency is firmly grounded in the long-established principle of entity separateness. This principle results in the demarcation of a pool of assets of a company from the assets and liabilities of its owners (shareholders), representing the entity shielding function of a corporate veil.[8] In insolvency this means that assets in the group are separated along entity lines and creditors have legal rights (recourse) only against particular entities and their respective asset pools.

5 E. Göretzlehner, *Maritime Cross-Border Insolvency: An Analysis for Germany, England & Wales and the USA* (Springer, 2019), p. 14. During the second decade of the 21st century, the insolvency law paradigm seems to have shifted from the exclusive focus on the interests of creditors to the rise of the rescue culture with increased attention on the interests of debtors and other stakeholders (e.g. employees). In Europe, this shift has recently culminated in the adoption of the Directive (EU) 2019/1023 of the European Parliament and of the Council of 20 June 2019 on preventive restructuring frameworks, on discharge of debt and disqualifications, and on measures to increase the efficiency of procedures concerning restructuring, insolvency and discharge of debt (Restructuring Directive). While being a major achievement in the process of harmonizing substantive (pre)insolvency law in the EU, it lacks developed rules targeting restructuring of multinational enterprise groups. As a result, the effectiveness of group reorganizations may be undermined.

6 It should be noted that some European jurisdictions allow for the pooling of assets and liabilities of some or all members of a corporate group, so that a creditor of one member becomes, in essence, a creditor of all members. For instance, Art. L. 621-2 of the French Commercial Code (*Code de commerce*) provides for a consolidation of insolvency proceedings against companies whose property is intermixed or where the corporate body is a sham. However, due to entity shielding and legal separability, substantive consolidation remains extremely rare in Europe. In Case C-191/10, *Rastelli Davide e C. Snc v. Jean-Charles Hidoux*, ECLI:EU:C:2011:838 (Dec. 15, 2011), the CJEU had to decide whether the court, having opened the main insolvency proceedings in one Member State (France), could join to those proceedings a second company whose registered office was in another Member State (Italy) solely on the basis that the property of the two companies had been intermixed. The Court noted that the legal personality of the two debtors should be respected and that each debtor constituting a distinct legal entity, was subject to its own court jurisdiction.

7 B. Wessels and S. Madaus, Rescue of Business in Insolvency Law, Instrument of the European Law Institute, 2017, p. 342.

8 H. Hansmann, R. Kraakman and R. Squire, 'Law and the Rise of the Firm'. (2006) 119(5) *Harvard Law Review*, p. 1338 noting that 'entity shielding is the *sine qua non* of the legal entity'.

Appointed insolvency practitioners act in the interests of such separate estates and creditors. The fact that before insolvency the group acted as one enterprise plays no role.

Second, the concept of a 'group of companies' has not been comprehensibly developed or widely recognized in company laws worldwide. While some jurisdictions apply general corporate and/or civil law (e.g. the UK), other jurisdictions have adopted special corporate group laws (e.g. Germany, Portugal, the Czech Republic, Slovenia).[9] Still there is some convergence of approaches when it comes to agency conflicts arising in corporate groups, i.e. conflicts between controlling and minority shareholders and between shareholders and creditors. This convergence manifests itself in rules concerning related-party transactions. In the vast majority of EU Member States, but also outside the EU, insolvency laws establish special treatment of transactions involving related parties, such as shareholders and their affiliates, sometimes referred to as 'insiders'. Such insiders usually enjoy lesser, minimal or no protection against transaction avoidance. In practice this materializes in the extension of suspect periods,[10] acceptance of certain mental elements[11] or a rebuttable presumption of the harm caused to creditors.[12] **3.04**

Recognition of the economic reality of corporate groups faces significant obstacles and even resistance whenever the principle of entity separateness is at stake. A good example is the discussion about the recognition of a 'group interest' in European company law that has taken place since the 1990s, first solely among academics[13] and then under the EC Consultation on the Future **3.05**

---

9 K. Hopt, Groups of Companies. A Comparative Study on the Economics, Law and Regulation of Corporate Groups, Law Working Paper No. 286/2015, ECGI Working Paper Series in Law, 2015, p. 9.

10 For instance, in England and Wales the suspect period for preference transactions is two years for connected persons, compared to otherwise applicable six-month period, see s. 240 UK Insolvency Act 1986. In Estonia, gratuitous transactions can be revoked if concluded within one year before the appointment of an interim trustee. This period is extended to five years if the donee was a person connected to the debtor. See s. 111 Bankruptcy Act (Estonia).

11 According to §131(2) German Insolvency Code (*Insolvenzordnung*), a person with a close relationship to the debtor on the date of [preference] transaction (s. 138) shall be presumed to have been aware of the disadvantage to the creditors in insolvency proceedings. Under s. 239 UK Insolvency Act 1986, a company which has given a preference to a person connected with the company 'is presumed [...] to have been influenced in deciding to give it by such a desire as is mentioned in subsection (5)' [desire to create advantage to a counterparty]. In Greece, avoidance of preferences requires knowledge of the counterparty about the detrimental effects of the transactions. Such knowledge is presumed for connected persons, see Art. 43(2) Bankruptcy Code (Greece). The knowledge of prejudice in related-party transactions is codified in Art. 43(1) (3, 4, 5) Bankruptcy Act (Netherlands).

12 Art. 71 Insolvency Act (Spain).

13 A group of scholars, Forum Europaeum Corporate Group Law, has recommended the introduction of a modified *Rozenblum* doctrine at the European level. See Corporate Group Law for Europe, *European Business Organization Law Review*, Vol. 1, 2000, pp. 165–264. See also Report of the High-Level Group of Company Law Experts on Model Regulatory Framework for Company Law in Europe ('Winter report'), 2002.

of European Company Law, which was launched in 2012. The latter resulted in Company Law Action Plan, which included an initiative to recognize the concept of a 'group interest'.[14] Despite the generally positive attitude of scholars and business community,[15] these initiatives have not resulted in any legislative proposals.

3.06 In practical terms the entity-by-entity approach to group insolvencies may cause a complete break-up and disintegration of vital intra-group financial and operational links and the loss of synergies. This leads to a decrease of the insolvency estate value. A well-known example where the atomistic treatment of group entities and the lack of cooperation between separate proceedings has resulted in dismemberment of the debtor's business and a loss of value is insolvency of KPN Qwest. KPN Qwest was a telecom group, which owned and operated rings of fibre-optic cable around Europe and the USA. The parts of the cable were owned by different group entities (the French part by the French subsidiary, the German by the German subsidiary, etc.). When the Dutch holding company of KPN Qwest group collapsed in 2002, its subsidiaries were forced into insolvency and their assets were sold on a separate country-by-country basis.[16] This result was suboptimal as the value of the ring was much higher compared to the value of its isolated sections. The opposite outcome was reached in the insolvency of Nortel Networks, a global networking and telecommunications firm that went insolvent in 2009. As a result of cooperation between parallel proceedings running in Canada, the US and Europe, and prompted by the entry into a cross-border insolvency protocol, the group's assets (most important, its patent portfolio) were sold for USD 7.3 billion – USD 2.8 billion on account of business lines and USD 4.5 billion for intellectual property rights.[17]

---

14 EC, Action Plan: European company law and corporate governance – a modern legal framework for more engaged shareholders and sustainable companies (2012) COM/2012/0740 final.

15 P.-H. Conac, 'Director's Duties in Groups of Companies – Legalizing the Interest of the Group at the European Level' (2013) 10(2) *European Company and Financial Law Review*, pp. 195–226. M. Winner, 'Group Interest in European Company Law: an Overview' (2016) 5(1) *Acta Universitatis Sapientiae: Legal Studies*, pp. 85–96.

16 N. Cooper, Insolvency Proceedings in Case of Groups of Companies: Prospects of Harmonisation at EU Level, Note to European Parliament, 2011, p. 7.

17 R. Mason and J. Martin, 'Conflict and Consistency in Cross border Insolvency Judgments', http://www.uncitral.org/pdf/english/congress/Papers_for_Programme/46-MASON_and_MARTIN-Conflict_and_Consistency_in_Cross_border_Insolvency_Judgments.pdf, citing Justice Newbould of the Ontario Superior Court of Justice, who noted that:

> Judge Gross in Wilmington and I have communicated with each other in accordance with the Protocol with a view to determining whether consistent rulings can be made by both Courts. We have come to the conclusion that a consistent ruling can and should be made by both Courts. [...] These insolvency

A coordinated going concern sale of an enterprise as a whole can maximize the estate value and benefit creditors of each entity involved.[18] Equally important is the fact that efficient business rescue and financial restructuring require group-wide solutions to prevent a domino-like collapse of enterprise group members as well as other non-group entities dependent on them.[19] Group entities are often integrated and interdependent. This interdependence stems from operational and financial links existing between group members. Such links can relate to funding arrangements (intra-group loans, cross-guarantees, access to capital markets), business commitments (supply of materials, provision of licences and know how, lease of premises), collaboration (information exchange, common client databases, development and implementation of a business strategy) and services (data management, IT, marketing). Successful restructuring needs to take these factors into account, which is only possible if proper communication and cooperation between group proceedings is maintained. **3.07**

B. CORPORATE GROUP INSOLVENCY AND 'GROUP INSOLVENCY SOLUTION'

1. Recognition of a corporate group in insolvency

The UNCITRAL Legislative Guide 2010 distinguishes two types of insolvency regulation applicable to corporate groups: (1) the separate entity approach (by far the most prevalent) and (2) the single enterprise approach.[20] Mevorach refers to them as 'entity law' and 'enterprise law' respectively.[21] As noted above, the separate entity approach relies on the principle of legal separability. Thus, insolvency estates and pools of creditors of legal entities are separated. This should limit the risks attached to a failure of a single company. However, the economic interconnectedness of companies in a group could **3.08**

proceedings have now lasted over six years at unimaginable expense and they should if at all possible come to a final resolution. It is in all of the parties' interests for that to occur.

On the history of the Nortel case see J. Pottow, 'Two Cheers for Universalism: Nortel's Nifty Novelty', in J. Sarra and B. Romaine (eds), *Annual Review of Insolvency Law* (Toronto: Carswell, 2015), pp. 333–68, available at https://papers.ssrn.com/sol3/papers.cfm?abstract_id=2697095.

18 *Black's Law Dictionary* defines 'going concern value' as the 'value of a commercial enterprise's assets or of the enterprise itself as an active business with future earning power, as opposed to the liquidation value of the business or of its assets'. This value is usually higher than the piecemeal liquidation value. *Black's Law Dictionary* (8th edn, Thomson Reuters, 2004), p. 1587.

19 I. Mevorach, 'Cross-Border Insolvency of Enterprise Groups: The Choice of Law Challenge' (2014) 9(1) *Brooklyn Journal of Corporate, Financial & Commercial Law*, p. 233.

20 Legislative Guide 2010, Ch. I, para. 31.

21 I. Mevorach, 'Transaction Avoidance in Bankruptcy of Corporate Groups' (2011) 8(2) *ECFR*, pp. 243–4.

make such an approach less appealing. In contrast, the single enterprise approach treats the group as a single economic unit that operates to further interests of the group as a whole. This latter approach has given rise to various rules and techniques, from less intrusive (e.g. communication and cooperation between insolvent group members) to the ultimate disregard of entity boundaries (substantive consolidation).[22]

3.09 Recent years have witnessed the rise of important initiatives and the emergence of new legal instruments that modernize insolvency law to enhance the effective administration of cross-border insolvency proceedings in the context of enterprise groups. The World Bank Principles (2015)[23] establish a range of benchmarks, based on international best practices. Among them, principles related to insolvency of international enterprise groups, including appointment of the same insolvency representative for all or several enterprise group members located in different jurisdictions, cooperation between courts and insolvency representatives and conclusion of cross-border insolvency agreements.[24] These principles have found their way into a number of hard and soft law instruments.

3.10 As noted above, the EIR 2000, the CIWUD and the original Model Law 1997 did not address the problem of enterprise group insolvency. This contrasts with more recent developments. The BRRD, the EIR Recast and the Model Law 2019 recognize the existence of corporate groups and offer special tools to address their insolvency. Notably, whereas such recognition by the EIR Recast and the Model Law 2019 pursues the goal of asset value maximization and business rescue, the BRRD is primarily concerned with matters of public interest, preservation of financial stability, protection of public funds and safeguarding of the rights of depositors and clients.[25]

3.11 A number of national legal regimes also contain a regulation of corporate group insolvency. For example, Germany reformed its insolvency law in 2017 to facilitate effective administration of insolvency proceedings through enhanced coordination. This may be achieved by means of concentration of

---

22 Substantive consolidation permits the court in insolvency cases involving related entities in appropriate circumstances to disregard the separate identity of the entities to consolidate and pool their assets and liabilities and treat them as though held and incurred by a single entity. See Legislative Guide 2010, Ch. II, para. 105.

23 The World Bank Principles for Effective Insolvency and Creditor/Debtor Regimes, 2015 (World Bank Principles).

24 Ibid., C17.

25 BRRD, Recital 45. M. Haentjens, 'National Insolvency Law in International Bank Insolvencies', in B. Santen and D. van Offeren (eds), *Perspectives on International Insolvency Law: A Tribute to Bob Wessels* (Kluwer: Deventer, 2014), p. 76.

insolvency proceedings of group members in one court, appointment of the same insolvency practitioner in separate insolvency proceedings and opening of group coordination proceedings.[26] France, Italy, Belgium, England and Spain have adapted general insolvency rules to provide for joint commencement of proceedings in cases of enterprise groups.[27] The English scheme of arrangements is frequently used to restructure debts of various group members at the same time, giving effect to a group-wide solution.[28] This is particularly evident from the sweeping approval by English courts of so-called third-party releases, which lead to a release (i.e. total or partial discharge or amendment) of claims against third parties, such as co-obligors, guarantors and collateral providers (typically, group members) in the insolvency or restructuring proceeding of the principal debtor. In the recent case of *Syncreon Group BV*, the court noted that such releases were necessary 'in order to give full effect to the schemes' and that they were 'a relatively regular feature of the schemes'.[29]

Modernization of insolvency law has been linked to better cooperation and communication between insolvency proceedings opened against enterprise group members. Thus, both the EIR Recast and the Model Law 2019 provide for communication between courts and insolvency practitioners, possibility to appoint the same insolvency practitioner in several proceedings and to initiate group coordination (EIR Recast) and planning (Model Law 2019) proceedings. **3.12**

This new generation of legal texts recognizes the need to adjust traditional approaches of insolvency law to the characteristics and business reality of corporate groups. Nevertheless, the extent of such recognition and its boundaries are not entirely clear. **3.13**

2. The rise of 'group insolvency solution'

The EIR Recast establishes that cooperation in the context of enterprise group insolvency 'should be aimed at finding a solution that would leverage synergies **3.14**

26 Gesetz zur Erleichterung der Bewältigung von Konzerninsolvenzen, 13.04.2017, Bundesgesetzblatt Jahrgang 2017 Teil I Nr. 22, ausgegeben am 21.04.2017, Seite 866.

27 S. Madaus, 'Abuse of Companies in Insolvency Law', in H. Birkmose, M. Neville et al. (eds), *Abuse of Companies* (Wolters Kluwer, 2019), p. 339. For the country-by-country study of approaches to company groups, see also R. Manóvil (ed.), *Groups of Companies: A Comparative Law Overview* (Springer, 2020).

28 A scheme of arrangement is a statutory procedure available under Part 26 (ss. 895–901) of the UK Companies Act 2006. It is not considered to be an insolvency procedure, as it falls under company rather than insolvency law. Nevertheless, in practice schemes are used by companies (and corporate groups) in distress as a mechanism for financial reorganization. Read further J. Payne, *Schemes of Arrangement: Theory, Structure and Operation* (CUP, 2014).

29 *In the matter of Syncreon Group BV* [2019] EWHC 2412 (Ch), 2019 WL 04279919.

across the group'.[30] In a like manner the Model Law 2019 aims at providing effective mechanisms to address cases of insolvency of groups of companies, inter alia, through facilitation of the development of group insolvency solutions for the whole or part of an enterprise group. 'Group insolvency solution' is defined as:

> a proposal or set of proposals developed [...] for the reorganization, sale or liquidation of some or all of the assets and operations of one or more enterprise group members, with the goal of protecting, preserving, realizing or enhancing the overall combined value of those enterprise group members.[31]

As explained in the Draft Guide to Enactment of the Model Law 2019, 'group insolvency solution' is a new term, which is intended to be flexible.[32] This flexibility is needed to take into account the circumstances of a specific enterprise group, its structure, business model, as well as the degree of integration between different group members.

3.15 For integrated groups of companies, a group solution often entails preservation of the business' going concern value, which requires prevention of group disintegration upon insolvency. Imagine the following (rather typical) scenario. A complex corporate group consists of a number of entities playing different roles: a company issuing debt instruments and lending the received funds to other group members (FinCo); a company managing and owning assets essential for the group's business, including intellectual property, licences, know how, real estate (SPV); a company exercising managerial control over the group as a whole and acting as a group treasury as a result of a centralized cash management strategy (HoldCo); and a number of operational companies offering services or producing goods (OpCos). Administering such companies separately in insolvency can be difficult and suboptimal in terms of maximizing insolvency estate value, as strict entity-by-entity approach may lead to a breakup of intra-group links and denial of the access to vital resources and lifelines.

3.16 A good example is Lehman Brothers. In the Lehman Brothers group, the US holding company, Lehman Brothers Holdings Inc. (LBHI), acted as the banker for the hundreds of its affiliates due to the established intra-group cash pooling system. According to the report, prepared by the examiner in the Chapter 11 proceedings of LBHI (also referred to as 'Valukas Report'), LBHI

30 EIR Recast, Recital 52.

31 Model Law 2019, Art. 2(g).

32 Enterprise group insolvency: draft guide to enactment, A/CN.9/WG.V/WP.165, 20 March 2019 (Guide to Model Law 2019).

controlled 'the cash disbursements and receivables for itself, its subsidiaries and its affiliates'.[33] This was done to track all cash activities, maximize investment opportunities and minimize transaction costs. The holding company lent money to its operating affiliates 'at the beginning of each day and then swept the cash back to LBHI at the end of each day'.[34] When LBHI filed for insolvency in the USA on 15 September 2008, most of the group funds became part of the US proceedings, and therefore – as was generally held – unavailable for supporting its subsidiaries.[35] Another problem that arose in the insolvency of Lehman Brothers related to the concentration of information on accounts and trades in one jurisdiction and access to such information by group entities established in other jurisdictions. Thus, Lehman Brothers International (Europe) (LBIE), the UK subsidiary of LBHI recorded information on financial notes relevant to other group members, including its Dutch subsidiary, Lehman Brothers Treasury. When the latter went insolvent in the Netherlands, the court needed such information to make asset distribution in the Dutch proceedings, as it was not readily available.[36]

A similar scenario can occur if in insolvency, entities lose their access to vital assets held by other entities in the group, including patents, licences, customer databases, real estate and raw materials. As a result, the operational activity of the group may be paralyzed, and group entities may end up in a piecemeal liquidation. Intra-group interdependence plays an important role in restructuring. Rescue attempts at an entity level without due consideration of a group context, position and interest of other group members risk being short-sighted and economically inefficient. Separateness of insolvency proceedings and the lack of communication and cooperation between them can also give rise to intra-group disputes concerning access to information, enforcement of intra-group claims, allocation of assets and liquidity within the group. **3.17**

Group insolvency solutions mentioned above aim at overcoming these problems by facilitating information flows and coordination of parallel insolvency proceedings. The question arises whether 'group insolvency solution' replaces the long-established entity-by-entity treatment of corporate groups in insolvency. This question is discussed below. **3.18**

---

33 Lehman Brothers Holdings Inc. Chapter 11 Proceedings Examiner's Report (Valukas Report), 2010, p. 1550.

34 R. Herring and J. Carmassi, 'The Corporate Structure of International Financial Conglomerates: Complexity and its Implications for Safety and Soundness', in A. Berger, P. Molyneux and J. Wilson (eds), *The Oxford Handbook on Banking* (1st edn, OUP, 2012), p. 225.

35 E. Avgouleas, *Governance of Global Financial Markets. The Law, the Economics, the Politics* (CUP, 2012), p. 254.

36 J. Kirshner, *International Bankruptcy: The Challenge of Insolvency in a Global Economy* (The University of Chicago Press, 2018), p. 5.

3. The limits of 'group insolvency solution'

3.19 In the last two decades a number of solutions have been proposed by legislators or have been worked out in practice to facilitate administration of insolvency estates in corporate groups and to ensure efficient group restructuring. Among such solutions, communication and cooperation between courts and insolvency practitioners, conclusion of cross-border insolvency protocols or agreements, opening of special coordination or planning proceedings. Despite the growing body of mechanisms and channels to exchange information and coordinate parallel insolvency or restructuring proceedings, important obstacles to and limitations of such activities remain.

3.20 Wessels lists some general obstacles to cross-border communication and conclusion of cross-border insolvency protocols. Among them, 'a general reciprocity provision, language, uncertainty about the meaning of certain procedural or substantial legal terms or an inadequate infrastructure that would impede local judges from participating in teleconferences'.[37] Courts may have different approaches towards communication with foreign courts and insolvency practitioners. The reasons for such divergence may come from different national (legal) traditions and even different philosophies.[38] For instance, the Irish constitutional principle that justice must be administered in public[39] can make it considerably more difficult to engage in direct (without prior open court hearing involving affected parties) communication with courts in other Member States.

3.21 The corporate group context may create additional obstacles. One of them relates to the requirement to avoid conflicts of interest. The EIR Recast, the Guide to Model Law 2019,[40] the UNCITRAL Legislative Guide,[41] many national laws and soft law instruments mention such a limitation. For example, the EIR Recast mandates insolvency practitioners and courts to cooperate to the extent that it does not entail any conflict of interest.[42] A common feature of these instruments is that they do not offer a general

37 B. Wessels, *International Insolvency Law Part I. Global Perspectives on Cross-Border Insolvency Law* (4th edn, Wolters Kluwer, 2015), 10118a.

38 See C. Paulus, 'Judicial Cooperation in Cross-Border Insolvencies: An outline of some relevant issues and literature', 2006, referring to Eidenmüller, Der nationale und der internationale Insolvenzverwaltungsvertrag, ZZP 114, 2001, 3, 'whereas the Common Law judiciary – in particular, in equity-related matters – understands statutory (so far) uncovered areas in the law as permission to rule, their Civil Law counterparts understand them as a prohibition in the sense that action by the Judge has not been explicitly permitted'.

39 Constitution of Ireland, Art. 34(1).

40 Guide to Model Law 2019, para. 103.

41 Legislative Guide 2010, Ch. II, para. 68.

42 EIR Recast, Arts 56(1), 57(1) and 58.

definition of a 'conflict of interest' and oftentimes instead consider cases in which the risks arising from conflicts of interest are particularly acute (e.g. appointment of the same insolvency practitioner or an intermediary). Carson suggests that a conflict of interest exists where (1) an individual has duties to another party in virtue of an office, (2) this individual is impeded or compromised in performing such duties, and (3) the impediment follows from that person's interest (broadly construed) that is incompatible or seemingly incompatible with fulfilling those duties.[43]

The main reason why conflicts between enterprise group members may intensify in insolvency proceedings is legal separability. Each enterprise group member has its own insolvency estate, whose value an insolvency practitioner appointed in the respective proceeding is tasked to safeguard and enhance. Also, each group member has its own pool of creditors, separate from the pool of creditors of other group entities. Thus, generally speaking, a conflict may arise from the impairment of the value of one group entity's insolvency estate to the benefit of another group entity's insolvency estate. This can also result from communication and cooperation. As an example, Moss and Smith, commenting on Article 56 of the EIR Recast ('Cooperation and communication between insolvency practitioners'), note that whenever there is a disputed claim between two group entities, an obligation of insolvency practitioners to cooperate may 'need to be circumscribed accordingly'.[44] This is due to the fact that such cooperation may result in the exchange of information that can prove instrumental in substantiating a claim of one group entity against the other, therefore potentially to the detriment of that other entity and its creditors.[45] Procedural consolidation,[46] the use of special coordination proceedings (i.e. group coordination and planning proceedings) **3.22**

43 T. Carson, 'Conflicts of Interest and Self-Dealing in the Professions: A Review Essay' (2004) 14(1) *Business Ethics Quarterly*, p. 165.

44 G. Moss and T. Smith, 'Commentary on Council Regulation 1346/2000 on Insolvency Proceedings and Regulation (EU) 2015/848 of the European Parliament and of the Council of 20 May 2015 on Insolvency Proceedings (Recast)', in G. Moss, I. Fletcher and S. Isaacs (eds), *Moss, Fletcher and Isaacs on the EU Regulation on Insolvency Proceedings* (OUP, 2016), para. 8.754. See also Mevorach, *supra* note 21, p. 254, noting that in the case of coordinated or centralized proceedings, 'problems of conflict of interests should be tackled as the avoidance of transactions could benefit one member and be detrimental to another'.

45 The same argument is made by Wessels, who notes that 'a conflict may occur where disclosing information to a foreign court or a foreign insolvency practitioner would be beneficial to creditors in one proceeding, but prejudicial to creditors in any other proceeding.' See B. Wessels, 'Secondary Insolvency Proceedings', in R. Bork and K. van Zwieten (eds), *Commentary on the European Insolvency Regulation* (OUP, 2016), para. 43.05.

46 In the case of procedural consolidation insolvency proceedings opened with respect to separate entities are consolidated for administration purposes to promote procedural convenience and cost efficiencies, but the assets and liabilities of the debtors remain separate and distinct. See UNCITRAL Working Group V, Treatment of corporate groups in insolvency, 4 October 2006, A/CN.9/WG.V/WP.74.

and cross-border insolvency agreements facilitate information exchange to a greater extent, further aggravating the risk of conflicts of interest.

3.23 The requirement to avoid conflicts of interest may present an obstacle to communication and cooperation in the context of enterprise group insolvency. It also highlights a boundary for the adoption of group insolvency solutions, which should not harm particular entities within a group and their creditors. The rise of group insolvency solutions does not change or affect the essence of entity separateness.[47] Instead it tries to ensure that in insolvency, important operational and financial ties, information links and contractual bonds between group members are preserved. These are crucial for the realization of any group-wide recovery and resolution plans, safeguarding operational continuity and going concern value of a group and its constituent members. In other words, a rigid entity-by-entity approach is transformed into a more flexible group coordination approach, which preserves entity separateness but appeals to economic reality of multinational enterprise groups. The development of this new approach has originated from case law and creative solutions embraced by insolvency practitioners, rather than from a top-down imposition by state authority. The next chapter introduces one of these creative cooperation solutions, namely cross-border insolvency protocols or agreements.

---

47 With the exception of substantive consolidation, the principle of 'five ones' is maintained ('one insolvent debtor, one estate, one insolvency proceeding, one court and one insolvency office holder'). This means that separateness of insolvency estates is preserved, and enterprise group members end up in separate insolvency proceedings. In the context of bank resolution, despite the existence of group recovery and resolution plans, resolution tools only apply at the entity (parent or subsidiaries) level pursuant to national law. Besides, the no-creditor-worse-off (NCWO) principle, established under Art. 34(1)(g) BRRD applies on the entity-by-entity and not the group basis.

4

CROSS-BORDER INSOLVENCY PROTOCOLS AND AGREEMENTS: INTRODUCTION AND EVOLUTION

A. PURPOSE AND GOALS OF CROSS-BORDER INSOLVENCY PROTOCOLS AND AGREEMENTS 4.01

B. EARLY CASES OF CROSS-BORDER INSOLVENCY PROTOCOLS: TARGETED CRISIS RESPONSE 4.09
1. Macfadyen Protocol 4.09
2. Maxwell Protocol 4.13
3. Commodore Protocol 4.18

C. CROSS-BORDER INSOLVENCY CONCORDAT AND EARLY HARMONIZATION PROCESS 4.23
1. Principles of Cross-border Insolvency Concordat 4.23
2. Application of Concordat Principles in insolvency protocols 4.30

D. LOEWEN AS A NEW MODEL INSOLVENCY PROTOCOL 4.36

E. EVOLUTION OF CROSS-BORDER INSOLVENCY PROTOCOLS: INITIAL OBSERVATIONS 4.42

A. PURPOSE AND GOALS OF CROSS-BORDER INSOLVENCY PROTOCOLS AND AGREEMENTS

It is widely recognized that communication and cooperation in international insolvency cases is necessary to ensure efficient administration of insolvency proceedings and insolvency estates. It is necessary on two levels: (1) the general level of national or regional legislation, to guarantee that such communication and cooperation have a clear basis in law, and (2) on an individual basis taking account of the individual cross-border case at hand and focusing on the needs of such an individual case. **4.01**

Bork highlights the value of communication and cooperation as a standalone principle of international insolvency law.[1] Certain regional and national legislation obliges courts and insolvency practitioners to cooperate and exchange information with each other. For example, the EIR Recast establishes that courts and insolvency practitioners appointed in proceedings **4.02**

1 R. Bork, *Principles of Cross-Border Insolvency Law* (Intersentia, 2017), p. 44.

concerning a member of the group *shall* cooperate with each other.[2] The Model Law 1997[3] and most jurisdictions which passed laws on its basis[4] also mandate cooperation with foreign courts and foreign representatives. Duty of cooperation and communication can also be found in some non-Model-law based national insolvency law regimes.[5]

4.03 There are many different tools to facilitate the management of transnational insolvencies and promote communication and cooperation among different stakeholders. One of these tools is known as a cross-border insolvency agreement or a protocol. While the Model Law 1997 only mentions 'agreements', the EIR Recast uses both terms (i.e. agreement and protocol) interchangeably. In practice, other names can also be found, including 'Stipulation', 'Memorandum of understanding', 'Cross-border cooperation arrangement', 'Cross-border liquidation protocol', 'Protocol Agreement'. This book attempts to compile these variations in practice with respect to as many forms of cross-border cooperation instruments as possible. Unless otherwise indicated, it uses various terms interchangeably. Nevertheless, it recognizes that the use of a generalized term may not reflect the diverse nature of the arrangements being used in practice. This chapter introduces cross-border insolvency protocols, explores the reasons for their adoption and discusses some of the early cases where protocols have been used.

4.04 According to the UNCITRAL Practice Guide, a cross-border insolvency agreement is 'an oral or written agreement intended to facilitate the coordination of cross-border insolvency proceedings and cooperation between courts, between courts and insolvency representatives and between insolvency representatives, sometimes also involving other parties in interest'.[6] While their exact nature is not entirely clear and will be dealt with in the following chapters of this book, the instrument of a protocol has evolved as a judicial

2 As applied to group insolvencies see EIR Recast, Arts 56–58. Wessels encourages active role of insolvency practitioners and courts in communicating and cooperating on cross-border insolvency cases, see B. Wessels, *International Insolvency Law Part II. European Insolvency Law*, Vol. X (4th edn, Wolters Kluwer, 2017), 10926e and 10926k.

3 Model Law 1997, Arts 25–27. The Guide to the Enactment and Interpretation of the Model Law 1997 (2013) on p. 95 emphasizes that the Model Law mandates cross-border cooperation by 'providing that the court and the insolvency representative "shall cooperate to the maximum extent possible". Note that the Model Law 1997 does not deal with a situation of a corporate group but concerns single-entity insolvency.

4 See e.g. 11 U.S. Code § 1525-1527; Chapter IV, The Cross-Border Insolvency Regulations 2006.

5 See e.g. § 269a (cooperation between IPs) and § 269b (cooperation between courts) German Insolvency Code (InsO). Art. 288 Italian Crisis and Insolvency Code. For more on the recent reform of Italian insolvency law, concerning insolvency of groups of companies, see L. Benedetti, 'Information Flows in the Insolvency of Enterprise Groups' (2019) 30(3) *European Business Law Review*, pp. 417–38.

6 UNCITRAL Practice Guide on Cross-Border Insolvency Cooperation, 2009 (Practice Guide), Introduction, para. 13(i).

innovation and as a response to the increasingly global scope of business interactions, highly divergent substantive insolvency laws and the absence of comprehensive national, regional or international rules. Protocols have been used in a wide variety of situations involving liquidation and restructuring proceedings, opened against a single entity or different members of a group of companies, localized in close geographical proximity (e.g. the USA and Canada) and far away from each other (e.g. the USA and Switzerland), coming from a similar legal tradition (e.g. common law jurisdictions, inter alia, England, the USA, Canada, the Cayman Islands) or from very different legal families (e.g. the Netherlands and India).

It has been argued that at an early stage, protocols were used with the purpose of information exchange, while later they have grown into an instrument to negotiate shared measures and solutions, mostly of procedural nature.[7] The identification of a single or primary purpose of cross-border insolvency protocols may be difficult or even futile. As the judge in *MacFadyen* noted (as early as in 1908), a protocol is a 'proper and common-sense business arrangement to make, and one manifestly for the benefit of all parties interested'.[8] One of the first examples of an insolvency protocol, the protocol reached in the course of insolvency proceedings concerning the Maxwell Communication Corporation and approved by the English and the US courts allocated functions between proceedings and provided for cooperative administration. Thus, it went far beyond facilitating information exchange. **4.05**

The American Law Institute (ALI) and International Insolvency Institute (III) have drafted Global Principles for Cooperation in International Insolvency Cases 2012.[9] The Principles represent a non-binding statement or a list of guidelines to be used both in civil-law and common-law jurisdictions around the world. Principle 26 (Cooperation) stipulates that a protocol between insolvency practitioners 'should address the coordination of requests for court approvals of related decisions and actions when required and communication with creditors and other parties'. When possible, 'it should also provide for timesaving procedures to avoid unnecessary and costly court hearings and other proceedings'. Specific principles concern maximization of **4.06**

7 G. Vallar, 'Protocols as Means of Coordination of Insolvency Proceedings of Cross-Border Banking Groups', in L. Cadiet, B. Hess and M. Requejo Isidro (eds), *Procedural Science at the Crossroads of Different Generations* (Nomos, 2015), p. 323.

8 *Re P. MacFadyen & Co, ex parte Vizianagaram Co. Ltd.* [1908] 1 K.B. 675.

9 ALI-III Global Principles for Cooperation in International Insolvency Cases 2012. Please note that these Principles focus on a situation of single debtor insolvency, rather than insolvency of an enterprise group. See Principle 2 (Aim): 'The aim of these Global Principles is to facilitate the coordination of the administration of international insolvency cases involving the *same debtor*, including where appropriate through the use of a protocol.'

aggregate value of the assets to be sold (Principle 29: Cross-Border Sales) and assistance in reorganization attempts (Principle 30: Assistance to Reorganization). In the European Communication and Cooperation Guidelines for Cross-border Insolvency (CoCo Guidelines, 2007) a similar description is used: 'Cooperation may be best attained by way of an agreement or "protocol" that establishes decision-making procedures, although decisions may continue to be made informally as long as they are compatible with the substance of any such agreement or "protocol".'[10] The use of insolvency protocols for efficient group resolution has been supported by the III Guidelines for Coordination of Multinational Enterprise Group Insolvencies.[11] These guidelines foresee that courts should direct, authorize, or permit a debtor or an IP to enter into agreements or protocols with other members of the enterprise group.[12] Where courts are not permitted to do so, IPs, debtors or creditors should 'initiate development of agreements or protocols to promote the orderly, effective, efficient and timely administration of the cases'.[13]

4.07 Due to the flexibility inherent in cross-border insolvency protocols as freely negotiated instruments of combined public-private nature, they can pursue multiple purposes. These may range from a simple facilitation of communication and information sharing between insolvency practitioners and courts (e.g. by way of joint hearing[14]) to covering submission and approval of winding-up and reorganization plans and setting up special rules for asset preservation, allowance, priority and valuation of creditors' claims or even establishing special procedures for resolution of intercompany claims. As a result, a 'joint transborder case management'[15] or 'a sort of transnational insolvency norm'[16] can be created.

4.08 Cross-border insolvency protocols are often adjusted to a particular factual scenario or a problem. As the court held in *Calpine*, 'a protocol cannot be

10 Guideline 12: Cooperation, European Communication and Cooperation Guidelines for Cross-border Insolvency, 2007 (CoCo Guidelines). Just like ALI-III Global Principles, CoCo Guidelines concentrate on a single-debtor insolvency.

11 International Insolvency Institute Guidelines for Coordination of Multinational Enterprise Group Insolvencies, 2012, https://www.iiiglobal.org/sites/default/files/draftmultinationalcorporaqtegroupguidelines.pdf.

12 Ibid., Guideline 7.

13 Ibid., Guideline 8.

14 The group-wide solution in the Nortel Networks case was reached through joint trials of the Ontario and Delaware courts. On this see D. Miller and M. Shakra, 'Nortel: The Long and Winding Road', in J. Sarra and Justice B. Romaine (eds), *Annual Review of Insolvency Law* (Carswell, 2015), pp. 281–310.

15 P. Schlosser, 'Jurisdiction and International Judicial and Administrative Cooperation' (2000) 284 Recueil des Cours de l'Académie de droit international, p. 396.

16 G. Vallar, 'Use of Cross-Border Insolvency Protocols in Banking and Financial Sector', in R. Parry and P. Omar (eds), *Banking and Financial Insolvencies: The European Regulatory Framework* (INSOL Europe, 2016), p. 168.

drafted in a vacuum, and must address the particular circumstances of the case at hand'.[17] For example, the Madoff protocol described the arrangements related to cooperation provided to law enforcement and other state agencies.[18] This was dictated by a substantial public interest in the investigation of stock and securities fraud, in which Bernard L. Madoff Investment Securities LLC was engaged. The protocol in the Lehman Brothers case sought to address the pressing issues and unique characteristics, including a truly global calibre and the complexity of the Lehman Brothers group. As explained in the Lehman Brothers protocol, '[o]ver many years [...] the relationships among the Debtors and Foreign Debtors have developed into a complex web of financial balances'.[19] In light of this, the determination of the common accounting records by the protocol pursued a pragmatic goal of avoiding protracted and unnecessary intercompany litigation. These unique *sui generis* protocols will be analysed in further chapters of this book.

B. EARLY CASES OF CROSS-BORDER INSOLVENCY PROTOCOLS: TARGETED CRISIS RESPONSE

1. Macfadyen protocol

It is argued that the first cross-border insolvency protocol was concluded as early as in 1908 in the case of *Macfadyen*.[20] Mr. Macfadyen was a member of two merchant partnerships, one in London, the UK (P. Macfadyen & Co.) and one in Madras, India (Arbuthnot & Co.). When Mr. Macfadyen died in 1906, his creditors filed an involuntary insolvency petition against the London partnership in the UK. Meanwhile, Macfadyen's partners initiated insolvency proceedings against the Madras partnership in India. There were about 1,036 creditors of the English partnership (debt of GBP 400,000) and 7,000 creditors of the Indian partnership (debt of GBP 1 million).[21] **4.09**

Quite extraordinarily, the trustee in the UK proceedings and the official assignee in the Indian case negotiated an agreement under which both partnerships were treated as one firm (*Macfadyen protocol*). As a result of this **4.10**

17 *In re Calpine Canada Energy Ltd.* 2006 A.B.Q.B. 743, 2006 CarswellAlta 1313.

18 *Securities Investor Protection Corp. v. Bernard L. Madoff Investment Securities LLC* (Bankr. S.D.N.Y.) Adv. Pro. No. 08-1789 (BRL) (9 June 2009).

19 *In re Lehman Brothers Holdings Inc., et al.* (Bankr. S.D.N.Y.) No. 08-13555 (JMP) (14 January 2009).

20 *In re P. Macfadyen & Co. ex parte Vizianagaram Co., Ltd.* [1908] 1 K.B. 675. See also E. Moustaira, *International Insolvency Law: National Laws and International Texts* (Springer, 2019), p. 109.

21 B. Wessels, B. Markell and J. Kilborn, *International Cooperation in Bankruptcy and Insolvency Matters* (OUP, 2009), p. 177.

substantive consolidation, assets of both partnerships had to be distributed proportionately to all creditors whose claims had been accepted, either by the London trustee or by the Madras official assignee. These insolvency practitioners agreed to share the lists of admitted claims and consented to be bound by the decisions of each other regarding claims acceptance. Interestingly, Article 41(1) EIR Recast leads to the same result, as it mandates insolvency practitioners to exchange information about the lodgement and verification of creditors' claims. In *Macfadyen* the practitioners also promised to remit the surplus of assets, remaining after the distribution with creditors, 'to the other [...] as may be necessary in order to ensure such rateable distribution'. The main principle behind this innovative solution is the equality of creditors. Such ratable cross-border distribution is in essence what is now known as the 'hotchpot' rule. According to this rule, a creditor who has received a payment in one proceeding can share in distributions made in another proceeding only where creditors in such a proceeding have obtained an equivalent dividend. Fletcher notes that the hotchpot rule redresses the 'distortion of the process of *pari passu* distribution of the estate among all creditors on a collective basis'. This rule is now established in Article 32 Model Law 1997[22] and Article 23(2) EIR Recast.

4.11 The courts in the UK and India approved the proposed arrangement. The English court rejected the objections made by one of the creditors, who was dissatisfied with the solution of sharing the combined estate value with other (i.e. Indian) creditors. The court concluded that the agreement constituted 'a proper and common-sense business arrangement [...] manifestly for the benefit of all parties interested'.[23]

4.12 While recognizing the advanced level of cooperation reached in *Macfadyen*, Mannan noted in 2016 – rightly at that time – that '[s]adly, such a spirit of cross-border civil cooperation does not continue to prevail in India or its neighbouring states'.[24] This might have changed in recent years. India reformed its insolvency law in 2016, when the new Insolvency and Bankruptcy Code was enacted. The insolvency law reform did not address the issue of cross-border insolvency. However, the Insolvency Law Committee constituted by the Ministry of Corporate Affairs of India has recommended the

22 See Guide to Enactment of Model Law 1997 (2013), para. 45, explaining that the hotchpot rule seeks 'to avoid situations in which a creditor might make claims and be paid in multiple insolvency proceedings in different jurisdictions, thereby potentially obtaining more favourable treatment than other creditors'.

23 *In re P. Macfadyen & Co. ex parte Vizianagaram Co., Ltd.* [1908] 1 K.B. 675.

24 M. Mannan, 'Are Bangladesh, India and Pakistan Ready to Adopt the UNCITRAL Model Law on Cross-Border Insolvency?' (2016) 25(3) *International Insolvency Review*, p. 205.

adoption of the Model Law 1997.[25] Another positive development is the approval in 2019 of the cross-border insolvency protocol in the *Jet Airways* case. The protocol was negotiated to promote international cooperation and the coordination of activities and proceedings, opened simultaneously in India and the Netherlands. This protocol is unique in many respects and will be closely studied in later chapters of this book.

2. Maxwell protocol

The practice of entering into insolvency protocols dates back long before the adoption of special regulation. One notable and, on a truly global scale, probably the first example comes from the *Maxwell* case.[26] Maxwell Communication Corporation plc. (Maxwell) was a UK-incorporated media holding company. The Maxwell group consisted of more than 400 subsidiaries worldwide with assets located in Bulgaria, Israel, Germany, Canada, as well as a large US presence with more than USD 700 million in value. **4.13**

Following the death of media tycoon Robert Maxwell in 1991, Maxwell experienced a wave of instability and, unable to perform its obligations under the UK credit facilities, it filed a pre-emptive Chapter 11 petition in the USA on 16 December 1991. The very next day, Maxwell's directors also petitioned for an administration order in the UK. As a result, one company was placed into administration in England and into Chapter 11 proceeding in New York, since both the UK and US courts had well-founded jurisdictional basis under national insolvency law. In the UK proceedings Joint Administrators were appointed. They assumed management and took control over the affairs of Maxwell. In the USA, in accordance with the Bankruptcy Code, the existing management was left in place as debtor in possession.[27] Nevertheless, the court had appointed an Examiner. In Chapter 11 examiners are usually appointed to investigate any allegations of fraud, misconduct, mismanagement, or irregularity in the management of the affairs of the debtor.[28] But in this case the Examiner, as a disinterested party, was appointed to fulfil the **4.14**

---

25 Report of Insolvency Law Committee on Cross Border Insolvency, October 2018.

26 *Maxwell Communications Corp.*, [1992] B.C.L.C. 465; 170 B.R. 800 (Bankr. S.D.N.Y. 1994); Aff'd B.R. 807 (Bankr. S.D.N.Y. 1995); 593 F.3rd 1036 (2nd Cir., 1996). Writing on the *Maxwell* case, Westbrook called the adoption of a protocol 'a remarkable arrangement' that 'permitted the case to be administered efficiently and without jurisdictional litigation'. See J. Westbrook, 'Comment: A More Optimistic View of Cross-Border Insolvency' (1994) 72(3) *Washington University Law Review*, p. 950. For a detailed overview of the Maxwell case see J. Pottow, 'The Maxwell Case', in R. Rasmussen (ed.), *Bankruptcy Law Stories* (New York: Foundation Press, 2007), pp. 221–37, available at https://papers.ssrn.com/sol3/papers.cfm?abstract_id=1000448.

27 11 U.S. Code §§ 1101(1), 1107 and 1108.

28 11 U.S. Code §§ 1104(c).

facilitation role to harmonize the insolvency proceedings across the Atlantic and to promote rehabilitation and reorganization of the debtor.[29]

4.15 Uncoordinated handling of two concurrent primary proceedings opened against Maxwell could have disturbed efficient administration of the insolvency estate. As a way to streamline crisis management and mitigate discrepancies between the proceedings, a protocol (agreement) was negotiated. In January 1992, the US court made a Final Supplemental Order Appointing Examiner and Approving Agreement Between Examiner and Joint Administrators (*Maxwell protocol*).[30] Under this agreement, English Joint Administrators and the US-appointed Examiner undertook to coordinate insolvency proceedings, inter alia, by requiring the consent of the Examiner for certain actions performed by the Administrators. For example, the Administrators were mandated to attempt, in good faith, to obtain the prior approval or consent of the Examiner or the Bankruptcy Court 'to borrow funds or pledge or charge any assets of the Debtor', to seek to 'convert the Debtor's case to a case under Chapter 7 of the Bankruptcy Code' and to filing a reorganization plan.[31]

4.16 The cross-border agreement in Maxwell was reached in the proceedings concerning a single debtor – Maxwell Communication Corporation plc. In other words, it was not insolvency of an enterprise group. However, it was mindful of a corporate group reality and considered other group members, including Macmillan Inc. (Macmillan) and Official Airline Guides Inc. (OAG).[32] The provisions of the protocol relating to these and other group companies concerned, inter alia:

---

29 E. Flaschen, A. Smits and L. Plank, 'Foreign Representatives in US Chapter 11 Cases: Filling the Void in the Law of Multinational Insolvencies' (2001) 17(1) *Connecticut Journal of International Law*, p. 9.

30 *In re Maxwell Communication Corp.* (Bankr. S.D.N.Y.) No. 91-15741 (TLB) 15 January 1992. See Lord Hoffmann, Cross-Border Insolvency, Address at the 1996 Denning Lecture: Cross-Border Insolvency, 18 April 1996, at 18–20. Reflecting on the approval of the Maxwell protocol, Lord Hoffmann noted the following:

> The administrators therefore found that to get anything done – for example, to raise interim finance to keep the subsidiary companies going – required a great deal of expensive and time-consuming negotiation. So they negotiated an overarching agreement with the Examiner, which was rather grandly called the Protocol, which laid down general lines of demarcation for running the proceedings on both sides of the Atlantic with a view to avoiding delay and duplication of effort. The New York judge had encouraged both the negotiation of the Protocol and co-operation between the Examiner and the English administrators. The Protocol was brought before me for approval. I think it took me about 20 minutes to read and approve it. I checked to see whether it contained anything which looked like an obvious mistake.

31 Maxwell protocol, para. G(1).

32 The list of the group members is given in Sch. 1 to the Maxwell protocol.

- *Board composition.* It was prescribed that '[t]he Joint Administrators and the Examiner shall consult and together agree as to the appropriate composition of the boards of directors of Macmillan and OAG'.[33]
- *Commencement of insolvency and other similar proceedings against group members.* It was agreed that the Joint Administrators 'shall, in good faith, attempt to obtain the consent of the Examiner and shall obtain the approval of the Bankruptcy Court prior to [...] commencing bankruptcy or insolvency proceedings with respect to any member of the [group]'.
- *Aligned management of the group.* It was agreed that the:

> Joint Administrators and the Debtor under the direction of the Joint Administrators shall, in good faith, attempt to obtain the consent of the Examiner and shall obtain the approval of the Bankruptcy Court prior to [...] (c) causing any member of the [group] to borrow funds; (d) causing any member of the [group] to pledge or charge any assets; (e) causing any member of the [group] to sell or dispose of any shares or other assets outside the ordinary course of business.[34]

The Maxwell Protocol did not set up a specific mode of communication between courts and insolvency practitioners. Neither did it touch upon the issues of the protocol modification or resolution of disputes arising from its performance – the topics that will subsequently become common in insolvency protocols. It was also argued that the Maxwell protocol intentionally left aside matters that would require resolution later in the proceedings, such as 'distribution and sharing of value, including priorities, as well as the choice of law in avoidance actions, which the courts were called upon to resolve later in the case'.[35] Despite these omissions, the protocol was an advanced, path-breaking and largely successful instrument addressing complex multinational insolvency in the absence of any developed state guidance or regulation. It allowed the administrators, the examiner and other interested parties 'to produce a common system for reorganizing Maxwell by disposing of assets as going concerns and distributing the proceeds to creditors'.[36] The protocol was also unique to the extent that it had an 'extension effect' and went beyond the interests and affairs of a single company, taking into consideration the enterprise group context. **4.17**

33 Maxwell protocol, para. D.

34 Ibid., para. G(2).

35 Wessels, Markell, Kilborn, *supra* note 21, p. 180.

36 *Maxwell Communication Corp.*, 93 F.3d 1036, 1042 (2nd Cir. 1996).

3. Commodore protocol

4.18 The protocol reached in 1994 in the case of Commodore (*Commodore protocol*) is notable for at least three reasons. First, unlike the protocols in *Macfadyen* and *Maxwell Communications*, the Commodore protocol applied to a group of companies.[37] Second, unlike the previous protocols, signed by insolvency representatives and approved by courts, the Commodore protocol had the unofficial committee of unsecured creditors (Creditors' Committee) as one of its signatories. Third, this protocol marked the 'beginning of a new era in which protocols evolved from one-time-use measures of crisis aversion into more generally applicable planning documents, much like a standard business operating agreement'.[38]

4.19 Commodore was founded in Canada in 1954 by the Polish-Jewish immigrant and Auschwitz survivor Jack Tramiel. It initially manufactured adding machines and electronic calculators, but then switched to home and personal computers. In the 1980s Commodore was one of the world's largest personal computer manufacturers. However, due to managerial mistakes and the competition from IBM PC and Apple Macintosh, Commodore began to fade from the consumer and business markets. Unable to stay afloat, Commodore Electronics Ltd. (CEL) and Commodore International Ltd. (CIL) filed for voluntary winding up in the Bahamas. In parallel, their creditors filed involuntary Chapter 7 petitions against both companies in New York. The joint Bahamian liquidators objected and filed motions for abstention and petitions for relief ancillary to foreign proceedings. The liquidators feared that uncoordinated insolvency proceedings would inhibit the orderly liquidation of the Commodore group, prevent orderly asset liquidation and damage the interests of creditors.[39] To resolve the potential jurisdictional conflict, the liquidators and the creditors agreed to allow the liquidators to convert the US proceedings to voluntary Chapter 11 cases, with the liquidators acting as debtors in possession.

4.20 When approving the Commodore protocol, the Bahamian court held that:

> [...] the idea behind the protocol [...] is not to subordinate the courts of one jurisdiction to the courts of another but to recognise the legitimate jurisdiction of each

37 Protocol in Re Commodore Electronics Ltd. between the United States Bankruptcy Court for the Southern District of New York (Hon. James L. Garrity, Jr.) and the Supreme Court of the Commonwealth of the Bahamas and Reasons for Decision, Supreme Court of the Bahamas (Case No. 473/1994, May 27, 1995).

38 Wessels, Markell, Kilborn, *supra* note 21, p. 182.

39 At the time of the protocol, around 32 liquidation or insolvency proceedings have been opened with respect to Commodore group members in some 17 jurisdictions.

> court over the subject matter within its jurisdiction and to encourage the liquidators who will also become the debtors in possession if the protocol is approved, to so manage the affairs of the companies in the United States and the liquidation in The Bahamas as to maximise the benefits to all creditors and to minimise conflicts which could arise on the adoption of a confrontational attitude between courts each of which are undoubtedly exercising their legitimate jurisdiction.[40]

The protocol quickly resolved the governance issue, as the joint liquidators became debtors in possession, and instead focused on the planning of transnational case administration. Among other things, it was agreed that the Bahamian court should alone govern the liquidators' tenure of office, the conduct of the liquidation proceedings under Bahamian law and the hearing and determination of matters arising in the liquidation proceedings under Bahamian law.[41] At the same time, the US court was to govern the conduct of the Chapter 11 cases and the hearing and determination of matters arising in the Chapter 11 proceedings.[42] **4.21**

Separate provisions of the protocol related to the filing and allowance of claims (timing, forum, recognition),[43] appointment of accountants and retention of counsel,[44] commencement of insolvency or similar proceedings with respect to Commodore group companies,[45] rights of the liquidators and their limitations,[46] composition of the Creditors' Committee[47] and information exchange between liquidators and the Creditors' Committee.[48] Thus, the level of detail and the scope of regulation imposed by the Commodore protocol far exceeded any of the previous protocols. It also facilitated standardization of cross-border insolvency protocols, which was accelerated with the adoption in 1996 of the Cross-Border Insolvency Concordat. **4.22**

---

40 *In the Matter of Commodore Electronics Ltd. and In the Matter of the International Business Companies Act, 1989* (No. 2 of 1990) and *In re Commodore International Ltd. and In re the International Business Companies Act, 1989* (No. 2 of 1990), Supreme Court of the Commonwealth of the Bahamans, No. 473, 8 December 1994.

41 Commodore protocol, para. C.

42 Ibid., para. D.

43 Ibid., para. G.

44 Ibid., paras H. and I.

45 Ibid., para. L.

46 Ibid., para. M. For example, the liquidators are authorized to deposit funds of the estates of CEL and CIL in accounts outside the USA. With the consent of the Creditors' Committee, they can also borrow funds, pledge or charge any assets of CEL or CIL; sell or dispose of any assets outside the ordinary course of business worth more than USD 250,000; lend funds of CEL or CIL to any of their subsidiaries.

47 Ibid., para. Q.

48 Ibid., para. N. Books, records, reports, and other information relating to asset sales and litigation of CEL and CIL were to be exchanged between the liquidators and the Creditors' Committee, 'subject to appropriate confidentialities'.

C. CROSS-BORDER INSOLVENCY CONCORDAT AND EARLY HARMONIZATION PROCESS

1. Principles of Cross-border Insolvency Concordat

4.23 At the beginning of the 1990s members of the International Bar Association (IBA) were actively involved in a number of large-scale international insolvency cases. The most famous example, discussed above, was the *Maxwell* case. Another well-known case involving a protocol, concerned the financially troubled Olympia & York Developments Ltd. (Olympia & York), a real estate investor and developer whose registered office was in Canada and whose operations extended to London (developing the office area now known as Canary Wharf) and New York (construction of the World Financial Center in New York City).

4.24 Facing an impending liquidity crisis, Olympia & York filed a petition under the Canadian Companies' Creditors Arrangement Act (CCAA). In parallel, together with a number of subsidiaries it filed a Chapter 11 petition in the USA. The insolvency protocol, *Olympia & York protocol*, was developed to (almost exclusively) deal with the corporate governance issues (e.g. composition, authority, actions, removal and re-election of directors).[49] When approving the protocol, the court in Canada noted that:

> Insolvency disputes with international overtones and involving property and assets in a multiplicity of jurisdictions are becoming increasingly frequent. Often there are differences in legal concepts – sometimes substantive, sometimes procedural – between the jurisdictions. The Courts of the various jurisdictions should seek to co-operate amongst themselves, in my view, in facilitating the trans-border resolution of such disputes as a whole, where that can be done in a fashion consistent with their own fundamental principles of jurisprudence. The interests of international co-operation and comity, and the interests of developing at least some degree of certitude in international business and commerce, call for nothing less.[50]

4.25 The members of the IBA took the commendable initiative to collect the individual protocols and to share their experience of negotiating and concluding such protocols. As a result, the working party consisting of lawyers from some 25 countries and judges from eight jurisdictions drafted the Cross-Border Insolvency Concordat (Concordat), which was officially approved by

---

49 Ontario Court of Justice, Toronto, Case No. B125/92 (26 July 1993), and United States Bankruptcy Court for the Southern District of New York, Case Nos. 92-B-42698-42701 (15 July 1993).

50 *Olympia & York Developments Ltd. v. Royal Trust Co.* (1993), 20 C.B.R. (3d) 165 (Ont. Gen. Div.), at p. 167.

the IBA Council in 1996.[51] The Concordat is a prime example of 'best practices' developed mainly by (international) practitioners, working together in Committee J (Insolvency and Creditors' Rights, now the Insolvency Section) of the IBA.

The Concordat was created with the objective of compensating for the absence of any global convention or treaty addressing pressing issues of cross-border insolvency. It was devised as a 'framework for harmonizing cross-border insolvency proceedings' and was intended as a set of flexible guidelines or principles rather than a list of developed rules.[52] This was a conscious choice, driven by the complexities and great variance of international insolvencies. **4.26**

The Concordat has a short introduction explaining its purpose. Following the introduction, there are ten principles supplemented with a concise explanation and a Glossary of Terms, which contains suggestions with regard to the preferable wording to be used when drafting a protocol in a specific case. In principle both corporations and individuals could fall within the Concordat's scope. Its Principle 1 states that '[i]f an entity or individual with cross-border connections is the subject of an insolvency proceeding, a single administrative forum should have primary responsibility for coordinating all insolvency proceedings relating to such entity or individual'.[53] This forum should be responsible for administration and collection of assets (Principle 2). Thus, the Concordat strongly endorses the principle of universalism. In case of parallel proceedings, the Concordat argues that all creditors should be treated as creditors of a single worldwide estate, even though the estate is administered by more than one forum. Principle 4 establishes that 'where there is more than one plenary forum and there is no main forum [...] each forum should coordinate with each other, subject in appropriate cases to a governance protocol'. Other notable provisions, which will find their way in future protocols concerned recognition, right to be heard, notification, access to information, hotchpot rule and asset distribution. **4.27**

It is clear from the text of the Concordat that it was meant to address a situation of a single debtor insolvency. This is why it referred to 'an entity [...] with cross-border connections'. As a result, insolvency of multinational enterprise groups was left out. This is despite the fact that the majority of cases in **4.28**

51 B. Wessels, *International Insolvency Law Part I. Global Perspectives on Cross-Border Insolvency Law* (4th edn, Wolters Kluwer, 2015), 10114.

52 Introduction to the Committee J Cross-Border Insolvency Concordat, 1996.

53 Committee J Cross-Border Insolvency Concordat, adopted by the Council of the International Bar Association on 31 May 1996.

which protocols were used involved groups of related companies (e.g. Commodore, Olympia & York, Everfresh, AIOC Corporation). Even protocols reached in cases concerning a single debtor oftentimes took notice of a corporate group context (e.g. Maxwell). The omission of corporate groups from the scope of the Concordat may be explained by the difficulty of questions that arise in corporate group insolvency, the diversity of enterprise groups and the lack of consensus or special regulation of groups in national insolvency regimes. Nevertheless, most of the guidelines or principles enshrined in the Concordat (and many subsequent soft law instruments, such as ALI-III Global Principles and CoCo Guidelines[54]) with respect to a single company can be used for coordination of parallel proceedings opened against separate legal entities comprising a corporate group.[55]

4.29 It is hence generally correct to say that many modern instruments applied in corporate group insolvency (e.g. cooperation and communication between group insolvency proceedings, group coordination and planning proceedings, insolvency protocols) derive their inspiration from a single-debtor insolvency perspective. Both single debtor and group insolvency rules pursue the same (international) insolvency law principles, including optimal realization of debtor's assets (preservation of going concern value),[56] protection of legitimate expectations and certainty of transactions and ensuring the equal (*pari passu*) treatment of creditors. Nevertheless, realization of such principles in the context of a corporate group requires certain readjustments and a careful balancing. Since enterprise group insolvency involves multiple debtors with different sets of creditors and separate pools of assets, conflicts of interest are much more likely to arise, compared to a situation of a single debtor with main and non-main (secondary) proceedings.[57]

---

54 Notably, the drafters of CoCo Guidelines initially intended to include a separate guideline, addressing communication and cooperation between parallel proceedings involving a subsidiary and a parent company. This guideline covered issues such as information exchange, participation rights, agreements on a common position concerning avoidance of any pre-insolvency transactions, coordination of certain actions (i.e. actions, which are intended to or the reasonable anticipated consequences of which would have a material adverse impact in the group). Ultimately, the group guideline was withdrawn as being ahead of time, since the EIR 2000 had no legal or theoretical basis for intra-group cooperation or group insolvency.

55 R. van Galen, 'Insolvent Groups of Companies in Cross Border Cases and Rescue Plans', Report to the Netherlands Association for Comparative and International Insolvency Law (conference of 8 November 2012), p. 17.

56 UNCITRAL Legislative Guide on Insolvency Law, Parts I and II (2004) (Legislative Guide 2004), Part one, Ch. 1, para. 5.

57 van Galen, *supra* note 55.

2. Application of Concordat Principles in insolvency protocols

Everfresh was one of the first protocols in which a reference was made to the Concordat and which was drafted under the guidance of many of its principles.[58] Everfresh Beverages Inc. and its affiliated company Sundance Beverages Inc. (debtors) engaged in manufacturing and distribution of beverage products. Everfresh produced 'juices, juice drinks, lemonade and related products throughout the United States and Canada under the brand name Everfresh'.[59] Sundance manufactured sparkling juice products. The debtors 'distributed their products via a network of more than 250 distributors who purchased the product from the Debtors and then distributed it to retail stores'.[60] When the debtors encountered financial difficulties, they filed for reorganizations proceedings in the USA and Canada. In the early stage of the proceedings, the Ontario Court of Justice (General Division) and the United States Bankruptcy Court S.D.N.Y. encouraged coordination of parallel proceedings. Shortly, the debtors and their creditors negotiated a cross-border insolvency protocol (*Everfresh protocol*), which was approved by both courts in late 1995.[61] **4.30**

The Everfresh protocol strongly and specifically endorsed the Concordat and implemented many of its principles.[62] It encouraged the US debtors in possession and the Canadian interim receivers to have regard to the proceedings initiated in another jurisdiction, cooperate with each other and coordinate administration of parallel insolvency proceedings.[63] In line with the Concordat, it contained rules related to notification, right to appear, information availability and the hotchpot rule. However, unlike its predecessors, the Everfresh protocol had provisions regulating issues of jurisdiction and distribution of proceeds. In particular, it prescribed the jurisdiction for **4.31**

58 The Concordat was explicitly mentioned in the protocol concerning AIOC group of companies (USA – Switzerland, see below) and relied on in the motion of debtors for interim and final orders approving cross-border insolvency protocol in the case of Federal-Mogul Global Inc. *In re Federal-Mogul Global Inc., T&N Ltd., et al.* Case No. 01-10578 (Bankr. D. Delaware, 2001).

59 *In Re Everfresh Beverages, Inc.*, 238 B.R. 558 (Bankr. S.D.N.Y. 1999).

60 Ibid.

61 Ontario Court of Justice, Toronto, Case No. 32-077978 (20 December 1995), and the United States Bankruptcy Court for the Southern District of New York, Case No. 95 B 45405 (20 December 1995).

62 The case came before Judge Lifland (USA) and Justice Farley (Canada), both of whom were involved in the development of the Concordat. For this reason, it was no surprise that 'the judges on both sides of the border enthusiastically supported the concept of developing a more general protocol based on the Concordat principles'. J. Farley, B. Leonard and J. Birch, 'Cooperation and Coordination in Cross-Border Insolvency Cases', INSOL International Annual Regional Conference, 2006.

63 Everfresh protocol, s. 1.

approval of transactions involving debtor's assets,[64] jurisdiction over claims,[65] jurisdiction over the conduct of insolvency practitioners and the general administration of the respective proceedings.[66] The distribution of assets and proceeds was to be carried out in accordance with the principle of territorialism. Assets arising from the Canadian business were to be disposed of and distributed pursuant to Canadian law (i.e. Canadian ranking of claims) and Canadian court approval, and vice versa for US assets.[67] Nevertheless, the protocol to some extent furthered universalism by mandating the insolvency practitioners to endeavour to pursue reorganization in different jurisdictions in a coordinated manner and in substantially similar way.[68]

4.32 The Everfresh protocol was innovative in several respects. Compared to earlier protocols, it also contained new provisions that will be repeated in many other subsequent protocols. For example, it established procedural rules for its amendment and modification,[69] confirmed jurisdictional independence of courts,[70] provided for entry into force[71] and highlighted its binding character for the parties.[72] In all, the protocol was clearly a success, as by some estimates there was a 40 per cent enhancement of preservation of value of the insolvency estate as a result of the use of the protocol and the ensuing cooperation among the parties.[73] Interestingly, despite the fact that the Everfresh protocol applied to two separate debtors (Everfresh Beverages Inc. and Sundance Beverages Inc.), it lacked provisions reflecting the specificity of a corporate group context (e.g. limitations related to potential conflicts of interest, adoption of a group reorganization plan, resolution of intra-group claims, extension of group financial support). The debtors were in fact treated as if they were one and the same company, as the protocol almost exclusively used the term 'Debtors' instead of referring to a particular group member. This may at least partially be explained by the fact that the Concordat, underlying the Everfresh protocol, did not consider a group insolvency context.

---

64 Ibid., para. 6. It was agreed that transactions relating to the Canadian assets were subject to the sole approval of the Canadian Court and transactions relating to the US assets were subject to the sole approval of the US Bankruptcy Court. Transactions involving assets located both in Canada and the US were subject to joint jurisdiction.

65 Ibid., para. 8. For example, it was agreed that the US court had jurisdiction over all claims governed principally by the laws of the US or any of its states.

66 Ibid., paras 14 and 15.

67 Ibid., para. 10.

68 Ibid., para. 13.

69 Ibid., para. 17.

70 Ibid., para. 21.

71 Ibid., para. 23.

72 Ibid., para. 16.

73 Justice J.M. Farley, 'A Judicial Perspective on International Cooperation in Insolvency Cases', (1998) 17 *American Bankruptcy Institute Journal*, p. 13.

The Concordat facilitated further development of insolvency protocols, which implemented some of its principles, even if to a lesser extent than the Everfresh protocol. In the relevant cases, insolvency practitioners who periodically participated in international conferences, explained pros and cons of using a protocol in transnational insolvency situations. The general take in the mid-1990s was that, although protocols may seem an uncertain instrument, they work in practice, especially when lawyers demonstrate self-constraint by not playing out all contingencies that may happen. **4.33**

A good example is the *AIOC protocol* (1998).[74] It involved the Swiss and the US proceedings concerning the metal commodities-trading company AIOC Resources AG. Among its goals, the AIOC protocol mentions promotion of international cooperation, facilitation of fair and efficient administration of cross-border insolvency proceedings, establishment of a coordinated claims reconciliation process and a mechanism for assets distribution.[75] In furtherance of Principle 4C of the Concordat and in line with the solution in *Commodore*, the AIOC protocol provided for cross recognition of claims.[76] It confirmed the right to be heard in all the proceedings for creditors and insolvency practitioners.[77] It also established a joint jurisdiction of the US Bankruptcy Court and the Swiss Bankruptcy Office over transactions related to the disposition of debtor's assets.[78] In order to coordinate parallel proceedings, it was agreed that the insolvency practitioners shall attempt in good faith to obtain each other's consent prior to selling assets or disposing of shares in the group companies, seeking substantive consolidation or adopting any measures that can have a material adverse impact on any member of the group.[79] The Chapter 11 trustee was given the primary role in administering the orderly wind-down of non-Swiss subsidiaries, while the Swiss insolvency practitioner was responsible for proceedings opened with respect to Swiss subsidiaries. **4.34**

Thus, just like the Maxwell protocol, the AIOC protocol extended its coordination effects (i.e. 'extension effect') to cover non-participating group members, a list of which was given in the annex to the protocol. **4.35**

---

74 *Re AIOC Corporation and AIOC Resources AG*, Case nos. 96 B 41895 and 96 B 41896 (Bankr. S.D.N.Y. 1996).
75 AIOC protocol, para. I. E.
76 Ibid., para. II. C.
77 Ibid., para. II. F.
78 Ibid., para. III. A.
79 Ibid., para. III. B.

D. LOEWEN AS A NEW MODEL INSOLVENCY PROTOCOL

4.36 Standardization of cross-border insolvency protocols continued in the second half of the 1990s. This standardization reached a new level with the adoption of the protocol in Loewen. The Loewen Group Inc., a Canadian corporation, was the ultimate parent company of a multinational enterprise group that operated, through hundreds of its subsidiaries and affiliates, in the USA, Canada and other countries. Loewen's operations covered three major business lines: funeral homes, cemeteries and life insurance. In 1999 it was the second largest funeral company in North America. Through an aggressive acquisition, Loewen expanded its network of funeral homes and cemeteries. This led to the growing operating expenses and the debt level exceeding USD 2.3 billion. To restructure this debt, the Loewen Group Inc. and certain of its direct and indirect subsidiaries commenced insolvency and reorganization proceedings in the USA and Canada.[80]

4.37 To harmonize and coordinate parallel proceedings and to promote orderly and effective administration of insolvency estates, the US Bankruptcy Court for the District of Delaware and the Ontario Superior Court of Justice approved the Cross-border insolvency protocol for the Loewen Group Inc. and its affiliates (*Loewen protocol*). This protocol will become a model for many other cross-border insolvency protocols, most of them concluded in the proceedings involving Canada and the USA. For example, the following protocols have largely followed the Loewen model: Philip Services Corp. (Canada-USA, 1999), Matlack Systems Inc. (Canada-USA, 2001), PSINet Inc. (Canada-USA, 2001), Laidlaw Inc. (Canada-USA, 2001), 360Networks Inc. (Canada-USA, 2001), Systech Retail Systems Corp. (Canada-USA, 2003), Calpine Corporation (Canada-USA, 2007), Pope & Talbot Inc. (Canada-USA, 2008), Quebecor World Inc. (Canada-USA, 2008), Progressive Moulded Products Limited (Canada-USA, 2008), Masonite International (Canada-USA, 2009), Abitibibowater Inc. (Canada-USA, 2009), Eddie Bauer (Canada-USA, 2009), Graceway Canada (Canada-USA, 2011), Montreal, Maine & Atlantic (Canada-USA, 2013), Aralez Pharmaceuticals (Canada-USA, 2018), Payless Holdings (Canada-USA, 2019).

4.38 It therefore makes sense to study the Loewen protocol a bit further. It consists of 11 sections.

---

80 For the role of ad hoc creditors' committees in promoting a coordinated approach in developing strategy and in plan negotiations concerning Loewen, see James M. Peck, 'Introduction', in Howard Morris, J.M. Peck and S. van de Graaff, *The Art of the Ad Hoc* (GRR, 2017), https://globalrestructuringreview.com/benchmarking/the-art-of-the-ad-hoc/1151047/introduction.

- *Background.* This section introduces participating debtors and courts and provides general information about insolvency proceedings.
- *Purpose and goals.* This section covers what a protocol tries to achieve. Most of the time this includes such objectives as: harmonization and coordination of proceedings, promotion of orderly and efficient administration of insolvency proceedings to reduce costs and avoid duplication of effort, honouring the independence and integrity of courts, promotion of international cooperation and respect for comity, facilitation of fair, open and efficient administration of insolvency proceedings.
- *Comity and independence of the courts.* This section confirms that the approval of a protocol does not divest or diminish courts' independent jurisdiction over the subject matter of the respective (national) proceedings. It also affirms the obligation of debtors, creditors and insolvency practitioners to respect and comply with independent non-delegated duties imposed on them by courts and applicable laws.
- *Cooperation.* This section establishes that debtors, creditors and insolvency practitioners shall cooperate with each other in connection with actions taken by the courts and make any other appropriate steps to coordinate the administration of proceedings. To this end courts shall also use their best efforts to coordinate their activities, which can be facilitated with the help of joint hearings[81] (via a telephone or a video link) and court-to-court communication, including *ex parte* communication.
- *Retention and compensation of estate representatives and professionals.* According to this section, each country should have the sole and exclusive jurisdiction to regulate insolvency representatives appointed in the respective country. This includes the matters of tenure, retention, compensation and liability.
- *Rights to appear and be heard.* This section confirms that debtors, their creditors and other interested parties shall have the right and standing to (i) appear and be heard in the insolvency proceedings to the same extent as creditors and other interested parties domiciled in the forum country and (ii) file notices of appearance or other papers. The latter, however, may subject the respective party to the court's jurisdiction.
- *Notice.* In line with some previous protocols, this section establishes that notice of any motion, application or other pleading or paper filed in one or both proceedings shall be given by appropriate means to all creditors

81 Joint hearings were used even before the Loewen protocol. For example, in the case Solv-Ex Canada Limited and Solv-Ex Corporation (Canada-USA, 1998) simultaneous joint hearings were organized. In the case of Livent Group (Canada-USA, 1999) joint cross-border hearings were conducted via a closed-circuit satellite TV/video-conferencing facility.

and other interested parties in accordance with the practice of the jurisdiction where the papers are filed or where the proceedings are to occur.

- *Joint recognition of stays of proceedings.* To preserve the integrity and completeness of the debtors' insolvency estates, the protocol provides that courts shall extend and enforce the stay introduced in other (foreign) insolvency proceedings, to the same extent and scope as in the originating jurisdiction. The importance of the cross-border recognition of stays is difficult to overestimate. Its significance is obvious. An enforcement and execution stay is explicitly mandated by Article 20 Model Law 1997, as one of the major effects of recognition of a foreign (main) proceeding.[82] Since at the time of the Loewen protocol, the Model Law 1997 was not yet adopted in either the USA or Canada, the protocol played a leading instrumental and gap-filling role.
- *Effectiveness and modification.* This section prescribes that the protocol becomes effective only upon its approval by both courts. It also adds that the protocol may not be supplemented, modified, terminated or replaced in any manner except by the courts.
- *Procedure for resolving disputes under the protocol.* The section on the resolution of disputes related to the terms, intent or application of the protocol is quite innovative. A dispute may be addressed to one of the courts or both courts. Whenever an issue is filed with only one court, such court: (a) shall consult with the other court; and (b) may, in its sole and exclusive discretion, either (i) render a binding decision after such consultation, (ii) defer to the determination of the other court by transferring the matter, in whole or in part, to that court or (iii) seek a joint hearing of both courts.
- *Preservation of rights.* This section confirms that neither the protocol nor actions taken under its terms shall prejudice or affect the powers, rights, claims and defences of the debtors, insolvency practitioners or any creditors under applicable law.

4.39 The Loewen protocol was negotiated to restructure the debts of a multinational enterprise group with operations and proceedings extending to several jurisdictions. The majority of other protocols following the Loewen model (see above) also apply in a corporate group setting. This is why it may be surprising that the Loewen protocol lacks any provisions addressing the specific relations between group members (e.g. financial and operational interdependencies) and other features characteristic of a corporate group (e.g.

82 A stay is also given as an option (the court 'may') by Art. 20 of the Model Law 2019, to the extent 'needed to preserve the possibility of developing or implementing a group insolvency solution'.

management of a corporate group). Instead, it adheres to the approach proposed in the Everfresh protocol to effectively treat a group as a single debtor. The explanation for this approach comes from the fact that the Loewen protocol is a sort of a framework agreement that does not address the most problematic or conflict-ridden issues.

For example, the protocol leaves open the questions related to asset disposition, resolution of intra-group claims, distribution of sale proceeds, law applicable to avoidance actions, set-off and the effects of insolvency proceedings on current contracts. In the practice of protocols, it is often the case that such points are deliberately and strategically left open as negotiators just cannot agree on them at a certain point or consider them not to be urgent enough. These questions therefore need to be further discussed (in the spirit of true cooperation) and agreed by insolvency practitioners or decided by courts. This can take years after the conclusion of the original protocol and may result in additional protocols. **4.40**

The framework-like nature of the Loewen protocol can explain why it turned out to be very successful and why until now it continues to serve as a standard for many cross-border insolvency protocols. **4.41**

E. EVOLUTION OF CROSS-BORDER INSOLVENCY PROTOCOLS: INITIAL OBSERVATIONS

In over 30 years of their existence and use, cross-border insolvency protocols have developed in insolvency cases as a practical and flexible response to the needs of international commercial enterprises. The stimulus for international cooperation especially by insolvency practitioners has been the need for predictability and stability in transnational cases in the absence of an adequate legal framework to support cross-border liquidations and restructurings. They are the embodiment of the culture of trust and cooperation, adopted to maximize the estate value, realize equal treatment of creditors and implement effective cross-border liquidation and reorganization plans. **4.42**

While the first use of protocols can be traced back to the early 20th century,[83] their rise and proliferation has occurred only in the 1990s. This coincided with **4.43**

---

83 Note, that cross-border insolvency cooperation dates back long before the 20th century. For example, the first treaties and conventions addressing certain insolvency-related issues date from the Middle Ages. Wood mentions the treaty between Verona and Trent (1204) that provided for the transfer of debtor's assets, and the treaty between Verona and Venice (1304) that governed the extradition of fugitive offenders. P. Wood, *Principles of International Insolvency* (Sweet & Maxwell, 1995), para. 1-059. Wessels discusses the 1689 Treaty

(or: logically followed from) the processes of globalization, the growth of multinational enterprise groups, regional economic integration between blocks of countries, the availability of cross-border IT-facilities (from fax to Facebook) and the increased interest in the matters of international insolvency law.[84] As the court in *Hunt v. T & N* noted:

> the old common law rules relating to recognition and enforcement were rooted in an outmoded conception of the world that emphasized sovereignty and independence, often at the cost of unfairness. Greater comity is required in our modern era when international transactions involve a constant flow of products, wealth and people across the globe.[85]

With these international trends came the risks of pervasive financial distress, overstepping the boundaries of a single jurisdiction. Cross-border insolvency protocols came as a tool to address such risks.

4.44 Initially, a protocol was used as an ad hoc solution or a targeted response to a particular problem arising from international insolvency. Oftentimes, this was a governance problem and the solution entailed alignment of managerial functions and administration of parallel proceedings across national borders. The evolution of cross-border protocols in the 1990s was characterized by three major trends or characteristics.

4.45 First, protocols had become increasingly standardized. This process was facilitated by the growing expertise of insolvency lawyers, practitioners and judges in matters of cross-border insolvency, and by the adoption of the early non-binding guidelines. These include the IBA Cross-Border Insolvency Concordat (1996) and the ALI-III Guidelines Applicable to Court-to-Court Communications in Cross-Border Cases (2001). The former was explicitly referred to in cases of *Everfresh* and *AIOC Corporation*. The latter are incorporated by reference and form part of the protocols in Matlack Systems Inc., PSINet Inc., Systech Retail Systems Corp., Calpine Corporation, Quebecor World Inc., Progressive Moulded Products Limited, Abitibibowater Inc., Masonite International, Nortel Networks (Canada-USA, 2009), Lehman Brothers (multijurisdictional, 2009) and others. A novel chapter of the

---

between the State of Holland and the State of Utrecht, which established mutual recognition of declarations of bankruptcy as the earliest form of international insolvency law in the Netherlands. Wessels, *International Insolvency Law Part I*, *supra* note 51, 10034. See also P. Omar, 'The Landscape of International Insolvency Law' (2002) 11 *International Insolvency Review*, pp. 173–200.

84 See also J. Westbrook, 'The Globalisation of Insolvency Reform' (1999) 3 *New Zealand Law Review*, pp. 401–14.

85 *Hunt v. T & N plc.*, Supreme Court of Canada, 1993 CarswellBC 294.

protocol standardization had begun with the approval in 1999 of the Loewen protocol, which served and continues to serve as a model for new protocols.

Second, standardization of insolvency protocols had resulted in the development of framework protocols,[86] much like a standard business operating agreement. On the one hand, such protocols replaced the one-time-use measures of crisis aversion or crisis response (i.e. specific-purpose protocols with a narrow focus). On the other hand, framework protocols, while setting out the general structure for cross-border communication and cooperation, avoided provisions addressing the most complex or objectionable issues, such as law applicable to transaction avoidance and set-off, allocation of assets and distribution of proceeds between insolvency proceedings. However, this 'simplification' did not stop the appearance of more detailed and in-depth insolvency protocols, focusing on specific vulnerabilities and pressing issues. These *sui generis* insolvency protocols have been negotiated, inter alia, in insolvencies of Sendo International Limited (UK-France, 2006), Lehman Brothers (17 jurisdictions worldwide), Bernard L. Madoff Investment Securities (UK-USA, 2009) and Jet Airways (the Netherlands-India, 2019). **4.46**

Third, a vast number of cross-border insolvency protocols was negotiated in the context of corporate group insolvency. As a result, such protocols frequently list several legal entities (typically, group members) as participants. Nevertheless, the group specificity is rarely addressed in any detail. A number of protocols seem to extend their effects to group members other than those indicated in the introductory or background section (i.e. participating debtors), either explicitly mentioning them in the annex to a protocol[87] and the motion to approve a cross-border protocol,[88] or vaguely referring to them as to 'certain [...] direct and indirect subsidiaries'.[89] In other words, a few protocols adopt the extension model, first applied in the Maxwell protocol, when the personal and material scope of a protocol is extended to a range of legal entities. **4.47**

The fact that many insolvency protocols do not distinguish between particular legal entities within the group, their respective roles and positions in a group structure may create an impression that a protocol is dealing with a single debtor. This approach was utilized in the Everfresh protocol and protocols **4.48**

86 Loewen protocol is a good example of such a protocol.

87 AIOC protocol, Sch 1 (14 companies in nine jurisdictions).

88 Motion of debtors for interim and final orders approving cross-border insolvency protocol in Federal-Mogul Corporation. *In re Federal-Mogul Global Inc., T&N Ltd., et al.* Case No. 01-10578 (Bankr. D. Delaware, 2001).

89 Loewen protocol, paras 2 and 3.

based on the Loewen model. The treatment of an enterprise group as if it is one company, in the absence of procedural or substantive consolidation, is noteworthy. It facilitates coordinated administration of insolvency on a group-wide level and can be instrumental in reaching group-wide solutions, promoted by both the Model Law 2019 and the EIR Recast. At the same time, it brings up questions linked to entity separateness, as each group entity keeps its separate legal identity, separate insolvency estate and a separate pool of creditors.

4.49 Protocols were invented to overcome the lack of statutes, treaties and – in the early days as of the 1980s – even soft law instruments for cross-border cooperation in the context of insolvency. Such instruments have gradually been created in the 1990s and the 2000s. A leading role in this process has been played by UNCITRAL, which stands behind the Model Law on Cross-Border Insolvency (1997) and the Model Law on Enterprise Group Insolvency (2019), as well as many other soft law guidelines and recommendations (e.g. UNCITRAL Legislative Guides and the Practice Guide on Cross-Border Insolvency Cooperation). The next chapter discusses these important instruments and analyses their position and approaches to coordination and cooperation in transnational insolvency cases and the role of cross-border insolvency protocols.

5

UNCITRAL AND FACILITATION OF CROSS-BORDER INSOLVENCY COOPERATION: FROM ENTITY TO ENTERPRISE

A. MODEL LAW ON CROSS-BORDER INSOLVENCY 1997 5.01
B. PRACTICE GUIDE ON CROSS-BORDER INSOLVENCY COOPERATION 2009 5.11
C. LEGISLATIVE GUIDE ON INSOLVENCY LAW, PART III 2010 5.17
D. MODEL LAW ON ENTERPRISE GROUP INSOLVENCY 2019 5.25
1. Purpose and goals of Model Law 2019 5.25
2. Scope and tools of Model Law 2019 5.29
3. Model Law 2019 and insolvency agreements 5.34

A. MODEL LAW ON CROSS-BORDER INSOLVENCY 1997

This chapter describes and comments on several documents produced by the United Nations Commission on International Trade Law (UNCITRAL). It is undisputable that at the moment, UNCITRAL plays an active and leading standard-setting role in the development of international insolvency law. Below four of its work products will be discussed, namely the Model Law 1997, the Practice Guide on Cross-Border Insolvency Cooperation 2009, the Legislative Guide on Insolvency Law, Part III (2010) and the Model Law 2019. The analysis of these instruments will, within the scope of this study, focus on the issues of cross-border communication and cooperation, cross-border insolvency protocols and their operation in a corporate group environment. **5.01**

In May 1997 UNCITRAL adopted the Model Law on Cross-Border Insolvency (Model Law 1997).[1] Among its objectives, the Model Law 1997 mentions promotion of cooperation between courts and other competent authorities involved in cases of transnational insolvency, facilitation of greater legal certainty for trade and investment and enabling fair and efficient **5.02**

1 UNCITRAL Model Law on Cross-Border Insolvency (1997) with Guide to Enactment and Interpretation (2013), https://uncitral.un.org/en/texts/insolvency/modellaw/cross-border_insolvency.

administration of cross-border insolvencies that protects the interests of all creditors and other interested persons, including the debtor.[2] The Model Law 1997 also aims to protect and maximize the value of the debtor's assets and to ensure rescue of financially troubled businesses. Unlike the EIR Recast, the Model Law 1997 is itself non-binding and needs to be incorporated in national law to acquire the binding force.

5.03 As of July 2020, legislation based on the Model Law 1997 has been adopted in 48 states in a total of 51 jurisdictions. Among such jurisdictions are Japan (2000), Poland (2003), the USA (2005), Canada (2005), the UK (2006), Australia (2008), Greece (2010), the 17 African countries that constitute OHADA (2015),[3] Singapore (2017), Israel (2018), Dubai International Financial Centre (2019) and Myanmar (2020).[4] Several other countries have implemented international insolvency rules which are rather similar to or strongly inspired by the Model Law 1997, including Spain, Germany, Belgium and (under the volatile pre-draft) the Netherlands.[5]

5.04 While the EIR Recast has unified certain aspects of cross-border insolvency law in the EU, the Model Law 1997 has contributed significantly to harmonization of insolvency laws around the world.[6] At the same time, the Model Law 1997 respects the differences between national procedural and conflict of law rules and does not attempt to substantively harmonize national insolvency law. It is also sometimes adopted with significant differences, departing from the original text.[7] The soft law nature of the Model Law 1997 and the divergence in its application and interpretation at the national level have been criticized in literature.[8] Nevertheless, the widespread adoption of

---

2 Ibid., preamble.

3 Enacting the *Acte uniforme portant organisation des procédures collectives d'apurement du passif* (OHADA), adopted on 10 September 2015 at Grand-Bassam, Côte d'Ivoire.

4 Status: UNCITRAL Model Law on Cross-Border Insolvency (1997), available at https://uncitral.un.org/en/texts/insolvency/modellaw/cross-border_insolvency/status.

5 On the Model Law 1997, see B. Wessels, *International Insolvency Law Part I. Global Perspectives on Cross-Border Insolvency Law* (4th edn, Wolters Kluwer, 2015), Chapter III; B. Wessels, 'Should the EU Adopt UNCITRAL Model Law on Cross-Border Insolvency?' Blog of Bob Wessels, 28 October 2016.

6 R. Bork, 'The European Insolvency Regulation and the UNCITRAL Model Law on Cross-Border Insolvency' (2017) 26(3) *International Insolvency Review*, p. 248.

7 One of the most significant departures from the original text of the Model Law 1997 is the reciprocity requirement, absent in the original text, but introduced in a number of jurisdictions (e.g. Romania, South Africa, Mexico). India is now also considering adopting the Model Law 1997 with the provision requiring reciprocity, see Report of Insolvency Law Committee on Cross Border Insolvency, October 2018. It is our view that this requirement unjustifiably limits the recognition of foreign insolvency judgments and should not be added. See on the topic K. Yamauchi, 'Should Reciprocity Be a Part of the UNCITRAL Model Cross-Border Insolvency Law?' (2007) 16 *International Insolvency Review*, pp. 145–79.

8 S. Chandra Mohan, 'Cross-Border Insolvency Problems: Is the UNCITRAL Model Law the Answer?' (2012) 21(3) *International Insolvency Review*, p. 223, concluding that 'the Model Law does not appear to be able to provide States with what they need'. See also K. Pistor, 'The Standardization of Law and Its Effects on

the Model Law 1997 by some of the world's leading economies, its crucial role in fostering convergence of law and practice, and in the promotion of cross-border cooperation and communication and the realization of solutions based on the principle of modified universalism should not be underestimated. Furthermore, the experience shows that the Model Law in its key role can assist both developed and developing economies and is feasible for jurisdictions with different legal traditions (i.e. common law, civil law and mixed regimes). Moreover, the soft/hard law divide lacks nuance and must be approached with caution and suspicion since many soft law instruments might in fact be 'harder' and more practical than some general or vague binding legislation.[9] The line between hard and soft law becomes even less clear when the mandatory law explicitly refers to soft law guidelines.[10]

The Model Law 1997 centres around four major concepts: (1) access of foreign representatives and creditors to courts; (2) recognition of a foreign proceeding; (3) granting of relief in support of a foreign proceeding; and (4) cooperation with foreign courts and foreign representatives. This book focuses on the latter element. The Guide to Enactment of Model Law 1997 (2013) explains that many courts may be reluctant to cooperate with each other and with foreign insolvency practitioners in the absence of express authorization to do so.[11] In this respect the Model Law 1997 fills the gap by expressly empowering courts and insolvency practitioners to communicate and cooperate in cross-border insolvency cases. Under the Model Law 1997, cooperation is not dependent on recognition and may occur even before the application for recognition has been satisfied.[12] **5.05**

Articles 25 and 26 of the Model Law 1997 do not simply recommend, but mandate cooperation and direct communication between courts and insolvency practitioners ('shall cooperate to the maximum extent possible'). In line with this, US Chapter 15 prescribes that 'the court shall cooperate to the maximum extent possible with a foreign court or a foreign representative, **5.06**

Developing Economies' (2002) 50(1) *The American Journal of Comparative Law*, p. 102, arguing that soft law guidelines cannot ensure full standardization, yet 'the aim of standardization is to minimize deviations from the standards, lest the very purpose of standardization is undermined'.

9 I. Mevorach, 'A Fresh View on the Hard/Soft Law Divide: Implications for International Insolvency of Enterprise Groups' (2019) 40(3) *Michigan Journal of International Law*, p. 509. B. Wessels and G-J. Boon, 'Soft Law Instruments in Restructuring and Insolvency Law: Exploring its Rise and Impact' (2019) 2 *TvOB*, p. 64, highlighting that 'soft law instruments on restructuring and insolvency law lead to less politicised compromises, provide for more flexibility, and are developed more quickly and at lower cost than hard law'.

10 See e.g. EIR Recast, Recital 48, referring to 'guidelines prepared by the United Nations Commission on International Trade Law (Uncitral)'.

11 Guide to Enactment of Model Law 1997, para. 213.

12 Ibid., para. 212.

either directly or through the trustee'.[13] The Canadian Companies' Creditors Arrangement Act uses similar words.[14] In contrast, the UK's Cross-Border Insolvency Regulations 2006 contain a slightly different wording, stating that 'the court *may* cooperate to the maximum extent possible with foreign courts or foreign representatives'.[15] This 'relaxed' approach is also adopted in Singapore.[16] Japan has also departed from the original text and decided not to adopt Article 25 at all and to limit the application of Article 26 to cooperation between foreign and local representatives, thus excluding courts.[17]

5.07 Article 27 (non-exhaustively) lists various forms of such cooperation, including (1) appointment of a person to act at the direction of the court, (2) sharing of information by any court-approved method of communication, (3) coordination of administration and supervision of the debtor's assets and affairs, (4) *approval or implementation by courts of agreements* concerning the coordination of proceedings, and (5) coordination of concurrent proceedings regarding the same debtor.

5.08 Thus, the Model Law 1997 endorsed conclusion of cross-border insolvency agreements or protocols. Nevertheless, it did not provide any further guidance on the matter. The practice and experience with the use of cross-border insolvency agreements or protocols is compiled in another document, called the UNCITRAL Practice Guide on Cross-Border Insolvency Cooperation, which we will discuss below. Before we do so, it is important to stress that the Model Law 1997 does not concern situations of group insolvency. Facilitation of cooperation and communication, including by way of protocols, established by the Model Law 1997 applies, first of all, to parallel proceedings (main, non-main and other[18]) opened with respect to the same debtor company. However, this does not mean that the Model Law had no effect on administration of group insolvencies.

---

13 11 US Code § 1525.

14 Companies' Creditors Arrangement Act (R.S.C., 1985, c. C-36), sec. 52(1).

15 The Cross-Border Insolvency Regulations 2006, Art. 25. Note that unlike courts which 'may cooperate', under Art. 26 of the Cross-Border Insolvency Regulations 2006, insolvency officeholders 'shall to the extent consistent with his other duties, [...] cooperate to the maximum extent possible with foreign courts or foreign representatives'.

16 Companies Act, Tenth Schedule, ss. 354B and 354C, Art. 25. In line with the UK approach, insolvency officeholders in Singapore 'must [...] cooperate' pursuant to Art. 26.

17 For explanation of the Japanese approach, see K. Yamamoto, 'New Japanese Legislation on Cross-border Insolvency as Compared with the UNCITRAL Model Law' (2002) 11(2) *International Insolvency Review*, p. 91, arguing that the 'cooperation between representatives of both proceedings is not only necessary but also sufficient'. For an overview of nearly all countries having implemented their version of the Model Law, see Look Chan Ho (ed.), *Cross-Border Insolvency: A Commentary on the UNCITRAL Model Law* (4th edn, Global Law and Business, 2017).

18 For example, proceedings opened at the presence of the debtor's assets and therefore not qualifying as either main or non-main proceedings.

Based on the analysis of real cases, Mevorach concluded that 'courts applying the Model Law tend to facilitate centralisations of group proceedings'.[19] In 94 per cent of the group cases, courts recognized foreign proceedings in regard to a number of group members in the same jurisdiction. Recognition was oftentimes granted even in cases where group members were not all registered in a single foreign jurisdiction (*forum concursus*).[20] In other words, the Model Law 1997 by promoting cross-border cooperation and recognition of insolvency judgments facilitated group solutions. This finding confirms our observations made in Chapter 4 that the mechanisms and instruments initially created for single-debtor insolvencies can be useful and effective in addressing insolvency of corporate groups. **5.09**

However, insolvency instruments of general nature have their limitations and are incapable of offering tailor-made solutions to problems characteristic of enterprise groups. In this respect, Mevorach noted that the 'application of the general cross-border insolvency framework [of the Model Law 1997] in cases of groups has not been fully consistent. Some courts took account of the group circumstances and promoted group solutions while others were more inclined to consider each entity in a group separately'.[21] This is one of the reasons why the development of a new model law, the Model Law 2019, was necessary. The Model Law 2019 is analysed in subchapter D below. **5.10**

B. PRACTICE GUIDE ON CROSS-BORDER INSOLVENCY COOPERATION 2009

The Practice Guide project arose from a proposal made to UNCITRAL by the International Insolvency Institute (III) in 2005. The III recommended UNCITRAL to take a position of leadership in developing a higher use of cross-border insolvency protocols. Among the suggested approaches, the proposal mentioned creation of a standard form or forms of insolvency protocols to be used in a transnational setting.[22] It was recognized that while the Model Law 1997 authorized the use of protocols, it did not provide much detail – a gap that needed to be filled. The work focused on the standards for the substance of a protocol (e.g. control and protection of assets, coordination of asset disposition, filing and classification of claims) and on making the **5.11**

19 I. Mevorach, 'On the Road to Universalism: A Comparative and Empirical Study of the UNCITRAL Model Law on Cross-Border Insolvency' (2011) 12(4) *European Business Organization Law Review*, p. 539.

20 Ibid.

21 I. Mevorach, 'A Fresh View on the Hard/Soft Law Divide: Implications for International Insolvency of Enterprise Groups' (2019) 40(3) *Michigan Journal of International Law*, p. 517.

22 UNCITRAL, Proposal by the International Insolvency Institute (III), Committee on Cross-Border Communications, 15 April 2005, A/CN.9/582/Add.3, https://undocs.org/en/A/CN.9/582/Add.3.

examples of protocols more widely available.[23] As a result of consultations with judges and insolvency practitioners in 2006 and 2007, the Working Group V presented the first draft of the practice guide in November 2008. This draft was also circulated to governments. A revised version of the guide was presented in 2009 and adopted by consensus on 1 July 2009.[24] This chapter offers a general description of the Practice Guide and draws special attention to the issues specific to groups of companies.

5.12 The Practice Guide aims at providing relevant information to practitioners and judges on practical aspects of communication and cooperation in cross-border insolvency cases and specifically on the conclusion of insolvency protocols. It is not prescriptive in nature and instead it illustrates available options and solutions, which can be tailored to meet the specific needs of a concrete case. Importantly, the Practice Guide does not restrict its application to single-debtor insolvency and expressly recognizes that international insolvencies typically involve enterprise groups. Even more so, it stresses that a 'complex debtor structure (for example, an enterprise group with numerous subsidiaries) or complex intertwining of the operations of the debtor' make conclusion of cross-border agreements particularly useful.[25] An additional factor that justifies entering into a protocol may be the existence of a cash management system involving the pooling of cash on a centralized basis and the allocation of liquidity among enterprise group members. This type of a cash pooling system was, for instance, used by Lehman Brothers.

5.13 The Practice Guide discusses insolvency protocols in two sections. Section A deals with preliminary issues. In particular, it addresses contents, timing, parties, capacity to enter into an insolvency agreement, format, common provisions, legal effect, safeguards and means of dispute resolution. Section B provides an overview of the contents and structure of insolvency agreements and suggests sample clauses.[26] These clauses are grouped in nine categories:

- Recitals (Parties; Background/Insolvency History; Scope of the insolvency agreement; Purpose; Language of the agreement and of communication).
- Terminology and rules of interpretation.

---

23 UNCITRAL, Insolvency law: possible future work, 7 March 2006, A/CN.9/596, https://undocs.org/en/A/CN.9/596.

24 UNCITRAL Practice Guide on Cross-Border Insolvency Cooperation, 2009 (Practice Guide).

25 Ibid., Ch. III, para. 10.

26 For the general overview see D. Shah and J. Snead, 'The UNCITRAL Practice Guide on Cross-border Insolvency Cooperation: A Good Practice Guide to Cross-border Insolvency Agreements', *International Corporate Rescue*, Vol. 7, Issue 5, 2010, pp. 325–327.

- Courts (Comity and independence of courts; Allocation of responsibilities between courts; Treatment of claims; Avoidance proceedings; Powers with respect to insolvency representatives; Resolution of disputes arising from the insolvency agreement; Deferral by courts; Right to appear and to be heard; Future proceedings).
- Administration of the proceedings (Priority of proceedings; Stays of proceedings; Applicable law).
- Allocation of responsibilities between the parties to the cross-border insolvency agreement (General means of cooperation; Supervision of the debtor; Reorganization plans; Treatment of assets; Allocation of responsibility for commencing proceedings; Treatment of claims; Post-commencement finance).
- Communication (Communication between courts; Joint or coordinated hearings; Communication between the parties; Information-sharing between insolvency representatives; Notice; Confidentiality of communication).
- Effectiveness, amendment, revision and termination of cross-border insolvency agreements (Effectiveness and conditions precedent to effectiveness; Amendment, revision and termination of a cross-border insolvency agreement).
- Costs and fees.
- Safeguards (Preservation of rights and jurisdiction; Limitation of liability; Warranties).

The sample clauses offered by the Practice Guide are based on a comparative analysis of around 40 insolvency protocols concluded since the early 1990s. They reflect the common topics appearing in these protocols. As there are different views on a number of matters, the sample clauses provide different options for dealing with certain topics. **5.14**

The Practice Guide does not separately deal with issues specific to enterprise group insolvency. However, it does highlight some of them in different sections. For example, in 'Recitals' it recognizes that protocols usually provide the names of debtors-parties to the agreement and their places of incorporation.[27] It is less common to see a description of a corporate group and the allocation of responsibilities within it. Nevertheless, some protocols indicate which company is a (direct or indirect) group parent[28] and explain global and **5.15**

27 Practice Guide, Ch. III, para. 41.

28 Protocols in Quebecor (para. 4), Smurfit-Stone Container (Canada-USA, 2009) (paras 1–2), Progressive Moulded (para. 1), PSINet Inc. (paras 1–3). See also Systech protocol, para. 1, noting that 'Systech Retail Systems Corp. [...] is the parent company in a North American business that operates, through various

complex nature of an enterprise group.[29] This can be done either in the preamble or the main body of a protocol. Group specificity can also be reflected in the provisions related to the allocation of responsibilities between courts. For example, protocols may establish the agreed (exclusive) jurisdiction for resolution of claims and approval of transactions.[30] Some of them may even create or offer an opportunity to create in the future a special *sui generis* mechanism for the resolution of intercompany claims.[31] We will discuss these protocol-based arrangements in later chapters of this book.

5.16 The group reality is at times visible in the mechanics of insolvency administration, inter alia, where insolvency practitioners agree to give prior notice before initiating insolvency proceedings against group members or seeking substantive consolidation with them,[32] or where a protocol seeks to promote group reorganization or to maximize the realizable value of assets to which multiple debtors have an interest.[33] Where the value of assets is at risk, interested group members may consider providing funding to other group entities to preserve such value or assist in the recovery of respective assets[34] ('Allocation of responsibilities between the parties to the cross-border insolvency agreement'). The enterprise group context can also affect decisions regarding the allocation of responsibilities for the use and disposal of assets. The UNCITRAL Practice Guide highlights that in groups with a high level of managerial and operational interdependence (i.e. integrated groups), it may be appropriate to make sales of certain assets subject to the joint approval of the courts involved, regardless of the location of those assets.[35] To facilitate such joint approval and the allocation of proceeds between different group companies, some protocols permit joint hearings.[36]

Canadian and American subsidiaries and affiliates in the United States and Canada'. This protocol also adds that 'approximately 90 per cent of the Systech Companies' revenue [is] generated in the United States'.

29 Lehman Brothers protocol, para. B.

30 Protocols in Solv-Ex (para. 6), AIOC Corporation (para. III(E)), AgriBioTech Canada (Canada-USA, 2000) (paras 4.01–4.02), Pioneer Companies Inc. (Canada-USA, 2001) (para. 10) and Quebecor (paras 22–23).

31 Lehman Brothers protocol (para. 9.3); Madoff protocol (para. 7.1.).

32 AIOC protocol, para. III(B); Maxwell protocol, para. E.; Commodore protocol, para L.

33 Lehman Brothers protocol, para. 7.4.

34 Ibid. Quebecor and Commodore protocols also contain provision related to rescue financing and intra-group lending. The former protocol divided jurisdiction over DIP-related matters between Canadian and US courts, so that Canadian courts have jurisdiction over matters affecting Canadian debtors, and US courts should consider issues affecting US debtors. The second protocol authorized the liquidators, with consent of the creditors' committee to 'lend monies of the estates [...] to any of their subsidiaries, with or without security'.

35 Practice Guide, Ch. III, para. 122.

36 E.g. protocols in PSINet (para. 13), Quebecor (para. 10), Payless Holdings (para. 12) and Loewen (para. 11).

C. LEGISLATIVE GUIDE ON INSOLVENCY LAW, PART III 2010

The project of the UNCITRAL legislative guide arose from the proposal to the Commission in 1999 to undertake further work on corporate insolvency law to foster and encourage the adoption of effective national corporate insolvency regimes. Australia proposed creation of a model national corporate insolvency law, which would contain a menu of legislative measures on various matters that countries could select from and modify to suit their individual circumstances.[37] However, it was felt that a universally acceptable model law was not feasible and that any work to be done needed to take a flexible approach. A legislative guide adopting such an approach to the implementation of key objectives and core features of a strong insolvency regime was agreed to be a better alternative.[38] **5.17**

The first draft of the Legislative Guide was prepared by the Working Group V in 2001 and in 2004 the text of the Legislative Guide on Insolvency Law (Parts I and II) was approved.[39] This document contained a chapter titled 'Treatment of corporate groups in insolvency', which noted that the treatment of the group companies in insolvency as separate legal personalities may operate unfairly.[40] Recognizing the complexity of the topic, the Legislative Guide 2004 limited itself to a brief introduction to some of the issues specific to group insolvencies. Among them were treatment of intra-group debts, responsibility of group members for external debts of other group members (e.g. arising from cross-guarantees) and commencement of insolvency proceedings by a group company against a related group company.[41] It was also recognized, however, that the analysis of current treatment and identification of possible solutions to group insolvencies would have undoubtedly distracted the attention from the main body of work on the Legislative Guide. Accordingly, the subject was not pursued in any great detail and no recommendations were proposed. **5.18**

The Guide did not touch upon communication and cooperation in group insolvencies or the use of cross-border insolvency protocols. Nevertheless, the work on these topics was just starting. In 2005 the International Association **5.19**

37 UNCITRAL, Possible future work in the area of insolvency law: Proposal by Australia, 13 April 1999, A/CN.9/462/Add.1, https://undocs.org/en/A/CN.9/462/Add.1.

38 Report of UNCITRAL, Thirty-third session, 12 June–7 July 2000, Supplement No. 17 (A/55/17), para. 409, https://undocs.org/en/A/55/17.

39 Legislative Guide 2004.

40 Ibid., part two, Ch. V, para. 82.

41 Ibid., part two, Ch. V, para. 83.

of Restructuring, Insolvency and Bankruptcy Professionals (INSOL) proposed to focus on the issue of treatment of corporate groups in insolvency,[42] while the III suggested to explore the practice of cross-border insolvency protocols (which has resulted in the Practice Guide reviewed above).[43] Thus, the discussions of these two topics went hand in hand, affecting and enriching each other.

5.20 The continued engagement of the Working Group V has led to the adoption of the UNCITRAL Legislative Guide on Insolvency Law, Part III: Treatment of enterprise groups in insolvency (Legislative Guide 2010). Unlike the previous documents produced by UNCITRAL, Legislative Guide 2010 focuses exclusively on the treatment of enterprise groups in insolvency, complementing the positions and recommendations given in the context of a single-debtor insolvency. It consists of three main chapters: (1) General features of enterprise groups (nature of enterprise groups, reasons for conducting business through enterprise groups, definition and regulation of enterprise groups); (2) domestic issues in insolvency of enterprise groups (application and commencement, treatment of assets on commencement of insolvency proceedings, remedies, participants, reorganization of two or more enterprise group members); and (3) international issues in insolvency of enterprise groups (promotion of cross-border cooperation, forms of cooperation involving courts and insolvency representatives, use of cross-border insolvency agreements).

5.21 The Legislative Guide 2010 starts by explaining that there are enterprise groups in which separate insolvency proceedings may be a feasible option (e.g. decentralized horizontal groups), but for many integrated groups 'cooperation may be the only way to reduce the risk of piecemeal insolvency proceedings that have the potential to destroy going-concern value and lead to asset ring-fencing, as well as asset shifting or forum shopping by debtors'.[44] It

42 UNCITRAL, Proposal by International Association of Restructuring, Insolvency and Bankruptcy Professionals (INSOL), Treatment of corporate groups in insolvency, 26 April 2005, A/CN.9/582/Add.1, https://undocs.org/en/A/CN.9/582/Add.1.

43 UNCITRAL, Proposal by the International Insolvency Institute (III), Committee on Cross-Border Communications, Cross-border insolvency protocols in transnational cases, 15 April 2005, A/CN.9/582/Add.3, https://undocs.org/en/A/CN.9/582/Add.3.

44 Legislative Guide 2010, Ch. III, para. 7. Forum shopping refers to the practice whereby companies transfer assets or judicial proceedings from one jurisdiction to another seeking to obtain a more favourable legal position or a bankruptcy regime. On the discussion of forum shopping in the European context, see W-G. Ringe, 'Insolvency Forum Shopping, Revisited', in V. Lazić and S. Stuij (eds), *Recasting the Insolvency Regulation: Improvements and Missed Opportunities. Short Studies in Private International Law* (Asser Press, 2020), pp. 1–19. Forum shopping is typical for cross-border group reorganizations. See J. Dengler, 'Debt Restructuring in the UK and Spain: Is the Grass Still Greener on the Other Side?' III Prize submission, 2019, https://www.iiiglobal.org/iiiprizehistory.

therefore encourages courts and insolvency practitioners in insolvency proceedings concerning enterprise group members 'to cooperate to the maximum extent possible'.[45] This may be realized through direct communication, coordination of hearings (e.g. joint or simultaneous video hearings), the appointment of a person to act at the direction of the court or to represent multiple debtors, or with the help of cross-border insolvency agreements.[46]

As regards the latter, the Legislative Guide 2010 stresses their utility in reducing the cost of litigation and enabling parties to focus on the conduct of the insolvency proceedings. They can clarify legitimate expectations and assist in the preservation of the debtor's assets and the maximization of their value.[47] Importantly, the Legislative Guide 2010 makes it clear that the adoption of cross-border agreements should not be limited to a single-debtor situation, but could in principle be extended to the group context. Such group-wide protocols might be required to facilitate the global resolution of a group's financial difficulties.[48] In sum, the Legislative Guide 2010 supports the application of the principles of cooperation and communication underpinning the Model Law 1997 to enterprise group insolvency. **5.22**

However, the Legislative Guide 2010 (perhaps, for the first time so explicitly) recognizes that there are important limitations to communication and cooperation in the group context. For example, one of the limitations mentioned concerns information exchange. The Legislative Guide 2010 accepts that sharing of commercially sensitive or confidential information may be justifiably restricted, inter alia, to protect a debtor in reorganization proceedings 'where its continued ability to operate in the market and the protection of value may require confidentiality'.[49] Another significant limitation stems from the need to avoid conflicts of interest, which may arise in situations where the interests of the group as a whole conflict with the potentially different interests of individual group members. The risk of conflicts of interest is magnified in the context of intra-group financing (post-commencement finance),[50] resolution of intra-group claims[51] and in **5.23**

45 Legislative Guide 2010, recommendations 240–245.
46 Ibid.
47 Ibid., Ch. III, para. 48.
48 Ibid., recommendations 253–254.
49 Ibid., Ch. III, para. 30.
50 Ibid., Ch. II, para. 57.
51 Ibid., Ch. II, para. 144.

cases where a single or the same insolvency practitioner is appointed to administer insolvency proceedings of a number of group members.[52]

5.24 The main reason behind these limitations on communication and cooperation is the separate legal personality or legal separateness of companies comprising a corporate group. Neither the Practice Guide, nor the Legislative Guide change this long-standing maxim. Cross-border insolvency protocols, while bringing some level of universalism in the group context[53] and allowing the adjustment of crisis responses to the economic realities of corporate groups, cannot change it either.

D. MODEL LAW ON ENTERPRISE GROUP INSOLVENCY 2019

1. Purpose and goals of Model Law 2019

5.25 The discussion of the contribution made by UNCITRAL to the development of approaches to insolvency of enterprise groups would be incomplete without its most recent instrument, namely the UNCITRAL Model Law on Enterprise Group Insolvency (Model Law 2019). During the first decade of this century, corporate groups and the possible solutions to deal with them in transnational insolvency cases had been subject to many corridor chats and informal discussions in smaller groups of academics and practitioners. The idea to create a new legal instrument, specifically addressing the issue of insolvency of enterprise groups emerged in 2013.[54] Since then the Working Group V has been engaged in drafting legislative provisions, which concentrated on the most salient areas, such as coordination and cooperation between group insolvency proceedings, mechanisms for development and approval of a group insolvency solution and the use of synthetic proceedings.

5.26 It soon became clear that insolvency of enterprise groups deserved a distinct model law, building on the Model Law 1997 and working with its foundation in the five basic ground rules ('one insolvent debtor, one insolvency estate, one insolvency proceeding, one court and one insolvency office holder'). According

---

52 Ibid., Ch. III, para. 47. For similar concerns, see The World Bank Principles, C16.5, noting that a system permitting a single or the same insolvency representative to be appointed with respect to two or more enterprise group members, should include provisions addressing situations involving conflicts of interest.

53 Mevorach asserts that encouraging maximum cooperation is crucial for integrated groups and 'might be dubbed as a type of modified universalism albeit a weakened one'. I. Mevorach, 'Towards a Consensus on the Treatment of Multinational Enterprise Groups in Insolvency' (2010) 18(2) *Cardozo Journal of International and Comparative Law*, p. 419.

54 UNCITRAL, Report of Working Group V (Insolvency Law) on the work of its forty-third session, 26 April 2013, A/CN.9/766, para. 106, https://undocs.org/en/A/CN.9/766.

to the drafters of the Model Law 2019, 'the text should be prepared as a stand-alone model law, in the light of its distinct scope'.[55] That approach, it was noted, would 'accord more prominence to the text and facilitate its promotion, as well as highlight its importance for cross-border inter-State cooperation and coordination in insolvency-related matters'.[56] Finally, in July 2019 UNCITRAL approved the Model Law 2019.[57] This model law is supplemented by the guide to enactment, which at the moment of writing of this study (April/May 2020) continues to be a draft, rather than an approved document.[58]

The purpose of the Model Law 2019 is to 'provide effective mechanisms to address cases of insolvency affecting the members of an enterprise group'.[59] Among its key objectives: (i) fair and efficient administration of insolvencies; (ii) protection and maximization of the overall combined value of the assets and operations of enterprise group members and of the group as a whole; and (iii) facilitation of group rescue and restructuring (thus entailing preservation of employment). The achievement of these objectives is envisioned through the creation and application of tools and mechanisms to improve communication and cooperation between courts and insolvency practitioners and to facilitate the development of a group insolvency solution and its cross-border recognition and implementation. **5.27**

One of the fundamental goals of insolvency law is the imposition of collectivism, which should lead to the reduction of strategic costs and the increase of the collective pool of assets to the extent that it prevents a race to the court, individual enforcement of claims and piecemeal liquidation.[60] Coordination problems arising in a situation of financial distress and premised on the plurality of creditors having a natural desire to enforce their claims ahead of other creditors (common pool problem) intensify in a group context. Essentially, a creditor run to the court in fact in a group situation turns into multiple **5.28**

---

55 UNCITRAL, Report of Working Group V (Insolvency Law) on the work of its fifty-third session, 18 May 2018, A/CN.9/937, para. 48, https://undocs.org/en/A/CN.9/937.

56 Ibid.

57 UNCITRAL Model Law on Enterprise Group Insolvency, https://uncitral.un.org/en/texts/insolvency. For general analysis of the Model Law 2019 and its comparison with the current EIR Recast approach, see I. Mevorach, 'A Fresh View on the Hard/Soft Law Divide: Implications for International Insolvency of Enterprise Groups' (2019) 40(3) *Michigan Journal of International Law*, pp. 505–30.

58 UNCITRAL, Enterprise group insolvency: draft guide to enactment, 20 March 2019, A/CN.9/WG.V/WP.165, https://undocs.org/en/A/CN.9/WG.V/WP.165. We note that the final Guide to the Model Law 2019 has been published, as approved in 2020, and is available at https://uncitral.un.org/sites/uncitral.un.org/files/media-documents/uncitral/en/19-11346_mloegi.pdf.

59 Model Law 2019, preamble.

60 T. Jackson, *The Logic and Limits of Bankruptcy Law* (HUP, 1986), pp. 16–17, viewing the role of insolvency law as one of 'ameliorating a common pool problem created by a system of individual creditor remedies'. See also H. Eidenmüller, What is an Insolvency Proceeding? ECGI Working Paper Series in Law, No. 335/2016, 2016, arguing that only fully collective proceedings should be qualified as insolvency proceedings.

creditors running to multiple courts. In the absence of a group-level regulation and decision-making, aligning the interests of creditors of multiple entities in the group is unlikely. To turn around this outcome, the Model Law 2019 provides for such group-level regulation and attempts to align the economic self-interest with the goals of collective action, now on a group level.

2. Scope and tools of Model Law 2019

5.29 The scope of the Model Law 2019 extends to three main issues or tools: (1) cooperation and direct communication between insolvency representatives, courts and group representatives with respect to multiple insolvency proceedings concerning members of an enterprise group; (2) opening, conduct and recognition of planning proceedings and relief available to them; (3) granting of an undertaking or synthetic insolvency proceedings.

5.30 The use of these tools should stimulate the adoption of a 'group insolvency solution', defined by the Model Law 2019 as:

> a proposal or set of proposals developed in a planning proceeding for the reorganization, sale or liquidation of some or all of the assets and operations of one or more enterprise group members, with the goal of protecting, preserving, realizing or enhancing the overall combined value of those enterprise group members.[61]

Thus, the exact contours of a group solution may differ depending on the specific characteristics of an enterprise group – its structure, business model, degree and type of integration between enterprise group members, intra-group financing and other factors.[62] It may, for instance, include a negotiated sale of a part of the business or the sale of a combination of assets belonging to different group members, the subsequent adoption of a single reorganization plan involving several group members or a series of entity-level plans complementing each other. The concept of a group insolvency solution does not affect separate legal personality of group entities as such and does not entail substantive consolidation. It also does not specifically sanction procedural consolidation, although such consolidation is not ruled out.

5.31 A group insolvency solution is contemplated to be developed and implemented through a so-called 'planning proceeding', which is defined as either a main proceeding commenced in respect of an enterprise group member (with

61 Model Law 2019, Article 2(f).

62 Guide to Model Law 2019, para. 42.

additional requirements)[63] or a proceeding that has been approved by a court in the main proceeding. 'Planning proceeding' is a new *sui generis* term in the global world of restructuring and insolvency. Over several meetings of the Working Group V the definition and the mode of operation of a planning proceeding have been widely discussed. The idea behind the planning proceeding is to establish and identify a proceeding that should play a leading role and liaise with proceedings opened with respect to other participating group members in order to come to an acceptable group insolvency solution.[64] This model of allocation of all or many of the strategic functions within a group is also supported by the appointment of a 'group representative'[65] and the relief that may be granted upon the recognition of a planning proceeding. Such relief may include, inter alia, a stay of execution against the assets of the enterprise group member, suspension of the right to transfer, encumber, or otherwise dispose of any assets of the enterprise group member, approval of the arrangements concerning intra-group financing.[66]

The adoption of a coordinated group solution is dependent on the initiative and willingness of group members to communicate, cooperate and, ultimately, participate in a planning proceeding. While such participation is voluntary and group companies are free to opt in or out at any time,[67] cooperation and communication are mandatory ('shall cooperate to the maximum extent possible'[68]). In this respect the Model Law 2019 follows the steps of the Model Law 1997. Cooperation can be implemented by any appropriate means, including coordinated hearings[69] and the approval and implementation of insolvency agreements.[70] It draws upon recommendations 253–254 of the Legislative Guide 2010 and recognizes the utility of such agreements for developing group insolvency solutions. **5.32**

63 For the main insolvency proceeding to be a planning proceeding: (i) one or more other group members should participate in it for the purpose of developing and implementing a group insolvency solution; (ii) the enterprise group member subject to the main proceeding should be a necessary and integral participant in that group insolvency solution; and (iii) a group representation has to be appointed. Model Law 2019, Art. 2(g).

64 Guide to Model Law 2019 in para. 44 clarifies that it is not intended that there should be only one planning proceeding. Especially for groups organized horizontally in relatively independent units or geographical areas or where different plans are required for different parts of the enterprise group, more than one planning proceeding can be envisaged.

65 Model Law 2019, Art. 2(e).

66 Ibid., Art. 24.

67 Ibid., Art. 18(3).

68 Ibid., Arts 9, 13, 14.

69 Ibid., Art. 12. Interestingly, the Model Law 2019 provides for the possibility of parties reaching a separate agreement on the conditions to govern the coordinated hearing. This agreement may address: use of pre-hearing conferences; conduct of the hearing, including the language to be used and need for interpretation; requirements for the provision of notice; methods of communication; conditions applicable to the right to appear and be heard; the courts to which participants may make submissions; questions of confidentiality.

70 Ibid., Art. 16.

5.33 In all, the adoption by UNCITRAL of the Model Law 2019 is a crucial step in recognizing the existence of corporate groups and developing practical tools and approaches to handling their insolvencies. It also marks a logical outcome in the evolution of the UNCITRAL's vision of international insolvencies, which has started with consideration of a single entity with cross-border operations and assets (Model Law 1997) and has gradually, step-by-step, come to the group insolvency context.

3. Model Law 2019 and insolvency agreements

5.34 The Model Law 2019 encourages cooperation to the maximum extent possible, inter alia, by way of approval and implementation of agreements concerning the coordination of insolvency proceedings relating to two or more enterprise group members. In this respect, it has a number of important aspects which are worth mentioning.

5.35 First, the Model Law 2019 acknowledges that insolvency agreements may involve enterprise group insolvency proceedings opened in the same jurisdiction (so-called domestic groups).[71]

5.36 Second, it does not require agreements to be approved by the court, leaving the issue to domestic law and decisions of insolvency practitioners.[72]

5.37 Third, the Model Law 2019 assumes that a group solution may require the participation of all or the majority of group members, irrespective of their financial status. As a result:

> it makes no distinction between an enterprise group member that might be subject to insolvency proceedings and an enterprise group member that is not, avoiding any distinction based upon financial status, such as between what might be described as an 'insolvent' or 'solvent' enterprise group member.[73]

For example, the engagement of a solvent group member holding valuable assets (e.g. intellectual property rights or real estate relied on by other group members) may be necessary to effectuate a going concern sale of the whole business and avoiding suboptimal liquidation of assets owned by individual insolvent group entities. Participation by solvent group members is, in fact,

71 Guide to Model Law 2019, para. 93.

72 Ibid., para. 95.

73 Ibid., para. 110.

not unusual in practice.[74] Thus, solvent group members should also be able (and in some cases, encouraged) to take part in the insolvency protocols.[75]

Fourth, the Model Law 2019 reiterates that cooperation arrangements cannot diminish or remove the obligations insolvency practitioners have under the law governing their appointment, including professional rules and ethical guidelines.[76] Thus, their allegiance to a particular enterprise group and its respective (pool of) creditors, as may be sanctioned by the applicable national law, remains unaffected. **5.38**

Fifth, the Model Law 2019 and the guide to its enactment cover certain limitations on communication and cooperation in the group context. For example, the latter subjects the implementation of cooperation to the mandatory rules applicable in insolvency proceedings, including rules restricting information exchange for the reasons of protection of privacy or confidentiality.[77] However, it further clarifies that the need to ensure confidentiality 'should not be interpreted as providing a basis for declining to share information'.[78] Instead, appropriate safeguards need to be put in place to guarantee protection of such information. While the Model Law 2019 does not mention the issue of conflicts of interest, its guide addresses it, but only in the scenario where a single or the same insolvency representative is appointed to administer several members of an enterprise group.[79] **5.39**

Sixth, the Model Law 2019 establishes that participation by a court in communication does not imply a waiver of any powers, responsibilities or authority, a substantive determination of any matter before the court, or a waiver by any of the parties of any of their substantive or procedural rights.[80] The latter may be problematic, since insolvency protocols frequently establish and regulate procedural and (sometimes) substantive rights of participating parties. Should such agreements be invalid or unenforceable, their practical **5.40**

74 Legislative Guide 2010, Ch. II, para. 152.

75 Participation of solvent companies in group insolvency solutions (e.g. group reorganization plans) may create problems with their cross-border recognition. In the recent case of *Re Sturgeon Central Asia Balanced Fund Ltd. (in liquidation)* [2019] EWHC 1215 (Ch), the High Court of Justice of England and Wales held (among many other things) that solvent proceedings cannot be recognized under the English Cross-Border Insolvency Regulations 2006 (CBIR), implementing the Model Law 1997. In other words, a court-approved reorganization plan involving both insolvent and solvent companies risks not being recognized in the UK, potentially undermining the effectiveness of such a plan. The adoption of the Model Law 2019 and its express acceptance of insolvent/non-insolvent group solutions may address this problem.

76 Guide to Model Law 2019, para. 91.

77 Ibid., para. 80.

78 Ibid., para. 93.

79 Ibid., para. 103.

80 Model Law 2019, Art. 11(2).

value will be significantly diminished. Undoubtedly, reaching an enforceable compromise can help achieve certainty and avoid the burdens and costs of protracted litigation. The guide somewhat clarifies this situation by stating that 'it should be possible for the courts to explicitly reach agreement on a range of matters'.[81]

5.41 The use of cross-border insolvency protocols (or agreements, as referred to by UNCITRAL) has initially been embraced to deal with a single-debtor insolvency, but naturally, first in practice and then in the UNCITRAL's instruments, insolvency protocols have been applied in the context of enterprise groups and are now an integral part of the model legislation. A similar evolution has occurred in the EU, although in practice the use of insolvency protocols in Europe has been rather limited. The next chapter traces this development in more detail.

81 Guide to Model Law 2019, para. 83.

6

EUROPEAN INSOLVENCY REGULATION (RECAST) AND GROUP INSOLVENCIES

A. BACKGROUND OF EIR RECAST AND TREATMENT OF CORPORATE GROUPS IN INSOLVENCY 6.01

B. EIR RECAST AND COORDINATED SOLUTION TO GROUP INSOLVENCIES 6.07

1. Cooperation and communication in group insolvencies 6.09
2. Group coordination proceeding 6.16

C. CROSS-BORDER INSOLVENCY PROTOCOLS UNDER EIR RECAST 6.21

A. BACKGROUND OF EIR RECAST AND TREATMENT OF CORPORATE GROUPS IN INSOLVENCY

Harmonization of conflict-of-laws aspects of insolvency law in Europe has been discussed since the 1960s, when the Brussels Convention of 27 September 1968[1] (the predecessor of the modern Brussels I Recast[2]) was adopted. The Brussels Convention harmonized rules on jurisdiction and recognition and enforcement of judgments in civil and commercial matters, but explicitly excluded from its scope matters of bankruptcy, winding-up, judicial arrangements, compositions and analogous proceedings. It took more than 30 years for the EU to agree on a harmonized regulation of transnational insolvencies. The adoption of unified rules on matters of international insolvency jurisdiction and applicable law was determined by the need to improve the efficiency and effectiveness of insolvency proceedings having cross-border effect, ensure equal treatment of creditors (*pari passu* principle), and protect legitimate expectations and certainty of transactions.[3] **6.01**

The first major instrument dealing with cross-border insolvencies was the EIR 2000. It was adopted in 2000 and entered into force on 31 May 2002. Directly applicable in all Member States (except Denmark), it contained uniform rules **6.02**

1 1968 Brussels Convention on jurisdiction and the enforcement of judgments in civil and commercial matters, Consolidated version CF 498Y0126(01).

2 Regulation (EU) No. 1215/2012 of the European Parliament and of the Council of 12 December 2012 on jurisdiction and the recognition and enforcement of judgments in civil and commercial matters (recast).

3 Report on the Convention of Insolvency Proceedings, Brussels, 3 May 1996 (also known as Virgos-Schmit Report), http://aei.pitt.edu/952/.

on international jurisdiction, recognition of insolvency judgments and applicable law in insolvency matters. It also contained one provision, mandating cooperation and communication between insolvency practitioners in main and secondary proceedings (Art. 31). Just like the Model Law 1997, the EIR 2000 did not contain rules dealing with insolvency of multinational enterprise groups.[4] For example, there was no compulsory coordination of the independent insolvency proceedings opened for a parent company and its subsidiaries that would allow maximizing both the value of the group's assets and the prospects for a successful restructuring. This was seen as a considerable drawback, as a large number of cross-border insolvencies in the EU involved groups of companies.[5] The basic premise of the EIR 2000 was that separate proceedings must be opened for each individual member of the corporate group and that these proceedings ought to be entirely independent of each other.

6.03 Legal distinction of debtors in an enterprise group has been stressed in the jurisprudence of the Court of Justice of the European Union (CJEU). For example, in the case of *Eurofood IFSC Ltd.*,[6] it was noted that in a situation of a group of companies, COMIs of its members shall be determined separately (entity-by-entity) and rather independently of the group structure and group interdependencies. The CJEU's function is to provide answers to questions posed by national courts. Such answers determine the way certain issues with relation to EU law have to be interpreted. The actual implementation of the CJEU authoritative guidelines is to be done by the national court which has posed the question. In literature is has been submitted that the CJEU did not pay enough attention to the context of a complex multinational enterprise (i.e. Parmalat group), experiencing financial difficulties in multiple jurisdictions at the same time and trying to pursue restructuring in a single point of entry.[7]

4 In the EIR 2000 corporate groups were deliberately left out. One would expect that within European company and insolvency law special rules would have been developed, but the tension between the strict judicial approach (i.e. 'five ones') and the economic (group) reality is not easy to tackle. The discussions about the recognition of the group interest in European company law have taken place since the 1990s and resulted in a number of initiatives (see, for instance, the Company Law Action Plan, referred to above). Despite the generally positive attitude of scholars and business community, these initiatives have not resulted in any legislative proposals. C. Teichmann, 'Towards a European Framework for Cross-Border Group Management' (2016) 13(5) *European Company Law*, p. 150, pointing out that 'the company law of most jurisdictions is still focused on the single legal entity and does not expressly acknowledge the fact that the corporate group may create legal challenges which are different from those of an independent company'.

5 Report from the Commission to the European Parliament, the Council and the European Economic and Social Committee on the application of Council Regulation (EC) No 1346/2000 of 29 May 2000 on insolvency proceedings, Strasbourg, 12.12.2012, COM(2012) 743 final, p. 14.

6 Case C-341/04, *Eurofood IFSC Ltd.*, 2 May 2006, ECLI:EU:C:2006:281.

7 The CJEU's failure to address the treatment of related entities in a corporate group with systemic insolvency problems was highlighted by Bufford. See S. Bufford, 'Center of Main Interests, International Insolvency Case Venue, and Equality of Arms: The Eurofood Decision of the European Court of Justice' (2007)

The approach taken by the CJEU could be partially explained by the liquidation-oriented nature of the EIR 2000. However, even if the company is destined to be liquidated, the highest possible realization of its value could certainly depend on whether a coordinated group-wide solution (e.g. going-concern sale) is available. It is true that in none of the legal systems involved (i.e. Ireland and Italy) was such coordination available in legislation or supported by the wealth of case law. **6.04**

The atomistic vision of a corporate group is also evident in another CJEU case – the *Rastelli* case.[8] In that case the CJEU had to decide whether the court, having opened the insolvency proceedings in one Member State (France), could join to those proceedings another company whose registered office was in another Member State (Italy), on the basis that the two companies formed a de facto unit and their property had been intermixed. The court noted that the legal personality of the two debtors had to be respected and that each debtor constituting a distinct legal entity was subject to its own court jurisdiction. Indeed, the CJEU had its hands tied by what has historically been the meaning of a European measure (such as a Regulation or a Directive) and to what was conceivable or possible in the legal systems of the (majority) EU Member States.[9] **6.05**

According to Article 46 EIR 2000, no later than 1 June 2012 the European Commission had to present a report on the application of the EIR 2000 with a proposal for its adaptation (if necessary). Despite the general acknowledgement of the EIR 2000's success, after 15 years of its existence, it has become clear that some of its provisions needed adjustment, while other developments required totally new rules.[10] As a result, a new insolvency regulation was adopted in 2015, the EIR Recast. This new regulation entered into force on 26 June 2017 and replaced the original EIR 2000.[11] While keeping the **6.06**

---

27 *Northwestern Journal of International Law & Business*, pp. 351–420. For the criticism of the CJEU's approach to corporate groups in insolvency see also I. Kokorin, 'Contracting Around Insolvency Jurisdiction: Private Ordering in European Insolvency Jurisdiction Rules and Practices', in V. Lazić and S. Stuij (eds), *Recasting the Insolvency Regulation: Improvements and Missed Opportunities. Short Studies in Private International Law* (Asser Press, 2020), pp. 21–58.

8 Case C-191/10, *Rastelli Davide e C. Snc v. Jean-Charles Hidoux*, 15 December 2011, ECLI:EU:C:2011:838.

9 See B. Wessels, 'The Ongoing Struggle of Multinational Groups of Companies under the EC Insolvency Regulation' (2009) 6(4) *European Company Law*, pp. 169–77, explaining ten ways in which in practice more group-oriented approaches could be achieved.

10 Proposal for a Regulation of the European Parliament and of the Council amending Council Regulation (EC) No 1346/2000 on insolvency proceedings, COM(2012) 744 final, 12 December 2012.

11 For an overview and commentary on the EIR Recast, see B. Wessels and I. Kokorin, *European Union Regulation on Insolvency Proceedings: An Introductory Analysis* (Alexandria: American Bankruptcy Institute, 2018). For detailed analysis of the EIR Recast, see B. Wessels, *International Insolvency Law Part II. European Insolvency Law* (4th edn, Wolters Kluwer, 2017). See also Moritz Brinkmann, *European Insolvency Regulation. Article-by-Article Commentary* (C.H. Beck/Hart/Nomos, 2019).

fundamental principles and the framework of the EIR 2000 (COMI, main and secondary proceedings, extent of *lex concursus*, automatic recognition of insolvency and related judgments, etc.), the EIR Recast has a wider scope and covers proceedings that promote the rescue of economically viable but distressed businesses and that give a second chance to entrepreneurs. It also introduces new extended communication and cooperation duties and the rules on group coordination proceedings.

B. EIR RECAST AND COORDINATED SOLUTION TO GROUP INSOLVENCIES

6.07 The EIR Recast contains an extensive chapter (Chapter V) dedicated to group insolvencies, with more than 20 articles. It aims to achieve efficient administration of insolvency proceedings relating to different companies forming part of a group of companies.[12] To that end, it provides two sets of tools. Articles 56–60 prescribe cooperation and communication duties for courts and insolvency practitioners involved in insolvency proceedings opened against members of an enterprise group. Articles 61–77 introduce a distinct mechanism of the so-called group coordination proceeding.

6.08 The starting point is that the EIR Recast adheres to the notion of separate legal personalities of the companies comprising a corporate group. Therefore, it does not promote either substantive or procedural consolidation. However, unlike its predecessor, it recognizes that special rules may be necessary to allow for a group restructuring[13] or finding another solution that would leverage synergies across the group.[14] The EIR Recast aims at achieving these goals through coordinated administration of insolvency proceedings by way of enhanced communication and cooperation standards and a centralized group-level coordination via group coordination proceedings.

1. Cooperation and communication in group insolvencies

6.09 The legal framework for cooperation and communication in the context of group insolvencies greatly resembles the rules for cooperation and communication between main and secondary proceedings (Arts 41–43). Recital 52 EIR Recast explicitly states that the various insolvency practitioners and the courts involved in group insolvencies should be under similar obligations to cooperate and communicate with each other as those involved in main and secondary

12 EIR Recast, Recital 51.
13 Ibid., Recital 54.
14 Ibid., Recital 52.

insolvency proceedings relating to the same debtor. In our opinion, such duties shall not be limited to intra-EU group insolvencies but extend to cooperation and communication with courts and insolvency practitioners in non-EU countries.

The duties of cooperation and communication in the context of group insolvencies apply in three major scenarios, namely between: insolvency practitioners, courts and insolvency practitioners and courts. All of these actors *shall* cooperate and communicate with each other. **6.10**

Insolvency practitioners appointed in insolvency proceedings opened against members of the same corporate group shall cooperate to the extent that such cooperation is appropriate to facilitate the effective administration of those proceedings, and insofar as it is compatible with the rules applicable to them and does not entail any conflict of interest.[15] In any case, insolvency practitioners must (i) as soon as possible communicate to each other any information that may be relevant to the other proceedings;[16] (ii) consider whether possibilities exist for coordinating the administration and supervision of the affairs of the group members, and if so, coordinate such administration and supervision;[17] and (iii) consider whether possibilities exist for restructuring group members and, if so, coordinate with regard to the proposal and negotiation of a coordinated restructuring plan.[18] In order to achieve a successful group restructuring, the EIR Recast grants the insolvency practitioners the power to request a stay of any measure related to the realization of the assets in the proceedings opened with respect to any other member of the same group.[19] **6.11**

As to courts, they should also cooperate to the extent that the cooperation facilitates the effective administration of the proceedings, is not incompatible with the rules applicable to them and does not entail any conflict of interest.[20] The EIR Recast lists cases in which cooperation may be desirable.[21] For example, cooperation may concern: (i) coordination in the appointment of insolvency practitioners; (ii) communication of information by any means considered appropriate by the court; (iii) coordination of the administration and supervision of the assets and affairs of the members of the group; **6.12**

15 Ibid., Art. 56(1).
16 Ibid., Art. 56(2)(a).
17 Ibid., Art. 56(2)(b).
18 Ibid., Art. 56(2)(c).
19 Ibid., Art. 60.
20 Ibid., Art. 57(1).
21 Ibid., Art. 57(3).

(iv) coordination of the conduct of hearings; and (v) coordination in the approval of protocols where necessary.

6.13 Thus, cooperation and communication are generally limited by matters of practicality (i.e. they should facilitate effective administration of insolvency proceedings), rules and limitations imposed by the *lex concursus* of the jurisdictions concerned, and obligations to avoid conflicts of interest.[22] The EIR Recast does not provide a definition of a conflict of interest. Nevertheless, conflicts oftentimes arise in a situation of a dispute between group members. Such a dispute may concern enforcement of intra-group claims, transaction avoidance actions and the allocation or transfer of assets within the group. Schmidt notes that a conflict may appear if the cooperation entails the (gratuitous) 'transmission of valuable know-how, patents, or business secrets, or making assets available to other group members which could have been disposed of with a large profit for the individual group member'.[23]

6.14 The main idea behind restricting communication and cooperation in a situation of a conflict of interest is to avoid or minimize the potential harm that can be caused by such communication to the interests of individual group members (and their creditors), which preserve their separate legal identity.[24] However, in our opinion, in order to ensure efficient cooperation within corporate groups in insolvency, these limitations should be interpreted narrowly and applied on a case-by-case basis, taking into account all the facts of the case. The principle of the most complete and uninhibited exchange of information comes from the trust, underpinning the operation of the EU.[25]

6.15 To improve cooperation in the absence of one dominant insolvency proceeding, as in the context of groups all pending insolvency proceedings function on the same footing (in contrast to the relationship between main and secondary proceedings), the EIR Recast allows insolvency practitioners to agree to grant additional powers to an insolvency practitioner appointed in one of the

---

22 Ibid., Arts 56(1), 57(1) and 58.

23 J. Schmidt, 'General Duty of Cooperation and Communication (Article 56(1))', in R. Bork and K. Van Zwieten (eds), *Commentary on the European Insolvency Regulation* (OUP, 2016), para. 56.22.

24 B. Hess et al., *The Implementation of the New Insolvency Regulation: Improving Cooperation and Mutual Trust* (Nomos/Hart, 2018), p. 162, noting that since:

> insolvency practitioners still owe their duties towards the creditors of 'their' respective insolvency proceeding, they should and will normally refrain from entering a protocol that may hamper local creditors, even when a refusal may reduce the total welfare of the creditors involved in all the relevant proceedings.

25 The principle of mutual trust supports the automatic recognition of insolvency judgments in the EU and is based on Art. 4(3) of the Treaty on the Functioning of the European Union (TFEU).

proceedings.[26] They may also divide certain tasks among themselves. However, in practice, without a developed regulatory framework, purely voluntary cooperation may be stalled by high transaction costs and collective-action problems. Therefore, a new group coordination proceeding was added by the EIR Recast.

2. Group coordination proceeding

With a view to improving the efficiency in administration of insolvency proceedings in the group context and to allow for a group restructuring, the EIR Recast has introduced procedural rules on coordination of insolvency proceedings. Such coordination, however, shall not affect separate legal personality of group members.[27] This latter requirement, as we will show, has led to a rather modest (for some, disappointing) result. **6.16**

As noted above, the EIR Recast does not sanction or even mention the possibility of substantive or procedural consolidation regarding group members' insolvency. Instead, it offers a coordination mechanism – 'group coordination proceeding'. In essence, a group coordination proceeding is separate from any other insolvency proceedings and can be seen as a legal superstructure, available to (all or some) insolvency proceedings of corporate group members. The idea behind a group coordination proceeding is similar to that of a planning proceeding under the Model Law 2019, discussed above.[28] **6.17**

'Group coordination proceeding' can be compared with software that steers towards the procedures of the entities to achieve a group solution or a group coordination plan. Such a plan may contain measures to re-establish economic performance and financial soundness of the group or any part of it, such as through an increase of equity capital, simplification of the financial structure of the group, and the elimination of deficiencies in the intra-group cash pooling system. Measures might aim to improve business performance, including through the reorganization of the group structure, the realignment **6.18**

26 EIR Recast, Art. 56(2).

27 Ibid., Recital 54.

28 At the same time, there are important differences between 'group coordination proceedings' and 'planning proceedings'. For example, while group coordination proceedings are always separate from insolvency proceedings opened with respect to group members, a planning proceeding may coincide with a (main) insolvency proceeding. Additionally, under the Model Law 2019 a group representative may be one of the insolvency practitioners appointed in an insolvency proceeding of a group member. According to the EIR Recast, a coordinator shall not be one of the insolvency practitioners appointed to act in respect of any of the group members (Art. 71(2) EIR Recast). For further discussion see I. Kokorin, 'Conflicts of Interest, Intra-group Financing and Procedural Coordination of Group Insolvencies' (2020) 29(1) *International Insolvency Review*, pp. 32–60.

and refocusing of business activities, replacement of management, and personnel reduction. A plan may also include solutions to settle intra-group disputes and avoidance actions related to, for instance, intra-group sales on the basis of transfer pricing, performance of services by one group member for another below market price, and gratuitous allocation of means of production and licences. Other plans could see agreements between insolvency practitioners of the insolvent group members, for example, to incorporate a group coordination plan in the insolvency plans of the individual group members, to reconsider the treatment of intra-group contracts or to provide security.[29]

6.19 Coordinated treatment of insolvency proceedings in a group context should be achieved with the help of a 'coordinator',[30] an independent person, whose main tasks consist of identifying and outlining recommendations for the coordinated conduct of the insolvency proceedings and drafting a group coordination plan.[31] The role of a group coordinator can be compared to that of a mediator, who assists parties in reconciling divergent positions in order to achieve the best possible (agreeable) solution.

6.20 A coordinator can suggest recommendations to insolvency practitioners of the individual insolvency proceedings of the members of the group that are pending in different Member States. In the EIR Recast, the whole coordination mechanism is voluntary in nature and group members are free to opt-out from participating in it at any time. They are also free to disregard the recommendations of the coordinator or the group coordination plan.[32] For these reasons, the new set of rules on group insolvency have had a mixed reception in legal literature, with the majority of authors expressing doubts as to their effectiveness and practical value, as well as to the high costs the group coordination proceedings may bring with them and their complex character.[33]

---

29 Wessels and Kokorin, *supra* note 11, p. 137.

30 EIR Recast, Art. 71.

31 Ibid., Art. 72(1). A group coordinator has the right to be heard and participate in any of the proceedings opened in respect of any member of the group (Art. 72(2)(a)). He may also request information and mediate or suggest mediation of any dispute arising between two or more insolvency practitioners of group members (Art. 72(2)(b)). Importantly, the group coordinator may ask for a stay for a period of up to six months of the proceedings opened in respect of any member of the group if it is necessary to ensure the proper implementation of the plan and would be to the benefit of the creditors in the proceedings for which the stay is requested. The request shall be made to the court that opened the proceedings for which the stay is asked (Art. 72(2)(e)). The stay seems to be the most powerful tool in the hands of the coordinator, as it relates to the whole of the group member's proceedings (and not only to asset realization) and has a direct effect on the course of the individual insolvency proceedings. It is particularly in contrast to the fact that, as a general rule, actions by the coordinator are recommendatory in nature, and insolvency practitioners are not obliged to follow recommendations coming from the coordinator.

32 Ibid., Art. 70(2).

33 C. Thole, M. Dueñas, 'Some Observations on the New Group Coordination Procedure of the Reformed European Insolvency Regulation' (2015) 24(3) *International Insolvency Review*, p. 214, noting that while a

Additional problems may arise if the corporate group has members located in non-Member States, meaning that the EIR Recast will not bind courts and insolvency practitioners in such non-Member State proceedings, and that the latter cannot form part of the group coordination proceedings. As of the moment of this study (April/May 2020), we have not seen the application of group coordination proceedings in practice.

C. CROSS-BORDER INSOLVENCY PROTOCOLS UNDER EIR RECAST

Whereas the EIR 2000 did not mention cross-border insolvency protocols, the EIR Recast encourages their conclusion in a corporate group setting. It notes that insolvency practitioners and courts should be able to enter into agreements and protocols for the purposes of facilitating cross-border cooperation of multiple insolvency proceedings. The EIR Recast accepts that protocols 'may vary in form, in that they may be written or oral, and in scope, in that they may range from generic to specific, and may be entered into by different parties'.[34] They can reflect the agreement between the parties to take, or to refrain from taking, certain steps or actions.[35] To assist courts and insolvency practitioners in their cooperation tasks (including in the conclusion of insolvency protocols), the EIR Recast points out that they should take into account best practices in cross-border insolvency cases, as set out in principles and guidelines on communication and cooperation adopted by European and international organizations.[36] Among such guidelines are, the already-mentioned CoCo Guidelines, EU JudgeCo Principles and Guidelines and JIN Guidelines.[37] **6.21**

Despite the vast (and positive) experience of entering into cross-border insolvency protocols, mainly in the US, Canada, the UK and, more recently, in **6.22**

new coordination procedure is 'a step into the right direction, the procedure has significant shortcomings such as the weak position of the coordinator, a liberal opt-in and opt-out mechanism and the problem of forum shopping'. See also S. Madaus, 'Insolvency Proceedings for Corporate Groups under the New Insolvency Regulation' (2015) *International Insolvency Law Review*, p. 241, concluding that group coordination proceedings 'can be considered a rather soft approach intended to incentivise stakeholders more than making them bound to perform specific duties'. See also I. Mevorach, 'On the Road to Universalism: A Comparative and Empirical Study of the UNCITRAL Model Law on Cross-Border Insolvency' (2011)12(4) *European Business Organization Law Review*, p. 523, summarizing that while coordination under the EIR Recast is possible, 'it is not mandatory or binding as might have been expected from a hard law instrument'.

34 EIR Recast, Recital 49.

35 Ibid.

36 Ibid., Recital 48.

37 Guidelines for Communication and Cooperation between Courts in Cross-Border Insolvency Matters (JIN Guidelines), 2016, http://www.jin-global.org/content/jin/pdf/Guidelines-for-Communication-and-Cooperation-in-Cross-Border-Insolvency.pdf.

Asian jurisdictions,[38] and despite the explicit recognition of protocols in the EIR Recast, in practice their adoption in Europe has been rather limited. There are only a few cases, in which EU civil law jurisdictions have been engaged in an insolvency protocol. There may be several reasons for this outcome. We have identified six:

(1) *Language barriers.* The EU has 24 official languages.[39] The language barrier can be a significant obstacle to communication between insolvency practitioners and courts, and in negotiations over an insolvency protocol. However, this is not an unsurmountable obstacle and cannot solely explain the rarity of protocols. After all, there are examples of cross-border protocols concluded between countries with different official languages.[40] In the current international practice, most of the lawyers and financial restructuring advisers master the English language. An obstacle for using another language, however, may lie in national procedural rules.[41] Besides, considering the rapid pace of technological development and digitization, the practicalities and technicalities will be playing an even lesser role in hindering cross-border communication. You no longer need to travel across borders to be able to negotiate with other parties, who can be put at one table virtually via platforms like Skype, Zoom or Microsoft Teams.

(2) *Differences in legal systems and cultures and the roles played by courts.* The largest majority of cross-border insolvency protocols engage countries with common law systems (i.e. the USA, Canada, the UK, Hong Kong[42]). In common law, alongside the various statutory mechanisms, the inherent power of courts to provide assistance in insolvency matters has been in existence for decades and is embraced to empower court-to-court communication.[43] Such inherent power is related to the concept of comity, which has been described as 'neither a matter of absolute obligation, on the one hand, nor of mere courtesy and good will upon the other', as 'the recognition which one nation allows within its territory to

38 Corporate Restructuring and Insolvency in Asia 2020, ABLI Legal Convergence Series, joint project of the Asian Business Law Institute and the III, 2020, https://info.sal.org.sg/insolvency/.

39 EU languages, https://europa.eu/european-union/about-eu/eu-languages_en.

40 For example, see protocols in Sendo International Limited (French and English), Jet Airways (Dutch and Hindi as the official language of the Union, Art. 343(1) of the Indian constitution).

41 In some countries it is uncertain whether information to be transferred by a foreign insolvency practitioner or a foreign court should be accompanied by official translation in the language used by the receiving court.

42 Corporate Restructuring and Insolvency in Asia 2020, *supra* note 38, p. 264, noting that 'the Hong Kong liquidators may and often do enter into a protocol with their foreign counterparts, and the use of protocols is an increasingly common feature of international insolvencies'.

43 A. Godwin, T. Howse and I. Ramsay, 'The Inherent Power of Common Law Courts to Provide Assistance in Cross-Border Insolvencies: From Comity to Complexity' (2017) 26(1) *International Insolvency Review*, pp. 5–39.

the legislative, executive, or judicial acts of another nation, having due regard both to international duty and convenience'.[44] In civil law countries the idea of courts communicating with foreign courts and insolvency practitioners in the absence of a clear statutory permission or authority has been unusual.[45] In addition, certain parts of a protocol need to be aligned with or included in national insolvency laws, many of which are rather detailed and procedural in nature. Such procedural details may be hard to synchronize with details of a cross-border protocol.[46] In this respect, the adoption of the EIR Recast and the implementation of the Model Law 1997 by a number of civil law countries (e.g. Serbia, Greece, Poland, Romania, Slovenia) should serve as the necessary statutory authority. In many other European countries, transnational communication and coordination between courts of different states has been a rarity. Since 2017 the related provisions apply in countries with a less developed tradition of judicial activism, especially those where procedural rules lack the tenor to exercise any power that is not explicitly sanctioned by a specific legislative provision. Arguably, a cultural change, promoting initiative and 'opening up' to court-to-court communication and the adoption of insolvency protocols may take longer.

(3) *Differences in substantive insolvency law.* Despite tendencies of the harmonization and unification of private international law rules related to insolvency, national substantive insolvency law has not been harmonized in Europe. For example, the rules on directors' liability, transaction avoidance, and ranking of claims diverge from one jurisdiction to another.[47] As a result, negotiating a common approach or solution may be challenging. Yet, recent developments could bring some level of harmonization. In the summer of 2019, the EU adopted the Directive 2019/1023 on preventive restructuring frameworks, on discharge of debt and disqualifications, and on measures to increase the efficiency of procedures concerning restructuring, insolvency and discharge of debt (Restructuring Directive). While not leading to a full harmonization of

44 *Hilton v. Guyot*, 159 U.S. 113 (1895).

45 D. Arner et al. (eds), *Research Handbook on Asian Financial Law* (Edward Elgar Publishing, 2020), p. 270. See also E. Moustaira, *International Insolvency Law: National Laws and International Texts* (Springer, 2019), p. 56, pointing out that common law courts were 'much more accustomed to the idea of cooperation and their systems permit that, while civil law courts are constrained by cultural and legal obstacles to do so, in cross-border insolvency cases'.

46 For example, in Germany, protocols between insolvency practitioners are permitted, however, depending on their scope, they may require the consent of the creditors' committee, see Skauradszun, Spahlinger, in M. Brinkmann (ed.), *European Insolvency Regulation. Article-by-Article Commentary* (C.H. Beck/Hart/Nomos, 2019), Art. 41, nr. 6.

47 G. McCormack, A. Keay and S. Brown, *European Insolvency Law: Reform and Harmonization* (Edward Elgar Publishing, 2017).

insolvency law, it nevertheless facilitates the adoption of similar restructuring frameworks and rules related to them (e.g. on new and interim finance, content of restructuring plans and cross-class cram-down).[48] As a result, at least slowly and gradually this obstacle to cross-border insolvency protocols may be cleared to one extent or another.

(4) *Protocols are not needed because the EIR Recast provides all necessary rules.* Unlike the Model Law 1997 or the Model Law 2019, the EIR Recast contains detailed rules on international insolvency jurisdiction, applicable law, related actions, relations between main and secondary insolvency proceedings, powers of insolvency practitioners and rights of creditors. Therefore, one may argue that insolvency protocols are simply not necessary, as all complex questions have been resolved by the regulation itself. We do not support this position. At a closer look, the EIR Recast leaves many issues unanswered, which in practice could lead to disputes, the unwillingness to share information, cooperate or fully realize the potential of the regulation. For example, the EIR Recast mandates that insolvency practitioners communicate to each other any information which may be relevant to other proceedings.[49] However, the exact scope of such 'relevant' information is unclear. It is also uncertain how the coordinated administration and supervision of group insolvency proceedings, promoted in Article 56(2)(b) should be realized in practice. The lack of clarify and detail may also inhibit cross-border coordination of joint hearings or the appointment of insolvency practitioners. In this respect, protocols can play an important gap-filling role, tailoring the form and content of communication and cooperation to particular circumstances. Besides, they may obtain particular relevance for administration and coordination of groups with members and proceedings (partially) outside the EU, and therefore outside the territorial scope of the EIR Recast.

(5) *Lack of knowledge and experience with protocols.* As described in Chapter 4 of the book, insolvency protocols have originated in the common law world as an innovation of insolvency practitioners and judges and have been facilitated by the accumulation of considerable knowledge and expertise of dealing with complex cross-border insolvency cases and resorting to protocols in practice (like a snowball effect). However, this alone cannot explain the unpopularity of insolvency protocols in the EU. First, there are protocols involving European jurisdictions, including the Netherlands, the UK, France, Germany and Switzerland. Still, they have

48 See T. Richter and A. Thery, 'INSOL Europe Guidance Note on the Implementation of Preventive Restructuring Frameworks under EU Directive 2019/1023: Claims, Classes, Voting, Confirmation and the Cross-Class Cram-Down', April 2020, https://www.insol-europe.org/download/documents/1705.

49 EIR Recast, Art. 56(2)(a).

not triggered any significant growth. Second, there is vast knowledge related to the resolution of international insolvencies. Third, such knowledge is advanced by the wealth of various soft law guidelines and recommendations (e.g. CoCo Guidelines, EU JudgeCo Principles and Guidelines),[50] but also the continued investment in research in the area of insolvency cooperation and communication.[51]

(6) *Protocols have an unclear legal nature and raise more questions than answers.*[52] This may be true, as the EIR Recast does not define insolvency protocols or provide comprehensive rules related to their conclusion, content or enforcement. As a result, there may be natural hesitation to negotiate and enter into such protocols. This was noted by the Conference on European Restructuring and Insolvency (CERIL), which has posed the following questions: (i) which parties have permission to agree on a protocol (e.g. including the approval by creditors or a creditors' committee)?; (ii) which clauses may a protocol contain (whether a protocol can include a choice of law clause or a clause waiving the right to sue directors, or a clause providing that costs of creating/drafting the protocol will be borne by creditors)?; (iii) how to deal with clauses that infringe rules of mandatory law (e.g. related to confidentiality, procedural rights of creditors, protection of creditors' information rights)?; (iv) what are the consequences of not using the agreed protocol and, thus, acting in conflict with the court's approval?[53] The situation is further complicated by the fact that the EU Member States introduce different rules of varying detail and prescribing the process in which communication and cooperation should take place.[54]

---

50 During the creation of these soft law instruments, practitioners and judges of a large number of European countries were involved.

51 JCOERE Project (Judicial Co-Operation supporting Economic Recovery in Europe) funded by the EU Justice Programme (2014-2020). This project (due to be completed at the end of 2020) concerns cross-border cooperation between courts and practitioners in insolvency and restructuring. See more https://www.ucc.ie/en/jcoere/. Two other projects, not specifically dealing with cross-border insolvency cooperation, but exploring different topics of European insolvency law (including certain aspects of insolvency of enterprise groups), include the ELI Business Rescue Project (https://www.europeanlawinstitute.eu/about-eli/bodies/membership/default-title/rescue-of-business-and-insolvency-law/), completed in 2017, and the CODIRE project (https://www.codire.eu/), completed in 2018. For the monograph setting out the findings and recommendations of the CODIRE project team, see L. Stanghellini et al., *Best Practices in European Restructuring: Contractualised Distress Resolution in the Shadow of the Law (CODIRE)* (Wolters Kluwer, 2018).

52 B. Hess et al. conducted a survey in the preparation of the study concerning the implementation of the EIR Recast. They have found out that the majority of respondents (53 per cent) considered the lack of a clear legal basis for the validity of protocols or for their approval (47 per cent) as the most mentioned legal impediment to concluding insolvency protocols, together with the uncertain legal nature (47 per cent). Hess et al., *supra* note 24, p. 172.

53 CERIL Report 2018-1 on Insolvency Regulation (Recast) and National Procedural Rules, 4 June 2018, p. 8.

54 Ibid., p. 13.

7

LEGAL NATURE OF CROSS-BORDER INSOLVENCY PROTOCOLS

A. WHAT ARE INSOLVENCY PROTOCOLS? 7.01
1. Insolvency protocols and issue of jurisdiction 7.12
2. Insolvency protocols and issue of applicable law 7.19

B. LEGAL EFFECT OF INSOLVENCY PROTOCOLS 7.31

A. WHAT ARE INSOLVENCY PROTOCOLS?

7.01 Despite the fact that modern insolvency protocols (since the Maxwell protocol) have been in existence for almost three decades, their legal nature is not entirely clear. In cross-border practice they are negotiated and concluded. Their result is used to guide certain steps in the administration of international insolvency cases. However, what are insolvency protocols? To what extent (and if at all) are they binding on the parties and what are the limitations on their scope and content? The difficulty of determining the nature of insolvency protocols can be attributed to their unique characteristics. These are mainly of three kinds.

7.02 First, protocols originate in a multi-actor environment. Therefore, they may establish rights and lay down obligations for different parties. Who are these actors?

7.03 Typically, the following actors are engaged at different stages in the process of a protocol negotiation and conclusion: (i) insolvency practitioners appointed in separate insolvency proceedings, nearly always opened in different jurisdictions; (ii) courts approving protocols and sometimes urging parties to enter into them; (iii) creditors and creditors' committees, which may be consulted with and in rare cases are involved in the approval and signing of protocols;[1]

1 Lehman Brothers protocol, para. 14.6, stating that 'This Protocol shall be deemed effective [...] upon execution by all Official Representatives [...] and its approval by the Tribunal with jurisdiction over such estates or the relevant Committee (or similar body), where such approval is required under applicable law.' See also Commodore protocol with the unofficial Committee of unsecured creditors as one of the signatories. See

(iv) debtors themselves, as the debtors' management is not always replaced in the insolvency proceedings and may continue exercising most of its rights and functions (debtor-in-possession), including preparation of a rescue or pre-packaged plan and negotiation of an insolvency protocol. Many protocols are in fact negotiated prior to the commencement of insolvency proceedings.[2]

Second, insolvency protocols operate within a regulated regime of two or more separate insolvency or restructuring proceedings. As a result, parties to a protocol are inherently placed in a certain national legal framework and a set of legal boundaries within such a framework, within which they must operate. This framework is naturally more restrictive, compared to a situation of a freely negotiated commercial contract. This is due to the fact that insolvency law aims at protecting the collective interest of creditors, as well as the separateness of insolvency estates and pools of creditors. As a result, an insolvency protocol that unjustifiably limits procedural rights of creditors, treats them unequally, unduly harms the interests of a single legal entity (and its creditors) within an enterprise group for the benefit of other group members, would as a matter of principle not be permissible. We will discuss the potential limitations on the scope and content of insolvency protocols later in this book. **7.04**

Third, ambiguity around the nature of protocols stems from the variety of purposes pursued by them, and therefore by the diversity of clauses and provisions found in them. As we will discuss below, some of these provisions indicate the binding force of protocols, while other stress their non-binding soft law character or do not provide any indication about their binding nature. This diversity makes it difficult to develop a coherent theory of insolvency protocols or devise a single harmonized set of rules, which would ensure legal certainty and facilitate their use in countries with different legal cultures and traditions. **7.05**

These are difficulties indeed. In transnational practice in most cases the parties involved seem purely focused on their practical use. It is possible to refer to such behaviour as functional-pragmatic. We do not condemn or praise this practice. What we try to do is to find the legal dimension of what parties are achieving with concluding an insolvency protocol. On the basis of our analysis of around 50 protocols we have identified two main legal approaches to **7.06**

also the IFSA (Nortel Networks), sec. 18(a) stating that both Creditors' Committee and the Bondholders' Committee have voted in favor of the IFSA.

2 Practice Guide, Ch. III, para. 11.

cross-border insolvency protocols. For this we used findings from international standard-setting institutions, academic literature and the text of insolvency protocols themselves.

7.07 The first approach embraces a public law perspective and qualifies an insolvency protocol as a 'court-created treaty'[3] or a 'mini-treaty regarding each side's role in resolving the dispute'.[4] In a similar way, cross-border insolvency protocols have been referred to as 'case-specific, private international insolvency treaties'.[5] This approach is partially premised on the fact that insolvency protocols are frequently approved by a court, which affirms their validity and grants them additional state-authorized weight with a possibility of state enforcement. It also reduces the risk that a protocol will be successfully challenged by the dissenting creditors, which could otherwise create uncertainty and potentially undermine its effectiveness.[6] It should be acknowledged that the literature referring to protocols as mini-treaties mostly dates from nearly two decades ago. At that time in international insolvency practice the dominant topic in conversations and discussion was that states did not have (for whatever reason) an appropriate answer for complex cross-border insolvency cases and that international practice should try to fill that gap.

7.08 It is not uncommon for protocols to explicitly state that they become binding and enforceable only after the approval by the courts concerned and/or signing by the parties.[7] In this respect a range of possibilities can occur, from simple approval (in the meaning of 'support') to the incorporation of a protocol in a form of a judgment (e.g. a court order). Depending on the content of the judgment and the protocol itself, the judgment may be qualified as an insolvency-related judgment. Under the EIR Recast, an insolvency-related judgment is a judgment which derives directly from the insolvency proceedings and is closely linked with them.[8] The UNCITRAL Model Law on Insolvency-Related Judgments defines an insolvency-related judgment as a judgment that 'a. Arises as a consequence of or is materially associated with an insolvency proceeding [...]; and b. Was issued on or after the commencement

3 S. Dargan, 'The Emergence of Mechanisms for Cross-border Insolvencies in Canadian Law' (2001) 17(1) *Connecticut Journal of International Law*, p. 124.

4 A-M. Slaughter, 'A Global Community of Courts' (2003) 44(1) *Harvard International Law Journal*, p. 193.

5 E. Flaschen and R. Silverman, 'Cross-border Insolvency Cooperation Protocols' (1998) 33(3) *Texas International Law Journal*, p. 589.

6 Practice Guide, Ch. III, para. 33.

7 See e.g. protocols in Jet Airways, para. 4.1.1., stating that the terms of the Protocol 'shall come into effect upon receiving an approval [...] from (i) NCLT/NCLAT; and (ii) the Dutch Bankruptcy Court', and para. 12.1.1., adding that 'this Protocol does not have legal effect until each Party has validly signed this protocol'. See also protocols in PSINet Inc. (para. 29), AgriBioTech Canada (para. 6.01), Calpine Corporation (para. 31).

8 EIR Recast, Art. 6(1).

of that insolvency proceeding'.[9] The characterization of a judgment approving and incorporating a protocol in its body as insolvency-related would make it enforceable under the above insolvency instruments.

The second approach treats protocols as contracts or agreements, concluded by key parties to the proceedings.[10] This approach is recognized in the UNCITRAL Legislative Guide 2010, which notes that cross-border insolvency agreements 'can be regarded as contracts between the signatories'.[11] The UNCITRAL Practice Guide describes a cross-border insolvency protocol as 'an oral or written agreement'.[12] A reference to the contractual nature of an insolvency protocol can also be found in court cases.[13] Similar to contracts, protocols arise from the negotiations and are not directly imposed by some authority. Some of them do not require a court order.[14] In other words, they originate from true cooperation by key parties rather than from confrontation or prescription. In principle, the parties are free to agree on the scope and content of a protocol, provided that they do not violate mandatory rules of the jurisdictions involved. Insolvency protocols also have a layout similar to contracts to the extent that they may contain the following information and sections: date, parties, rights and obligations, procedure for resolving disputes under a protocol, effectiveness and modification of a protocol, number and validity of copies (or counterparts), governing law and jurisdiction, term, representation and warranties, severability and signatures.[15] **7.09**

Among the benefits of classifying protocols as contracts is the potential applicability of rules of private international law and contract law, which may **7.10**

---

9 UNCITRAL Model Law on Recognition and Enforcement of Insolvency-Related Judgments, 2018, https://uncitral.un.org/en/texts/insolvency/modellaw/mlij.

10 A. Sexton, 'Current Problems and Trends in the Administration of Transnational Insolvencies Involving Enterprise Groups: The Mixed Transnational Insolvencies Involving Enterprise Groups: the Mixed Record of Protocols, the UNCITRAL Model Insolvency Law, and the EU Insolvency Regulation' (2012) 12(2) *Chicago Journal of International Law*, p. 818. Sexton disagrees with characterizing insolvency protocols as treaties, pointing out that '(i) protocols are not binding on the courts, while a treaty would be; and (ii) each principal may refuse to adopt the Protocol'.

11 Legislative Guide 2010, Ch. III, para. 50.

12 Practice Guide, Introduction, para. 13(i).

13 *Re Performance Investment Products Corp. Ltd.*, 2014 WL 6443 (CFI), [2014] HKEC 465, 'liquidators in Hong Kong and Bermuda have consensually adopted by way of *contract*, subject to approval by the courts in the two jurisdictions, protocols for the purpose of co-ordinating the concurrent liquidations'. *Olympia & York Developments Ltd. v. Royal Trust Co.* (1993), 20 C.B.R. (3d) 165 (Ont. Gen. Div.), holding that the 'protocol is, in essence, an *agreement* between the parties, and binding upon them'.

14 M. Maltese, 'Court-To-Court Protocols In Cross-Border Bankruptcy Proceedings: Differing Approaches Between Civil Law And Common Law Legal Systems', submission to 2013 III PRIZE In International Insolvency Studies, p. 21, noting that the Sendo protocol 'was entered into by the representatives of the two proceedings in the form of a private agreement and was not approved by an order of either of the two courts involved'.

15 See e.g. IFSA (Nortel Networks).

play an important gap-filling role, therefore promoting legal certainty and predictability.[16] For instance, such rules might regulate the issues of *force majeure*, consequences of a breach of contract, contract termination, etc. At the same time, it is important to keep in mind that contract law has not been harmonized on a global scale. This is why the treatment of an insolvency protocol as a contract will ultimately depend on the applicable contract law.

7.11 Inherent to this view is the notion that certain provisions in a protocol may, under applicable law, signal a specific type of a contract. A protocol itself or its certain provisions related to two or more proceedings may qualify as a 'procedural agreement', to the extent that they introduce a dispute resolution clause or an arbitration clause.[17] Such procedural agreements should generally be available for contractual obligations. Other modalities may cover the means of evidence, the burden of proof and the assessment of evidence. In this respect a protocol may constitute an 'evidence agreement'. Evidence agreements are in principle enforceable under French, Belgian and Dutch law. Under German and Swiss law, they may reverse the burden of proof, but cannot affect the means of evidence or its assessment.[18] Inclusion of provisions governing the storage of certain information or assets may result in the characterization of a protocol as a deposit or custody agreement.

1. Insolvency protocols and issue of jurisdiction

7.12 Classification of an insolvency protocol as a contract or as an insolvency-related judgment goes beyond a purely doctrinal discussion and may have important consequences in practice. This comes from the application of different insolvency and contract law instruments. In the EU, pursuant to the EIR Recast, insolvency-related judgments are automatically recognized and enforced in all EU Member States (except Denmark). The only ground on which such recognition can be denied relates to public policy considerations, which are strictly interpreted and rarely applied.[19] On the other hand, if protocols are viewed as contracts, jurisdictional issues related to them should generally be governed by the Brussels I Recast. This was confirmed by the CJEU in the case of *Nortel Networks SA and Others*.[20]

16 F. Van de Ven, 'The Cross-Border Insolvency Protocol: what it is and what is in it?' Leiden University Master Thesis, 2015.

17 A. Belohlávek, *Rome Convention – Rome I Regulation: Commentary* (New EU Conflict-of-Law Rules for Contractual Obligations, Juris Publishing Inc, Vol. 1, 2010), paras 01.881–01.885.

18 M. Fontaine and F. de Ly, *Drafting International Contracts* (Transnational Publishers, 2009), p. 140.

19 EIR Recast, Art. 33.

20 Case C-649/13, *Comité d'entreprise de Nortel Networks SA and Others v. Cosme Rogeau, and Cosme Rogeau v. Alan Robert Bloom and Others*, 11 June 2015, ECLI:EU:C:2015:384.

The case concerned the insolvency of the company Nortel Networks SA (NNSA), a French subsidiary of the Canadian parent company Nortel Networks Limited, provider of technical solutions for telecommunications networks. Whereas the (original) European Insolvency Regulation (i.e. EIR 2000) applied, NNSA was subject to main insolvency proceedings in the UK and secondary insolvency proceedings in France. On 1 July 2009, a protocol coordinating the main and secondary proceedings was signed by the persons responsible for the two sets of proceedings, under which, in particular, the administration expenses had to be paid in full, in priority, wherever the assets sold were situated. In addition, NNSA also joined the Interim Funding and Settlement Agreement (IFSA),[21] entered into between different members of the Nortel group and prescribing that the proceeds from the sale of the group's assets needed to be placed in a centralized escrow account ('lockbox') in the USA.[22] They could not be distributed without an agreement concluded by all the relevant entities in the group (so-called Selling Debtors). The dispute in the proceedings arose from the disbursement of the deferred severance payments and the jurisdiction of courts in main and secondary proceedings to rule on the determination of the debtor's assets falling within the scope of the effects of the secondary proceedings and the relevant applicable law. 7.13

Deciding on the latter, the CJEU noted that the disputes at hand fell within the context of the application of a large number of agreements concluded by or between the parties before it, including, in particular, the IFSA and the coordinating protocol. The jurisdictional rules for the interpretation of such agreements, according to the court, could in principle be found in the predecessor of the Brussels I Recast – the Brussels Regulation.[23] This is despite the fact that the dispute was between the liquidators in two sets of insolvency proceedings, one main and the other secondary, each of which fell under the EIR 2000. Nevertheless, looking at the substance of the dispute (i.e. allocation of sale proceeds in line with the EIR 2000 and unaltered by the protocol[24]), the CJEU concluded that the action before it derived directly from insolvency proceedings and was closely connected to them. In other words, it was an insolvency-related matter. This led to the application of the EIR 2000. 7.14

21 Interim Funding and Settlement Agreement (IFSA, Nortel Networks) (Canada-USA, 2009), 9 June 2009, available at http://bankrupt.com/misc/NortelInterimFundingAgreement.pdf.

22 Ibid., para. 12(b).

23 Council Regulation (EC) No 44/2001 of 22 December 2000 on jurisdiction and the recognition and enforcement of judgments in civil and commercial matters.

24 In para. 30 the court noted that it appeared from the protocol that it was agreed by the parties that the proceeds were to be allocated by applying the EIR 2000 and that the protocol or the other agreements at issue before the court were not intended to modify its content.

Despite this ultimate outcome, the CJEU recognized the potential applicability of a specific non-insolvency 'civil and commercial' regulation (i.e. the Brussels Regulation) to insolvency agreements.

7.15 It may be argued that not all disputes arising from or issues regulated by insolvency protocols derive directly from insolvency – instead, they may be qualified as contractual. For instance, disputes related to the terms, intent, interpretation or application of a protocol may be primarily connected to and arise from the protocol itself, rather than from insolvency proceedings. The same applies to an agreement on the distribution of costs incurred in the process of protocol negotiation or an arrangement to share particular information or use specific communication tools or channels. Other issues that are not necessarily closely linked with insolvency proceedings include a compromise to use a common set of financial accounting records or set up a special mechanism for the resolution of intercompany claims. For such non-insolvency-related matters, the applicability of the Brussels I Recast cannot be ruled out. If the Brussels I Recast applies to an insolvency protocol and disputes arising therefrom, then its rules on prorogation of jurisdiction (Art. 25), *lis pendens* and related actions (Art. 29), provisional measures (Art. 35), recognition and enforcement of judgments (Chapter III) and other rules become particularly relevant.

7.16 The Brussels I Recast recognizes the choice-of-court or prorogation agreements, by which parties determine a court or courts to have exclusive or alternative jurisdiction for the resolution and settlement of disputes. Choice-of-court clauses are presumed to be exclusive unless otherwise specified.[25] The analysis of protocols has revealed that a number of them establish a dispute resolution procedure. For instance, the Loewen model-based protocols[26] typically contain the following (or similar) alternative jurisdiction clause:

> Disputes relating to the terms, intent or application of this Protocol may be addressed by the interested parties to either [the U.S. Court], [the Canadian Court] or both Courts upon notice. [...] When an issue is addressed to only one Court, in rendering a determination in any such dispute, such Court: (a) shall consult with the other Court; and (b) may, in its sole and exclusive discretion, either (i) render a binding decision after such consultation, (ii) defer to the determination of the other Court by transferring the matter, in whole or in part, to the Court or (iii) seek a joint hearing of both Courts.[27]

25 Brussels I Recast, Art. 25.

26 See e.g. protocols in Systech (para. 27), Progressive Moulded (para. 27), Masonite International (para. 28), Aralez (para. 36), Payless Holdings (para. 36).

27 Loewen protocol, para. 27.

Some protocols include jurisdictional agreements detailing the chosen (exclusive or alternative) jurisdiction for the resolution of certain enlisted matters. This could apply to the debtors' obligations under specific contracts.[28] Other jurisdictional agreements are phrased more generally. For example, parties may agree that all claims against Debtor 1 should be resolved by courts of Country 1 and all claims against Debtor 2 by courts in Country 2.[29] The same approach might also be taken with regard to the direction and approval of particular transactions. For instance, a protocol may stipulate that any transaction outside the ordinary course of business for the sale, lease or use of property of Debtor 1 shall be subject to the sole discretion or approval of Court 1, while such transactions for Debtor 2 shall be subject to the sole discretion and approval of Court 2.[30] The extent to which such jurisdictional agreements are enforceable depends on mandatory national law and regional regulation, such as the EIR Recast. We will deal with the potential limitations on the scope of insolvency protocols in chapters below. **7.17**

Back to the core jurisdictional question. By admitting that an insolvency protocol could be governed by the Brussels Regulation and by not subjecting it to the EIR 2000 for the sole reason that it was an insolvency protocol agreed during the insolvency proceedings by the insolvency practitioners, the CJEU in *Nortel Networks* seems to have presumed the complex nature of insolvency protocols. This nature can be insolvency-related (protocol as an insolvency-related judgment) and non-insolvency related (protocol as a civil and commercial matter). **7.18**

2. Insolvency protocols and issue of applicable law

The dual nature of insolvency protocols is also relevant for determining the law applicable to such protocols. If an insolvency protocol, due to its specific insolvency-related content (i.e. matters deriving directly from insolvency), falls under the EIR Recast, its private international law rules become applicable. As **7.19**

---

28 Pioneer protocol, para. 10.

29 PSINet protocol, para. 10(iv), establishing that:

> the Inter-Company Claims of the Chapter 11 Debtors against CCAA Debtors, including their priority in the Canadian Proceedings, will be determined, valued and resolved by the Canadian Court; the Inter-Company Claims of the CCAA Debtors against the Chapter 11 Debtors, including their priority in the US Cases, shall be determined, valued and resolved by the US Court.

30 Quebecor protocol, para. 22. This protocol has also divided the jurisdiction between the US and Canadian courts on matters of DIP financing (para. 23). Thus, it was agreed that the US court shall have the exclusive jurisdiction to hear and determine all matters relating to the DIP documents as they affect the US Debtors, while the Canadian court shall have the exclusive jurisdiction to hear and determine all matters relating to the DIP documents as they affect the Canadian Debtor.

the CJEU in the *Nortel Networks* case has pointed out, such rules are meant to be uniform and replace national rules of private international law.[31]

7.20 The EIR Recast lays down the main rule that the law of the state of the opening of insolvency proceedings (*lex concursus*) determines the effects of such proceedings, both procedural and substantive, on the persons and legal relations concerned. *Lex concursus* determines the conditions for the opening of insolvency proceedings, their conduct and their closure. Article 7(2) EIR Recast contains a number of subject matters explicitly falling within the boundaries of the *lex concursus*. For instance, this concerns the determination of assets that form part of the insolvency estate,[32] the availability of set-off in insolvency and its conditions,[33] and the effects of insolvency on current (executory) contracts.[34] Despite the EIR Recast being largely an instrument of procedural nature, it introduces several provisions of substantive character, directly regulating a particular issue or relationship. For example, the EIR Recast sets out uniform rules on asset localization,[35] the effects of insolvency on rights based on reservation (retention) of title,[36] the consequences of performance in good faith of an obligation for the benefit of the debtor instead of the insolvency practitioner[37] and the duties for involved IPs and courts to cooperate and communicate across borders.[38]

7.21 In matters of direct regulation by the EIR Recast, parties' contractual freedom is substantially curtailed. Nevertheless, the EIR Recast does not aim at introducing a comprehensive framework of uniform substantive norms across the EU. Thus, in principle it does not prohibit parties to (contractually) agree on a set of special arrangements related to the administration of parallel insolvency proceedings, provided that such rules do not breach the mandatory law of the jurisdictions concerned.

7.22 In practice, there have been cases where protocols were used to enhance the effectiveness of cross-border cooperation in instances where the EIR Recast was silent. For example, the Sendo protocol, reached between the UK joint administrators and the French liquidators appointed in the insolvency of Sendo International Limited in 2006, accepted that the insolvency regulation (at that time, the EIR 2000) established only very general operating principles.

---

31 Case C-649/13, *Comité d'entreprise de Nortel Networks SA and Others supra* note 20, para. 49.

32 EIR Recast, Art. 7(2)(b).

33 Ibid., Art. 7(2)(d).

34 Ibid., Art. 7(2)(e).

35 Ibid., Art. 2(9).

36 Ibid., Art. 10.

37 Ibid., Art. 31.

38 Ibid., Arts 56–58.

Therefore, an (informal) agreement was concluded to define a 'practical means of functioning which would allow for the efficient coordination of the two insolvency proceedings'. Among other things, the Sendo protocol clarified and elaborated how the provisions of the EIR 2000 related to creditor notification obligations, lodgment and verification of claims, advance payment of costs and expenses and stay of liquidation proceedings should be realized in practice. One could say that the Sendo protocol is inspired by (or maybe even limited to) a public law perspective providing a case related mini-treaty on specific procedural matters.

For those subjects that are not governed by the EIR Recast, specifically its rules on applicable law, another EU regulation becomes relevant, namely the Rome I Regulation (Rome I).[39] This regulation determines the law applicable to contractual obligations in civil and commercial matters. It does not provide a definition of a 'contractual obligation'. In literature it has been argued that an extensive interpretation of this concept is intended.[40] A broad interpretation of the term 'contract' is also supported by the jurisprudence of the CJEU.[41] Given this broad interpretation, insolvency protocols could fall under the scope of the Rome I. Classifying protocols as contracts within the meaning of this regulation would lead to the application of its uniform rules on determining the law application to a contract, its performance and interpretation.[42] 7.23

The starting point of the Rome I is the freedom of parties to choose the applicable law. Such choice shall be made expressly or clearly demonstrated by the terms of the contract or the circumstances of the case.[43] The UNCITRAL Practice Guide acknowledges that in cross-border insolvency cases complex questions may arise with respect to the law that should apply to determine the validity and effectiveness of claims or the rights of parties located in different jurisdictions.[44] This is why an insolvency protocol could seek to provide clarity and help avoid potential disputes by specifying in advance the law applicable to certain issues. However, our research demonstrates that predominantly insolvency protocols do not contain provisions on the choice of applicable law. Nevertheless, some of them indicate such a choice. 7.24

---

39 Regulation (EC) No 593/2008 of the European Parliament and of the Council of 17 June 2008 on the law applicable to contractual obligations (Rome I).

40 M. Bogdan and M. Pertegás Sender, *Concise Introduction to EU Private International Law* (4th edn, Europa Law Publishing, 2019), p. 122.

41 Case C-27/02, *Petra Engler v. Janus Versand GmbH*, 20 January 2005, ECLI:EU:C:2005:33, para. 48, noting that 'the concept of "matters relating to contract" referred to in Article 5(1) of the Brussels Convention is not interpreted narrowly by the Court'.

42 Rome I Regulation, Art. 12.

43 Ibid., Art. 3(1).

44 Practice Guide, Ch. III, para. 100.

7.25 For example, the protocol in AgriBioTech Canada Inc. stipulates that:

> Sections 544, 547 and 550 of the [US] Bankruptcy Code shall be the governing substantive law as to all transfers made to entities located in the United States. Canadian law shall be governing substantive law as to all transfers made to entities in Canada.[45]

7.26 Another example is the AIOC protocol, which establishes in reference to the claims filed in the US and/or Swiss proceedings that 'the claims reconciliation process shall be administered in accordance with the procedural and substantive laws (both bankruptcy and nonbankruptcy) governing the respective case in which the Party is appointed unless considerations of comity otherwise require'.[46]

7.27 In both cases the choice of substantive law relates to the submission and resolution of creditors' claims. Therefore, the chosen law does not extend to such issues as the validity and interpretation of the insolvency protocol itself. In other words, in the sense of Article 3(1) Rome I Regulation, no choice of law is made to the protocol as a whole.[47]

7.28 In the absence of such a choice, the Rome I prescribes that the contract shall be governed by the law of the country with which it is most closely connected.[48] It is a challenge to identify a jurisdiction with which a cross-border insolvency protocol has the closest relationship, as it typically provides for equal bilateral obligations and reaffirms independent jurisdiction and authority of courts on both sides. Some protocols even confirm the equal treatment of insolvency practitioners.[49] Van de Ven suggests that in case of a protocol concluded between main and secondary proceedings, the forum of the main insolvency proceedings may be presumed as having the closest connection to a

45 AgriBioTech Canada protocol, sec. 8.01.

46 AIOC protocol, para. III(E)(1)(b).

47 A rare example of an insolvency protocol that specifies governing law is the IFSA (Nortel Networks), which in sec. 16 provides that '[t]his Agreement shall be governed exclusively by the laws of the State of New York without regard to the rules of conflict of laws of the State of New York or any other jurisdiction; *provided, however*, that Section 17 shall be governed exclusively by English law'. Another example is the Urbancorp Group protocol (Canada-Israel, 2016), stipulating in para. 7 that '[t]his protocol shall be governed by laws of Ontario and the laws of Canada as applicable and all disputes or requests for direction in connection with this Protocol shall be determined by the Canadian Court'.

48 Rome I Regulation, Art. 4(4). Insolvency protocols do not seem to fall under any other clauses of this article. Protocols cannot be qualified as contracts for sale of goods, provision of services, tenancy, franchise or distribution (Art. 4(1)). It is quite difficult to establish which of the contractual obligations contained in insolvency protocols are 'characteristic'. It is also impossible to determine under Art. 4(2) the jurisdiction where 'the party required to effect the characteristic performance of the contract has his habitual residence'.

49 Jet Airways protocol, para. 10.1.2.

protocol.[50] This view is premised on the fact that in the context of the EIR Recast (but also under the Model Law 1997), main insolvency proceedings play a leading or dominant role.[51] We hold Van de Ven's view as persuasive.

In principle it is possible to argue that the law of the jurisdiction of the main insolvency proceedings should be the governing law of the protocol. Despite the appeal of this approach, it can however hardly be applied in the context of enterprise group insolvency, where separate legal entities enter into a protocol. As a result, the insolvency protocol related to group members' insolvencies may lack a particularly strong connection to a single jurisdiction. This is why an explicit choice of law in a protocol may be considered (see Box 7.1). 7.29

Box 7.1 Choice of law

In order to avoid complications and potential disputes around determining law applicable to an insolvency protocol (e.g. law governing its validity, interpretation, amendment and termination), insolvency practitioners and other contracting parties should be able to explicitly agree on such law in an insolvency protocol as *lex contractus*.

It is also important to keep in mind that questions governed by company law, including creation, legal capacity, internal organization or winding-up of companies, as well as personal liability of officers and members for the obligations of the company are excluded from the scope of the Rome I Regulation.[52] According to the CJEU, these exclusions apply 'to the structural aspects of [...] companies' and extend to 'complex acts which are necessary to the creation of a company or firm and to the regulation of its internal 7.30

50 F. Van de Ven, *supra* note 16, Leiden University Master Thesis (supervised by Prof. B. Wessels and Dr. B. Santen), 2015.

51 The leading role of main insolvency proceedings is evident in the provisions granting the possibility to stay (Art. 38(3) EIR Recast) or refuse the opening of secondary proceedings (Arts 36 and 38(2) EIR Recast) at the request of main insolvency practitioner, or giving him the right to request a stay of the realization of assets in secondary proceedings (Art. 46 EIR Recast). The predominance of main insolvency proceedings has also been confirmed by the CJEU. In Case C-116/11, *Bank Handlowy w Warszawie SA, PPHU 'ADAX'/Ryszard Adamiak, v. Christianapol sp. z o.o.*, 22 November 2012, ECLI:EU:C:2012:739, para. 62, the court noted that:

> The principle of sincere cooperation [...] requires the court having jurisdiction to open secondary proceedings [...] to have regard to the objectives of the main proceedings and to take account of the scheme of the Regulation, which [...] aims to ensure efficient and effective cross-border insolvency proceedings through mandatory coordination of the main and secondary proceedings guaranteeing the priority of the main proceedings.

52 Rome I Regulation, Art. 1(2)(f).

organization and winding-up'.[53] These issues typically fall within the scope of company law (*lex societatis*). They may also be covered by insolvency law (*lex concursus*) to the extent that they relate to the conduct of insolvency proceedings and their effects. For example, insolvency law would normally apply to determine the liability of directors for wrongful conduct in the context of insolvency.[54]

B. LEGAL EFFECT OF INSOLVENCY PROTOCOLS

7.31 The complexity of the legal nature of insolvency protocols manifests itself in their effects and potential enforceability. Whether protocols are qualified as court-approved treaties acquiring the force of a court judgment, or are treated as contracts freely and willingly reached by the relevant parties, they aim at facilitating effective and efficient administration of insolvency proceedings in the context of an enterprise group. In other words, they seek to produce real effect on the parties and proceedings concerned.

7.32 The UNCITRAL Practice Guide summarizes that though in different form, insolvency protocols 'tend to regulate a similar range of issues and are *nearly always intended to be binding* [italics added by the authors] on the parties that enter into them'.[55] In practice the outcome may be less coherent or conclusive. Some insolvency protocols are intended to have binding effect on the parties. For example, the Madoff protocol states:

> This Protocol shall be binding on, and inure to the benefit of, the Representatives' respective successors and assigns, including any liquidator subsequently appointed over MSIL [Madoff Securities International Limited]. This Protocol shall not create any right for any person or entity that is not a party hereto.[56]

7.33 Another example is the protocol (referred to as Stipulation) in InverWorld, which gives even more details:

> This Stipulation shall be binding on and inure to the benefit of the parties hereto and their respective successors, assigns, representatives, heirs, executors, administrators, trustees (including any trustees under chapters 7 or 11 of the Bankruptcy Code), and

53 Case C-25/18, *Bryan Andrew Kerr v. Pavlo Postnov, Natalia Postnova*, 8 May 2019, ECLI:EU:C:2019:376, paras 33–34.

54 Case C-594/14, *Simona Kornhaas v. Thomas Dithmar*, 10 December 2015, ECLI:EU:C:2015:806, para. 19.

55 Practice Guide, Ch. III, para. 5.

56 Madoff protocol, paras 12.1 and 12.2.

> receivers, receiver managers, or custodians appointed under US law, Cayman law, or English law, as the case may be.[57]

Other protocols explicitly state that they should not be enforceable or impose legal obligations on the parties. For example, the Lehman Brothers protocol contains the following paragraph: **7.34**

> The parties acknowledge that this Protocol represents a statement of intentions and guidelines designed to minimize the costs and maximize recoveries for all creditors of the Proceedings. In recognition of substantive differences among the Proceedings in each jurisdiction, this Protocol shall not be legally enforceable nor impose on Official Representatives any duties or obligations.[58]

Based on our empirical analysis of the insolvency protocols, we have divided them into three groups: **7.35**

(a) *Binding effect.* Protocols with provisions specifically establishing their binding nature (e.g. 'this protocol shall be binding').
(b) *Non-binding effect.* Protocols with provisions specifically highlighting their non-binding nature (e.g. 'the protocol shall not be legally enforceable').
(c) *No special indication.* Protocols without provisions that explicitly and unambiguously confirm either binding or non-binding character (nevertheless, protocols in this group may contain provisions indicating their obligatory nature, e.g. 'the liquidators shall', 'claims shall be determined', 'claimants shall vote' etc.).

The results of this review are presented in Table 7.1 below. It is clear that the majority of protocols surveyed belong to the third category and do not directly state their binding or non-binding character. This by itself should not be interpreted as confirming or refuting either binding or non-binding effects of these insolvency protocols. Many protocols in this group follow the Loewen model and are general in their scope and content (i.e. framework agreements). Protocols in the other two categories are typically more detailed and tailored to addressing the issues characteristic to a specific case. **7.36**

57 InverWorld protocol (UK-USA-Cayman Islands, 1999), para. 29.

58 Lehman Brothers protocol, paras 1.1. and 1.2.

Table 7.1 Legal effects of insolvency protocols

Binding effect	Non-binding effect	No special indication
Madoff protocol	Sendo protocol	Loewen protocol
InverWorld protocol	Lehman Brothers protocol	Mosaic protocol
Everfresh protocol	Jet Airways protocol	PSINet protocol
Financial Asset Management protocol[a]		Philip Services protocol
		Maxwell protocol
		Matlack protocol
		Aralez protocol
		Pioneer protocol
		Quebecor protocol
		Commodore protocol
		Nakash protocol
		Urbancorp Group protocol
		Barzel Industries protocol[b]
		Payless Holdings protocol
		Progressive Moulded protocol
		Calpine protocol
		Masonite protocol
		Abitibibowater protocol
		Eddie Bauer protocol
		AIOC protocol
		AgriBioTech Canada protocol
		Graceway Canada protocol
		Montreal, Maine & Atlantic protocol

Notes:
a. Financial Asset Management protocol (Canada-USA, 2001).
b. Barzel Industries protocol (Canada-USA, 2009).

7.37 Discussing why in Europe, parties may be less inclined to acknowledge the binding nature of insolvency protocols, Queirolo and Dominelli refer to the general limitation on cooperation established in the EIR Recast, namely that such cooperation must not be incompatible with the rules applicable to the respective proceedings. They argue that 'the more formal an agreement on cooperation is, the more limits it might encounter'.[59] Thus, where parties cannot reach a binding agreement (either because of legal or practical limitations, or due to psychological factors), they may still be willing to pursue informal cooperation between themselves and utilize a non-binding protocol for that purpose. Especially in continental Europe with drastically different procedural rules applicable in insolvency proceedings and less experience of negotiating and executing insolvency protocols, a non-binding protocol may be a preferred option.

The classification of insolvency protocols as either binding or non-binding **7.38** naturally leads to some degree of oversimplification. In fact, protocols, which are generally intended to be non-binding, may effectively contain provisions imposing obligations or creating legal rights. These usually concern the responsibilities of the insolvency practitioners, allocation of costs or the procedure to render an insolvency protocol effective. A revealing example is the Jet Airways protocol. On the one hand, it recognizes that it shall not impose on the Indian and Dutch insolvency practitioners any duties and obligations.[60] On the other hand, for instance, it prescribes that 'the Dutch Trustee shall collate all claims received by him and shall forward these claims to the RP [Indian Resolution Professional], who shall then verify and admit such claims in accordance with Indian law'.[61] It also provides that 'No Party may suspend (*opschorten*) performance of its obligations under or in connection with this Protocol on any ground whatsoever'.[62] If parties cannot suspend performing their obligations under the protocol, it is logical to assume that such obligations have been created in the first place. For the purpose of promoting legal certainty, a protocol may unambiguously state whether it is intended to be binding or not, and in which part (Box 7.2).

Box 7.2 Legal force

For the sake of clarity, contracting parties may divide the insolvency protocol into binding and non-binding sections or otherwise unambiguously state which provisions are meant to be binding and which provisions are mere statements of good faith or intent.

59 I. Queirolo and S. Dominelli, 'Cooperation and Communication Between Parties in the Management of Cross-Border Parallel Proceedings Under the European Insolvency Regulation Recast', in V. Lazić and S. Stuij (eds), *Recasting the Insolvency Regulation: Improvements and Missed Opportunities. Short Studies in Private International Law*, (The Hague: Asser Press, 2020), p. 123.

60 Jet Airways protocol, paras 2.1.1(a) and 2.1.1(c).

61 Ibid., para. 9.1.2.

62 Ibid., para. 12.8.1.

7.39 Contrarily, the protocols expressly stipulating their binding nature may contain statements of good faith or intent, including provisions on the intent of the protocol,[63] which are not meant to be binding in a strict sense. For example, the Everfresh protocol contains the provision related to the adoption of a reorganization plan, which states that the IP and the Debtors 'shall endeavor' to submit substantially similar reorganization plans and 'shall endeavor to coordinate all procedures in connection therewith'.[64]

7.40 It is important to separate the issue of enforcement of duties and rights under the protocol from the issue of their existence. The fact that in practice the enforcement of a protocol may be complicated does not undermine the validity of rights and obligations created by it. The power of non-binding and non-enforceable protocols should also not be undermined or underestimated. Such protocols can be seen as a case-specific soft law instrument offering practical solutions and facilitating parties to engage in a dialogue and cooperation. Although perceived to be non-binding, insolvency protocols might be concluded with a high degree of detail and precision, reflecting the specificity of a concrete case, as well as a common position and consensus reached between the parties. The dialogue may reinforce trust and mutual confidence, further generating a strong compliance pull. According to Finch and Milman, '[w]ithout mutual confidence, even the best informed, most astute commercial judgments will come to nothing'.[65] To the extent that protocols could reinforce mutual confidence and trust, they can in fact be 'harder' than some hard law instruments.

63 Madoff protocol (para. C), InverWorld protocol (paras 17–19).

64 Everfresh protocol, para. 13.

65 V. Finch and D. Milman, *Corporate Insolvency Law: Perspectives and Principles* (3rd edn, CUP, 2017), p. 432.

8

GENERAL FEATURES AND LIMITATIONS OF INSOLVENCY PROTOCOLS

A. PROCEDURAL PRINCIPLES AND INSOLVENCY PROTOCOLS 8.01
1. Procedural efficiency 8.03
2. Fair trial and procedural justice 8.07
3. Transparency and access to information 8.16

B. COMPATIBILITY WITH NATIONAL LAW AND EIR RECAST FRAMEWORK 8.30
1. Agreement on jurisdiction for claims against debtors 8.32
2. Agreement on COMI and jurisdiction for related actions 8.37
3. Agreement on law applicable to claims 8.41

C. INFORMATION EXCHANGE AND CONFLICTS OF INTEREST 8.45

A. PROCEDURAL PRINCIPLES AND INSOLVENCY PROTOCOLS

Most protocols follow a certain pattern in terms of their overall structure and separate clauses. They usually include provisions explaining the background of a protocol, its aims and purposes, elaborating cooperation and participation rights, confirming comity and independence of courts, setting the rules on notices, retention and compensation of IPs and resolution of disputes arising from the protocol. These provisions need to be integrated in and should be compatible with the procedural systems of the countries for which they are employed. **8.01**

Insolvency proceedings exist and function within the systems of national procedural law aimed at protecting important procedural principles and rights of parties. Insolvency protocols too are not immune from protections guaranteed by such instruments as the European Convention on Human Rights (ECHR).[1] Recently, Bork has investigated the following principles governing cross-border insolvency proceedings: efficiency, transparency, predictability and procedural justice.[2] While these principles are not unique to an insolvency process, they can find specific application in insolvency cases. **8.02**

1 The Convention for the Protection of Human Rights and Fundamental Freedoms, 1950.

2 R. Bork, *Principles of Cross-Border Insolvency Law* (Intersentia, 2017), p. 78.

1. Procedural efficiency

8.03 The principle of efficiency underlies the operation of the EIR Recast, the Model Law 1997 and the Model Law 2019. The EIR Recast states that the 'proper functioning of the internal market requires that cross-border insolvency proceedings should operate efficiently and effectively'.[3] The Model Law 1997 has among its purposes promotion of '[f]air and efficient administration of cross-border insolvencies that protects the interests of all creditors and other persons, including the debtor'.[4] A similar purpose is stated in the Model Law 2019, even though with an emphasis on administration of insolvencies concerning enterprise group members.[5]

8.04 Efficient administration of transnational insolvency proceedings entails reduction of transaction costs and delays (thus, maintaining or even enhancing the value of insolvency estates) and facilitation of cooperation and communication, which enable courts and IPs from two or more countries to achieve the optimal results.

8.05 As noted above, insolvency protocols are manifestations of the desire to improve efficiency of cross-border insolvency proceedings. Nevertheless, they may not be appropriate or necessary in every case. For example, when it comes to insolvency of decentralized enterprise groups with little to no interaction or synergies between group members, the costs of negotiating an insolvency protocol may clearly outweigh its potential benefits. It may also be the case that conflicting interests of group members and high risk of conflicts of interest make the adoption of a protocol impractical.

8.06 To emphasize that the primary goal of the rules on cooperation and communication in the context of group insolvency is efficiency, the EIR Recast prescribes that IPs and courts shall cooperate only to the extent that such cooperation is appropriate to facilitate the effective administration of the insolvency proceedings.[6] Thus, an insolvency protocol should promote procedural efficiency. Otherwise its conclusion loses a practical purpose.

3 EIR Recast, Recital 3.

4 Model Law 1997, Preamble.

5 Model Law 2019, Preamble.

6 EIR Recast, Arts 56–58.

2. Fair trial and procedural justice

In addition to being efficient, insolvency proceedings must be organized and conducted in a fair, predictable and just way, ensuring equal treatment of all relevant parties (including safeguarding equality of arms), absence of arbitrariness and protection of the right to be heard. These norms are usually incorporated in national legislation, but can also be found in various conventions, treaties and soft law instruments.[7] The EIR Recast acknowledges the respect for the fundamental rights recognized in the EU Charter of Fundamental Rights, including the right to an effective remedy and to a fair trial.[8] The CJEU in the case of *Eurofood IFSC Ltd.*, discussed above in Chapter 6, is clear in stressing that the general principle that everyone is entitled to a fair legal process: **8.07**

> is inspired by the fundamental rights which form an integral part of the general principles of Community law [...], drawing inspiration from the constitutional traditions common to the Member States and from the guidelines supplied, in particular, by the European Convention for the Protection of Human Rights and Fundamental Freedom.[9]

The ECHR, one of the major instruments for the protection of human rights and political freedoms in Europe, guarantees that '[i]n determination of his civil rights and obligations [...] everyone is entitled to a fair and public hearing within a reasonable time by an independent and impartial tribunal established by law'.[10] The concept of 'civil rights and obligations' has an 'autonomous' meaning and does not depend on the parties' status, the nature of the legislation governing the 'dispute' (civil, commercial, administrative, etc.), or the authority having jurisdiction over the matter (ordinary court, administrative authority, etc.).[11] In the jurisprudence of the European Court of Human Rights (ECtHR), insolvency proceedings clearly fall within the civil limb of the Article 6(1) (Right to a fair trial).[12] Even though the ECHR is not **8.08**

---

7 See e.g. EU JudgeCo Principles and Guidelines, Principle 6 (Equality of Arms), providing that '[e]ach party should have a full and fair opportunity to present evidence and legal arguments and each party shall receive reasonable time to do so'. Equality of arms is also incorporated in Principle 5 of the ALI-III Global Principles.

8 EIR Recast, Recital 83.

9 C-341/04, *Eurofood IFSC Ltd.*, 2 May 2006, ECLI:EU:C:2006:281, para. 65. In this case the CJEU ruled that a Member State may refuse to recognize insolvency proceedings opened in another Member State where the decision to open the proceedings was taken in flagrant breach of the fundamental right to be heard.

10 ECHR, Art. 6(1).

11 Guide on Article 6 of the European Convention on Human Rights, Right to a fair trial (civil limb), 31 August 2019, p. 6, https://www.echr.coe.int/Documents/Guide_Art_6_ENG.pdf.

12 For an in-depth study, see J.C. van Apeldoorn, *Human Rights in Insolvency Proceedings* (Kluwer Legal Publishers, 2012).

a part of the EU institutions' system, all EU Member States are parties to the ECHR and are therefore bound by the authoritative interpretation of the ECtHR.

8.09 Improper notification of a creditor in insolvency proceedings about the hearing on the distribution of the estate was seen as a violation of the right to a fair trial (*Zavodnik v. Slovenia*).[13] The ECtHR held that the manner in which notice of the hearing was given (it was announced on the court's notice board and in the Official Gazette) was inappropriate and had prevented the applicant from challenging estate distribution. Excessive length of insolvency proceedings may also lead to such a violation. In the case of *Affaire Cipolletta v. Italy*,[14] the court found that the unreasonable length of the Italian administrative liquidation proceedings (*liquidazione coatta amministrativa*) (more than 25 years!) contravened the right to a fair trial. The ECtHR has also held that under certain conditions, the lack of reasoning in a judgment can constitute a violation of the right to a fair trial (*Bochan v. Ukraine*[15]). Therefore, a complete absence of reasoning in the judgment opening insolvency proceedings (or in the related actions judgment), which amounts to the neglect of the procedural guarantees, might constitute a breach of a fair trial.[16] Its violation may also be triggered by the lack of independence and impartiality on the side of the court, as well as corruption or fraud involved in the course of insolvency proceedings.

8.10 It is rather unlikely that the adoption of an insolvency protocol would by itself negatively affect procedural justice or lead to a violation of the right to a fair trial. To the contrary, the protocols analysed in this book, do not seek to restrict participation rights, but instead promote equality (i.e. equality of arms and non-discrimination of creditors and other parties), access to justice and establish rights to appear and be heard. For instance, the Loewen protocol provides that:

> The Debtors, their creditors and other interested parties in the Insolvency Proceedings, including the Committee, the Estate Representatives and the U.S. Trustee, shall have the right and standing to (a) appear and be heard in either the U.S. Court or the Canadian Court in the Insolvency Proceedings to the same extent as creditors and other interested parties domiciled in the forum country, subject to any local rules or regulations generally applicable to all parties appearing in the forum and (b) file

13 *Zavodnik v. Slovenia*, Application no. 53723/13, ECtHR 2015.

14 *Affaire Cipolletta v. Italy*, Application no. 38259/09, ECtHR 2018.

15 *Bochan v. Ukraine*, Application no. 7577/02, ECtHR 2007.

16 Under Art. 4(1) EIR Recast, a court seised of a request to open insolvency proceedings 'shall of its own motion examine whether it has jurisdiction pursuant to Article 3'. In a judgment opening insolvency proceedings the court must 'specify the grounds on which the jurisdiction of the court is based'.

notices of appearance or other papers with the Clerk of the U.S. Court or the Canadian Court in the Insolvency Proceedings.[17]

Other protocols may be less detailed or extensive in their coverage. For example, the Madoff protocol only establishes the right of representatives to appear in all proceedings[18] – creditors are not specifically mentioned. The same applies to the Lehman Brothers protocol.[19] This, however, should not be interpreted as limiting the participation rights of creditors, which may be granted by the applicable (national) insolvency law. Participation rights established by protocols are largely in line with the Model Law 2019, which promotes participation of enterprise group members in insolvency proceedings 'for the purpose of facilitating cooperation and coordination […], including developing and implementing a group insolvency solution'.[20] Such enterprise group members are given the right to appear, make written submissions and be heard.[21] The right to be heard in any of the insolvency proceedings opened in respect of members of the same group of companies is also granted by the EIR Recast.[22] It is noteworthy that insolvency protocols in extending participation rights in the group insolvency context, preceded the development of special insolvency instruments and rules, dealing with enterprise group insolvency. **8.11**

In practice, there may be disagreements relating to the exact scope of participation rights granted to a foreign insolvency practitioner and other parties. In 2019, in the case of Jet Airways, a dispute arose around the right of the Dutch Trustee to attend the meetings of the Committee of Creditors (CoC). The latter objected to such attendance. The conflict was ultimately resolved by the National Company Law Appellate Tribunal, which held that the 'Dutch Trustee' was equivalent to the 'Resolution Professional' of India, and therefore under law had a right to attend the meetings of the CoC, even though without voting rights.[23] Despite the fact that the Jet Airways protocol concerned a single-debtor insolvency, similar problems are likely to arise in a situation of enterprise group insolvency. **8.12**

---

17 Loewen protocol, para. 20. Similar provisions can be found in the protocols concerning Systech Retail Systems Corp. (para. 24), Pioneer Companies Inc. (para. 16), PSINet Inc. (para. 27), Mosaic Group Inc. (Canada-USA, 2003) (para. 23), Aralez Pharmaceuticals (para. 26).

18 Madoff protocol, para. 3.

19 Lehman Brothers protocol, para. 3. Despite the heading 'Rights of Official Representatives and Creditors to Appear', the respective provision only deals with rights of Official Representatives.

20 Model Law 2019, Art. 18(1).

21 Ibid., Art. 18(4).

22 EIR Recast, Art. 60(1)(a).

23 *In the matter of Jet Airways (India) Ltd. v. State Bank of India and Another.*, National Company Law Appellate Tribunal, Company Appeal (AT) (Insolvency) No. 707 of 2019, 26 September 2019.

8.13 Procedural efficiency and fair trial cannot exist without proper notification of the parties concerned. Notification allows creditors and IPs to express their position, timely file a claim or an objection, coordinate the adoption of a reorganization or a liquidation plan, facilitate non-conflicting court decisions and ensure ratable cross-border distribution of assets and sale proceeds among insolvency proceedings and creditors. The CJEU in *Eurofood* emphasized that the right to be notified of procedural documents occupies 'an eminent position in the organization and conduct of a fair legal process'.[24]

8.14 While insolvency protocols cannot circumvent the notification requirement set in the applicable law (e.g. by opting out from notification when it is prescribed), they may extend or clarify such requirements to improve the administration of insolvency proceedings. Many insolvency protocols contain provisions on notification. They vary in length and detail and may specify a party that shall give a notice, a recipient of such a notice, a method of giving notice, the timing of notification and its content. Notice provisions may be general in phrasing, simply referring to the applicable law and listing the recipients[25] or stating that a notice shall be given on matters in which the relevant insolvency practitioner has an interest.[26] The Loewen protocol prescribes that:

> Notice of any motion, application or other pleading or paper filed in one or both of the Insolvency Proceedings and notice of any related hearings or other proceedings mandated by applicable law in connection with the Insolvency Proceedings, or the Protocol shall be given by appropriate means (including, where circumstances warrant, by courier, telecopier or other electronic forms of communication) to the following: (a) all creditors, including the Committee, and other interested parties in accordance with the practice of the jurisdiction where the papers are filed or the proceedings are to occur; and (b) to the extent not otherwise entitled to receive notice under subpart (a) of this sentence, the Monitor, to its counsel […], and such other parties as may be designated by either of the Courts from time to time.[27]

8.15 Notice provisions can also be more nuanced and prescriptive. For example, the Sendo protocol specifies the means for the implementation of Article 40 EIR 2000 (Duty to inform creditors). It establishes that the Joint Administrators in the main proceedings (UK) 'will notify by regular mail […] all of the debtor's creditors based in France, without exception. Such notice shall be in the form

---

24 *Eurofood IFSC Ltd.*, para. 66.

25 AgriBioTech Canada protocol, sec. 3.02.

26 Madoff protocol, para. 2.

27 Loewen protocol, para. 21. Similar provisions can be found in the protocols concerning Quebecor (para. 24), Payless Holdings (para. 28), Nortel Networks (para. 21), Smurfit-Stone Container (para. 21), Montreal, Maine & Atlantic (para. 20).

of an individual notice and shall set forth the required formalities and penalties provided by English law and applicable to the main proceedings'.[28] The mirror provision was included with regard to notice given by the French liquidators.

3. Transparency and access to information

Transparency of public proceedings is closely linked to the principles of fair trial and procedural justice. It ensures fairness and legitimacy of insolvency proceedings. It is also indispensable for building public trust in the judiciary and the realization of participation rights. When it comes to insolvency protocols, the issues of transparency may arise with respect to the negotiations and conclusion of a protocol and its effect on the insolvency proceedings. **8.16**

It is not always clear who initiates the adoption of a protocol, who takes part in its negotiations, who drafts a protocol and, finally, who signs or otherwise adopts it. There are many approaches to resolving these questions in practice. While some protocols result from pre-insolvency (private) negotiations,[29] others are the product of collaboration taking place inside insolvency proceedings, sometimes even on the advice from and direction by a court.[30] As a result, the level of stakeholder engagement may vary. Such engagement is determined by the applicable law, urgency of a protocol, as well as the lack of practical guidelines concerning conclusion of insolvency protocols. **8.17**

Most often, protocols are entered into by insolvency practitioners and debtors (i.e. debtors in possession). In rare cases committees of creditors or individual creditors (e.g. large lenders) are engaged.[31] Explaining this pattern, the Practice Guide mentions practical difficulties associated with negotiating an agreement between potentially large numbers of creditors.[32] This is further complicated by the fact that in group insolvency there are creditor pools of several legal entities that would need to be consulted with. It is also likely that when insolvency proceedings are commenced and the adoption of a protocol is a top priority, not all creditors are yet known to insolvency practitioners. Despite these noteworthy considerations, the Practice Guide recognizes that since creditors play an important role in global reorganization, close cooperation with them is highly desirable. We support this view (see Box 8.1).[33] **8.18**

---

28 Sendo protocol, sec. I-1.

29 Federal-Mogul protocol (Canada-USA, 2001).

30 Protocols in Maxwell, Nakash (Israel-USA, 1996), Jet Airways.

31 Financial Asset Management protocol.

32 Practice Guide, Ch. III, para. 17.

33 Ibid.

> *Box 8.1 Notification*
>
> To the extent that creditors and other stakeholders may have a legal or economic interest in the adoption of a protocol and its specific provisions, they should at least be informed about its negotiation and, ideally, have an opportunity for comment or objection.
>
> The early involvement of and supervision by courts and their approval of an insolvency protocol in an open hearing with due notification should be sought to mitigate concerns over transparency.

8.19 Transparency is ensured though the access to and the availability of relevant information. Such access is an essential component of the right to a fair trial.[34] The task of guaranteeing the access to information is primarily addressed at the national level. Thus, questions of who can receive information, what type of information and under which conditions are typically answered by national law. In the cross-border insolvency context, some harmonized notification and publication requirements have also been imposed.[35] To the extent that insolvency protocols aim to facilitate information flows and encourage data exchange between parallel insolvency proceedings, they can promote transparency.

8.20 Some protocols do not specifically deal with the issue of information sharing and contain a general undertaking of debtors to cooperate (or 'reasonably' cooperate) with each other and to take any other steps to coordinate the administration of insolvency proceedings.[36] Other protocols are very brief so far as the access to and sharing of information are concerned. They may simply confirm that information publicly available in either forum shall be publicly available in both forums[37] or add that to the extent permitted, non-public information shall be made available to official representatives of the debtors, subject to appropriate confidentiality arrangements and privileges under the applicable rules of evidence.[38]

---

34 Bork, *supra* note 2, p. 91.

35 See e.g. EIR Recast, Arts 24–25, prescribing the establishment of national insolvency registers with certain relevant information concerning the proceedings and a decentralized system for the interconnection of insolvency registers. See also Recital 12 EIR Recast, explaining that publicity is needed 'to allow creditors to become aware of the proceedings and to lodge their claims, thereby ensuring the collective nature of the proceedings'.

36 Protocols in Quebecor (para. 9), Payless Holdings (para. 10), Systech (para. 11), Philip Services (para. 11).

37 Masonite protocol (para. 13), Calpine protocol (para. 16).

38 Everfresh protocol, para. 5.

Yet a few protocols establish detailed provisions on communication, access to data and information exchange between insolvency practitioners, courts and committees of creditors.[39] A good example is the Lehman Brothers protocol, which provides that: **8.21**

> Official Representatives should share information regarding the Debtors, and their assets and liabilities, which each may lawfully share with the other; provided, however, that with respect to work product or other privileged information, Official Representatives may, but are not obliged, to share such information with each other, subject to all privileges under the applicable rules of evidence or applicable law, and provided that sharing work product or privileged information shall not be deemed a waiver of any attorney-client privilege or work product protections under the applicable rules of evidence or applicable law.[40]

The Lehman Brothers protocol further clarifies that insolvency practitioners should cooperate in the gathering and sharing of certain data and share analysis of certain transactions by exchanging via free, read-only access all relevant information and data relating to material interest holders of an asset, restitution of assets, and relevant information that can assist other insolvency practitioners to fulfil their duties, except where litigation has commenced or is contemplated or where disclosure is prohibited.[41] Cooperation may also cover sharing of books, records, correspondence,[42] coordination in the investigation of pre-filing activities,[43] and liaising on matters of significant mutual interest, such as exit from the proceedings.[44] **8.22**

Since under the applicable rules of evidence and relevant provisions of applicable law certain information may be non-public, privileged and commercially sensitive, limitations imposed on its disclosure and unwillingness of insolvency practitioners or courts to share or exchange it should not per se be considered as causing unjustified lack of transparency. However, this situation is quite different from the process of judicial decision-making (i.e. actual court proceedings and making a judgment), which needs to be credible and transparent. **8.23**

39 See e.g. Commodore protocol, para. N ('It is expected that upon reasonable request all books, records, reports and opinions of experts other than those of legal counsel will be exchanged by and between the Liquidators and the Committee in connection with the sale of assets and litigation.'). See also Madoff protocol, para. 4.

40 Lehman Brothers protocol, para. 4.2.

41 Ibid., para. 4.6.1.

42 Ibid., para. 4.6.2.

43 Ibid., para. 4.6.3.

44 Ibid., para. 4.6.4.

8.24 In this respect the ALI-III Guidelines Applicable to Court-to-Court Communications in Cross-Border Cases accept that '[c]ommunications by judges directly with judges or administrators in a foreign country [...] raise issues of credibility and proper procedures. The context alone is likely to create concern in litigants unless the process is transparent and clearly fair'.[45] This is why its Guideline 7 establishes that:

> [i]n the event of communications between the Courts [...] by means of telephone or video conference call or other electronic means, unless otherwise directed by either of the two Courts: (a) Counsel for all affected parties should be entitled to participate in person during the communication and advance notice of the communication should be given to all parties [...]; (b) The communication between the Courts should be recorded and may be transcribed.

Guideline 8 adopts the same approach to communication between courts and insolvency practitioners.[46]

8.25 The EU Cross-Border Insolvency Court-to-Court Communications Guidelines (EU JudgeCo Guidelines) provide that a 'court may communicate with another court in connection with matters relating to proceedings before it for the purposes of coordinating and harmonising proceedings before it with those in the other jurisdiction'.[47] They also point out that a 'court should obtain in advance the consent of all parties affected by these communications before disclosing the information communicated'.[48] When it comes to electronic communication, the EU JudgeCo Guidelines, in line with the ALI-III Guidelines establish that in the event of e-communication, 'Counsel for all affected parties should be entitled to participate in person during the communication with advance notice of the communication being given to all parties.'[49] The JIN Guidelines adopt a less prescriptive approach and state that in the event of communication between courts '[i]n the normal case, parties *may* be present'.[50]

---

45 ALI-III Guidelines Applicable to Court-to-Court Communications in Cross-Border Cases (2001), Introduction.

46 These recommendations have been kept in ALI-III Global Principles and Guidelines 2012. See Guideline 8 (E-communication to Court) and Guideline 9 (E-communication to Insolvency Administrator).

47 EU JudgeCo Guidelines, Guideline 3, para. 3.1.

48 Ibid., para. 3.2. The commentary to the EU JudgeCo Guidelines explains that the flow of information between courts or between courts and administrators may be limited by confidentiality concerns and restrictions on communication with third parties, especially if proceedings are treated as 'private' under applicable law. See II EU Guidelines for Court-to-Court Communications in Cross-Border Insolvency Cases [Full Black Letter Text Without Commentary], available at https://www.universiteitleiden.nl/binaries/content/assets/rechtsgeleerdheid/fiscaal-en-economische-vakken/guidelines.pdf.

49 Ibid., Guideline 8.

50 JIN Guidelines, Guideline 8.

There can be situations where the engagement of creditors, IPs and other parties in an open court hearing during court-to-court e-communication (e.g. via video or audio calls) is not possible or feasible, for example, where communication aims to resolve an urgent matter or seeks to address a highly technical question, which does not affect rights and obligations of insolvency stakeholders. In such cases, no significant issues related to transparency of court proceedings and fair trial arise. This view is supported by the ECtHR, which has repeatedly held that, having regard to the demands of efficiency and economy, forgoing a hearing may be justified in certain circumstances, for example, where the case is of technical nature[51] or raises merely legal issues of a limited nature.[52] At the same, the court has recognized that 'notwithstanding the technical nature of some discussions and depending on what is at stake in the proceedings, public scrutiny may be viewed as a necessary condition for transparency and for the protection of litigants' rights'.[53] **8.26**

To the extent that protocols determine the procedure for and shape the process of court-to-court communication, they may affect transparency of insolvency proceedings. The analysis of the insolvency protocols has revealed an area which may potentially be a cause of concern. In particular, this relates to the practice of *ex parte* court-to-court communication authorized by some protocols (i.e. direct communication between courts without the presence of the parties or their counsel). Many cross-border insolvency protocols (especially between the USA and Canada) contain the following provision establishing the procedure for joint hearings: **8.27**

> [Courts] shall be entitled to communicate with each other during or after any joint hearing, with or without counsel present, for the purposes of determining whether consistent ruling can be made by both Courts, coordinating the terms upon of the Courts' respective rulings, and addressing any other procedural or administrative matters.[54]

A number of protocols provide more generally that courts 'may communicate with one another, with or without counsel present, with respect to any **8.28**

51 *Schuler-Zgraggen v. Switzerland*, Application no. 14518/89, ECtHR 1993, para. 58.

52 *Allan Jacobsson v. Sweden (no. 2)*, Application no. 16970/90, ECtHR 1998, para. 49.

53 *Ramos Nunes de Carvalho e Sá v. Portugal* [GC], Applications nos. 55391/13, 57728/13 and 74041/13, ECtHR 2018, para. 208.

54 See e.g. Montreal, Maine & Atlantic protocol, para. 11(d)(vi). For similar provisions, see also protocols in Smurfit-Stone Container (para. 10(d)(vi)), Eddie Bauer (para. 10(d)(vi)), Masonite International (para. 10(d)(vi)), Quebecor (para. 10(d)(vi)). A protocol in PSINet Inc. is slightly different, as it approves in para. 13(v) *ex parte* communication 'after consultation with counsel for the Debtors and any other counsel that represents a party in the relevant matter, if any'.

procedural or *substantive* matter relating to Insolvency proceedings'.[55] Some protocols restrict such communication to *procedural* matters.[56]

8.29 There are three main issues with *ex parte* communication between courts. First, it decreases the transparency of insolvency proceedings, since the content of communication may be hidden from the parties. Second, it replaced the active role of parties in the proceedings with that of courts.[57] Third, it could give rise to legitimate concerns over judicial impartiality and procedural fairness (see Box 8.2). The idea that courts can freely audio- or video-call each other to discuss the judgment or agree on other substantive or procedural matters without parties being notified or present appears to be foreign to many European legal regimes. Commenting on this arrangement, Moss noted that '[f]rom an English law point of view, the idea of the judges in the different courts chatting together without the presence of parties (at least by telephone or video-conference) would seem very strange, although this apparently occurs in North America'. He concluded that the 'ability of parties to attend such discussions would seem to be a matter of elementary justice'.[58]

Box 8.2 Procedural fairness

In order to guarantee procedural fairness, judicial impartiality and transparency of insolvency proceedings, court-to-court and court-to-IP communication under a protocol should be premised on timely notification and granting an opportunity for parties (e.g. creditors) to be present during such communication.

In exceptional circumstances, having regard to the demands of efficiency, economy and urgency, court-to-court and court-to-IP communication may take place on an *ex parte* basis, but only on matters of procedural or administrative nature.

B. COMPATIBILITY WITH NATIONAL LAW AND EIR RECAST FRAMEWORK

8.30 Communication and cooperation under insolvency protocols should comply with the rules of national law and the applicable regional instruments, such as

55 Aralez Pharmaceuticals protocol (para. 12(a)), Barzel Industries protocol (para. 10(a)).

56 Abitibibowater protocol (para. 11(a)), Progressive Moulded protocol (para. 11(a)).

57 See ALI-III Global Principles and Guidelines 2012, Principle 5 (Equality of arms), holding that each party in an international insolvency case 'should have a full and fair opportunity to present evidence and legal arguments'.

58 G. Moss, 'Are JIN Guidelines a Tonic for Cross-border Insolvencies?' (2017) 30(7) *Insolvency Intelligence*, p. 102.

the EIR Recast. The latter establishes uniform conflict of law rules regulating such issues as: (i) international insolvency jurisdiction for decisions opening insolvency proceedings (Art. 3) and for actions deriving directly from insolvency proceedings and closely linked with them (Art. 6); (ii) determination of the law applicable to insolvency proceedings and their effects (Art. 7); (iii) asset localization (Art. 2(9)); (iv) exercise of creditors' rights, including the right to simultaneously file their claims in any proceedings (whether main or secondary) concerning a debtor (Art. 45); (v) powers of the insolvency practitioner in proceedings concerning members of a group of companies (Art. 60).

Problems could arise if a protocol introduces rules, which differ or depart from the stated provisions of the EIR Recast or non-discretionary rules of national law (e.g. rules applicable to the resolution of claims against an insolvent debtor). To the extent that a protocol sets out different rules, it may potentially contravene the EIR Recast or national law. Any such conflict should be addressed via the substantial and procedural rules of the state(s) concerned. **8.31**

1. Agreement on jurisdiction for claims against debtors

A number of protocols contain provisions confirming the agreement between the parties as to the exclusive forum for the resolution of certain claims. For example, the protocol in Pioneer Companies Inc. divided the jurisdiction between the Canadian and the US courts, so that 'any claims against any of the Debtors [whether American or Canadian] arising under or in connection with [notes, guarantees, loan agreements and other specific contracts] shall be determined by the U.S. Court in the U.S. Cases'.[59] Thus, under this arrangement even certain claims against the Canadian debtor had to be resolved in the insolvency proceedings of the US debtors (members of the same enterprise group). The protocol in AgriBioTech Canada (ABTC) stipulates that: **8.32**

> [i]n order to be entitled to participate in any distribution or vote upon any Proposal or Plan of Reorganization involving ABTC [debtor], claimants must file proofs of their claims [...] with ABTC in Canada and the claims procedure shall be conducted by the Canada Court pursuant to an Order of the Canada Court.[60]

The protocol has also stated that claims timely filed in the US proceedings shall be transmitted to Canada and decided upon in the CCAA proceedings.

59 Pioneer protocol, sec. D. ('Matters relating to the Proving of Claims against the Debtors').

60 AgriBioTech Canada protocol, section 4.01(a) ('Claims process').

8.33 There are two potential problems with such forum selection provisions, revealed by the above insolvency protocols.

8.34 First, it is often the case that the jurisdiction to hear claims against insolvent debtors is set by law and cannot be altered by the parties' choice of an alternative forum. The exclusive jurisdiction of the insolvency forum might be dictated by the doctrine of *vis attractiva concursus*, under which all claims against the insolvent debtor are 'attracted' to and need to be filed in the insolvency proceedings of such a debtor. Any agreement to the contrary may therefore be held void or otherwise unenforceable pursuant to national (insolvency) law.

8.35 In several recent cases, courts in the EU Member States had to decide whether choice of forum clauses that granted jurisdiction to courts other than the courts of the opening of insolvency proceedings could trump the insolvency court's jurisdiction where the relevant national insolvency law said that only the insolvency court had the competence to decide on claims against the insolvent debtor.[61] In the case of the insolvent Icelandic bank Kaupthing, the English court (i.e. the court of the chosen forum) held that the insolvency court's jurisdiction (*forum concursus*) should prevail over contractual arrangements with respect to the jurisdiction, including a dispute resolution clause.[62] This conclusion relied on Article 10(2)(e) CIWUD, which prescribes the application of *lex concursus* to the effects of winding-up proceedings on proceedings brought by individual creditors, and is identical to Article 7(2)(f) EIR Recast. The English court ruled that if the *lex concursus* (i.e. Icelandic insolvency law) established that only Icelandic courts had the competence to rule on all monetary claims against the insolvent debtor, parties' choice for an alternative forum is trumped by the authoritative force of *vis attractiva concursus*.

8.36 Second, limitations imposed by insolvency protocols on creditors (e.g. on their jurisdictional position, rights to file claims, complaints and objections) can lead to a violation of their rights, granted by the EIR Recast or national law. The EIR Recast stipulates that '[a]ny creditor may lodge its claim in the main insolvency proceedings and in any secondary insolvency proceedings'.[63] Any

---

61 Z. Fabok, 'Vis Attractiva Concursus Throughout the EU? New Ruling of the Hungarian Curia on the Jurisdiction for Post-opening Actions Against an Insolvent Debtor', Oxford Business Law Blog, 31 October 2017, available at https://www.law.ox.ac.uk/business-law-blog/blog/2017/10/vis-attractiva-concursus-throughout-eu-new-ruling-hungariancuria (accessed 20 June 2020).

62 *Tchenguiz v. Grant Thornton UK LLP*, [2017] EWCA Civ 83.

63 EIR Recast, Art. 45(1).

agreement to the contrary (e.g. an agreement stipulating that all claims against the debtor shall be filed in one proceeding) would be contrary to the EIR Recast, provided it is applicable to the case at hand. If the EIR Recast does not apply, an agreement to 'accumulate' all creditors' claims in one (e.g. main) insolvency proceeding can be cost-efficient and help avoid duplication of efforts for the confirmation or establishment of claims in several proceedings simultaneously taking place in different jurisdictions. However, one needs to make sure that such an agreement complies with applicable law determining rights and position of creditors.

2. Agreement on COMI and jurisdiction for related actions

Similar to the choice of a jurisdiction for claims against an insolvent debtor are arrangements for the selection of the jurisdiction for insolvency-related actions and determination of the status of the relevant proceedings (i.e. whether such proceedings are main or non-main). While such a choice may promote legal certainty and cost efficiency (e.g. preventing unnecessary litigation over the status of the proceedings and facilitating early planning for a group solution) in the administration of parallel insolvency proceedings,[64] it may run into problems when it comes to the EIR Recast. **8.37**

For example, the Jet Airways protocol specifies that the 'Parties recognize that the Company being an Indian company with its centre of main interest in India, the Indian Proceedings are the main insolvency proceedings and the Dutch Proceedings are the non-main insolvency proceeding'.[65] While the parties can make an agreement on the status of the respective proceedings and on the location of the debtor's COMI, the enforceability of such an agreement and its determinative role are highly doubtful, at least under the EIR Recast regime. The status of the proceeding (i.e. main or non-main/secondary) is dependent on the presence of the debtor's COMI (or establishment). In turn, COMI depends on the factual situation ('place where the debtor conducts the administration of its interests on a regular basis and which is ascertainable by third parties'[66]) and cannot be changed purely on the basis of the parties' agreement. Nevertheless, parties' choice for a COMI jurisdiction in a protocol can be taken into account by courts when they independently assess the factual situation. In the case of *Videology Limited* the court held that the express **8.38**

64 For this argument, see I. Kokorin, 'Contracting Around Insolvency Jurisdiction: Private Ordering in European Insolvency Jurisdiction Rules and Practices', in V. Lazić and S. Stuij (eds), *Recasting the Insolvency Regulation: Improvements and Missed Opportunities. Short Studies in Private International Law* (The Hague: Asser Press, 2020), p. 53, pointing out the benefits of the contractual selection of the COMI-jurisdiction.

65 Jet Airways protocol, sec. 3.

66 EIR Recast, Art. 3(1).

representations in the financing documents with respect to the debtor's COMI gave strong support of finding the debtor's COMI in the agreed jurisdiction.[67]

8.39 When it comes to the jurisdiction over insolvency-related matters, the EIR Recast lays down that the *forum concursus* 'shall have jurisdiction for any action which derives directly from the insolvency proceedings and is closely linked with them, such as avoidance actions'.[68] It has been pointed out that such jurisdiction is exclusive.[69] An exception is made for cases where an insolvency-related action is related to an action in civil and commercial matters against the same defendant. In the latter case both actions can be brought in the jurisdiction of the defendant's domicile.[70] Insolvency-related actions include, inter alia, actions to set a transaction aside based on insolvency,[71] to hold debtor's directors liable on special insolvency-related grounds (e.g. failure to timely file for insolvency),[72] to hold members of the creditors' committee liable for their voting on a restructuring plan in insolvency proceedings.[73] The rules of the EIR Recast on insolvency-related actions purport to centralize insolvency-related disputes in one jurisdiction, therefore enhancing the proceedings' effectiveness and efficiency.[74]

8.40 Any agreement between the parties on an alternative jurisdiction for resolution of insolvency-related disputes cannot deprive the insolvency forum of its exclusive jurisdiction as granted by Article 6 EIR Recast or national law, as the case may be.[75] The analysis of insolvency protocols has revealed that they sometimes encompass an agreement on the jurisdiction for the resolution of

---

67 *In the matter of Videology Ltd. and In the matter of the Cross-Border Insolvency Regulations* [2018] EWHC 2186 (Ch).

68 EIR Recast, Art. 6(1).

69 B. Hess et al., *The Implementation of the New Insolvency Regulation: Improving Cooperation and Mutual Trust* (Nomos/Hart, 2018), p. 101. The CJEU has also confirmed the exclusivity of the *forum concursus* over related actions. See Case C-296/17, *Wiemer & Trachte*, 14 November 2018, ECLI:EU:C:2018:902, para. 36; Case C-493/18, *UB v. VA and others*, 4 December 2019, ECLI:EU:C:2019:1046, para. 29.

70 EIR Recast, Art. 6(2).

71 Case C-339/07, *Christopher Seagon v. Deko Marty Belgium NV*, 12 February 2009, ECLI:EU:C:2009:83.

72 *Simona Kornhaas v. Thomas Dithmar*, Case C-594/14, 10 December 2015, ECLI:EU:C:2015:806.

73 Case C-649/16, *Peter Valach and others v. Waldviertler Sparkasse Bank AG and others*, 20 December 2017, ECLI:EU:C:2017:986.

74 P. Mankowski (ed.), *Research Handbook on the Brussels Ibis Regulation* (Edward Elgar, 2020), p. 192. See also Z. Fabok, 'Jurisdiction Concerning Annex Actions in the Context of the Insolvency and Brussels *Ibis* Regulations' (2020) 29(2) *International Insolvency Review*, p. 213, arguing that one of the major upsides of granting exclusive jurisdiction to the courts of the opening state 'is that by doing so in most cases, the unity of the *jus* and *forum* can be achieved'. For an account of the debate about 'exclusive' or 'elective' (or: optional, facultative or competing) jurisdiction, see B. Wessels, *International Insolvency Law Part II: European Insolvency Law* (4th edn, Wolters Kluwer, 2017), 10622x et seq.

75 This issue has been raised by the court in *Olympia & York Developments Ltd. v. Royal Trust Co.* (1993), 20 C.B.R. (3d) 165 (Ont. Gen. Div.). While approving the protocol, the court warned that it does not 'take its

specific insolvency-related matters. For example, the InverWorld protocol allocates the sole jurisdiction over English insolvency practitioners (e.g. their tenure in office, conduct, retention) and over matters arising in the respective English proceedings to English courts.[76] In principle, the alignment of insolvency-related issues with the jurisdiction of the *forum concursus* should not cause any problems. Nevertheless, when drafting an insolvency protocol, it is crucial to check that such an agreement is in line with national law and the applicable regional regulation, such as the EIR Recast.

3. Agreement on law applicable to claims

The Pioneer protocol, referred to above, has specified the law applicable to the validity, amount and treatment of claims. It provided that 'any person filing a proof of claim against the Canadian Debtor in both the U.S. Cases and the Canadian Case shall be deemed to have elected to have the validity, amount and treatment of such claim determined by the U.S. Court'.[77] The AgriBioTech Canada protocol established that 'the validity and quantum of claims shall be determined in accordance with the proper law governing the obligation underlying the claim'.[78] When it comes to transaction avoidance law, it provided that the US law 'shall be governing substantive law as to all transfers made to entities located in the United States. Canadian law shall be the governing substantive law as to all transfers made to entities located in Canada'.[79] The Everfresh protocol also contains the agreement as to the avoidance laws, noting that: **8.41**

> all creditors subject to the jurisdiction of the Bankruptcy Court [USA] shall be subject to the avoiding laws set forth in the Bankruptcy Code, and other applicable laws of the United States which shall be the controlling law of each case to the extent permitted by applicable international law.[80]

When choosing law applicable to certain issues in an insolvency protocol, one should keep in mind that the EIR Recast establishes a number of uniform rules dealing with applicable law. It provides for the general rule, according to which the law applicable to insolvency proceedings and their effects shall be that of the Member State within the territory of which such proceedings are **8.42**

approval to be binding upon the Court in the sense of committing it unequivocally to an ouster of its jurisdiction in the future without regard to the circumstances'.

76 InverWorld protocol, para. 21. For a similar approach see protocols in Everfresh (para. 14) and Commodore (para. C).

77 Pioneer protocol, para. 10.

78 AgriBioTech Canada protocol, sec. 4.01(b).

79 Ibid., sec. 8.01.

80 Everfresh protocol, para. 12.

opened (*lex concursus*).[81] This law determines the effects of the insolvency proceedings, both procedural and substantive, on the persons and legal relations concerned.

8.43 The EIR Recast contains a number of subject matters clearly falling within the boundaries of *lex concursus*. They include powers of the debtor and the insolvency practitioner, conditions under which set-off may be invoked, effects of insolvency proceedings on current contracts to which the debtor is a party, rules governing the lodging, verification and admission of claims, rules governing the distribution of proceeds from the realization of assets and the ranking of claims, rules relating to the voidness, voidability or unenforceability of legal acts detrimental to the general body of creditors, etc. Thus, if the law chosen by the parties in the protocol differs from or is at odds with the law applicable under the guidance of the EIR Recast, the latter shall prevail. For instance, if a protocol (following the example of the Pioneer protocol) establishes that the validity, verification, admission and treatment of claims shall always be subject to the law, different from main *lex concursus* (e.g. law of secondary proceedings – *lex concursus secondarii*), such a choice will contravene Article 7(2)(h) and 7(2)(m) EIR Recast. This also applies to the special rules and exceptions contained in Articles 8–18 EIR Recast.[82]

8.44 The provisions of the protocols cited above do not easily fit in the scheme of the EIR Recast, especially to the extent that they separate *lex concursus* from *forum concursus*. Thus, if insolvency proceedings governing such protocols would have fallen under its scope, these provisions would most likely be held unenforceable and ignored by European courts. This is why it is crucial to ensure the full compliance of a protocol with applicable national and supra-national law (Box 8.3).

Box 8.3 Compliance with applicable law

When drafting an insolvency protocol, insolvency practitioners and other contracting parties shall ensure that the protocol complies with national laws of the proceedings concerned (*lex concursus*) and any applicable regional regulation (e.g. the EIR Recast).

Particular attention should be paid to provisions of insolvency protocols which restrict creditors' rights related to filing of claims (i.e. allocating creditors' claims to

81 EIR Recast, Art. 7(1).

82 These special rules concern rights *in rem*, set-off, detrimental acts, employment contracts, etc.

one proceeding or one jurisdiction), introduce differentiated treatment of creditors or determine law applicable to claim resolution or validity of claims.

A protocol shall not interfere with independent exercise of jurisdiction by courts involved, including in their authority or supervision over insolvency practitioners, nor shall it interfere with national rules or ethical standards by which insolvency practitioners are bound pursuant to applicable law and professional rules.

C. INFORMATION EXCHANGE AND CONFLICTS OF INTEREST

Chapters 5 and 6 above have noted the problem of conflicts of interest in the context of group insolvencies. They pointed out that many instruments of international insolvency law discourage the appointment of the same insolvency practitioner and mandate restricted communication and cooperation in a situation of a conflict of interest.[83] This is premised on the fact that due to legal separability (resulting in separateness of pools of assets and creditors along entity lines), such communication and cooperation may harm the interests of one group member for the benefit of another group member or the group as a whole. **8.45**

The analysis of insolvency protocols has shown that the majority of them do not introduce limitations as to the categories or the scope of information to be shared between proceedings. For example, the Mosaic protocol simply states that the 'Canadian Court and the U.S. Court may communicate with one another with respect to any matter relating to the Insolvency Proceedings'.[84] Some protocols add that communication shall be conducted in accordance with the ALI-III Guidelines (2001).[85] The Madoff protocol specified that insolvency practitioners shall 'share with the other Representative non-public information available to it regarding the Debtors, their pre-appointment activities and transactions, and their assets and liabilities'.[86] The only limitation imposed by the Madoff protocol related to undertaking not to transfer non-public information to third parties.[87] However, the absence of specific **8.46**

83 EIR Recast, Arts 56–58; Guide to Model Law 2019, para 103; Legislative Guide 2010, Ch. II, para. 68.

84 Mosaic protocol, para. 11(b). For a similar approach, see protocols in Calpine (para. 13(a)), Financial Asset Management (para. 13), Systech (para. 12(b)), Philip Services Corp. (para. 12). Some protocols limit such communication to procedural matters only, see protocols in Montreal, Maine & Atlantic (para. 11(a)), Masonite International (para. 10(a)), Quebecor (para. 10(a)).

85 Protocols in Matlack Systems Inc. (para. 11), Systech (para. 12(c)), Graceway Canada (preamble).

86 Madoff protocol, para. 4.1.2.

87 Ibid., para. 4.2.

provisions related to information exchange – its scope, conduct and restrictions, does not mean that sharing of information between insolvency practitioners and courts is unlimited. It only means that such limitations are not agreed in the protocol but may instead be imposed by applicable national law. This is also confirmed by the protocols themselves, some of which establish the priority of applicable law over provisions of a protocol[88] and almost always confirm independent jurisdiction and authority of courts.[89]

8.47 Only a few protocols restrict cooperation in cases where the interests of parties (i.e. group members and their creditors) diverge or where the information is confidential or otherwise privileged. A good example is the Lehman Brothers protocol, which lays down that each Official Representative should cooperate in the gathering and sharing of certain data and share analysis of certain transactions by:

> 4.6.1. sharing, via free, read-only access, all relevant information and data that it has the right to disclose [...]
>
> 4.6.3. coordinating in good faith the investigations of pre-filing activities with any other Official Representative with an interest in such activities, so long as the interests of the Official Representatives coordinating such investigations do not diverge; and
>
> 4.6.4. liaising with any other Official Representatives on matters [...] in which such other Official Representatives have a significant mutual interest, so long as their interests do not diverge.

8.48 The analysis of the selected protocols has not revealed any significant threats of conflicts of interest linked to information exchange. In any case, the flexible character of protocols, priority of national law over them, independence and impartiality of insolvency practitioners should serve to control and minimize risks of conflicts of interest. If broadly interpreted, conflicts of interest could present a significant impediment to efficient cross-border insolvency communication and cooperation, promoted by insolvency protocols. It is important to keep in mind that communication and cooperation to the maximum extent possible is the rule, while restrictions based on the risk of conflicts of interest is an exception (see Box 8.4).

---

88 InverWorld protocol, para. 36, noting that '[t]his Stipulation is not intended to otherwise circumvent, alter, or otherwise affect the rights, obligations, or laws of any jurisdiction'. See also the Madoff protocol, para. 4.1., prescribing that communication and information sharing shall be carried out to 'the extent appropriate having regard to [...] respective duties under applicable law'. See also protocol in Financial Asset Management, para. 11.

89 See e.g. protocols in Loewen (para. 6), Commodore (para. T), Jet Airways (paras 13.1.1. and 13.1.3.), Philip Services Corp. (para. 7), Eddie Bauer (para. 5), AgriBioTech Canada (sec. 1.02), Lehman Brothers (para. 11.1.), Madoff Investment Securities (para. 10.1.).

Box 8.4 Information exchange

One of the primary purposes of insolvency protocols is to streamline information flows between insolvency practitioners and courts engaged in separate insolvency proceedings. Information sharing and data exchange are a precondition for the adoption of synchronized restructuring plans, development of a mechanism for the resolution of intercompany claims, coordination of proceedings for the purposes of asset preservation and maximization of insolvency estates value.

This is why under an insolvency protocol insolvency practitioners should agree to timely communicate to each other any information which may be relevant to the other proceedings and inform each other of any material developments. To facilitate information exchange, a protocol may specify subjects on which information should be communicated. This might relate, inter alia, to the contemplated restructuring or liquidation plans, planned disposition of material assets and other transactions outside the ordinary course of business, termination of key contracts and resolution of certain claims. Sharing of non-public (e.g. commercially sensitive) information should be subject to confidentiality arrangements and applicable privileges.

At the same time, information should not be unjustifiably withheld. While communication may be restricted in a situation where such communication entails a conflict of interest, any limitations based on the risk of conflicts of interest should be strictly and narrowly interpreted, well justified and rarely and cautiously used in practice. Communication and cooperation to the maximum extent possible is the rule, while restrictions based on the risk of conflicts of interest is an exception.

9

CROSS-BORDER INSOLVENCY PROTOCOLS AND NATIONAL LAW

A. MODEL LAW 1997 AND COMMON LAW JURISDICTIONS	9.01
B. INSOLVENCY PROTOCOLS AND CIVIL LAW JURISDICTIONS	9.09
1. The Netherlands	9.09
2. Germany	9.13
3. Other jurisdictions	9.19

A. MODEL LAW 1997 AND COMMON LAW JURISDICTIONS

9.01 In Chapter 5 above we emphasized that the Model Law 1997 authorizes for each individual case the conclusion of a cross-border insolvency agreement as a tool to improve administration of parallel insolvency proceedings, which fall under its scope. As a result, countries that base their legislation on the Model Law 1997 should have a direct legislative basis to approve insolvency protocols.

9.02 For example, in the USA insolvency protocols are consistent with sections 1526 and 1527 of the Bankruptcy Code.[1] Section 1526 requires a trustee to, subject to the supervision of the court, cooperate to the maximum extent possible with a foreign court or a foreign insolvency practitioner. Further, section 1527 provides that the cooperation described in section 1526 may be implemented by any appropriate means, including the 'approval or implementation of agreements concerning the coordination of proceedings'. Interestingly, the practice of entering into insolvency protocols in the US proceedings was formed prior to incorporation of the Model Law 1997 as chapter 15 in 2005.[2] While the US courts have been approving cross-border insolvency

1 11 U.S. Code § 1526, § 1527.

2 For discussion of the authority for insolvency protocols under US law before 2005, see R. Chapman, 'Judicial Abstention in Cross-Border Insolvency Proceedings: Recent Protocols in Simultaneous Plenary Cases' (1998) 7(1) *International Insolvency Review*, pp. 1–38. See e.g. *Stonington Partners v. Lernout & Hauspie Speech*, 310 F.3d 118, 133 (3rd Cir. 2002), stating that:

> [w]e strongly recommend, in a situation such as this, that an actual dialog occur or be attempted between the courts of the different jurisdictions in an effort to reach an agreement as to how to proceed or, at the very least, an understanding as to the policy considerations underpinning salient aspects of the foreign laws.

protocols before the enactment of chapter 15 in 2005, the latter conveys the explicit and direct statutory authority to do so.[3] Some authors conclude that chapter 15 'has significantly changed the legal environment, emphasizing communication and cooperation between the U.S. court and the foreign judiciary or administrator'.[4]

9.03 The Federal Rules of Bankruptcy Procedure, a set of rules directing procedures in the US bankruptcy courts, stipulate that approval of an insolvency agreement shall be sought by motion with at least 30 days' notice of any hearing on the motion.[5] It has been noted, however, that in practice parties have not sought authority under the Federal Rules of Bankruptcy Procedure to implement a protocol, but instead they continued to move under section 105 ('Power of court')[6] in seeking such a relief.[7] This section grants broad discretionary powers to courts to 'issue any order, process, or judgment that is necessary or appropriate to carry out the provisions of' the Bankruptcy Code. The all-encompassing omnibus character of section 105 has been accepted by courts.[8]

9.04 In Canada the approval of cross-border insolvency protocols is based on the CCAA, which, following the language of the Model Law 1997, lays down that 'cooperation may be provided by any appropriate means, including [...] the approval or implementation by courts of agreements concerning the coordination of proceedings'.[9] Just like the US courts, Canadian courts have commonly approved insolvency protocols prior to the incorporation of the Model Law 1997 in Canadian law in 2005. 'Pre-Model-Law' CCAA contained a general provision allowing a court to 'make such orders and grant such

Also stressing that cooperation can be initiated by the court itself, 'especially if the parties (whose incentives for doing so may not necessarily be as great) have not been able to make progress on their own'.

3 See B. Wessels, *International Insolvency Law Part I. Global Perspectives on Cross-Border Insolvency Law* (4th edn, Wolters Kluwer, 2015), 10328ff.

4 K. Beckering, 'United States Cross-Border Corporate Insolvency: The Impact of Chapter 15 on Comity and the New Legal Environment' (2008) 14(2) *Law and Business Review of the Americas*, p. 308.

5 Federal Rules of Bankruptcy Procedure, Rule 5012 ('Agreements Concerning Coordination of Proceedings in Chapter 15 Cases'), available at https://www.uscourts.gov/rules-policies/current-rules-practice-procedure/federal-rules-bankruptcy-procedure.

6 11 U.S. Code § 105.

7 A. Resnick and H. Sommer (eds), *Collier Guide to Chapter 11: Key Topics and Selected Industries* (Lexis Nexis, 2016), sec. 11.06(1). See Debtor's Motion Pursuant to Section 105 and 363 of the Bankruptcy Code for Approval of a Cross-Border Insolvency Protocol, *In re Lehman Brothers Holdings Inc.*, No. 08-13555 (Bankr. S.D.N.Y. May 26, 2009).

8 *Casse v. Key Bank Nat'l Ass'n (In re Casse)*, 198 F.3d 327, 342 (2d Cir.1999); *Davis v. Davis (In re Davis)*, 170 F.3d 475, 492 (5th Cir. 1999); *In re Earl*, 140 B.R. 728, 741 n. 4 (Bankr. N.D. Ind. 1992), noting that § 105 'empowers a court to issue such commands as are necessary and appropriate to prevent frustration of orders it has previously issued, and to permit the fashioning of extraordinary remedies when the need arises'.

9 Companies' Creditors Arrangement Act (R.S.C., 1985, c. C-36), sec. 52(3)(d).

relief as it considers appropriate to facilitate, approve or implement arrangements that will result in a co-ordination of proceedings under [CCAA] with any foreign proceeding'.[10]

9.05 Mr. Justice Farley of the Ontario Court of Justice, in approving the Everfresh protocol (1995), stated that that the protocol 'demonstrates the "essence of comity" between the courts of Canada and the United States of America'.[11] In an earlier case concerning cross-border Olympia & York re-organization, Blair J. had no hesitation in concluding that the Canadian court had 'the jurisdiction to approve a vehicle such as the Protocol, negotiated and agreed to by all of the affected parties, and designed to facilitate the implementation of a re-organization Plan by providing some certainty regarding cross-jurisdictional issues'. According to the court, such jurisdiction 'can be founded on the principles of international comity between nations, or, if necessary upon the Court's inherent jurisdiction'.[12]

9.06 Another jurisdiction which has based its law on the Model Law 1997 is Australia. Australian Cross-Border Insolvency Act 2008 almost word-by-word repeats the Model Law 1997, stating that cooperation and direct communication between courts and IPs 'may be implemented by any appropriate means, including [...] approval or implementation by courts of agreements concerning the coordination of proceedings'.[13] Additionally, many national courts, including the Supreme Court of New South Wales and the Federal Court of Australia have adopted similar practice notes specifying the operation of Australian law when it comes to cross-border insolvency cooperation.[14]

---

10 Companies' Creditors Arrangement Act (R.S.C., 1985, c. C-36), sec. 18.6(2). Version of document from 2004-12-15 to 2005-09-27.

11 *Everfresh Beverages, Inc., Re* (1995) 1995 CarswellOnt 2336, para. 4.

12 *Olympia & York Developments Ltd. v. Royal Trust Co.* (1993), 20 C.B.R. (3d) 165 (Ont. Gen. Div.), para. 7. It is appropriate to mention here the boundlessness of a Canadian practitioner, Bruce Leonard, in promoting cross-border communication and cooperation. In 2000, Bruce Leonard was a founder of the International Insolvency Institute (III) and its chairman till his passing away in 2017. See e.g. B. Leonard, 'The Everfresh Reorganisation: Advancing Co-operation in Cross-Border Insolvencies', in J.S. Ziegel and D. Baird (eds), *Case Studies in Recent Canadian Insolvency Reorganisations (In Honour Of The Honourable Lloyd William Houlden)* (Carswell, 1997), pp. 325–44; B. Leonard, 'The Development of Court-to-Court Communications in Cross-Border Cases' (2008) 17 *Norton Journal of Bankruptcy Law and Practice*, pp. 619–42.

13 Cross-Border Insolvency Act 2008 No. 24, 2008, Art. 27(d). See Wessels, *International Insolvency Law Part I*, *supra* note 3, 10360.

14 Practice notes and directions for cross-border cooperation in insolvency have been adopted by other Australian Supreme Courts. See e.g. Supreme Court of Tasmania, Cross-Border Insolvency – Cooperation with Foreign Courts or Foreign Representatives, No. 2 of 2009, 27 February 2009; Supreme Court of the Northern Territory, Cross-Border Insolvency, Practice Direction No. 4 of 2017.

9.07 The practice note of the Supreme Court of New South Wales states that cooperation between courts in the context of international insolvency should 'generally occur within a framework or protocol that has previously been approved by the Court, and is known to the parties, in the particular proceeding'.[15] It also points out that when drafting the framework or protocols, parties should have regard to the ALI-III Guidelines (2001) and the UNCITRAL Practice Guide. JIN Guidelines are also mentioned. The practice note of the Federal Court of Australia is more detailed. First, in addition to the JIN Guidelines, the UNCITRAL Practice Guide and the ALI-III Guidelines (2001), it refers to the Modalities of Court-to-Court Communication[16] and the ALI-III Global Principles for Cooperation in International Insolvency Cases (2012) and Global Rules on Conflict-of-Laws Matters in International Insolvency Cases.[17] Second, it adds that parties should have regard to the aspects of these instruments designed to provide transparency and accord procedural fairness to all parties, including communication between courts with advance notification of the counsel, advance notice of telephone or video conference communications between courts and between a court and IPs.[18] These clarifications are of paramount importance, as they aim to address some of the concerns regarding fair trial highlighted in chapter 8 above. Third, the practice note lays down that a protocol 'should generally address the processes for coordination of: notification of creditors; submission of creditor claims; the administration of claims; and the hearing of appeals where claims are rejected.'[19]

9.08 Despite this solid legislative basis, there is no decided case law where an Australian court would be involved in the approval of a cross-border insolvency protocol.[20] This shows that the adoption of a developed regulatory framework for insolvency protocols or solely belonging to the common law tradition do not guarantee the use of protocols in practice. Nevertheless, direct communication between courts and joint hearings have been authorized in recent cases involving Australia. In *Parbery; Re Lehman Brothers Australia*

15 Supreme Court of New South Wales Equity Division, Practice Note SC EQ_6: Cross-Border Insolvency: Cooperation with Foreign Courts or Foreign Representatives, 15 September 2017.

16 JIN Modalities of Court-to-Court Communication, http://jin-global.org/modalities.html. While JIN Guidelines focus on the principles of court-to-court communication, the Modalities seek to provide the mechanics for initiating, receiving and engaging in such communication. As of July 2020, the JIN Guidelines have been endorsed by 12 courts globally (e.g. US Bankruptcy Court for the Southern District of New York, Chancery Division of England and Wales, Seoul Bankruptcy Court, District Court Midden-Nederland) and the JIN Modalities have been accepted by the Supreme Court of Singapore.

17 Federal Court of Australia, Cross-Border Insolvency Practice Note: Cooperation with Foreign Courts or Foreign Representatives (GPN-XBDR), 31 January 2020, para. 2.5.

18 Ibid., para. 2.8.

19 Ibid., para. 2.9.

20 Corporate Restructuring and Insolvency in Asia 2020, p. 69.

Limited, Jacobs J of the Federal Court of Australia agreed to communicate with Judge Peck of the US Bankruptcy Court for the Southern District of New York. Jacobs J also considered a possibility of establishing a protocol for future communications 'as the necessary parties are consulted about the terms of any communication'.[21] More recently, in the cases of Halifax Investment Services Pty Ltd. (Halifax AU) and Halifax New Zealand Ltd. (New Zealand), a joint hearing of the Federal Court of Australia and the High Court of New Zealand took place (by way of Microsoft Teams) on 3 April 2020.[22]

B. INSOLVENCY PROTOCOLS AND CIVIL LAW JURISDICTIONS

1. The Netherlands

9.09 While the use of cross-border protocols or agreements in international insolvency cases is supported by the provisions of the Model Law 1997, the vast majority of (civil law) jurisdictions in the EU have not transposed it into national insolvency regimes. The Dutch Bankruptcy Act (*Faillissementswet*) dates from 1896 and has been amended several times since. However, it does not provide a developed framework for administering transnational insolvencies. This is why a question may arise whether a Dutch court has the judicial authority to provide assistance to a foreign court or to approve (in a similar way as a Dutch court 'approves' (*homologatie*) a composition (*akkoord*)) an insolvency protocol. In the Netherlands, prior to the EIR 2000 entering into force, courts and supervisory judges were unlikely to demonstrate an active attitude in communicating with foreign courts or insolvency practitioners. This was because in general the courts and practitioners' awareness of tools developed in cross-border insolvency was still in its infancy, whilst the system of Dutch national insolvency law did not leave much room for creditors' and courts' initiatives and the legal basis for the approval of insolvency protocols was insufficient.[23] The situation was further complicated by the longstanding 'territorialist' approach adhered to by Dutch courts, according to which '[u]nless a Convention, binding the Netherlands, provides otherwise, insolvency proceedings opened in another country have territorial effect'.[24]

---

21 *Parbery; Re Lehman Brothers Australia Ltd.* [2011] FCA 1449.

22 *In the matter of Halifax Investment Services Pty Ltd.* (No 5) [2019] FCA 1341, in which the Federal Court of Australia held that it could make a request to the New Zealand High Court that there be a joint hearing of those courts.

23 B. Wessels, *International Insolvency Law Part I*, *supra* note 3, 10118.

24 Hoge Raad 19 Dec. 2008, NJ 2009/456 in re *Yukos Finance I*, citing earlier cases in Hoge Raad 2 juni 1967, NJ 1968, 16 and Hoge Raad 31 mei 1996, nr. 16007, NJ 1998, 108. On these and other cases, see Wessels, ibid., Chapter II.

However, recent developments may indicate that the Netherlands is becoming more open to foreign insolvencies. This is not the result of the national law reform concerning cross-border insolvency. It can instead be (at least partially) attributed to the modern European and international trends. First, the EIR 2000 imposed a duty to cooperate and communicate information between insolvency practitioners.[25] Second, the EIR Recast extended such a duty to cooperation and communication between courts and between courts and IPs, also in the context of group insolvencies.[26] Third, the growth of international best practices and cases of international insolvency cooperation (including by way of insolvency protocols), as well as the increasing number of countries transposing the Model Law 1997 have had an indirect influence on the position held by Dutch practitioners and courts.[27] **9.10**

The changing attitude of Dutch courts to foreign insolvencies is evident from the evolving case law. For example, in the *Yukos* case, the Dutch Supreme Court ruled that the insolvency practitioner appointed in Russian insolvency proceedings could in principle and subject to the recognition of such proceedings (i.e. provided that a foreign insolvency judgment was not arrived at in a manner contrary to Dutch public policy), exercise the power to sell the debtor's (unencumbered) assets located in the Netherlands.[28] Thus, Dutch 'territorialism' has effectively given way to (modified) universalism.[29] Apart from recognition of foreign insolvency proceedings, Dutch courts appeared to be among the first in the EU to show the openness for transnational communication and cooperation in insolvency cases under the aegis of the EIR Recast. The website of courts (https://www.rechtspraak.nl/) mentions that the Netherlands takes into account best practices for cooperation in cross-border insolvency cases, including EU JudgeCo Principles and Guidelines.[30] The Dutch District Court Midden-Nederland is the first continental European court to have accepted the JIN Guidelines. Dutch courts and insolvency practitioners have also engaged in the adoption of insolvency protocols. There are at least three cases, in which such protocols were used. **9.11**

25 EIR 2000, Art. 31.

26 EIR Recast, Arts 56–58.

27 I. Mevorach, 'Modified Universalism as Customary International Law' (2018) 96(7) *Texas Law Review*, pp. 1403–36, discussing how the set of norms of modified universalism may be elevated to a recognized legal source, specifically to the status of customary international law. This idea was further developed in I. Mevorach, *The Future of Cross-Border Insolvency: Overcoming Biases and Closing Gaps* (OUP, 2018).

28 Hoge Raad 13 Sept. 2013, ECLI:NL:HR:2013:BZ5668; JOR 2014/50. The judgment is available in English at http://www.insol.org/emailer/Oct_2013_downloads/Yukos%20decision%20e%20translation.pdf.

29 For discussion of the evolution of the Dutch approach to recognition of foreign insolvencies, see I. Kokorin and B. Wessels, 'Recognition of Foreign Insolvency Judgments: The Case of Yukos' (2017) 14(6) *European Company Law*, pp. 226–33.

30 International Insolvency, www.rechtspraak.nl/English/Pages/International-Insolvency.

These are the very early case of Eurodis Electron plc. (2006, unreported),[31] Lehman Brothers (2009) and Jet Airways (2019).

9.12 At the same time, outside the EU (EIR Recast) context, Dutch law does not set out clear rules on communication and cooperation, and on the approval of insolvency protocols. Instead, it seems to rely on soft law instruments and the initiative of the parties involved. In practice this may inhibit cross-border insolvency cooperation in complex group insolvencies, where open and expedient communication may be most needed. In a recent interview, Dutch insolvency practitioners, engaged in insolvency proceedings concerning the Dutch entities belonging to the Oi Group stressed uncertainty in dealing with international insolvencies and the desirability of clear international insolvency rules.[32] As a way to close this gap, the insolvency practitioners attempted to draw an insolvency protocol with the Brazilian administrator, which also involved communication between Dutch and Brazilian judges by email and telephone. However, according to one of the insolvency practitioners, the irreconcilable differences between the proceedings and noncommittal nature of a protocol prevented its conclusion.[33]

2. Germany

9.13 Germany has recently reformed its insolvency law and, among other things, has incorporated rules on group insolvencies. New provisions of German Insolvency Code (§§ 269a, 269b InsO) set a legal basis for local courts and insolvency practitioners to communicate and cooperate when handling insolvency of domestic corporate groups.[34] The InsO prescribes coordination

31 In this case three from a group of eight companies were subject to English administration proceedings and Dutch insolvency liquidation (*faillissement*) proceedings. When the English administrator had filed for the opening of secondary proceedings in the Netherlands, by way of a protocol both the UK and the Dutch IPs agreed that the claim handling process would be dealt with by the Dutch IP. The latter had to recognize an agreement already made by the English IP (as main IP) with a Dutch bank. In the protocol, the main IP and the secondary IP agreed on the way to realize the assets and the handling of the claims of the creditors and to subsequently arrange for the distribution process to be in compliance with both English and Dutch law. Noteworthy in this protocol is that the activity of making distributions was to be done by the IP in the secondary proceeding, which is the mirror situation with what happened in *Collins & Aikman Europe SA, Re* [2006] EWHC 1343 (Ch); [2007] 1 B.C.L.C. 182. Read further A. Al-Attar, 'Using and Losing Secondary Proceedings' (2009) 22(5) *Insolvency Intelligence*, pp. 76–8.

32 J.H. Overduin and J.M.W. Pool, 'De curator in de spagaat: tussen Nederlandse taakuitoefening en het belang van een internationale herstructurering. Interview met curatoren Marcel Groenewegen (PTIF) en Jasper Berkenbosch (Oi Coop) over de voorlopige surseances en faillissementen van de financieringsmaatschappijen van Oi Telecom', TvI 2020/9, 2020, pp. 58–67.

33 Ibid.

34 According to § 3e InsO, a group of companies consists of legally independent companies with COMIs in Germany, which are directly or indirectly connected with each other through the possibility of exercising dominant influence or through a single leadership. The term 'group of companies' thus encompasses both horizontal and vertical groups as well as hybrid forms of both, in accordance with the expressly intended broad

between insolvency practitioners of group companies (§ 269a). In particular, such practitioners must immediately provide all information on request that may be important for the other procedure. Cooperation between courts in a group insolvency context is imposed by § 269b, which specifies that cooperation should be sought in relation to provisional measures, opening of a proceeding, appointment of an IP, essential procedural decisions, etc.

A core element of the German reform on group insolvency is the introduction of a 'coordination procedure' (*Koordinationsverfahren*, §§ 269d et seq.). The mechanism of a coordination procedure seeks to supplement the general communication and cooperation duties and to facilitate coordination of parallel insolvency proceedings, which shall retain their separate and independent character. It represents a uniform cross-procedural group planning tool of non-binding[35] (or indirectly-binding)[36] soft law character. Coordination procedure under German Insolvency Code can be compared to a group coordination proceeding under the EIR Recast. It involves a coordination court (*Koordinationsgericht*) and a coordinator (*Verfahrenskoordinator*). The latter prepares a coordination plan (*Koordinationsplan*), which requires a court confirmation and the approval by a group creditors' committee (§ 269h). It can record the measures necessary for the reorganization (or liquidation) of the group or part(s) of the group. These then need to be implemented at the level of the individual insolvency proceedings. 9.14

Importantly for the purposes of our discussion, § 269h in para. 2 lays down that a coordination plan may contain suggestions (proposals) for agreements between insolvency practitioners. Such agreements are essentially insolvency protocols, which allow IPs to coordinate insolvency proceedings with contractual means.[37] Insolvency agreements can specify how the requirements of the coordination plan should be implemented in the insolvency plans of the individual proceedings. They can also set cooperation obligations in writing and establish fixed procedures for certain future actions.[38] At the same time, it has been pointed out that due to the non-binding nature of a coordination 9.15

scope. Uhlenbruck/Pape, 15. Aufl. 2019, InsO § 3e Rn. 4. However, in a situation of a cross-border enterprise group with entities having their COMI both in and outside Germany, the rules of the EIR Recast concerning insolvency proceedings of members of a group of companies, including those related to cooperation, communication and coordination, take precedence over national rules.

35 Eidenmüller/Frobenius, Münchener Kommentar zur Insolvenzordnung, 4. Auflage 2020, InsO § 269h Rn. 1. MüKoInsO/Eidenmüller/Frobenius.

36 P. Esser in E. Braun, Insolvenzordnung, 8. Auflage 2020, InsO § 269h Rn. 7–9.

37 Gelbrich/Flöther in Fridgen/Geiwitz/Göpfert, BeckOK InsO, 19. Auflage 2020, InsO § 269h Rn. 9–12.

38 Ibid.

plan, binding agreements and legal measures are not the subject of a coordination plan.[39] This is why a coordination plan can only contain proposals for the insolvency agreements. Nevertheless, the explicit mentioning of such agreements, even if in the domestic insolvency context, is noteworthy. Prior to the insolvency law reform concerning group insolvency, German law was silent on insolvency protocols, but scholars and practitioners have generally accepted the possibility of concluding them in an international context under German law.[40]

9.16 Having analysed insolvency protocols against the background of (pre-reform) German Insolvency Code, Braun and Tashiro make several insightful conclusions, which remain topical nowadays.[41]

9.17 First, insolvency practitioners in Germany cannot rely on the insolvency court alone to authorize execution of insolvency protocols. This comes from rather limited (e.g. compared to the USA and the UK) and well-defined functions of courts in German insolvency proceedings,[42] as well as the leading role of creditors in such proceedings. Second, insolvency practitioners are entitled to enter into non-binding cooperation agreements that address issues of communication and information exchange. This is explicitly authorized by Article 56 EIR Recast and may be derived from §§ 269a, 269h and 357 InsO. Third, in case of a binding insolvency protocol addressing communication and cooperation without any monetary consequences or effects on insolvency estates, insolvency practitioners might seek consent of creditors' meeting (or at least consent of the creditors' committee) to act as a party to a protocol. However, if a protocol is considered a significant or important act pursuant to § 160 InsO, it would require an approval by the creditors' committee or, if none has been formed, by the creditors' meeting.[43] Fourth, protocols that affect the insolvency estate or creditors' rights, and thereby differ from the

39 Eidenmüller/Frobenius, *supra* note 35, Rn. 38–42.

40 P. Busch, A. Remmert, S. Rüntz and H. Vallender, 'Kommunikation zwischen Gerichten in grenzüberschreitenden Insolvenzen – Was geht und was nicht geht [Communication between courts in cross-border insolvencies – What works and what does not]'. Neue Zeitschrift für Insolvenz- und Sanierungsrecht, 2010, 13: 417–30; C. Paulus, 'Protokolle' – ein anderer Zugang zur Abwicklung grenzüberschreitender Insolvenzen', Zeitschrift für Wirtschaftsrecht (ZIP) 1998, 997.

41 E. Braun and A. Tashiro, 'Cross-border Insolvency Protocol Agreements between Insolvency Practitioners and their Effects on the Rights of Creditors (unpublished)', available at https://www.iiiglobal.org/sites/default/files/BraunTashiroandBraunCBProtocols.pdf.

42 Commenting on the differences between approaches to court-to-court communication in common and civil law jurisdictions, Balz pointed out that in civil law countries judges 'generally have no discretion to embark upon legally unstructured communications with foreign judges in order to delineate each other's jurisdiction and relief powers in a protocol'. See M. Balz, 'The European Union Convention on Insolvency Proceedings' (1996) 70 *American Bankruptcy Law Journal*, p. 489.

43 § 160 InsO aims to ensure that creditors are involved in key decisions regarding handling of insolvency proceedings. The exact criteria for determining 'significance' or 'importance' of an act are not set by law and

statutory procedural law (e.g. regulating lodging and verification of claims or asset distribution among creditors), need to be approved as or through an insolvency plan procedure. In this case, according to Braun and Tashiro, a protocol itself may be treated as an insolvency plan under German law, hence requiring the necessary court confirmation and authorization by creditors. In practice, this may take considerable time, while all-encompassing general approvals for the future are problematic and can cause liability issues.[44] Fifth, and finally, German courts tend to be very strict when it comes to statutory rights and guarantees, including those related to claims processing.[45] As a result, special procedures for resolution of intercompany claims or agreements regarding jurisdiction for filing of claims, such as those established or foreseen in the Lehman Brothers protocol, would most likely be held void and unenforceable in Germany.

While conclusion of insolvency protocols is permissible under German insolvency law, we have not found published cases where this has happened. Commenting on why this might be the case, one commentary has pointed out that when it comes to general procedural rules related to exchange of information and cooperation, they remain subject to the condition that they do not harm the insolvency estate and interests of creditors. It concluded that due to a significant risk of liability (§ 60 InsO),[46] hardly any insolvency practitioner would agree to an obligation that restricts his freedom to act without at least granting equivalent benefits with sufficient certainty.[47] It has been submitted that the obligation to cooperate ends where an insolvency practitioner's duty of care in relation to the insolvency estate and the risk of personal liability arise.[48] It remains to be seen whether, in view of the cooperation duties now imposed at both the European and the national levels, **9.18**

should be determined on a case-by-case basis. See C. Janssen in Münchener Kommentar zur Insolvenzordnung 4. Auflage 2019, InsO § 160 Rn. 5–11. It is certain that conclusion of an insolvency protocol may impact the further course of insolvency proceedings (e.g. facilitate restructuring or sale as a going concern) and therefore can in principle fall under § 160 InsO.

44 D. Andres in Andres/Leithaus, Insolvenzordnung, 4. Aufl. 2018, InsO § 160 Rn. 2–4.

45 A. Baumart and F. Schmitt, 'Phoenix Kapitaldienst – ein Verfahren schreibt BGH-Rechtsprechung', NZI 2012, 394–402, discussing the case of Phoenix Kapitaldienst GmbH. The case involved an insolvency plan, which provided for a calculation method for investors' claims. The plan was approved by the vast majority of creditors both in number and value. Nevertheless, while being commercially sensible and practical, it was not supported by the court, which reasoned that, among other things, an insolvency plan must not regulate the mode in which creditors' claims are to be calculated as such a mode is set by law.

46 § 60 InsO provides that an insolvency administrator shall be liable for damages to all parties to the proceedings if he intentionally or negligently breaches the duties incumbent upon him under the Insolvency Code. In carrying out his duties an insolvency practitioner shall exercise the due care of a prudent and conscientious insolvency administrator.

47 Esser, *supra* note 36, Rn. 20–22.

48 Ibid.

insolvency practitioners will start using the instrument of an insolvency protocol more frequently.

3. Other jurisdictions

9.19 The review of the available literature has revealed that different jurisdictions adopt different approaches to insolvency protocols. In this section we provide a general and concise overview of such approaches. We cover Sweden, France and Spain.

9.20 Discussing cross-border insolvency agreements or protocols from a Swedish law perspective, Millqvist argues that 'if a protocol makes it easier to apply and uphold the rules that in any case would be applicable, there is authority for both the administrator and the courts to take part in such an agreement with binding effect on the relevant party'.[49] According to Millqvist, Swedish law does not lay down any serious obstacles for an insolvency practitioner to participate in a protocol concerning coordination of proceedings in a group insolvency scenario.[50] To the extent that insolvency practitioners have a rather independent position and possess wide discretion to make business decisions to maximize insolvency estate value, they should be free to negotiate and conclude an insolvency agreement. The only limitation seems to be that such an agreement must comply with the formal administration rules and procedures established by the Bankruptcy Act 1987. In particular, an insolvency practitioner shall comply with reporting obligations to creditors and the supervisory authority.

9.21 French law provides detailed rules for engagement in transnational insolvency communication and conclusion of insolvency protocols.[51] It requires an insolvency practitioner to inform the supervising judge (*juge commissaire*) of any requests for cooperation and communication that he or she has received from a foreign insolvency practitioner, whether appointed in proceedings concerning the same debtor or a member of an enterprise group, opened in another Member State by virtue of Articles 41 and 56 EIR Recast. Permission of the supervising judge is required for authority to communicate confidential information to any practitioner in such proceedings, provided the debtor, any

49 G. Millqvist, 'Cross-border Insolvency Agreements – Protocols from a Swedish Perspective', *Essays in Honour of Michael Bogdan* (Juristförlaget, Lund, 2013), p. 334.

50 Ibid., p. 335.

51 These rules were introduced by way of Ordonnance n°2017-1519 du 2 novembre 2017 – art. 2.

other practitioner appointed in the same proceedings, the monitors (*contrôleurs*) and the Public Prosecutor are notified of the request for communication.[52] French law also requires an insolvency practitioner to submit for the supervising judge's approval any agreement or protocol that is proposed to be agreed by virtue of the same provisions of the Recast EIR in respect of the same debtor or another entity that is a member of the same group as the debtor.[53] As far as we are aware, the experience of entering into insolvency protocols in France predates the introduction of special rules, e.g. protocols in Sendo International Limited and Nortel Networks SA.[54]

When it comes to transnational cooperation in insolvency cases, Spanish law **9.22**
lays down a general cooperation duty between a Spanish insolvency practitioner and an insolvency practitioner appointed in a foreign proceeding concerning the same debtor. Insolvency practitioners shall cooperate in the exercise of their functions, under the supervision of their respective judges, courts or competent authorities.[55] The law adds that the refusal to cooperate by a foreign administrator or representative, or a foreign court or authority, should release the corresponding Spanish bodies from this duty.[56] Cross-border insolvency cooperation may also entail the approval by courts or competent authorities of agreements related to coordination of insolvency proceedings.[57] Thus, Spanish courts are legally entitled to approve insolvency protocols. However, this has not yet occurred.[58] In addition to insolvency-specific cooperation obligations (*lex specialis*), additional rules dealing with judicial communication may be found in the Law 29/2015 of 30 July 2015 (in force since 20 August 2015) on international legal cooperation in civil matters (*lex generalis*).[59] This law authorizes direct court-to-court communication without the involvement of an intermediary, but subject to the limits set in the respective jurisdictions and considerations related to preservation of judicial independence.[60] It is unclear to what extent these rules authorize conclusion

52 Commercial Code, Art. L695-2-I.

53 Ibid., Art. L695-2-II. See also CERIL Report 2018-1 on Insolvency Regulation (Recast) and National Procedural Rules, 4 June 2018, p. 13.

54 This protocol has been referred to in *Re Nortel Networks SA (No. 2)* [2010] B.C.C.21.

55 Ley 22/2003, de 9 de julio, Concursal, Artículo 227(1).

56 Ibid.

57 Ibid., Artículo 227(2)(3).

58 C. Umfreville et al., 'Recognition of UK Insolvency Proceedings Post-Brexit: The Impact of a "No Deal" Scenario' (2018) 27(3) *International Insolvency Review*, p. 440.

59 Ley 29/2015, de 30 de julio, de cooperación jurídica internacional en materia civil. Isidro notes that 'where the [Spanish] Insolvency Act does not provide a solution [the general law] may be resorted to as "common" law for cooperation in cross-border civil matters'. See B. Hess et al., *The Implementation of the New Insolvency Regulation: Improving Cooperation and Mutual Trust* (Nomos/Hart, 2018), p. 149.

60 Ibid., Art. 4.

and approval of insolvency protocols in the scenario of insolvency of a multinational enterprise group, exceeding the scope of the EIR Recast.

10

RECOMMENDATIONS FOR USE OF INSOLVENCY PROTOCOLS IN GROUP INSOLVENCIES

A. CIRCUMSTANCES SUPPORTING CONCLUSION OF PROTOCOLS 10.01

B. SECURING PROTECTION OR BEST REALIZATION OF VALUABLE ASSETS 10.05

C. PARTICIPATION RIGHTS AND FACILITATION OF GROUP REORGANIZATION PLANS 10.13
1. Right to appear and be heard in group insolvency 10.13
2. Negotiation and implementation of group reorganization plans 10.17

D. TREATMENT OF CLAIMS 10.23
1. Resolution of intra-group claims 10.23
2. Agreement concerning common set of financial accounting records 10.28
3. Special intercompany claim resolution mechanism 10.30
4. Agreements addressing coordination of claims and transactions 10.36
(a) Jurisdictional agreements for claims against debtor(s) 10.37
(b) Jurisdictional agreements for certain (future) transactions 10.45
(c) Arrangements coordinating filing of claims 10.49

E. SUPPLEMENTING EXISTING COOPERATION FRAMEWORKS 10.54
1. Group centralization and group governance in insolvency 10.57
2. Structuring of court-to-court communication 10.71

A. CIRCUMSTANCES SUPPORTING CONCLUSION OF PROTOCOLS

Cross-border insolvency protocols may not be appropriate for every situation. **10.01** Negotiation of a protocol takes time and resources, both financial and intellectual. A protocol does not by itself guarantee the improvement of efficiency in the administration of cross-border insolvency proceedings. This is why, for instance, the EIR Recast lays down that cooperation should only be sought if such cooperation is appropriate to facilitate the effective administration of insolvency proceedings related to two or more members of a group of companies. Conclusion of an insolvency protocol may be less justified if it does not help preserve group synergies due to the decentralized character of an enterprise group, absence of intra-group operational and financial links, and separate and independent existence of group members. Adoption of an insolvency protocol may also be less justified in a situation where the interests of group members diverge to the extent that they cannot be reconciled. For example, where communication and cooperation are restricted by law due to the abundance of conflicts or conflicts of interest (e.g. as a result of the variety of disputes arising from related-party transactions), entering into an insolvency protocol may not lead to the expected results. In any case, an insolvency protocol cannot resolve the unresolvable and can only succeed in the environment of trust and openness.

10.02 To the contrary, if prior to financial distress an enterprise group has existed close to or merely as a single economic enterprise with an integrated business model and close operational and financial ties (e.g. facilitated by intra-group financial arrangements, such as intra-group loans, cross-guarantees, cash pooling or dependent supply-chains), the adoption of an insolvency protocol can bring significant benefits. Such benefits are manifold.

10.03 First, an insolvency protocol can lead to the preservation and maximization of the overall group insolvency estate value, as opposed to the alternative entity-by-entity asset liquidation value.[1] It may help safeguard key production assets and ensure continuous operational activity of the group and performance under existing contracts (i.e. thus helping avoid defaults and cross-defaults). Second, an insolvency protocol may lead to the reduction of costs by preventing disputes between IPs and bringing down administration expenses.[2] In the European context, this may result in the elaboration of rules contained in the EIR Recast. Protocols can also be a valuable alternative to unpopular synthetic proceedings.[3] Third, an insolvency protocol might facilitate business rescue and restructuring to the extent that it can coordinate the adoption of reorganization plans in a synchronized fashion. This is particularly valuable where national insolvency law regimes lack detailed rules on transnational cooperation and recognition of foreign insolvencies. If permitted under applicable national rules, an insolvency protocol might fill the gaps in international insolvency law and establish the framework similar to that offered by the

1 A good example or a success story is the Nortel protocol (dealing with communication and cooperation) and the Nortel Allocation protocol which governed the trial on asset allocation. In the case *In re Nortel Networks, Inc.*, 532 BR 494 Bankr. D. Del. 2015, the court noted that:

> where, as here, operating entities in an integrated, multi-national enterprise developed assets in common and there is nothing in the law or facts giving any of those entities certain and calculable claims to the proceeds from the liquidation of those assets in an enterprise-wide insolvency, adopting a pro rata allocation approach, which recognizes inter-company and settlement related claims and cash in hand, yields the most acceptable result.

2 Practice Guide (in footnote 17) gives an example of the Everfresh protocol. It has been estimated that this protocol, by involving the creditors and restraining unsecured creditors from taking detrimental actions, has led to the enhancement of value in the order of 40 per cent.

3 B. Hess et al., *The Implementation of the New Insolvency Regulation: Improving Cooperation and Mutual Trust* (Nomos/Hart, 2018), p. 170.

Model Law 1997 and the Model Law 2019.[4] Importantly, it can be much more geared to the specific needs of participating stakeholders and the peculiarities of the proceedings or the nature of certain businesses of stakeholders (e.g. in the airline industry, the energy sector or industrial manufacturing).

The sections below review the examples of provisions or clauses which can be considered for inclusion in insolvency protocols to achieve the above benefits. At the same time, in practice they should be adjusted to particular facts and needs of the case, and to guarantee their compliance with relevant law. While the selected provisions do not aim to be comprehensive or exhaustive, they address some of the pertinent issues or problems arising in the context of enterprise group insolvency. **10.04**

B. SECURING PROTECTION OR BEST REALIZATION OF VALUABLE ASSETS

An insolvency protocol can be used as a tool to preserve certain assets, which are valuable for the group business or for survival of certain group members. In this respect, the EIR Recast establishes that an insolvency practitioner appointed in insolvency proceedings opened in respect of a member of a group of companies may, to the extent appropriate to facilitate the effective administration of the proceedings, request a stay of any measure related to the realization of the assets in the proceedings opened with respect to any other member of the same group.[5] This is possible in the context of adoption and implementation of a restructuring plan for all or some group members. Importantly, should the conditions for a stay be satisfied, the court is under an obligation to impose it (i.e. the court 'shall'). **10.05**

A similar but more detailed and less prescriptive (i.e. the court 'may') provision can be found in the Model Law 2019, which recognizes that: **10.06**

4 See Webinar 'Cross Border Insolvency: Should India adopt the UNCITRAL Model Law?', organized by the UNCITRAL Regional Centre for Asia and the Pacific (RCAP), the UNCITRAL National Coordination Committee for India (UNCCI), and the Manav Rachna University in July 2020, at https://www.youtube.com/watch?v=t35iAJo_nLA. At the webinar Sumant Batra, who represented the Dutch IP in India, commented on how the Jet Airways protocol was inspired by the framework of the Model Law 1997 and how it tried to replicate this framework by way of a protocol, in a situation where neither of the participating states had a developed legal system for dealing with international insolvencies. See also L. Viswanathan and D. Kumar, 'Cross-border Insolvency Protocols: A New Beginning in India' (2020) 17(2) *International Corporate Rescue*, p. 95, submitting that the Jet Protocol echoes the principles and methods of the UNCITRAL Model Law.

5 EIR Recast, Art. 60(1).

> To the extent needed to preserve the possibility of developing or implementing a group insolvency solution or to protect, preserve, realize or enhance the value of assets of an enterprise group member [...] the court, at the request of the group representative, may grant any appropriate relief, including:
>
> (a) Staying execution against the assets of the enterprise group member;
> (b) Suspending the right to transfer, encumber, or otherwise dispose of any assets of the enterprise group member;
> (c) Staying the commencement or continuation of individual actions or individual proceedings concerning the assets, rights, obligations, or liabilities of the enterprise group member;
> [...]
> (g) Approving arrangements concerning the funding of the enterprise group member and authorizing the provision of finance under those funding arrangements;[6]

10.07 Despite the fact that the EIR Recast may be inapplicable to a particular case at hand and the Model Law 2019 has not yet been transposed in any jurisdiction, the mentioned relief can prove indispensable for efficient handling of integrated groups of companies in insolvency. In its less prescriptive form ('may') or as a statement of intentions ('the parties should endeavour to') such a relief may be included in an insolvency protocol, as an extension of the duty to communicate and cooperate to the maximum extent possible.

10.08 The provisions aimed at asset preservation can be found in the Lehman Brothers protocol, which should serve as an inspiration for future protocols. It provides as follows:

> If, in the course of a Proceeding, an Official Representative learns or believes that another Debtor could have a material interest in a particular asset whose value and/or recovery is at risk, such Official Representative may notify the Official Representative of the Debtor whose estate includes such asset and, where practicable and consistent with the duties of such Official Representative under applicable laws, the Official Representative of the Debtor whose estate includes such asset should consult with the Official Representative of the Debtor that may have such material interest prior to: (i) the sale, abandonment, or any disposition of such asset; (ii) the termination, suspension, or other transition of any employees managing such asset; or (iii) the commencement of any judicial, or non-judicial, proceeding affecting such asset.[7]

10.09 It may also be reasonable to define which assets are considered material, and subsequently set a separate regime for their treatment, including, inter alia, the requirement to notify insolvency practitioners in other proceedings before their disposal and/or get the necessary court approval. For example, the

---

6 Model Law 2019, Art. 20(1).

7 Lehman Brothers protocol, para. 7.2.

InverWorld protocol defines Material Assets as 'assets outside of Counterparty Accounts that have a gross estimated market value of $1,000,000.00 (US) or more'.[8] The assets with the value below that are considered Non-Material Assets. Another example is the Solv-Ex protocol, which determined that 'a material asset shall be an asset having realizable value to the Corporations in excess of $40,000 (US) or the equivalent amount in Canadian currency'.[9] While the market value of an asset can serve as an indicator of its 'materiality', it does not necessarily correspond to its real value and significance for the operation of a particular enterprise group. Thus, one needs to be mindful when determining the parameters of materiality. Regarding the manner of treatment of Material Assets, the InverWorld protocol lays down the approval requirements depending on the location of a material asset,[10] as well as certain notification obligations.[11]

Insolvency protocols rarely address the issue of intra-group rescue financing. The Lehman Brothers protocol is one of the few protocols recognizing that in certain situations one group member may be incentivized to extend rescue financing to another group entity to preserve the latter's sound operations or to ensure that certain key assets held by that group member are not disposed of and do not decline in value. In this respect the protocol maintains that: **10.10**

> [...] the Official Representative of the Funding Estate may wish to provide funding towards the asset held by the Funded Estate in order to preserve and maximize its realizable value. In such event, the Official Representative of the Funded Estate may, subject to applicable laws, allow such funding to be provided on mutually acceptable bilateral terms.[12]

The above provision on intra-group financing may be especially warranted in groups where one or several entities act as banks for other group members (e.g. as a result of physical cash pooling, as was the case in the Lehman Brothers group) or are established as special purpose financing vehicles attracting funding on capital markets for the benefit of other entities (e.g. operating companies) within an enterprise group. If properly implemented, intra-group rescue financing could lead to an efficient allocation of assets and liquidity in **10.11**

8 InverWorld protocol, para. 5.

9 Solv-Ex protocol, para. 3(a). The parties agreed that there should be no sale or disposition of material assets without approval of both of the US and Canadian courts.

10 InverWorld protocol, paras 7 and 8.

11 Ibid, paras 15–18.

12 Lehman Brothers protocol, para. 7.4.

the group.[13] Approval of a protocol by courts and/or creditors can reduce the risks of such intra-group support transactions being challenged and avoided in the future. It can also make intra-group financing more transparent.

10.12 Prescribing specific rights and duties related to protection and value maximization of certain assets may contribute to efficient group restructuring (see Box 10.1). However, arguably, granting of certain rights and powers to insolvency practitioners and other parties under the protocol may cause reasonable concerns as to its compatibility with applicable national law. To address them, the Lehman Brothers protocol incorporated a 'saving clause', stipulating that: 'Where applicable, compliance with sections 7.2. through 7.6. by Official Representatives is subject to approval from their respective Tribunals or Committees, as the case may be under local law.'[14]

Box 10.1 Assets

To the extent justified by the integrated and interdependent operation of group members, and subject to applicable law of jurisdictions involved, an insolvency protocol should prescribe cooperation duties for insolvency practitioners and relief targeted at preservation of certain assets. Cooperation duties may be described in general terms, as in the case of Madoff Investment Securities:

> To the extent appropriate having regard to their respective duties under applicable law, and to the extent that a Representative learns or believes that the other representative may have a material interest in a particular asset, the Representatives shall coordinate and cooperate expeditiously with each other regarding the identification, preservation and realization of that asset.[1]

A protocol may establish or elaborate additional duties (e.g. duty to notify other IPs before disposing of certain assets or establishing security rights over them) and rights of insolvency practitioners (e.g. right to request a stay of execution against assets of another enterprise group member or an approval of intra-group financing to preserve such assets). The application of these rights and duties may be restricted to 'material'

13 A number of guidelines produced by standard-setting organizations encourage granting of financial assistance to a distressed group member by another group member, itself in distress. For example, the World Bank stipulates that the insolvency system should 'permit an enterprise group member subject to insolvency proceedings to provide or facilitate post-commencement finance or other kind of financial assistance to other enterprises in the group which are also subject to insolvency proceedings'. See World Bank Principles, C16.2. Similarly, UNCITRAL accepts that insolvency law should permit an enterprise group member subject to insolvency proceedings to advance post-commencement finance or grant a security interest/ provide a guarantee to another enterprise group member subject to insolvency proceedings. Legislative Guide 2010, Recommendations 211–213.

14 Lehman Brothers protocol, para. 7.6.

assets as defined in a protocol by way of reference to their market price and/or group-specific criteria (e.g. interest in such assets from one or more entities in the group).

Note:
1. Madoff protocol, para. 6.1.

C. PARTICIPATION RIGHTS AND FACILITATION OF GROUP REORGANIZATION PLANS

1. Right to appear and be heard in group insolvency

Participation rights are to be considered a precondition necessary for the development of any group insolvency solution. In this respect, the EIR Recast obliges insolvency practitioners to consider whether possibilities exist for restructuring insolvent group members and prescribes coordination with regard to the proposal and negotiation of a coordinated restructuring plan.[15] To facilitate such cooperation, the EIR Recast grants insolvency practitioners participation rights.[16] It also provides that all or some of the insolvency practitioners may agree to give additional powers to an insolvency practitioner appointed in one of the proceedings where such an agreement is permitted by the rules applicable to each of the proceedings. Additionally, insolvency practitioners may agree on the allocation of certain tasks amongst them.[17] **10.13**

The Model Law 2019 promotes cooperation between insolvency practitioners and courts with respect to the development and implementation of a group insolvency solution,[18] which extends to a proposal or set of proposals or options for reorganization, sale or liquidation of some or all of the assets and operations of one or more enterprise group members. It does so by establishing that an enterprise group member 'has the right to appear, make written submissions and be heard in [insolvency] proceeding on matters affecting that enterprise group member's interests and to take part in the development and implementation of a group insolvency solution'.[19] In principle, participation is not restricted to insolvent group members, since the engagement of solvent group members may be necessary for the realization of a group turnaround strategy or **10.14**

15 EIR Recast, Art. 56(2)(c).
16 Ibid., Art. 60(1)(a).
17 Ibid., Art. 56(2).
18 Model Law 2019, Art. 15(e).
19 Ibid., Art. 18(4).

sale of business as a going concern.[20] The Model Law 2019 also lays down that a 'participating enterprise group member shall be notified of actions taken with respect to the development of a group insolvency solution'.[21]

10.15 Chapter 8 above discussed the right to appear and to be heard. It concluded that many insolvency protocols contain provisions, allowing insolvency practitioners to participate in insolvency proceedings opened with respect to other enterprise group members. The exact scope of participation rights may be detailed in a protocol (e.g. whether a foreign insolvency practitioner is authorized to attend creditors' meetings) and should be consistent with the law applicable to each of the proceedings concerned (see Box 10.2). For the most part, the analysed protocols use general wording, when describing participation rights. For example, the Lehman Brother protocol provides that:

> Subject to the laws of each Forum, Official Representatives shall have the right to appear in all of the Proceedings, whether before a Tribunal or in statutory meetings convened pursuant to applicable law. If required and available in a particular Forum, an exequatur or similar proceeding may be utilized to implement recognition of the Official Representative.[22]

10.16 The InverWorld protocol, extending to three jurisdictions (the USA, England and the Cayman Islands) establishes that the 'Cayman Liquidators, the English Provisional Liquidators, and the SEC Receivers and any other representative that may be appointed [...] shall receive and give notice of all proceedings in accordance with the practices of the respective Courts and have the right to appear in all proceedings in any forum'.[23]

Box 10.2 Participation rights

Insolvency protocols seek to promote cooperation between insolvency practitioners for the purpose of improving administration of insolvency proceedings. They should therefore authorize cross-procedural participation by insolvency practitioners, allowing them to influence negotiations, to convey and test certain ideas, to communicate with creditors in various jurisdictions, to present and explain plans for group reorganization or liquidation to relevant persons or bodies. If permitted by applicable law and if justified by the group's organizational and financial structure, participation rights should be extended to solvent group members, and may cover attendance of court hearings and creditors' meetings.

20 Guide to Model Law 2019, para. 110.
21 Model Law 2019, Art. 18(5).
22 Lehman Brothers protocol, para. 3.1. See also Madoff protocol, para. 3.1.
23 InverWorld protocol, para. 14.

2. Negotiation and implementation of group reorganization plans

Efficient administration of insolvency proceedings related to two or more members of a group of companies operating in several jurisdictions may require the adoption of a coherent group-wide reorganization strategy and reorganization plan(s) aimed at business rescue. However, taking into account the separate and independent character of insolvency proceedings opened against group entities (entity-by-entity approach) in each jurisdiction involved, realization of such a strategy or a plan can face various practical and legal obstacles. Practical difficulties include avoidance of any contradictions and negotiation of substantially similar or complementary reorganization plans by insolvency practitioners. Legal complications involve the need to approve reorganization plans separately for each group entity in the respective proceedings, likely subject to different approval requirements. While insolvency protocols cannot completely change the dominant entity-by-entity approach, they can prove necessary in establishing the structured dialogue between insolvency proceedings[24] and in aligning the content of reorganization plans.[25] **10.17**

A few protocols prescribe coordination in the adoption of reorganization plans. For example, the Everfresh protocol states: **10.18**

> To the extent permitted by the laws of the respective jurisdictions and to the extent practicable, the Interim Receiver and the Debtor shall endeavor to submit a proposal in Canada and a plan of reorganization in the United States substantially similar to each other and the Debtors, the Interim Receiver and the Trustee shall endeavor to coordinate all procedures in connection therewith [...]. In order to coordinate the contemporaneous filing of the Proposal and the plan of reorganization, the Debtors shall take the actions necessary to seek extensions from time-to-time of the date for the filing of the Proposal.[26]

The Lehman Brothers protocol contains a similar provision: **10.19**

---

24 On the dialogic aspect of soft law instruments, see J. Pottow, 'The Dialogic Aspect of Soft Law in International Insolvency: Discord, Digression, and Development' (2019) 40(3) *Michigan Journal of International Law*, pp. 479–504, highlighting more generally how soft law instruments seek to further a conversation in a context where there is not yet uniform consensus.

25 Some insolvency protocols point out that they have been developed to harmonize and coordinate proceedings, minimize and avoid duplication of activities in parallel insolvency proceedings. See protocols in Pioneer Companies (para. 5), AIOC (para. E), Commodore (para. E), InverWorld (Purpose of Stipulation).

26 Everfresh protocol, para. 13. See also AgriBioTech Canada protocol, sec. 5.01. See also Livent protocol, stipulating that 'to the extent permitted by the laws of the respective jurisdictions and to the extent practicable and procedurally applicable, the plan(s) of arrangement filed by Livent in each proceeding will be substantially similar to each other'. See also Solv-Ex protocol, para. 9, providing that 'the Corporations shall submit a plan of arrangement in Canada and a plan of reorganization in the United States substantially similar to each other'.

> Where applicable and permitted under the law of the Forum in a proceeding, Official Representatives should endeavor to submit a winding-up plan, plan of reorganization or liquidation, or deed of company arrangement (a 'Plan') in their respective proceedings, or to amend a Plan once submitted (to the extent permitted by applicable law) so that each Official Representative's Plan is consistent with Plans filed by other Official Representatives.[27]

10.20 Insolvency practitioners may also provide certain undertakings in order to ensure implementation of common strategies and to avoid disruption of group reorganization. For that purpose, some protocols contain provisions related to commencement of insolvency proceedings with respect to other enterprise group members and other group-related coordination-driven clauses (see Box 10.3 below).

10.21 For example, the Maxwell protocol lays down that the Joint Administrators (UK) of the debtor shall give prior notice to the Examiner (USA) and shall, in good faith, attempt to obtain the consent of the Examiner prior to: commencing insolvency proceedings (whether in the USA or elsewhere) against members of the M&O Group; causing any member of the M&O Group to borrow funds; causing any member of the M&O Group to pledge or charge any assigns; causing any member of the M&O Group to sell or dispose of any share or other assets outside the ordinary course of business.[28] Despite the fact that the cross-border agreement in *Maxwell* was reached in the proceedings concerning a single debtor, it has effectively established a framework for the resolution of the whole group. This cooperation-based framework, bringing group-significant actions into the spotlight, can in principle be adopted in a situation where insolvency proceedings relate to two or more members of a group of companies.

10.22 Another example is the AIOC protocol. In that case it was agreed that each party (i.e. the US Chapter 11 trustee and the Swiss Bankruptcy Office):

> shall attempt in good faith to obtain the consent of the other Party prior to taking any of the following actions: 1. disposing of shares or interests in any entity [in the group]; 2. seeking or consenting to the substantive consolidation (or merger, if applicable) [of the debtor with any other entity]; 3. causing [the debtor] or entity in [the group] to take any action which is intended to or the reasonably anticipated consequences of which would have a material adverse impact on any member of [the group].[29]

---

27 Lehman Brothers protocol, para. 10.1.

28 Maxwell protocol, para. G(2). See also para. G(6), confirming the objective of the parties to provide for essentially similar arrangements with respect to the M&O Group and to be consulted with respect to and be involved in the formulation and negotiation of any plan of reorganization.

29 AIOC protocol, para. III(B). See also paras V(A) and VI(A).

Box 10.3 Reorganization and liquidation plans

Insolvency protocols can prove indispensable for aligning the content of reorganization or liquidation plans and for coordinating the timing of their adoption in separate proceedings concerning enterprise group members. If justified by the facts of the case, the parties should agree to (attempt or endeavour to) submit reorganization or liquidation plans that are principally aligned or are substantially similar to each other. An insolvency protocol may request that courts, in addressing the issues related to a plan confirmation, should, as far as possible seek and take into account the views of other courts and participants. To that end, courts may coordinate the timing of such confirmation or engage in a joint hearing.

An insolvency protocol may establish rules ensuring that negotiations of reorganization or liquidation plans and their subsequent implementation are not disrupted by uncoordinated actions of insolvency practitioners or creditors. In this respect, a protocol may prescribe that, to the extent appropriate and permitted under applicable law, certain actions should be taken by insolvency practitioners or creditors with prior notice and consultation/approval. These actions may include, among others:

(i) Commencement of insolvency or liquidation proceedings against other group members
(ii) Significant borrowing;
(iii) Causing a group member to pledge material assets;
(iv) Causing a group member to dispose of shares in other group members outside the ordinary course of business;
(v) Initiating liability claims against directors of other members of the enterprise group;
(vi) Taking action regarding contracts (e.g. contract termination) that can substantially harm the operation of the group, or a part of the group.

D. TREATMENT OF CLAIMS

1. Resolution of intra-group claims

Resolution of intra-group claims is probably one of the most contentious aspects in group insolvencies. The complexities arising from intra-group transactions are manifold. **10.23**

First, proper documentation of all intra-group transactions may be lacking, incomplete or scattered over several systems of contract documentation, making it extremely difficult to ascertain how much entities within the group owe to each other, and who exactly owes what to whom. Besides, intra-group **10.24** transactions can reach a substantial volume and be of informal nature that renders their policing in and outside insolvency even more complicated.[30] Moreover, cross-border intra-group transactions as part of a regional or global supply chain will typically involve complex tax issues, including value-added tax (VAT) and capital gains tax (CGT).

10.25 Second, depending on applicable law, intra-group transactions may be considered related-party transactions, subject to special avoidance provisions as undervalue, fraudulent or preferential transactions.[31] This has the potential of creating additional grounds for time-consuming and costly litigation, delaying the adoption of reorganization or liquidation plans and further depleting the insolvency estates of group entities concerned, ultimately resulting in value destruction.

10.26 Third, enforcement of cross-guarantees and collateral arrangements might serve as an obstacle to a successful group reorganization, since restructuring of financial obligations of one entity does not necessarily protect it from 'ricochet' (e.g. subrogation) claims pursuant to intra-group cross-liability arrangements.[32] The existence and scope of such claims in case the original debt is restructured (e.g. decreased, postponed) or written down may differ depending on applicable law, the character of discharge (voluntary/involuntary) and the nature of debt restructuring (pre-insolvency contractual or insolvency court-led restructuring). Additionally, most commonly, insolvency of the principal debtor does not affect the rights of creditors against guarantors, collateral providers or co-debtors.[33] Thus, even if debts of one group entity are restructured, this leaves other group entities exposed to creditors' claims. As a

30 J. Dammann, 'Related Party Transactions and Intragroup Transactions', in L. Enriques and T.H. Tröger, *The Law and Finance of Related Party Transactions* (CUP, 2019), p. 232.

31 G. McCormack et al., 'Study on a New Approach to Business Failure and Insolvency', 2016, p. 142, pointing out that nearly all EU Member States take a different approach to transactions with parties connected or related to the debtor company in some way. K. van Zwieten, 'Related Party Transactions in Insolvency', in Enriques and Tröger, ibid., p. 262, noting that the common feature of insolvency avoidance is the relaxation of substantive and/or procedural rules in cases where the counterparty is a related party. See also CERIL Report 201871 on Transactions Avoidance Laws, 26 September 2017, para. 24, stating that many European laws provide reduced protection for insiders.

32 See 11 U.S. Code § 509, providing that 'an entity that is liable with the debtor on, or that has secured, a claim of a creditor against the debtor, and that pays such claim, is subrogated to the rights of such creditor to the extent of such payment'. See also *Re Butlers Wharf Ltd.* [1995] 2 B.C.L.C. 43, [1995] B.C.C. 717, stating that subrogation in the case of guarantees 'is and has for over 150 years been part of English law and to such an extent that it has been given statutory clothing in s. 5 of the Mercantile Law Amendment Act 1856'.

33 Insolvency Act (Spain), Art. 135(1); German Insolvency Code (*Insolvenzordnung*), § 254(2); Dutch Bankruptcy Act (*Faillissementswet*), Art. 160, clarifying that notwithstanding the restructuring of debts in the proceedings against the debtor, creditors retain all their rights against the guarantors and co-debtors of the debtor.

result, group reorganization might be fruitless, since a successful restructuring of a group entity may require preservation of group synergies and survival of other group members. A debtor may need their assistance to both effect its reorganization and continue its operational activity in the future.[34]

Insolvency protocols – rather evidently – cannot fully replace the legal mechanism for resolution of intercompany claims. They can, however, streamline such process, making it more expedient and cost-efficient, and reducing the need for protracted value-destroying litigation over such claims. Following the analysis of protocols, we have found at least three types of arrangements addressing inter-company financial relations. These include: **10.27**

- Agreement on a common set of financial accounting records;
- Special intercompany claim resolution mechanism; and
- Jurisdictional agreements, outlining the agreed (exclusive) jurisdiction for resolution of intercompany claims and sometimes regulating applicable law.

2. Agreement concerning common set of financial accounting records

As explained in the Motion for the approval of the Lehman Brothers protocol, **10.28** '[o]ver many years [...] the relationships among the Debtors and Foreign Debtors have developed into a complex web of financial balances documented and managed through Lehman's integrated systems so as to allow Lehman to operate its global business seamlessly, quickly, and efficiently'.[35] Upon Lehman's insolvency filing, highly contentious disputes arose between members of the Lehman Brothers group of companies as to the nature and validity of intercompany claims and the enforceability of asserted guarantee claims by affiliates against LBHI as the principal debtor or guarantor. In order to avoid unnecessary intercompany litigation and to untangle the web of intercompany relationships and attempt to reconcile intercompany claims, the protocol has provided for special rules applicable to the treatment of intercompany claims, which have been referred to as 'the heart of the Protocol'.[36] In particular, it noted that:

> [...] resources and time should not be spent reviewing historical intercompany accounting records to resolve claims asserted in their respective Proceedings [...]; but

34 ABI Commission to Study the Reform of Chapter 11, Final Report and Recommendations, 2014, p. 255.

35 Debtor's Motion Pursuant to Section 105 and 363 of the Bankruptcy Code for Approval of a Cross-Border Insolvency Protocol, *In re Lehman Brothers Holdings Inc.*, No. 08-13555 (Bankr. S.D.N.Y. May 26, 2009), para. 23.

36 Ibid., para. 22.

that rather, it is in the best interests of the Debtors' creditors for Official Representatives to agree to a common set of financial accounting records that form the basis of Intercompany Claims, and that those financial records shall be *prima facie* valid unless there are elements of proof suggesting that a transaction was recorded in error, or that no such transaction ever occurred or it is inconsistent with the inter-company accounting records of the relevant Debtor(s).[37]

10.29 Negotiations over the protocol have resulted in the Global Close Balance Sheet, which was prepared between November 2008 and January 2009. This Global Close played an important role as it 'represented the last consolidated set of books and records of the Lehman Group prior to insolvency'.[38]

3. Special intercompany claim resolution mechanism

10.30 Among the mechanisms that can be implemented by insolvency practitioners to facilitate efficient administration of insolvency proceedings in enterprise groups, the Model Law 2019 mentions the '[u]se of mediation or, with consent of the parties, arbitration, to resolve disputes between enterprise group members concerning claims'.[39] UNCITRAL Practice Guide also supports the idea of establishing a special tribunal or committee to deal with disputes concerning certain claims, such as intercompany claims, or of an arbitration panel to handle issues that could otherwise involve difficult and uncertain questions of conflict of laws or choice of forum.[40]

10.31 The creation of such alternative mechanisms for resolution of inter-company disputes may contribute to efficiency and cost-saving, especially when parties can discuss and agree on the law according to which the dispute should be resolved, and to address potential problems regarding document production (i.e. issues of confidentiality and privilege). Nevertheless, in Europe mediation and arbitration are rarely used as a tool to assist insolvency proceedings.[41] This is in stark contrast to the USA, where mediation is frequently used in

37 Lehman Brothers protocol, para. 9.1. Under the protocol, insolvency practitioners also agreed to negotiate in good faith to attempt to reach a consensual resolution of any differences in their accounting of intercompany claims (para. 9.2.).

38 A. Lehavi, *Property Law in a Globalized World* (CUP, 2019), p. 269.

39 Model Law 2019, Art. 10(h).

40 Practice Guide, Ch. III, para. 72.

41 See Report from the Commission to the European Parliament, the Council and the European Economic and Social Committee on the application of Directive 2008/52/EC of the European Parliament and of the Council on certain aspects of mediation in civil and commercial matters, COM(2016) 542 final, para. 3.2., noting that '[o]ne area where mediation remains underdeveloped is that of insolvency proceedings.' However, mediation in matters of restructuring and insolvency is not unknown in the EU. For example, it occurs in Belgium and Spain and is provided for in the UK Chancery Guide. Read further B. Wessels and S. Madaus, 'Rescue of Business in Insolvency Law, Instrument of the European Law Institute', 2017, pp. 125–33.

insolvency procedures, including Chapter 11 cases.[42] It was contended that in the USA for complex multi-party restructuring, 'the use of mediation to reach consensual plans of reorganization, while not standard protocol in cases, has become common and is no longer controversial'.[43]

Some protocols include arrangements creating or offering an opportunity to create a special mediation- (or arbitration-) like mechanism aiding in resolution of intercompany claims. For instance, the Lehman Brothers protocol authorizes insolvency practitioners to establish a committee (referred to as the 'Procedures Committee'), whose members shall be jointly appointed by the insolvency practitioners and confirmed by courts (where applicable) to 'consensually resolve any differences in the accounting of Intercompany Claims'.[44] This Procedures Committee 'shall propose the (i) procedures, (ii) accounting methodologies, and (iii) elements of proof that it intends to use in its calculation and consensual resolution of Intercompany Claims'.[45] Among other things, the Procedures Committee shall measure and fix damages arising from rejection, termination or acceleration of intercompany derivative contracts.[46] After the Procedures Committee has agreed upon the accounting procedures and methodology for calculating derivatives-related damages, it was agreed that the insolvency practitioners shall, to the extent required by applicable law, seek courts' approval authorizing such procedures and methodology in the resolution of intercompany claims.[47] Essentially, a Procedures Committee constituted a mediation instrument tasked to assist parties in resolving certain disputes, which would otherwise be subject to full-scale litigation. **10.32**

It was reported that through multilateral meetings among Lehman's protocol members, a framework was developed and served as the basis for individualized bilateral settlement agreements, which were executed with affiliates in the UK, the Netherlands, Germany, Curaçao, Japan, Luxembourg, Hong Kong and Singapore.[48] According to Lehman's attorney Harvey Miller et al., such **10.33**

---

42 B. Wessels, 'Mediation in Restructuring and Insolvency', *Eurofenix*, Spring 2016, pp. 24–25. Cases in which mediation was used include, inter alia, insolvency of Residential Capital LLC, Cengage Learning Inc., Nortel Networks, Lehman Brothers, Radio Shack, Energy Future Holdings Corp. and Solar Millennium A.G.

43 J. Esher, 'Recent Use of Mediation for Resolution and Effective Management of Large Case Insolvencies' (2015) 12(6) *International Corporate Rescue*, p. 349.

44 Lehman Brothers protocol, para. 9.3.

45 Ibid., para. 9.4.

46 Ibid.

47 Ibid., para. 9.5.

48 H. Miller, L. Fife and M. Horwitz, In re Lehman Brothers Holdings Inc. From Chaos to Consensus, 22 June 2012, https://www.iiiglobal.org/sites/default/files/media/Miller_Fife_Horwitz_Lehmen_Bros_Holdings_From_Chaos_to_Consensus_0.pdf.

bilateral settlements resulted in '81% reduction of aggregate claims against Debtors (from $327.8B to $61.4B), including a reduction in guarantee claims from $223B to $11.2B'.[49]

10.34 The Madoff protocol stipulates that 'the Representatives shall cooperate and negotiate in good faith regarding any potential claims by either Debtor against the other Debtor' and at the appropriate stage 'the Representatives shall consider whether it is sensible to implement, subject to the approval of the Tribunals, a mechanism for resolution of intercompany claims'.[50] The protocol in the Payless Holdings LLC case contemplates the adoption of a specific claims protocol 'to address, among other things [...] the timing, process, jurisdiction and applicable governing law to be applied to the resolution of claims filed by the Debtors' creditors (including intercompany claims) in the Canadian Proceedings and the U.S. Proceedings'.[51] It further clarified that in such event, and 'in recognition of the inherent complexities of the intercompany claims that may be asserted in the Insolvency Proceedings, the Debtors shall submit a specific claims protocol'.[52]

10.35 It is argued that the success of mediated solutions in insolvency 'stems from facilitating parties' goals rather than simply evaluating the merits of their positions, [and in serving] the interests of all creditors for an expeditious resolution, rather than years of deadlocked litigation'.[53] We believe that insolvency protocols can promote the adoption of consensual mechanisms for efficient resolution of intercompany claims (see Box 10.4 below). In addition to intercompany/affiliate disputes, the use of mediation or arbitration should also be considered for disputes related to the allocation of assets between insolvency estates of enterprise group members and the allocation of enterprise group value following a coordinated sale of business (e.g. as it happened in the Nortel Networks case[54]), disputes concerning complex financial instruments

49 Ibid.

50 Madoff protocol, para. 7.1.

51 Protocol in Payless Holdings, para. 27.

52 Ibid.

53 B. Feder and D. Hahn, 'Mediation in Large Chapter 11 Cases', ABI Committee Newsletter, 2015, http://promo.abi.org/committees/newsletters/Mediation/vol2num3/feder.html.

54 In insolvency of Nortel Networks Limited (Canada) and a number of subsidiaries in the Nortel group in Canada, the USA and Europe, the Interim Funding and Settlement Agreement was negotiated in June 2009. Pursuant to this Settlement Agreement, the parties agreed that the sales proceeds should be deposited into an escrow account to be distributed upon (1) agreement by all of the selling debtors on a method of allocation, or (2) if the selling debtors could not agree, upon 'the determination of any dispute relating thereto by the relevant dispute resolver'. *Nortel Networks Corporation (Re)*, 2015 ONSC 2987, 12 May 2015. For discussion of Nortel insolvency, see J. Westbrook, 'Corporate Formalism in a Global Economy', in J. Sarra and B. Romaine (eds), *Annual Review of Insolvency Law* (Carswell, 2015), also available at

which would otherwise delay the bankruptcy process (e.g. derivatives transactions in case of Lehman Brothers,[55] clawback actions in the Madoff SIPA case), claim allowance disputes, negotiations over contentious or complex issues at creditors' meetings, seeking to align restructuring plans in parallel insolvency proceedings.[56]

Box 10.4 Resolution of intercompany claims

Resolution of intercompany claims very often constitutes a significant bottleneck for efficient administration of insolvency proceedings opened with respect to enterprise group members. Disputes around intercompany claims may concern their existence (and proof required), their validity, scope and amount (including currency and penalty issues), as well as the forum for their resolution and applicable law.

Insolvency protocols can be used as a practical tool to reduce related tension and deal with intra-group claims in an organized and expedient way. They can establish an agreement about a common set of financial accounting records to be relied on when calculating claims, the calculation methodology or the acceptance of certain rules of evidence with respect to such claims. They might also provide for a special mediation- or arbitration-like mechanism (e.g. by installing a claims committee) aiding parties and courts in resolution of intercompany claims. The establishment of such a mechanism may be particularly desirable where intercompany claims are complex and numerous and would result in the application of a myriad of different rules, leading to protracted and money-sucking litigation and bring about potentially contradictory judgments, or where adjudication of such claims requires special expertise (e.g. related to complex financial instruments). In addition to an insolvency protocol, stipulating the intention to create a special resolution mechanism, the parties may decide to conclude a separate claims protocol at a later stage.

Creation of a special aiding mechanism or a special resolution procedure for intercompany claims should, however, be formulated in such a way that it is in full compliance with applicable law of the relevant jurisdictions and should not deprive courts of their competence with respect to matters before them.

---

https://papers.ssrn.com/sol3/papers.cfm?abstract_id=2676232. See also L. Peacock, 'A Tale of Two Courts: The Nortel Cross-Border Bankruptcy Trial' (2015) 23 *American Bankruptcy Institute Law Review*, pp. 543–70.

55 *In re Lehman Bros. Holdings Inc.*, No. 08-13555 (SCC) (Bankr. S.D.N.Y. 2008).

56 E. Sussman and J. Gorskie, 'Capturing the Benefits of Arbitration for Cross Border Insolvency Disputes', in A. Rovine (ed.), *Contemporary Issues in International Arbitration and Mediation*, Martinus Nijhoff Publishers, (2013), pp. 158–72, discussing the categories of disputes in transnational insolvencies that could be best addressed by arbitration and mediation.

4. Agreements addressing coordination of claims and transactions

10.36 Many of the insolvency protocols analysed contain various types of agreements related to the treatment of claims and transactions. Such agreements may be divided into three categories: 1) arrangements establishing exclusive or alternative jurisdictions for claims against debtor(s), 2) arrangements for the approval of certain (future) transactions, and 3) arrangements facilitating coordination in filing of claims in several proceedings. We will now elaborate on each of these three categories.

(a) Jurisdictional agreements for claims against debtor(s)

10.37 A number of protocols contain jurisdictional agreements – agreements detailing the chosen exclusive or alternative jurisdiction for the resolution of claims against debtors, and sometimes, establishing governing substantive law. The idea behind such agreements is clear. Their provisions aim at bringing legal certainty around the claim resolution process by clarifying the proper jurisdiction and/or applicable law. They also seek to minimize transaction costs arising from the multiplicity of proceedings, duplication of efforts and irreconcilable judgments. Since most of the jurisdictional agreements do not single out specific claims, they should be able to extend to intercompany claims.

10.38 The UNCITRAL Practice Guide summarizes that the:

> responsibility for dealing with claims against the debtor may be allocated to the court of the State of which the debtor is a national, in which the claimants reside, are domiciled or carry on business and have offices or in which the claims arise from the supply of goods and/or services to the debtor, or according to the type of contract and the nationality of the contractual partner.[57]

The result is a multitude of possibly authorized courts. What is the experience from the set of protocols studied? A few examples follow.

10.39 The Pioneer protocol provides for a complex and elaborate arrangement, under which: (1) any claims against any of the Debtors arising under or in connection with the specifically identified contracts (e.g. notes and indentures, guarantees, loan agreements) shall be determined by the US Court in the US cases; (2) all claims against any of the US Debtors shall be determined by the US Court in the US cases; 3) all claims against the Canadian Debtor (with the exception of those mentioned under (1) shall be determined in accordance

57 Practice Guide, Ch. III, para. 62.

with certain principles, in fact establishing alternative jurisdiction, depending on the court in which a claim has been first filed.[58]

Another example is the Livent protocol, which states that: 10.40

> [US] Court will have jurisdiction over all claims asserted against Livent governed principally by the laws of the United States unless, with respect to any particular claim, the Canadian Court is a more appropriate forum in view of all the circumstances and that the Canadian Court will have jurisdiction over all claims asserted against Livent governed principally by the laws of Canada unless, with respect to any particular claim, the U.S. Court is a more appropriate forum in view of all the circumstances.[59]

The Lehman Brothers protocol also aims at decreasing the number of parallel filings by laying down the rule, under which: 10.41

> Where there are two or more Proceedings pending as to the same Debtor, those being one or more Plenary Proceedings and/or one or more Limited Proceedings, a claim should be filed only in the Proceeding(s) designated by the Official Representative of such Debtor (provided that certain Official Representatives may be required to make such designation in accordance with applicable law).[60]

The Solv-Ex protocol is more elaborate. It provides that quantification, allowance, classification and treatment of a claim in any plan or arrangement shall be dealt with in the Canadian proceedings under Canadian substantive and procedural law in the following circumstances. These are: (i) if a claim relates to the supply of goods and/or services directly to the debtors in Canada; (ii) if it arises from or in connection with a security right created under Canadian law; (iii) if it results from a tort committed in Canada; (iv) if it derives from a contract governed by Canadian law, etc.[61] In all other cases, unless a claim has a close connection with Canada, it must be resolved in the US proceedings and shall be governed by US substantive and procedural law.[62] In the Solv-Ex protocol it was also agreed that each 'individual claim shall be dealt with by one of the US or Canadian Courts, but not both'.[63] This arrangement seeks in simple but clear words to avoid duplicate filings. 10.42

58 Pioneer protocol, para. 10.

59 Livent protocol, cit. from L.W. Houlden and G. Morawetz, Bankruptcy & Insolvency Law Newsletters, November 16, 1999, Insolv. L. Nws. 1999-44.

60 Lehman Brothers protocol, para. 8.1.

61 Solv-Ex protocol, para. 6(a).

62 Ibid., para. 6(b).

63 Ibid., para. 6(g).

10.43 Very few protocols go beyond regulating jurisdiction for claim resolution and specify applicable law or a rule for its determination. We reviewed a number of such examples in Chapter 8, when discussing the limitations of insolvency protocols. For example, the protocol in AgriBioTech Canada contains a provision, under which claims against AgriBioTech Canada Inc. (ABTC) must be filed in Canada[64] and their validity and quantum 'shall be determined in accordance with the proper law governing the obligation underlying the claim'.[65] It also adds that the US Bankruptcy Code shall be the governing substantive law applicable to all transfers made to the entities located in the USA, while Canadian law shall apply to transfers made to the Canadian entities.[66] Another example is the AIOC protocol, which stipulates in rather broad terms that the 'claims reconciliation process shall be administered in accordance with the procedural and substantive laws (both bankruptcy and non-bankruptcy) governing the respective case in which the Party is appointed unless considerations of comity otherwise require'.[67]

10.44 In Chapter 8 above we noted that jurisdiction for claims against insolvent debtors and the respective rules governing the lodging, admission, verification of claims and distributions to be made may be imposed by insolvency law, often driven by the doctrine of *vis attractiva concursus*. This is why insolvency practitioners negotiating a protocol always need to make sure that jurisdictional agreements comply with applicable law (i.e. do not deprive courts of their jurisdiction) and do not violate creditors' rights (e.g. right to file claims in any proceeding, if applicable).

(b) Jurisdictional agreements for certain (future) transactions

10.45 Some of the reviewed insolvency protocols establish jurisdictional rules for future transactions, which can be entered into after insolvency proceedings have already been opened. The idea behind such agreements is to allocate the responsibilities among insolvency practitioners and courts to ensure efficient coordination of the proceedings, avoid overlaps and, possibly, to give a leading role to some of them in driving forward a group solution.[68] Thus, protocols may represent a consensus concerning group-wide (corporate) governance in insolvency.

---

64 AgriBioTech Canada protocol, sec. 4.01(a).

65 Ibid., sec. 4.01(b). This does not extend to issues of classification and priority of claims, which are to be determined in accordance with Canadian law. See sec. 4.01(c).

66 Ibid., sec. 8.01.

67 AIOC protocol, para. III(E)(1)(b).

68 The idea of role allocation between several insolvency proceedings in a group context is accepted in the EIR Recast, which recognizes that in order to facilitate information exchange, promote restructuring of group members and ensure coordination with regard to the proposal and negotiation of a coordinated restructuring

A good example is the Quebecor protocol. This protocol sets forth that all transactions outside the ordinary course of business for the sale, lease or use of property of the Canadian Debtor (Quebecor World Inc.), as well as all matters relating to the debtor-in-possession financing documents as they affect the Canadian Debtor shall be subject to the sole jurisdiction, direction and approval of the Canadian Court.[69] Importantly, these jurisdictional rules are also extended to transactions concerning any Non-Filing Subsidiaries, defined as subsidiaries controlled directly or indirectly by the Canadian Debtor, not parties to the insolvency proceedings.[70] And vice versa, transactions affecting the US Debtors should fall under the exclusive jurisdiction of the US Court. **10.46**

Provisions on the allocation of jurisdiction for the approval of certain transactions can be found in the Everfresh protocol, which links such jurisdiction to the place where a particular asset is manufactured, distributed or sold, as reflected in the debtor's books.[71] This jurisdiction should also determine the scheme for the distribution of proceeds from the respective transactions.[72] Another example is the Maxwell protocol, which contains detailed rules, covering rights and responsibilities regarding investigations into the financial dealing of the M&O Group members, disposition of shares in debtor's subsidiaries, filing of reorganization plans, etc.[73] As a result, the protocol allocates functions between the courts and provides for cooperative administration of the debtor and its group of companies under the lead of the UK administrators. **10.47**

As final examples, other protocols selecting jurisdiction for approval of certain transactions include InverWorld[74] and PSINet.[75] The latter is especially interesting, as it introduces a general rule that some so-called Cross-Border Matters should be resolved via joint hearings. Among such matters: (i) an allocation of proceeds between the US and Canadian Debtors; (ii) a reorganization plan involving both jurisdictions or entailing cross-border financial assistance; (iii) claims in respect of contracts in which one or more of the US Debtors share liability with one or more of the Canadian Debtors, either as joint or primary obligors, or as guarantors or sureties, etc.[76] The general rule is **10.48**

---

plan, IPs may agree to grant additional powers to an insolvency practitioner appointed in one of the proceedings or to allocate certain tasks amongst them. See EIR Recast, Art. 56(2).

69 Quebecor protocol, paras 22 and 23.

70 Ibid., para. 4.

71 Everfresh protocol, para. 6. The protocol defines 'Canadian Assets' and 'US Assets' in the Preamble.

72 Ibid., para. 10.

73 Maxwell protocol, para. G(4).

74 InverWorld protocol, para. 7.

75 PSINet protocol, paras 9–11.

76 Ibid., para. 9.

followed by the specific rules applicable to the matters not determined and resolved under a joint hearing.[77]

(c) Arrangements coordinating filing of claims

10.49 In the paragraphs above we noted that some insolvency protocols try to solve the coordination problem by prescribing a particular jurisdiction or jurisdictions for claims against the debtor(s). Nevertheless, in practice, it is almost unavoidable that the same claim is filed in multiple proceedings opened in different jurisdictions. Insolvency protocols often address this scenario and seek to coordinate filing of claims (Box 10.5 below). While not being specific to the group insolvency context, coordination of single-debtor filings can be conducive to reaching an efficient group solution, especially in a situation where main insolvency proceedings against group entities are concentrated in one jurisdiction, while secondary (non-main) proceedings cover other jurisdictions and could cause nuisance to a centralized group distress resolution.

10.50 One approach to contain multiple filings is to resort to 'synthetic' or 'reverse synthetic' proceedings, which seek to minimize the commencement of non-main or main insolvency proceedings respectively. This approach does not lead to the adoption of insolvency protocols in the traditional sense, since it altogether prevents the opening of insolvency proceedings.[78]

10.51 Another approach entails coordination in filing of claims to improve efficiency and avoid unequal, imbalanced, or unfair payments in violation of the 'hotchpot rule', introduced in Chapter 4 and already embraced by some of the early protocols. A more recent example is the Jet Airways protocol (2019), which explicitly recognizes that '[i]n order to ensure a complete and effective overview of claims and to enable each Party to fulfill his obligations, creditor claims should be submitted by the respective creditors in each Proceeding in accordance with the relevant applicable law'.[79] Each claim shall be exchanged, verified and accepted separately in each proceeding.[80] However, in order to streamline this process, the parties have agreed that the Indian Resolution Professional (RP) might be the best placed to investigate the admissibility of claims that were first submitted in the Indian Proceedings and that the Dutch

77 Ibid., para. 10.

78 While such proceedings are available both under the EIR Recast (Art. 36, only permitting 'synthetic' proceedings) and the Model Law 2019 (Arts 28 and 30), their use in practice remains limited. On the nature and operation of 'synthetic' proceedings see B. Wessels, 'Contracting Out of Secondary Insolvency Proceedings: The Main Liquidator's Undertaking in the Meaning of Article 18 in the Proposal to Amend the EU Insolvency Regulation' (2014) 9(1) *Brooklyn Journal of Corporate, Financial & Commercial Law*, pp. 63–110.

79 Jet Airways protocol, para. 9.1.1.

80 Ibid., paras 9.1.2. and 9.1.3.

Trustee might be the best placed to investigate the admissibility of claims first submitted in the Dutch Proceedings. Claims admitted in one proceeding may be 'randomly or otherwise, but *not unreasonably*', verified in another proceeding.[81] Thus, the protocol has effectively established the *prima facie* admissibility of claims, previously admitted in another (main or non-main) proceeding. This is a practical solution as it saves the parties from the need to do the duplicate work of claim verification, while leaving the window open for such verification, when justified by the facts of the case.

Another protocol containing elaborate provisions related to the treatment of claims lodged by creditors in parallel proceedings is the Sendo protocol. Among other things, this protocol confirmed the right of creditors to file their claims in both main (the UK) and secondary (France) proceedings[82] – the right then guaranteed by the EIR 2000 and now by the EIR Recast.[83] Like the Jet Airways protocol, the Sendo protocol also dealt with the exchange of claims between insolvency proceedings. In this respect, it is worth noting that both the EIR 2000 and the EIR Recast provide that insolvency practitioners in the main and any secondary insolvency proceedings shall lodge in other proceedings claims which have already been lodged in the proceedings for which they were appointed (sometimes called a system of multi-cross-border filings), provided that the interests of creditors in the latter proceedings are served by doing so.[84] Considering the lack of assets in the secondary proceeding, the Sendo protocol released the main insolvency practitioner from an obligation to lodge the received and accepted claims in the secondary proceeding, because such a lodgement would not further the interests of creditors in such proceedings.[85] Thus, we conclude, the protocol adjusted the operation of the EIR 2000 to the reality of a particular insolvency situation. **10.52**

81 Ibid., para. 9.1.4.

82 Sendo protocol, sec. I-2.

83 EIR 2000, Art. 32(1) and EIR Recast, Art. 45(1). Fletcher accepted that the fact that all creditors may file their claims in all insolvency proceedings 'may engender considerable administrative complexity in cross-accounting and record keeping'. See I. Fletcher, 'The European Union Convention on Insolvency Proceedings: An Overview and Comment, with U.S. Interest in Mind' (1997) 23 *Brooklyn Journal of International Law*, p. 44. In this respect, Wessels notes that Art. 45 EIR Recast is one of the most problematic articles in the EIR Recast. He suggests that insolvency practitioners should discuss measures to simplify the administration of claims and distributions of dividends. B. Wessels, *International Insolvency Law Part II. European Insolvency Law, Volume X* (4th edn, Wolters Kluwer, 2017), 10858. For this purpose, insolvency protocols may be utilized. Besides the Sendo protocol, another notable protocol concerning claims and proceeds in main and secondary insolvency proceedings is the Nortel Network SA protocol (UK-France, 2009). For discussion of this protocol see R. Dammann, 'Secondary Insolvency Proceedings', in R. Bork and K. van Zwieten (eds), *Commentary on the European Insolvency Regulation* (OUP, 2016), para. 45.06.

84 EIR 2000, Art. 32(2) and EIR Recast, Art. 45(2).

85 Sendo protocol, sec. I-2.

10.53 The Lehman Brothers protocol is also notable for the provisions addressing claim coordination in the context of multiple debtors. Two of them are worth mentioning. The first provision applies in a situation where the same claim is filed against the principal debtor and the guarantor. In this case, the IPs have agreed to seek to 'adjust distributions on the allowed Direct Claim and allowed Guarantee claim so that distributions [...] do not exceed in the aggregate the amount of the Direct Claim or the Guarantee, whichever is the highest'.[86] The protocol also reassures that distributions either under the main obligation or under the guarantee shall not reduce the amount of the respective claims – this is to protect the value of the main obligation and of the guarantee.[87] The second provision encourages insolvency practitioners, where possible and subject to the applicable laws, 'to coordinate notice procedures and establish the same deadlines for the filing of claims [...] and in all other matters regarding the filing, reviewing and objecting to claims'.[88]

Box 10.5 Claim coordination

To promote legal certainty, avoid duplication of efforts, save time and encourage efficient and simplified coordination of parallel insolvency proceedings, an insolvency protocol may contain various agreements related to the treatment of claims and future transactions. When claims concern a single debtor, such agreements often pursue a strategy of concentrating all or a set of claims in one jurisdiction, thus avoiding duplication of disputes around them and reducing the risk of conflicting judgments.[1] In a group scenario, an agreement about filing of claims may aim at facilitating a group solution. For instance, it can aid in setting common deadlines for filing of claims, making it easier to adopt aligned reorganization or liquidation plans.

Insolvency protocols could also address problems arising from multiple filings under cross-liability arrangements (e.g. cross-guarantees, co-debtorship arrangements and intra-group provision of collateral). In this context, it may be beneficial to agree and control that distributions to a creditor cannot exceed in the aggregate the amount under the main obligation and a related security arrangement. To do so, a sufficient level of communication concerning filing, admission and satisfaction of claims should be established. To facilitate non-conflicting judgments, joint or coordinated hearings can be considered.

When drafting provisions on claim coordination, it is important to keep in mind that the allocation of jurisdiction and applicable law for filing and resolution of claims, for transaction avoidance and approval of future transactions may depend upon (or be directly prescribed by) relevant provisions of applicable law, including conflict of laws provisions.

---

86 Ibid., para. 8.3.

87 Ibid., para. 8.3.

88 Ibid., para. 8.4.

Note:

1. See e.g. protocol in Laidlaw Inc. and Laidlaw Investments Ltd. (Canada-USA, 2001), para. 11(a), stating (in a group insolvency context!) that '[t]he Courts shall use their best efforts to coordinate activities in the Insolvency Proceedings so that the subject matter of any particular action, suit, request, application, contested matter or other proceeding may be determined in one Court only'.

E. SUPPLEMENTING EXISTING COOPERATION FRAMEWORKS

In Chapters 5 and 6 above we analysed the cooperation frameworks introduced by the Model Law 2019 and the EIR Recast. We also underlined the general understanding and acceptance of an idea that cooperation between insolvency practitioners and courts and coordination of insolvency proceedings related to two or more members of an enterprise group are key to efficient administration of such proceedings in pursuit of a group solution, protecting and even augmenting the total enterprise value. We concluded that despite this understanding, many relevant instruments within the cooperation frameworks are rarely used in practice. **10.54**

As of September 2020, the Model Law 2019 has not yet been adopted in any jurisdiction. As the experience of the Model Law 1997 shows, such adoption may take years or even decades. Thus, the Model Law 2019 cannot be (directly) relied on when implementing its cooperation rules. In contrast, the EIR Recast is mandatory law, directly applicable in all EU Member States, except Denmark. However, many of its provisions remain dormant or underutilized. For example, we are not aware of any instances where a group coordination proceeding has been opened to facilitate the effective administration of group insolvency. Another example is the so-called synthetic insolvency proceedings, introduced in Article 36 EIR Recast. To the best of our knowledge, it has only been relied on once or twice since 2017.[89] **10.55**

There are different reasons why these innovations have not taken off. Among them are excessive rigidity, complexity and ambiguity of relevant rules,[90] **10.56**

89 Art. 36 EIR Recast was relied on in 2018 in the case of the Hungarian company Küpper Hungária Kft. The COMI of the debtor was found to be in Germany and an undertaking was given by an insolvency practitioner in the main insolvency proceedings to avoid the opening of secondary proceedings in Hungary. The ultimate goal was to arrange for a coordinated sale of the productive and profitable parts of the Küpper group companies to an investor.

90 Wessels, *International Insolvency Law Part II: supra* note 83, 10836ff, concluding that 'Article 36 is over-regulated, with many vague terms and open questions, adds complexity, additional costs and time delay.' G. McCormack, A. Keay and S. Brown, *European Insolvency Law: Reform and Harmonization*

unclear prospects of their success[91] and high additional costs involved (e.g. remuneration for the coordinator). Nevertheless, we should not easily disregard the underlying ideas and goals pursued by them. Instead, we suggest that insolvency protocols with their benefits of flexibility, adjustability and relatively low costs, may be embraced to substitute or supplement these innovations, in full compliance with applicable law.

1. Group centralization and group governance in insolvency

10.57 Many multinational enterprise groups are strongly integrated and centrally managed. It is therefore recognized that preserving and maintaining a certain level of centralization in group governance and direction in insolvency may improve efficiency of insolvency proceedings and keep the group together.

10.58 The idea of centralized crisis resolution in the context of a group of companies is not new. Some scholars have proposed to address it by way of a group-COMI or an enterprise centre of main interests (ECOMI), allowing 'commencement of main proceedings for all members of an enterprise group in the home country of the enterprise group'.[92] The idea of group-COMI has found support in academic literature, accepting that it would make it more efficient, transparent and predictable to globally administer the group insolvency by allowing coordination from a single forum.[93] However, this approach was not endorsed in the legal instruments. Thus, neither the EIR Recast, nor the Model Law 2019 adopted the concept of a group-COMI. This, however, should not limit the possibility for a court to open insolvency proceedings for several companies belonging to the same group in a single

---

(Edward Elgar Publishing, 2017), p. 119, commenting that '[t]he new provision [...] comes with a lot of complexity in its detailed design'.

91 Group coordination proceedings are voluntary in nature and lead to nonbinding actions (recommendations) of a group coordinator and the proposal of a group coordination plan, which may or may not be adopted. Their success is therefore solely dependent on the willingness of IPs to cooperate with each other. See J. Schmidt, in R. Bork and K. Van Zwieten (eds), *Commentary on the European Insolvency Regulation* (OUP, 2016), para. 70.03, noting that some commentators perceive the lack of binding effects of group coordination proceedings as an inherent systemic weakness, but reminding that it was a deliberate compromise to 'have proceedings designed to achieve as much coordination as possible, while at the same time preserving the autonomy of the individual proceedings'.

92 S. Bufford, 'Coordination of Insolvency Cases for International Enterprise Groups: A Proposal' (2012) 86(4) *American Bankruptcy Law Journal*, pp. 685–748.

93 I. Mevorach, *The Future of Cross-Border Insolvency: Overcoming Biases and Closing Gaps* (OUP, 2018), p. 20, noting that '[m]odified universalism's emergent jurisdiction norm is still in rather early stages with regard to corporate, and even more so financial, groups', but that it can in principle accommodate group structures. D. Zhang, *Insolvency Law and Multinational Groups: Theories, Solutions and Recommendations for Business Failure* (Routledge, 2020), p. 85. For a different view see L. LoPucki, 'The Case of Cooperative Territoriality in International Bankruptcy' (2000) 98(7) *Michigan Law Review*, p. 2230, claiming – without providing clear evidence – that a 'rule that put the bankruptcy of the entire group in the home country of the group would lead to anomalous results and the resulting system would be manipulated easily'.

jurisdiction, provided that COMIs of those companies are located in that same jurisdiction.[94]

The latter is not uncommon in practice. For example, in the insolvency of the once leading supplier of automotive components, Collins & Aikman Group, the English High Court made administration orders for 24 of the group's European entities on the basis that their COMIs were in the UK.[95] Among them there was a Luxembourg holding company and trading companies operating in England and Wales, Sweden, Spain, Italy, Belgium, Germany and the Netherlands. Ultimately, Collins & Aikman liquidated for USD 45 million more than estimated, proving to be 'a model for how to complete single corporate group proceedings'.[96] Another example is the collapse of Nortel Networks Group, as a result of which 19 of the group's European entities (the EMEA sub-group of Nortel companies) were made the subject of administration orders in the UK.[97] The centre of main interests in respect of each of these companies was found to be in the UK. More recent examples of predominantly centralized group reorganizations include cases of large multinational groups, such as Oi Group (Brazil)[98] and Agrokor (Croatia).[99] **10.59**

---

94 This possibility is recognized in Recital 53 EIR Recast, stating that the

> introduction of rules on the insolvency proceedings of groups of companies should not limit the possibility for a court to open insolvency proceedings for several companies belonging to the same group in a single jurisdiction if the court finds that the centre of main interests of those companies is located in a single Member State. In such cases, the court should also be able to appoint, if appropriate, the same insolvency practitioner in all proceedings concerned, provided that this is not incompatible with the rules applicable to them.

Therefore COMI-coordination by one court can, if the criteria for establishing COMI of related companies have been met, function as a fallback option when the EIR Recast's group rules meet objections. Note that some legal instruments, such as the UK schemes of arrangement and private schemes under the Dutch WHOA, once enacted, permit group financial reorganization without COMI of all affected group members being present in the jurisdiction of the court, provided, however, that there is a sufficient nexus to the respective jurisdiction. In both cases such non-COMI based reorganizations will not fall under the EIR Recast.

95 *Re Collins & Aikman Corp. Group (Application for Administration Orders)* [2005] EWHC 1754 (Ch.).

96 N. Wouters and A. Raykin, 'Corporate Group Cross-Border Insolvencies Between the United States and European Union: Legal & Economic Developments' (2013) 29 *Emory Bankruptcy Developments Journal*, p. 410.

97 *Re Nortel Networks SA and other companies* [2009] EWHC 206 (Ch).

98 R. Cooper, F. Cestero and J. Mosier, 'Oi S.A.: The Saga of Latin America's Largest Private Sector In-Court Restructuring' (2018) 14(5) *Pratt's Journal of Bankruptcy Law*, pp. 209–21.

99 D. Djuric and V. Jovanovic, 'Too big to fail'? The Agrokor Case and its Impact on West Balkan Economies' (2019) 28(1) *International Insolvency Review*, pp. 22–43.

10.60 The COMI-based group insolvency centralization faces serious problems where COMIs of enterprise group members are located in different jurisdictions and a COMI shift (forum choice) to bring them together is not possible or feasible in the given circumstances.[100]

10.61 As an alternative and in departure from the focus on COMI, the III proposed in 2012 a concept of a Group Centre as a pathway to the coordination of proceedings involving multiple members of an enterprise group.[101] In the case of an integrated enterprise, a Group Centre was thought of as a coordination centre for the enterprise group. This centre was presumed to be the proper jurisdiction for the opening of main insolvency proceedings and for the filing of cases for affiliates of the group over which the Group Centre had jurisdiction.[102] To the extent permitted by local laws, courts in other countries 'should acknowledge the jurisdiction of the Group Center Court over the group enterprise'[103] and could only open secondary proceedings with respect to 'an affiliate of a multinational enterprise group for which a Group Center Court has been established'.[104] While the concept of a Group Centre aspires to solve the centralization problem in group insolvencies, it can hardly be implemented in practice due to the lack of flexibility when it comes to the rules determining international insolvency jurisdiction for the opening of insolvency proceedings, whether linked to COMI, registered office or establishment. Besides, determination of a Group Centre may be as difficult as finding COMI.

10.62 Yet another way to bring centralization in the governance of groups of companies in insolvency is through mutual consent and agreement to allocate the lead group member or members and give them additional tasks and powers to drive an insolvency solution. This approach has several advantages.

10.63 First, it does not deprive courts of their jurisdiction and does not interfere with typically rigid jurisdictional rules. Second, it has the inherent flexibility and is capable of being adjusted to the needs and characteristics of a particular enterprise group, taking into account its level of integration, presence of sub-groups and regional centres, geographical dispersion and division of roles

100 On the discussion of COMI relocation in the context of group reorganizations and recent cases of such relocation see I. Mevorach and A. Walters, 'The Characterization of Pre-insolvency Proceedings in Private International Law' (2020) *European Business Organization Law Review*, https://doi.org/10.1007/s40804-020-00176-x.

101 International Insolvency Institute Guidelines for Coordination of Multinational Enterprise Group Insolvencies, 2012.

102 Ibid., Guideline 13.

103 Ibid., Guideline 14.

104 Ibid., Guideline 18.

between group members. As Mevorach convincingly points out, an optimal approach to group insolvency requires 'non-neat, non-one-size-fits-all solutions because that is the reality of the global market and the businesses and institutions operating within it'.[105] Third, this approach is backed up by the existing international insolvency law instruments. Thus, according to the EIR Recast:

> all or some of the insolvency practitioners […] may agree to grant additional powers to an insolvency practitioner appointed in one of the proceedings […]. They may also agree on the allocation of certain tasks amongst them, where such allocation of tasks is permitted by the rules applicable to each of the proceedings.[106]

Similarly, the Model Law 2019 envisages that cooperation to the maximum extent possible may be implemented by any appropriate means, including by '[a]llocation of responsibilities between an insolvency representative appointed in this State, insolvency representatives of other group members and any group representative appointed'.[107] Fourth, and concluding, this approach can be implemented through the well-tried route of insolvency protocols.

We argue that insolvency protocols can serve as a tool to implement a group-wide governance framework in enterprise group insolvency without resorting to special coordination or planning proceedings. A protocol may seek a degree of centralization, allocate the roles and tasks between insolvency practitioners and preserve group leadership. In a single debtor insolvency, the dominant role is typically given to main insolvency proceedings, opened in the jurisdiction of the debtor's COMI. In group insolvency, insolvency proceedings concerning group members are legally equal. This legal equality does not necessarily reflect the actual economic power or a role of each entity within the group.[108] For example, centralized decision-making in a group may be concentrated at the level of the top parent company. In insolvency, this company (and its insolvency practitioner) may be best positioned to oversee and direct group reorganization, because it has the most complete information about the group's business and therefore can see the full picture (information advantage), or because it has the largest amount of resources and funds to manage group coordination, e.g. as a result of centralized cash management. 10.64

105 I. Mevorach, *The Future of Cross-Border Insolvency: Overcoming Biases and Closing Gaps* (OUP, 2018), p. 21.

106 EIR Recast, Art. 56(2). This is in line with the open approach of the EIR Recast towards mechanism to achieve a coordinated restructuring of the group. See Recital 60, EIR Recast.

107 Model Law 2019, Art. 15(c).

108 In this respect Wessels notes that in many cases it should be clear 'which of the IPs is or should be in the lead (e.g. in considering and proposing a restructuring plan)'. He also notes that 'there is no such thing as a "dominant" proceeding […], as in the context of groups all pending insolvency proceedings function on the same footing'. B. Wessels, *International Insolvency Law Part II, supra* note 83, 10926e.

10.65 Under an insolvency protocol, it may be agreed that an insolvency practitioner appointed in a particular proceeding ('lead insolvency proceeding') takes a coordinating role[109] and should:

(i) Identify and outline recommendations for the coordinated conduct of the insolvency proceedings.
(ii) Take on the task of drafting a reorganization plan and communicating it to IPs in other proceedings.[110]
(iii) Organize regular meetings or phone calls with other IPs to discuss group reorganization or liquidation strategies and to facilitate swift and coordinated decisions on other matters wherever possible.
(iv) Have the power to effect intra-group sales or purchases.[111]
(v) Consult with trade unions on certain issues.[112]
(vi) Participate in creditors' meetings of other group members.[113]
(vii) Recruit or dismiss employees of other group members.[114]
(viii) Be notified and/or consulted with on major decisions contemplated or made by other IPs,[115] or about significant developments in other group insolvency proceedings.
(ix) Decide, in agreement with other insolvency practitioners which insolvency practitioner is best placed to deal with any particular asset.[116]

10.66 The allocation of responsibilities between insolvency practitioners may relate to the following elements of group governance: adoption of recovery and liquidation plans; treatment of assets; resolution of claims; commencement of legal actions, including with respect to group affiliates; provision and approval of post-commencement finance; appointment, removal and terms of directors in group entities. In practice, insolvency protocols have long been employed to address these elements of group governance and management. Some examples were given in the previous chapters of this book. Below we provide a few

109 Legislative Guide 2010, Recommendation 250(c).

110 See e.g. Federal-Mogul protocol, para. 3.2., providing that the 'US Management shall have primary responsibility for (i) developing, confirming and implementing a Reorganization plan; [...] and (iv) the general strategy of the Debtors including Cross-Border Companies'.

111 Maxwell protocol, para. G(2), subject to a 'good faith attempt' or to consultation, or a court approval.

112 Ibid., 3.4(b)(ii).

113 This was agreed in the Jet Airways protocol, although in the context of a single debtor insolvency. In principle, similar participation rights may be considered for a situation of group insolvency.

114 J. Schmidt, in Bork and Van Zwieten, *supra* note 91, para. 56.29.

115 Such decisions may relate to post-commencement finance, safeguarding of assets, use and disposition of assets, exercise of avoidance powers, submission and admission of claims, including intra-group claims, distribution to creditors. See Legislative Guide 2010, Recommendation 250(d).

116 See Madoff protocol, para. 6.3, stipulating that insolvency practitioners 'shall provide assistance in respect of recovery of the identified assets, which may include enabling and/or confirmatory acts and instruments such as comfort letter, assignments and powers of attorney in favour of [the IP] who is pursuing recovery of such assets'.

additional examples showing how provisions of protocols undertake to regulate the issues of group governance in insolvency.

The Commodore protocol prescribed the opening of parallel Chapter 11 proceedings in the US in respect of a debtor's subsidiary, if it appears that 'such debtor holds substantial assets, conducted substantial business, or is incorporated in the United States'.[117] The Madoff protocol urged insolvency practitioners to 'endeavour to reach agreement expeditiously, on a case by case basis, as to which Representative is best placed to deal with any particular asset'.[118] The protocol agreement in *Manhattan Investment Fund Limited* included detailed provisions concerning asset identification and administration.[119] It 'obligated the parties to create a work plan for asset identification, collection, and management and to discuss any relevant actions that had taken place with respect to the debtors' assets in biweekly telephone calls'.[120] In AIOC protocol, the parties have agreed to attempt in good faith to obtain the consent of another party before taking actions which would have a material adverse impact on any group member.[121] The Federal-Mogul protocol established that the 'Cross-Border Management must consult with the Administrators or must obtain the Administrators' consent before taking certain actions with respect to the Cross-Border Companies'.[122] Coordination for the purposes of asset preservation is prescribed by the Lehman Brothers protocol, which also lays down the general rule that '[e]ach Tribunal should administer the assets subject to its jurisdiction'.[123] The Maxwell protocol sought to ensure a certain board composition for the ultimate parent company of the M&O Group and the enterprise group members.[124] **10.67**

We believe that these examples demonstrate that insolvency practitioners are competent in devising tailor-made insolvency protocols capable of facilitating cooperation and group insolvency governance, elaborating and supplementing the existing international and national insolvency law instruments or even filling the gaps in regulation. In this respect, the UNCITRAL Practice Guide **10.68**

117 Commodore protocol, para. L.

118 Madoff protocol, para. 6.2.

119 Protocol in *Manhattan Investment Fund Ltd.* (USA-BVI-Bermuda, 2000). US Bankruptcy Court for the Southern District of New York, Case No. 00-10922 (April 2000), the High Court of Justice of the British Virgin Islands (19 April 2000) and the Supreme Court of Bermuda, Case No. 2000/37 (April 2000).

120 As reported in K. Orr, D. Moss and A. Wetzel, 'Courts, Cooperation, and More: Incorporating U.S. Case-Specific Provisions in Insolvency Protocols – Part 2', Jones Day, 2017.

121 AIOC protocol, para. III(B).

122 Federal-Mogul protocol, para. 3.4. See also para. 3.6., setting the primary responsibilities of Administrators, including circulation for approval to creditors of any proposal for a reorganization plan, appointment and removal of directors, calling meetings of creditors or shareholders, etc.

123 Lehman Brothers protocol, para. 7.1.

124 Maxwell protocol, paras C and D.

mentions that in countries that have not adopted the Model Law 1997 and do not have developed rules dealing with international insolvencies or where there is doubt as to the standing of a foreign representative to commence insolvency proceedings, allocating the responsibility for commencement of such proceedings with respect to group entities in a protocol 'may facilitate commencement of those proceedings'.[125]

10.69 At the same time, it is important to note that we do not attempt to cover the whole variety of arrangements and provisions found in insolvency protocols, since there can be as many of them as there are types of groups of companies, their corporate structures, business models, peculiar requirements, needs and problems that need to be addressed in insolvency. Besides, not everything can or should be agreed in a protocol. Some agreements or disputes may be intentionally excluded from an insolvency protocol for reasons of sensitivity of the matter, absence of a clear legal mandate, ambiguity or inflexibility of national law, differences in legal cultures of relevant jurisdictions, unwillingness to leave a paper trail or a simple lack of a final decision or a consensus.[126] Controversial issues may be left out for further negotiations and separate protocols.[127] This has happened in practice and may be a good strategy, to first lay down the general cooperation framework to cement mutual agreement, and then concentrate on difficult or disputed questions.

10.70 Clearly, cooperation and communication can also exist outside an insolvency protocol. The UNCITRAL Practice Guide refers to the case of the Dutch cable and telecommunications operator United Pan-Europe Communications N.V.[128] The case involved parallel proceedings in the Netherlands and the USA. It did not lead to an insolvency protocol, but the parties (the US debtor in possession and the Dutch trustee) nevertheless (orally) agreed,[129] among other things, not to subordinate certain claims to the level of equity interests

---

125 Practice Guide, Ch. III, para. 127.

126 See, for instance, J. Pottow, 'The Maxwell Case', in R. Rasmussen (ed.), *Bankruptcy Law Stories* (New York: Foundation Press, 2007), p. 233, discussing how Maxwell protocol did not want to 'rock the cooperative boat' and deliberately avoided the issue of substantive law governing resolution of assets or law applicable to pre-insolvency transactions.

127 For example, the IFSA (Nortel Networks) provides in sec. 12(c) that 'the Debtors shall, as soon as reasonably practicable following the execution of this agreement, negotiate in good faith and attempt to reach agreement on a timely basis on a protocol for resolving disputes concerning the allocation of Sale Proceeds from Sale Transactions'. Having failed to do so, parties went to courts in the USA (Delaware) and Canada (Ontario), which cooperated and managed to avoid irreconcilable judgments. Another example is Payless Holdings protocol, stipulating in para. 41 that the 'question of the degree of standing of the U.S. Creditors' Committee in the Canadian Court remains an open issue. This Protocol is without prejudice to the question one way or the other'.

128 Practice Guide, Ch. III, paras 68, 104, 107, 130.

129 Since the debtor's Dutch counsel believed that conclusion of an insolvency agreement was not permissive under Dutch law.

(as such subordination is generally unavailable under Dutch law), not to consent to the disposition of any estate assets or funds until the court approval, to reject one burdensome contract in accordance with the US law and to arbitrate such rejection in the Netherlands, to coordinate retention and compensation of professionals. As a result of close cooperation, the proceedings in both jurisdictions were closed on the same day.

2. Structuring of court-to-court communication

Whereas the previous section applies mainly to insolvency practitioners coordinating the administration of parallel insolvency proceedings, this section concerns courts engaged in overseeing, guiding and directing such administration. **10.71**

The value of court-to-court communication in administering group insolvencies is undisputed. It is promoted by an array of soft law instruments (e.g. ALI-III Global Principles for Court-to-Court Communications in International Insolvency Cases, EU JudgeCo Guidelines and JIN Guidelines) and is prescribed by the EIR Recast,[130] the Model Law 1997[131] and the Model Law 2019.[132] Nevertheless, while in theory courts should communicate and cooperate with each other, in practice they may decide not to do so because of the variety of practical difficulties and factors, including language barriers, lack of understanding and/or awareness as to types of information that should be exchanged or absence of the mechanics for initiating, receiving and engaging in such communication. In this respect, insolvency protocols may serve to introduce the much-needed structure and clarity into cooperation and communication process, making it both smooth and transparent. Where the EIR Recast does not apply and the Model Law 1997 has not been adopted, protocols might both establish the framework for cooperation with foreign judges and IPs and offer the necessary practical detail.[133] **10.72**

When it comes to court-to-court communication, from existing protocol practice and legal literature, it flows that the following elements can be regulated in an insolvency protocol: **10.73**

130 EIR Recast, Art. 57.
131 Model Law 1997, Art. 25.
132 Model Law 2019, Art. 9.
133 Practice Guide, Ch. III, para. 146.

(i) Types of information to be exchanged.[134]
(ii) Means to exchange information.[135]
(iii) Frequency of communication between courts.
(iv) Provision of notice to parties to participate in communication.
(v) Safeguards to protect substantive and procedural rights of parties.
(vi) Organization of joint, simultaneous or coordinated hearings.[136]
(vii) Confidentiality and personal data protection.[137]

10.74 Many insolvency protocols provide for direct communication between courts, with or without a reference to the ALI-III Guidelines, approving such communication.[138] In a situation where there are more than two jurisdictions involved or where judges do not speak the same language or are not used to having direct communication,[139] communication may be facilitated through IPs or special intermediaries.

10.75 The EIR Recast stipulates that in order to facilitate communication a court may appoint an independent person or body to act on its instructions.[140] The

134 Provisions on court-to-court communication in insolvency protocols may have different levels of detail. Some protocols may simply state that courts should communicate with one another with respect to any matter relating to insolvency proceedings (see e.g. Pioneer protocol, para. 12(b)). See also para. 4 of the Nakash protocol, stating that the courts endeavour 'to consult with each other through the Official Receiver and the Examiner and/or via telephonic conference in order to attempt to coordinate their efforts and avoid (if possible) potentially conflicting rulings'. Other protocols may specify particular topics for communication. For example, pursuant to paras 27–28 of the Calpine protocol, courts agreed to consult with each other regarding interpretation and application of stays. See also Eddie Bauer protocol (para. 12), Abitibibowater protocol (para. 23).

135 E.g. telephonic and/or video conference capabilities, secure channel email capacity, etc.

136 Coordination of the conduct of hearings in the group insolvency context is envisaged in Art. 57(3)(d) EIR Recast. Queirolo and Dominelli note that whereas the EIR Recast allows courts to 'schedule their own hearings in light of the development of foreign proceedings (and, if appropriate schedule "parallel hearings"), the regulation does not grant courts the right to conduct joint hearings'. I. Queirolo and S. Dominelli, 'Cooperation and Communication Between Parties in the Management of Cross-Border Parallel Proceedings Under the European Insolvency Regulation Recast', in V. Lazić and Stuij S. (eds), *Recasting the Insolvency Regulation: Improvements and Missed Opportunities. Short Studies in Private International Law* (The Hague: Asser Press, 2020), p. 118.

137 Confidentiality-related provisions in protocols usually concern communications between IPs, rather than courts, see e.g. Everfresh protocol (para. 5), Federal-Mogul protocol (paras 4.6 and 4.7), Jet Airways protocol (para. 5.1.3.), mentioning a separate non-disclosure agreement.

138 See e.g. Madoff protocol (para. 5.1.), Masonite protocol (para. 10(a)), Calpine protocol (para. 10(a)), Pioneer protocol (para.12(b)).

139 See C. Paulus, 'Judicial Cooperation in Cross-Border Insolvencies: An Outline of Some Relevant Issues and Literature', 2006, underlining the division between Common Law world and the Civil Law world (with some exceptions), when it comes to direct court-to-court communication. According to Paulus, 'the former is in favour of direct communication, and the latter in opposition to, or at least reluctant to embrace, it'.

140 EIR Recast, Art. 57(1).

possibility to appoint a person to act at the direction of a court in communications is also envisaged in the Model Law 2019.[141] Insolvency protocols have in the past accommodated the assistance by such an intermediary to facilitate coordination of insolvency proceedings. For example, both Maxwell and Nakash protocols involved a court-appointed examiner. In the Maxwell case, the examiner (Richard Gitlin) was tasked 'to function as a mediator among the various parties', and to 'act to harmonize, for the benefit of all of [Maxwell's] creditors and stockholders and other parties in interest, [the proceedings] so as to maximize [the] prospects for rehabilitation and reorganization'.[142] Judge Brozman (USA) and Justice Hoffman (UK) subsequently authorized the examiner and the administrators to coordinate their efforts pursuant to an insolvency protocol. In the Nakash case, the examiner (again, Richard Gitlin) was directed to develop a protocol for harmonizing and coordinating proceedings concerning the debtor before the courts of the United States and Israel.

In the *Matlack* case, the Canadian court made an appointment of an information officer with various duties, including regular reporting on the status of the foreign proceedings and such other information as the court might order.[143] The duties of an information officer are not set out in the CCAA. In *Re Xinergy Ltd.*, the court described the role of the information officer as someone who would: '(i) act as a resource to the foreign representative in the performance of its duties; (ii) act as an officer to the Court, reporting to the Court on the proceedings, as required by the Court; (iii) provide stakeholders of [the debtor] with material information on [foreign proceedings].'[144] **10.76**

In the recent case concerning Urbancorp Group, a multinational enterprise group with the parent company in Israel and a number of subsidiaries in Canada, the CCAA monitor KSV Kofman Inc. (KSV), which was also appointed as an information officer, entered into a Protocol for Co-operation Among Canadian Court Officer and Israeli Functionary.[145] Under this insolvency protocol, KSV was given control over the 'ordinary course management **10.77**

141 Model Law 2019, Art. 9(1). In literature suggested by Bob Wessels, 'Judicial Co-operation in Cross-Border Insolvency Cases' (short version inaugural lecture Leiden 2008), in B. Wessels and P. Omar (eds), *Crossing (Dutch) Borders in Insolvency. Papers from the INSOL Europe Academic Forum and Meijers Institute of the Leiden Law School Joint Insolvency Conference*, Leiden, The Netherlands, 5–6 June 2008, Nottingham, Paris: INSOL Europe, 2009, pp. 105–17.

142 *In re Maxwell Communs. Corp.*, 93 F.3d 1036 (2d Cir. 1996).

143 On the role of information officers in Canadian law and insolvency practice, see A. Yandreski and B. Empey, 'Officer of the Court: Exploring the Role of the Information Officer', in J. Sarra (ed.), *Annual Review of Insolvency Law* (Carswell, 2016).

144 *Re Xinergy Ltd.*, 2015 ONSC 2692, 37 CBR (6th) 331.

145 Urbancorp Group protocol.

and receipts and disbursements of funds for Canadian debtors'.[146] KSV also undertook to provide the Israeli insolvency practitioner with regular and timely information updates regarding the ongoing status of the CCAA Proceedings as they unfold.[147] In return, the Israeli insolvency practitioner agreed to provide KSV, in its capacity as the information officer copies of all information pertaining to the Israeli proceedings, subject to some limitations.[148] Thus, the information officer accepted an intermediary role, keeping the Canadian court informed of developments in the foreign proceeding and acting as a resource to the foreign insolvency practitioner, who may not have had any experience with the Canadian insolvency system or courts.

10.78 Commenting on court-to-court communication (or lack thereof) in Europe, Wessels points out that many times the reluctance of courts to effectuate transnational cooperation and communication does not come from their unwillingness to do so. To the contrary, he stresses that '[j]udges will many times understand that their cross-border cooperation is necessary for the efficient administration of any given case. They will be prepared, in fact they must be as parties expect them to play their important role. Judges may, however, be unfamiliar with their new cross-border role'.[149] One way of addressing this problem is to raise the general awareness on the basics of cross-border insolvency cooperation and to provide special training to enhance courts' competence. Another way is to promote the use of insolvency protocols.

10.79 Having recognized the plethora of practical difficulties and obstacles related to court-to-court communication, the Judicial Insolvency Network has issued in 2019 the Modalities of Court-to-Court Communication, mentioned in Chapter 9. This instrument supplements the JIN Guidelines and offers 'mechanics' for initiation, receipt and engagement in communication, including arrangements as to the time, method and language of communication, the nature of the case (with due regard to confidentiality concerns) and the issue of parties' consent. We argue that insolvency protocols can themselves provide a similar framework, establishing sufficient level of detail and structure for cooperation and communication between courts. In other words, insolvency protocols can add substance to the frame of existing rules, and fill gaps in such rules, where necessary. They can specify the types of information to be shared,

146 Ibid., para. 2.
147 Ibid., para. 3(a).
148 Ibid., para. 3(e).
149 B. Wessels, *International Insolvency Law Part II*, *supra* note 83, 10926k.

language of communication, means and channels (e.g. technology) for information exchange, the role of court-appointed intermediaries and communication schedule. They can also outline the process of initiating and receiving communication and establish the safeguards to protect parties' interests, including notification, confidentiality and data protection arrangements (Box 10.6).

Box 10.6 Supplementing existing cooperation frameworks

Modern instruments in the area of international insolvency law contain a wide variety of rules aimed at improving administration of parallel insolvency proceedings related to two or more members of a multinational enterprise group. These rules may concern, inter alia, opening of special group coordination or planning proceedings, appointment of a single insolvency practitioner in separate insolvency proceedings of group members, close cooperation and communication between courts, an agreement between insolvency practitioners to grant additional powers to one of them or to decide on the allocation of certain tasks amongst them. Nevertheless, in practice the realization of these rules might be difficult, either due to their complexity, cost-inefficiency, ambiguity of applicable law or for any other reason.

Insolvency protocols may serve as a tool to elaborate, supplement or even substitute these 'dysfunctional' or 'low performing' rules and offer practical solutions to streamline court-to-court communication and introduce or improve group centralization and group governance in insolvency.

At the same one, it is important to keep in mind that any agreement on the allocation of tasks and roles in a group insolvency or/and on granting a leading coordinating role to one or several insolvency practitioner(s) shall not affect legal independence and equality of insolvency proceedings opened with respect to enterprise group members.

11

BANK INSOLVENCIES AND COOPERATION AGREEMENTS BETWEEN RESOLUTION AUTHORITIES

A. FROM SELF-INTEREST TO CLOSE COOPERATION 11.01

B. COOPERATION WITHIN RESOLUTION COLLEGES AND CRISIS MANAGEMENT GROUPS 11.05

C. COOPERATION AGREEMENTS BETWEEN RESOLUTION AUTHORITIES 11.10

A. FROM SELF-INTEREST TO CLOSE COOPERATION

11.01 The global financial crisis has clearly revealed the inadequacy of the rules for the resolution of international (cross-border) credit institutions and the deficiency with regard to these rules' cross-border effects. The Basel Committee on Banking Supervision (BCBS), the primary global standard setter for the prudential regulation of banks, concluded in its report from 2010 that the '[e]xisting legal and regulatory arrangements are not generally designed to resolve problems in a financial group operating through multiple, separate legal entities'.[1] This has resulted in the 'predominance of the territorial approach in resolving banking crises and insolvencies'.[2]

11.02 As a response, in 2011 the Financial Stability Board (FSB) issued the Key Attributes of Effective Resolution Regimes (Key Attributes),[3] the internationally agreed insolvency standards for credit institutions. According to the

1 BCBS, Report and Recommendations of the Cross-Border Bank Resolution Group, March 2010, para. 6.

2 Ibid. A good example of the territorial approach to insolvency of a banking group is the case of Icelandic banks. Following the crisis of Iceland's outsized banking system in summer-autumn 2008, the Icelandic government passed the emergency legislation that granted protection to domestic deposits, which had been transferred to new banks, while foreign operations remained in old banks, which were put into administration. Ultimately, foreign depositors had to be rescued by foreign (the UK and the Netherlands) governments. For discussion of this and other cases of poor cross-border cooperation in cross-border bank crises, see D. Schoenmaker, *Governance of International Banking* (OUP, 2013), Chapter 4.2. See also P. Davies, 'Resolution of Cross-border Groups', in M. Haentjens and B. Wessels (eds), *Research Handbook on Crisis Management in the Banking Sector* (Edward Elgar Publishing, 2015), pp. 263–5.

3 FSB, Key Attributes of Effective Resolution Regimes for Financial Institutions, October 2011.

Key Attributes, an effective resolution regime should include rules on and should encourage close cooperation, information exchange and coordination between resolution authorities before and during the resolution process. In the EU context, this has been implemented mainly through four sets of measures on: (i) group resolvability; (ii) adoption of group recovery and resolution plans; (iii) conclusion of group financial support agreements; and (iv) creation of resolution colleges by group-level resolution authorities. These novel instruments have been developed to ensure sufficient speed of intervention, continuation of banks' critical functions and preservation of financial stability. We will discuss them in more detail below.

In the EU, bank resolution is regulated by the BRRD and the SRMR, briefly **11.03** mentioned in Chapter 2 above. The BRRD was agreed in 2014 and entered into force on 1 January 2015 (with bail-in procedures applicable from 1 January 2016). The SRMR dates from 15 July 2014 and is in force since 14 August 2014. These instruments are unique as they represent the first major attempt to harmonize substantive rules on bank resolution across the EU/European Economic Area (EEA).[4] The BRRD applies to all EU Member States and provides for minimum harmonization rules, leaving the application of resolution tools to national authorities. The SRMR covers banks in the euro area and in those EU Member States which choose to join the Banking Union.[5] The resolution within the eurozone under the SRMR is centralized.[6] It is directed and managed by the Single Resolution Board (SRB), an independent, self-financed EU agency and the central resolution authority within the Banking Union.

Prior to this newly introduced system of rules, financial distress in the **11.04** European banking sector was addressed almost solely at the national level, inter alia, by way of general rules of each country's national insolvency law, with possible modifications, or via specific legislation tailored to insolvent financial institutions and their specific relationships.[7] Current rules on bank

---

4 Prior to the BRRD and the SRMR, some harmonization was facilitated by the Directive 94/19/EC of the European Parliament and of the Council of 30 May 1994 on deposit-guarantee schemes (repealed by the Directive 2014/49/EU of the European Parliament and of the Council of 16 April 2014 on deposit guarantee schemes), the Directive 98/26/EC of the European Parliament and of the Council of 19 May 1998 on settlement finality in payment and securities settlement systems, and the CIWUD.

5 SRMR, Recital 15. The eurozone consists of Austria, Belgium, Cyprus, Estonia, Finland, France, Germany, Greece, Ireland, Italy, Latvia, Lithuania, Luxembourg, Malta, the Netherlands, Portugal, Slovakia, Slovenia, and Spain.

6 See e.g. SRMR, Arts 8, 10 and 16. See also D. Busch, M. van Rijn and M. Louisse, 'How Single is the Single Resolution Mechanism?' EBI Working Paper Series, No. 30 (2019), p. 9.

7 For an overview of current approaches to bank insolvencies in the EU-28, Switzerland and the USA see S. Buckingham, S. Atanasova, S. Frazzani and N. Véron, 'Study on the Differences Between Bank Insolvency Laws and on Their Potential Harmonisation', Final Report, November 2019.

resolution are premised on the acceptance that cooperation between national authorities in the banking group context is key, both at the stage of drafting recovery and resolution plans, and during the actual resolution.[8] This acceptance is based on the fact that banking systems are highly interconnected, banking groups are usually international in their operations, holding a large percentage of foreign assets and liabilities. Most importantly, failure of a bank or banks in one country may affect the stability of the financial markets in other countries or destabilize the whole region.[9]

B. COOPERATION WITHIN RESOLUTION COLLEGES AND CRISIS MANAGEMENT GROUPS

11.05 While special procedures are implemented to coordinate insolvency in non-banking corporate groups (e.g. group coordination proceeding under the EIR Recast, planning proceeding under the Model Law 2019), coordination within banking groups is realized through special forums – resolution colleges and crisis management groups (CMGs).[10]

11.06 Resolution colleges were created for the most part during 2016, following the establishment of national resolution authorities in each EU Member State pursuant to the BRRD's implementation.[11] The BRRD lays down the requirement for group-level resolution authorities to set up resolution colleges to serve as a 'a forum for the exchange of information and the coordination of resolution actions'[12] between various participants, including the European

8 BRRD, Recitals 17 and 96, recognizing that further action is necessary to 'promote cooperation and prevent fragmented national responses'. SRMR, Art. 31, Recitals 38, 47, 54, providing that the SRB, national resolution authorities and competent authorities, including the European Central Bank (ECB) should, where necessary, conclude a memorandum of understanding (MOU) to promote cooperation with each other. MOUs can also be concluded with resolution authorities and competent authorities of non-participating Member States.

9 As rules regarding private international law may be vague or absent, cross-border effects of certain resolution measures are uncertain, see B. Wessels, International Insolvency Law and EU Bank Resolution Rules, in M. Haentjens and B. Wessels (eds), *Research Handbook on Cross-border Bank Resolution* (Edward Elgar Publishing, 2019), pp. 132–76. See also M. Haentjens, B. Wessels and S. Guo, *New Bank Insolvency Law for China and Europe, Volume 3: A Comparative Analysis* (The Hague: Eleven International Publishing, forthcoming), Chapter 10 ('Cross-border Issues in Bank Resolution').

10 On resolution colleges see V. Troiano, 'Cross-border Cooperation Between Resolution Authorities in the BRRD', in M. Haentjens and B. Wessels (eds), *Research Handbook on Crisis Management in the Bankruptcy Sector* (Edward Elgar Publishing, 2015), pp. 103–16. See also M. Lehmann, 'Bail-in and Private International Law: How to Make Bank Resolution Measures Effective Across Borders' (2017) 66(1) *International and Comparative Law Quarterly*, p. 141, arguing for more inclusive resolution colleges.

11 EBA Report on the functioning of resolution colleges in 2017, July 2018, p. 7.

12 BRRD, Recital 96. Group-level resolution authority means 'the resolution authority in the Member State in which the consolidating supervisor is situated'. Ibid., Art. 2(44).

Banking Authority (EBA) and the relevant resolution authorities.[13] Resolution authorities of third countries may also be invited to participate in the resolution college as observers, subject to confidentiality requirements.[14] Cooperation between these participants should facilitate the adoption of a group resolution scheme and prevent fragmented national responses.[15] At the same time, a resolution college is not an independent decision-making body, but rather a platform to enhance the decision-making process by national authorities.[16] Such decision-making can relate to the development of group resolution plans,[17] assessment of group resolvability,[18] establishment of a group resolution scheme,[19] or any issues concerning cross-border group resolution.[20]

The functions of resolution colleges can generally be compared with the activities (in cross-border restructuring of non-bank groups) of mediation colleges and their mediation sessions, in which decision makers are put at the same table to share information and discuss appropriate (coordinated) crisis-resolution measures (e.g. adoption of a group-wide resolution scheme) and their execution. What is particularly noteworthy for a resolution college is that: (1) it does not create new proceedings – resolution authorities remain in full control of the respective proceedings; (2) a resolution authority refusing to participate in a group resolution scheme must set out the reasons for the disagreement or the reasons to depart from the group resolution scheme ('comply or explain' basis);[21] and (3) exchange of information within a resolution college is mandatory and centrally coordinated by the group-level resolution authority.[22] While cooperating, respective authorities shall comply with the requirements of professional secrecy and confidentiality. Importantly, **11.07**

13 Ibid., Art. 88(2). Group resolution authorities are given a significant discretion as to which members and observers to invite to resolution colleges, which could potentially lead to exclusion of certain important parties and hinder resolution coordination. D. Singh, *European Cross-Border Banking and Banking Supervision* (OUP, 2020), para. 5.33.

14 Ibid., Art. 88(3). A special regime applies to cross-border groups primarily conducting business in a third country and having subsidiaries established in two or more EU Member States. In this case the resolution authorities of the Member States where the subsidiaries are located shall form a European resolution college. BRRD, Art. 89.

15 Ibid., Recital 96.

16 Ibid., Recital 98.

17 Ibid., Arts 12, 13.

18 Ibid., Art. 16.

19 Ibid., Arts 91, 92.

20 Ibid., Art. 88(1).

21 Ibid., Arts 91(8), 92(4). In any event, where a group resolution scheme is not implemented and resolution authorities take resolution actions in relation to any group entity, such resolution authorities are required to keep cooperating closely within the resolution college. Ibid., Art. 91(12).

22 According to Art. 90(1) BRRD, 'resolution authorities and competent authorities shall provide one another on request with all the information relevant for the exercise of the other authorities' tasks under this Directive'.

the BRRD stresses that such requirements should not prevent 'resolution authorities and competent authorities [...] from sharing information with each other and with other Union resolution authorities'.[23]

11.08 The FSB provides for the creation of crisis management groups (CMGs) by home and key host resolution authorities of all Global Systemically Important Financial Institutions (G-SIFIs),[24] as a forum for cooperation in recovery and resolution planning, as well as during the application of resolution measures. CMGs may also engage relevant supervisory authorities, central banks, ministries and public authorities responsible for guarantee schemes. Even though CMGs pursue functions similar to those of resolution colleges, unlike resolution colleges, they operate on a global scale and concern only selected (large) banks and banking groups, such as JP Morgan Chase, Citigroup, Deutsche Bank, HSBC, Bank of China.[25] The objective of CMGs is to enhance preparedness for, and facilitate the management and resolution of, a cross-border financial crisis.[26] CMGs have now been established for all G-SIFIs. This has facilitated the adoption of resolution plans with respect to all of them.[27]

11.09 The Key Attributes prescribe that participating jurisdictions 'should ensure that no legal, regulatory or policy impediments exist that hinder the appropriate exchange of information, including firm-specific information, between supervisory authorities, central banks, resolution authorities, [...]'.[28] In order to protect sensitive information, its communication may be restricted to the top officials of the relevant home and host authorities. Apart from this, the only explicit limitation to information sharing is the requirement to have a regime for the protection of confidential information.[29]

---

23 Ibid., Art. 84.

24 The overall number of G-SIFIs in 2018 was 29, rising to 30 in 2019. See 2018 list of global systemically important banks (G-SIFIs), FSB, 16 November 2018, https://www.fsb.org/wp-content/uploads/P161118-1.pdf. The list for 2019 dated 22 November 2019 is available at https://www.fsb.org/wp-content/uploads/P221119-1.pdf. The list for 2020 dated 11 November 2020 is available at https://www.fsb.org/2020/11/2020-list-of-global-systemically-important-banks-g-sibs.

25 FSB has stressed that authorities overseeing a non-G-SIB that is required to undertake recovery and resolution planning and has operations in foreign jurisdictions that are material to the group should also establish appropriate arrangements for cross-border cooperation and coordination, inter alia, through a cross-border coordinating forum (e.g. an extended supervisory college) to support the process of recovery and resolution planning. FSB, Key Attributes Assessment Methodology for the Banking Sector, 2016, p. 61.

26 Key Attributes, para. 8.1.

27 FSB 2018 Resolution Report: 'Keeping the pressure up', Seventh Report on the Implementation of Resolution Reforms, 15 November 2018, http://www.fsb.org/wp-content/uploads/P151118-1.pdf.

28 Key Attributes, para. 12.1.

29 The BRRD sanctions the exchange of information with authorities of third countries, provided that those third-country authorities are subject to the appropriate standards of professional secrecy (including data protection) and the requested information is needed for the performance by those authorities of their resolution functions and is not used for any other purposes. See BRRD, Art. 98.

C. COOPERATION AGREEMENTS BETWEEN RESOLUTION AUTHORITIES

When it comes to cross-border insolvency protocols or agreements, two different scenarios should be considered. The first scenario involves financial institutions operating within the euro area and intra-EU banking groups. In this case, mandatory rules on cooperation between resolution authorities apply,[30] and the use of cooperation agreements may be superfluous.[31] The second situation concerns non-EU banking groups or groups with substantial presence outside the EU, in which case the lack of internationally accepted rules for transnational bank resolution still persists. In this case, with no other regime establishing communication and cooperation on a global scale, other (soft law) instruments and arrangements can play an important role. **11.10**

Such instruments can take form of institution-specific cross-border cooperation arrangements (i.e. institution-specific agreements), cooperation agreements covering all relevant financial institutions or a defined group of institutions (i.e. non-firm-specific or framework agreements). Due to the specificity of the banking industry, and the corresponding need to ensure sufficient speed of intervention and continuation of critical functions, bank resolution is typically carried out with large state involvement. This is why both firm-specific agreements and general framework agreements are usually concluded by government authorities. For instance, the FSB suggests that institution-specific agreements should define the roles and responsibilities of authorities participating in the planning and resolution, make arrangements for the exchange of information and include the institution-specific details for the implementation of resolution measures.[32] **11.11**

The Principles for Cross-border Effectiveness of Resolution Actions, adopted by the FSB in 2015, mention coordination among relevant home and host jurisdictions by way of institution-specific cooperation agreements and memoranda of understanding, as a facilitator of supportive measures in cross-border bank resolution. Negotiation of an institution-specific cooperation agreement should create a more predictable and explicit framework dealing with information exchange for recovery and resolution planning purposes.[33] **11.12**

30 BRRD, Arts 87–92. SRMR, Art. 28, Chapter 4.

31 G. Vallar, 'Use of Cross-Border Insolvency Protocols in Banking and Financial Sector', in R. Parry and P. Omar (eds), *Banking and Financial Insolvencies: The European Regulatory Framework* (INSOL Europe, 2016), p. 174, arguing that under the BRRD and the SRMR there is no need for entering into cross-border insolvency protocols. We submit that other (soft law) instruments and arrangements can play a supplementary role as they could provide further detail gearing to the specific needs of the cooperation foreseen.

32 Key Attributes, KA 9.

33 FSB, Resolution of Systemically Important Financial Institutions, Progress Report, 2012, p. 12.

11.13 The example of an institution-specific cooperation agreement is the non-binding Cross-border Cooperation Arrangement among Authorities of the Crisis Management Group of LCH SA[34] (Arrangement).[35] It seeks to facilitate the 'exchange of information, views and assessments [...] among Authorities in order to allow for more efficient and effective resolution planning and timely resolution action in crisis situations'.[36] For this purpose, the Arrangement lays down the general commitment to cooperate both during 'business-as-usual' and 'in times of crisis'. The former concerns the assessment of the impact of resolution options in the relevant jurisdictions and identification of procedural requirements for cross-border recognition of resolution measures.[37] The latter introduces the commitment for authorities to inform and consult each other before taking resolution measures, and not to endeavour to pre-empt resolution actions by the main (home) authority.[38] The Arrangement recognizes that information pertaining to recovery and resolution plans is commercially and market sensitive. This and other non-public information is covered by special obligations of confidentiality.

11.14 Despite the fact that institution-specific cooperation agreements constitute an essential underpinning for cooperation and coordination in resolution planning and in resolution, they have not been adopted for all G-SIFIs.[39] It is difficult to explain why the conclusion of cross-border cooperation agreements remains slow. One possible explanation could be the entity-by-entity resolution strategy embraced by some of the banking groups. For instance, in its resolution plan, HSBC Group states that its resolution is 'facilitated by the separability embedded within the structure of the HSBC Group'.[40] As a result, the preferred resolution strategy is based on the 'resolution and restructuring of regional or national groups of affiliated companies'.[41] As long

34 LCH SA is licensed as a credit institution in France and is part of the LCH Group.

35 The Arrangement involves Autorité de contrôle prudentiel et de résolution (France), Banque de France, European Banking Authority, European Securities and Markets Authority (ESMA), SRB, Bank of England, Banca d'Italia, Deutsche Bundesbank, BaFin (Germany), National Bank of Belgium, Portuguese Securities Market Commission, Dutch National Bank, USA Commodity Futures Trading Commission (CFTC), Federal Deposit Insurance Corporation (FDIC, USA) and others. The Arrangement is available at https://www.cftc.gov/media/3661/cftc-acpr-arrangementmou091319/download.

36 Cross-border Cooperation Arrangement among Authorities of the Crisis Management Group of LCH SA, 2018, para. 14(b).

37 Ibid., para. 40.

38 In this case such authority is Autorité de contrôle prudentiel et de résolution as the home resolution authority. This authority is given the leading role in coordinating the activities covered by the respective Arrangement.

39 FSB, 2019 Resolution Report: 'Minding the Gap'. Eighth Report on the Implementation of Resolution Reforms, p. 9, noting that institution-specific cross-border cooperation agreements are still not in place for four G-SIBs. Available at https://www.fsb.org/wp-content/uploads/P141119-3.pdf.

40 HSBC Holdings plc, SIFI Plan, Section I – Public Section, December 2018, p. 8.

41 Ibid. This resolution strategy is typically referred to as a multiple point of entry (MPOE). This means that each entity within the group should be separately resolved in its own resolution proceeding. MPOE strategy is

as the resolution strategy is based on local resolution actions, the dependence on cross-border cooperation in resolution may be reduced.[42] At the same time, it may be argued that group entities cannot be completely separated and that some level of coordination and information sharing is important for the successful realization of a MPOE resolution strategy.

Another reason for the lack of firm-specific cooperative arrangements comes from the commitment of time and resources entailed by their negotiation and maintenance. Additional legal and procedural hurdles might relate to sharing of non-public firm-specific information, which state authorities may be eager to safeguard or exclusively control. Sometimes they can also be attributed to a simple reluctance or even resentment to cooperate with a foreign authority. **11.15**

The absence of institution-specific arrangements might be problematic for the access of host authorities to information. The Financial Stability Institute (FSI) has recently surveyed the authorities from 16 jurisdictions that are home or host to G-SIBs and/or domestic systemically important banks (D-SIBs). It concluded that while cooperation in supervisory colleges and non-firm-specific arrangements can be 'a useful source of information about frameworks and general resolution approaches, yet they may not provide host authorities with all the information they need to understand the impact of the resolution strategy on the local operations of a specific firm'.[43] **11.16**

Alongside institution-specific arrangements and in addition to the formal membership in CMGs, competent authorities may be engaged in general (non-firm-specific or framework) cooperation arrangements. For example, the Executives' Meeting of East Asia-Pacific Central Banks (EMEAP), launched in 1991 as a forum for central banks in the East Asia and the Pacific region to strengthen cooperative relationship among its members (e.g. Reserve Bank of Australia, People's Bank of China, Hong Kong Monetary Authority, Bank Indonesia, Bank of Japan), established in 2018 a multilateral resolution forum, **11.17**

---

also embraced by Banco Santander S.A., see Banco Santander, S.A., Resolution Plan for U.S. Operations, Public section, 31 December 2018, p. 6. The opposite strategy is called a single point of entry (SPOE) and entails the adoption of resolution measures at the holding (parent) company level, with no need to take separate resolution measures at the level of group (operating) subsidiaries. SPOE strategy is adopted by JPMorgan Chase, see JPMorgan Chase Resolution Plan Public Filing, 2019, p. 14.

42 Ibid. (HSBC Holdings plc, SIFI Plan), noting that cross-border cooperation in resolution 'cannot necessarily be relied upon in a systemic crisis'.

43 P. Baudino, T. Richardson and R. Walters, 'Cross-border Resolution Cooperation and Information-sharing: An Overview of Home and Host Authority Experience', FSI Insights on policy implementation No. 22, January 2020, para. 82. Another important conclusion made in this study emphasizes the correlation between the access of host authorities to adequate information about resolution strategies and their willingness to rely on or cooperate with the group resolution strategy. See para. 83.

the Focused Meeting on Resolution. This arrangement focuses on knowledge-sharing, capacity-building, cooperation and coordination in cross-border bank resolution.[44] In the Caribbean and Central America, non-firm-specific information-sharing, including on resolution-related topics is driven by the Caribbean Group of Banking Supervisors (CGBS) and the Central American College of Banking Supervisors (CCSBSO). Both are supported by multi-lateral memoranda of understanding. Various memoranda of understanding have also been concluded between the Nordic-Baltic countries, following the establishment of the Nordic-Baltic Stability Group (NBSG) in 2010.[45]

11.18 Another example of a framework arrangement is the bilateral agreement, referred to as the Memorandum of Understanding (MOU), reached between the US Federal Deposit Insurance Corporation (FDIC) and the Bank of England.[46] This MOU does not create any legally binding obligations, confer any rights, or supersede domestic laws.[47] Instead, it expresses the intent to enhance and strengthen consultation and cooperation. It does so by setting common principles regarding resolution of firms with cross-border operations. These principles include consistency of crisis resolution measures with supervisory frameworks, coordinating role of home country regulators, flexibility of arrangements and tools for cross-border crisis management.[48] The MOU recognizes the importance of close and effective communication and lays down provisions related to sharing of expertise and knowledge, notification of regulatory changes, exchange of information and execution of requests for assistance.

11.19 Another example of a non-firm-specific bilateral arrangement is the Trans-Tasman Council on Banking Supervision (TTBC), a working group established in 2005 for coordination in Trans-Tasman crisis resolution and planning arrangements.[49] Its members include the Reserve Bank of New

44 Ibid, para. 76.

45 See e.g. Memorandum of Understanding on Cooperation and Coordination on cross-border financial stability between relevant Ministries, Central Banks, Financial Supervisory Authorities and Resolution Authorities of Denmark, Estonia, Finland, Iceland, Latvia, Lithuania, Norway and Sweden, 31 January 2018. On the Nordic experience in cross-border crisis resolution, read further Report from the FSB Regional Consultative Group (RCG) for Europe, Nordic experience of cooperation on cross-border regulation and crisis resolution, 2016, available at https://www.fsb.org/2016/07/nordic-experience-of-cooperation-on-cross-border-regulation-and-crisis-resolution/.

46 Memorandum of understanding concerning consultation, cooperation and the exchange of information related to the resolution of insured depository institutions with cross-border operations in the United States and the United Kingdom, 2010, https://www.bankofengland.co.uk/-/media/boe/files/news/2010/january/bank-fdic-mou.pdf.

47 Ibid., para. 5.

48 Ibid., paras 10–12.

49 Read further D. Mayes, 'Bank Resolution in New Zealand and its Implications for Europe', in C. Goodhart et al. (eds), *Central Banking at a Crossroads: Europe and Beyond* (Anthem Press, 2014), pp. 123–39.

Zealand (RBNZ), the New Zealand Treasury and member agencies of the Australian Council of Financial Regulators (i.e. Australian Treasury, Australian Prudential Regulation Authority, the Reserve Bank of Australia and the Australian Securities and Investments Commission). For the purposes of assisting the participating parties in achieving a coordinated response to financial distress in any bank or banking group that has significant operations in Australia and New Zealand in a manner that promotes an effective resolution of the bank's financial distress, a Memorandum of Cooperation (MOC) was concluded.[50] The MOC underlines that it does not intend to bind the Australian or New Zealand governments, to pre-commit or to rule out any particular resolution option. It lays down the responsibilities of the participants in a case of a trans-Tasman bank distress, principles for responding to such distress (e.g. coordinated and cooperative approach, preference of private solutions over public support, protection of taxpayer interests, maintenance of market discipline, avoidance of actions that are likely to have a detrimental effect on the stability of the other country's financial system), rules on information sharing and early warning alerts, coordination in the process of investigating and assessing the bank's financial condition, providing liquidity and capital support, assessment of response options and implementation of resolution.

In case of a banking group consisting of entities established in the euro area, as **11.20**
well as entities from non-participating Member States or third countries, the SRB shall represent the national resolution authorities of the euro Member States for the purposes of consultation and cooperation with authorities of non-participating (i.e. non-euro) Member States and third countries.[51] One form of such cooperation is the conclusion by the SRB (on behalf of national resolution authorities) of non-binding cooperation agreements. In total, the SRB in the years 2017–2019 has signed seven cooperation arrangements with third countries. These arrangements involve the Canada Deposit Insurance Corporation (CDIC),[52] FDIC (the USA),[53] the Banco Central do Brasil (Brazil),[54] the National Bank of Serbia (Serbia),[55] the Institute for the

50 Memorandum of Cooperation on Trans-Tasman Bank Distress Management, 2010, available at https://www.cfr.gov.au/about/pdf/ttbc-memorandum-of-cooperation.pdf.

51 SRMR, Art. 32(1).

52 Cooperation Arrangement Concerning the Resolution of Institutions with Cross-Border Operations in Canada and the European Banking Union, 2017.

53 Cooperation Arrangement Concerning the Resolution of Insured Depository Institutions and Certain Other Financial Companies with Cross-Border Operations in the United States and the European Banking Union, 2017.

54 Cooperation Arrangement between the Banco Central do Brasil and the Single Resolution Board, 2018.

55 Cooperation Arrangement between the National Bank of Serbia and the Single Resolution Board, 2018.

Protection of Bank Savings (Mexico),[56] the Bank of Albania (Albania)[57] and the Financial Services Agency (Japan).[58]

11.21 The cooperation arrangements stress their non-binding nature and establish a set of common principles regarding resolution of financial entities with cross-border operations. These include careful *ex ante* crisis preparation, flexibility and adaptability of resolution arrangements and tools, division of responsibilities between authorities with the coordinating role of home country regulators, protection of financial stability and rights of retail customers. The cooperation arrangements represent a 'statement of intent' to consult, cooperate and exchange information related to the resolution planning and implementation of resolution measures. This may include information related to financial and operational conditions of a bank, its capital structure and liquidity, identification of materially significant subsidiaries, branches and affiliates, etc. Communication is further supported by the designation of persons to be involved in ongoing resolution and crisis management, as well as determination of the common working language (English). Among the limitations to information sharing, the cooperation agreements cite grounds of public interest, national security or the need to preserve an ongoing investigation.

11.22 To sum up, from the foregoing succinct analysis of various initiatives and arrangements for communication and cooperation in cross-border bank resolution and insolvency, it is possible to draw a general conclusion that some of the cooperation arrangements applicable to cross-border bank resolution may be compared to insolvency protocols, discussed in the previous chapters of this book. Memoranda of understanding and cooperation agreements may look like insolvency protocols in terms of their structure, with the sections covering parties, definitions, aims and principles, mechanism and scope of cooperation and information exchange, review and amendment, termination and signatures. Likewise, they may further supplement or detail national laws or regional (e.g. EU, eurozone) arrangements. Most importantly, they confirm the willingness of parties to communicate and cooperate in promoting efficiency and preserving value in the resolution of a financial institution, even if such goals are subordinate to the preservation of financial stability and avoidance of systemic risk.

---

56 Cooperation Arrangement between the Institute for the Protection of Bank Savings of the United Mexican States and the Single Resolution Board, 2018.

57 Cooperation Arrangement between the Bank of Albania and the Single Resolution Board, 2018.

58 Cooperation Arrangement between the Financial Services Agency and the Single Resolution Board, 2019. For text of cooperation agreements see the website of the SRB, https://srb.europa.eu/en/content/cooperation.

They, finally, accord to the extent that they represent (primarily) a flexible non-binding soft law instrument, providing for the general (non-specific) commitment to share information and coordinate activities pre-, during and post-resolution. As a result, in practice cooperation will hinge on good relationships and the acceptance of mutual interest in participating, in view of the risk exposure and an *ex ante* commitment to assist each other.[59] Where in many instances the risk exposure between home and host countries will likely diverge, the mutuality of interests may be weakened. It is also the case that in the absence of special rules for recognition of foreign resolution actions, the possibility and effectiveness of coordinated responses to banking crises may be seriously limited.[60] **11.23**

What distinguishes cooperation arrangements within banking groups from insolvency protocols is that the latter, without exception, are *ex post*-event instruments, rather than *ex ante* tools of crisis prevention and response. In contrast, cooperation arrangements in the banking area (CMGs, resolution and supervision colleges, MOUs, MOCs, etc.) usually pre-date a crisis. In other words, they constitute an *ex ante* (preparatory) instrument. This differentiates them from insolvency protocols, commonly concluded as a response to the unfolding crisis – thus, in the reactive mode. The *ex ante* format of establishing cooperation arrangements between resolution authorities to some extent explains their standardized character and the lack of unique case-specific provisions. **11.24**

On closer inspection, the following characteristics of cooperation arrangements in cross-border bank resolution are manifested. **11.25**

- Concluding parties are frequently resolution and other competent (e.g. supervisory) authorities (e.g. central banks), responsible for resolution planning and implementation of prudential supervision and resolution measures. This is in contrast to insolvency protocols, which are usually

59 Singh, *supra* note 13, para. 5.102.

60 Whereas recognition of resolution actions in the EU is automatic pursuant to the CIWUD and the BRRD, no similar statutory framework exists on a global scale. See FSB, Principles for Cross-border Effectiveness of Resolution Actions, 3 November 2015, discussing different approaches to give cross-border effect to resolution actions, including statutory approaches and contractual recognition. Under the latter, the International Swaps and Derivatives Association (ISDA) has developed a 2014 Resolution Stay Protocol, which lays down the limits on the exercise of early termination rights under OTC bilateral derivatives documented under the ISDA Master Agreement. Another example is inclusion of contractual bail-in recognition clauses in debt instruments. For further discussion, see S. Guo, 'Cross-border Resolution of Financial Institutions: Perspectives from International Insolvency Law', Submission for the III Prize in International Insolvency Studies, 2018. See also V. Chen, A. Godwin and I. Ramsay, 'Cross-Border Cooperation in Bank Resolution: A Framework for Asia' (2016) *Singapore Journal of Legal Studies*, pp. 1–28.

entered into by insolvency practitioners and are approved by the courts of 'cooperating' jurisdictions.

- These arrangements are typically established as a preventive measure and, as noted above, pre-date the crisis.
- They regulate both in and out of crisis cooperation, which is necessary for good preparation for a crisis (i.e. recovery and resolution planning). Preventive cooperation distinguishes cooperation and communication between resolution authorities from post-crisis cooperation and communication between insolvency practitioners and courts, which typically arise once insolvency or restructurings proceedings have already been opened.
- They can take forms of institution specific and/or general (industry) framework agreements, in contrast to non-bank insolvency protocols, concluded with the aim of coordinating insolvency of a specific group of companies or an entity, in which general (industry) models for such coordination may not exist.
- They generally lack specificity and detail found in some of the non-bank cross-border insolvency cooperation protocols.[61] For example, the reviewed bank cooperation arrangements contain no provisions related to resolution of intercompany claims or transaction avoidance and largely adhere to the same template. We therefore suggest the use in the banking industry of supplementary arrangements providing *ex post* further detail gearing to the specific needs of the cooperation laid down in an *ex ante* setting.
- They provide for additional grounds to refuse or restrict cooperation, which relate to the matters of public interest, national security and ongoing investigations. These grounds generally aim to minimize the risk of harm and could arise where cooperation adversely affects financial stability in a participating Member State, impedes an ongoing investigation concerning financial irregularities or suspected fraud, causes material fiscal implications, or where the treatment of depositors or creditors is not the same in a foreign jurisdiction.[62] These public-interest-driven grounds for the refusal or limitations of communication under cooperation arrangements for financial institutions cannot be found in (non-financial) insolvency protocols.

---

61 See e.g. Madoff protocol, describing the arrangements related to cooperation with law enforcement and other agencies, and dictated by a substantial public interest in the investigation of stock and securities fraud. See also the protocol in PSINet Inc. (para. 8) that lists seven matters (referred to as 'Cross-Border Matters'), which require cooperation (e.g. the approval of a sale of all or a substantial part of the assets, the allowance, priority and valuation of inter-company claims).

62 See SRMR, Art. 33(3), listing grounds, under which the SRB shall recommend refusing the recognition or enforcement of the resolution proceedings conducted by third-country resolution authorities.

Many of the cooperation arrangements in cross-border bank resolution are abstract efforts, as they have not been tested in a crisis. Unlike insolvency protocols, which have proven their efficiency in practice, many bank-specific cross-border cooperation arrangements (CMGs, MOUs, MOCs, etc.) are relatively recent. They were created in the wake of the global financial crisis and have not yet been relied on to facilitate early intervention or to promote coordinated adoption of resolution measures in the context of an international banking group. The gradual appreciation of the use of protocols in non-bank insolvency situations also reflects a legal-cultural shift towards the acceptance of coordinated solutions. In the cross-border banking area this cultural change may still be nascent. **11.26**

12

RECOMMENDATIONS FOR PROTOCOLS IN GROUP INSOLVENCIES

12.01 This chapter contains 15 recommendations relating to the use of protocols in insolvencies of multinational enterprise groups. These recommendations are based on the analysis of the most salient protocols widely used across the world and the conclusions made after the detailed study.

RECOMMENDATIONS FOR PROTOCOLS IN GROUP INSOLVENCIES

Preamble

These Recommendations for Protocols in Group Insolvencies (Recommendations) aim at raising awareness about cross-border insolvency protocols, at sharing knowledge and at offering suggestions on their application in the context of insolvency of multinational enterprise groups. They have been developed to facilitate and promote the use of protocols as an effective, pragmatic and workable solution which has arisen from international legal practice and cases where commercially minded insolvency practitioners and courts tried to overcome underdeveloped rules of international insolvency law and the lack of special rules on group insolvencies. Currently, the use of insolvency protocols is promulgated in several non-binding instruments and best practices. In the European Union, the European Insolvency Regulation (Recast) institutionalizes conclusion of protocols to assist courts and insolvency practitioners in their cross-border cooperation tasks.

The Recommendations are non-binding and seek to address a few general problems attached to the adoption of insolvency protocols as such, as well as to offer a number of suggestions for the improvement of group coordination through insolvency protocols. They reflect the gradual appreciation of the value of protocols in cross-border insolvencies.

The Recommendations embody the overriding objective of enabling courts and insolvency practitioners to efficiently cooperate and communicate in a complex environment of group insolvency. They aim to facilitate coordination in the administration of international insolvency cases involving several entities, comprising a group of companies. Nevertheless, they do not intend to present a comprehensive or an exhaustive list of guidelines to handle the variety of problems arising in the context of enterprise group insolvency.

The Recommendations may be found relevant to financial institutions (e.g. banks and banking groups) to the extent that they are compatible with rules applicable to insolvency and resolution of such financial institutions.

The Recommendations are grouped along the following headings, reflecting their scope:

- General recommendations
- Procedural fairness and participation rights
- Information exchange
- Assets
- Reorganization and liquidation plans
- Claims
- Group governance

General recommendations

Recommendation 1: circumstances justifying conclusion of protocols

1.1. Where insolvency proceedings relate to two or more members of a group of companies, insolvency practitioners and other parties, as the case may be, should endeavour to conclude an insolvency protocol to the extent that it is appropriate to facilitate the effective administration of the respective proceedings.

1.2. Conclusion of an insolvency protocol may be particularly justified in a situation where, prior to insolvency, group entities operated as a single economic enterprise. This can be determined by or result from an integrated business model, close operational and financial ties, facilitated by intra-group financial arrangements (e.g. intra-group loans, cross-guarantees, cash pooling), centralized data management and decision-making.

1.3. In the context of cross-border insolvency of enterprise groups, an insolvency protocol may seek, among other things, to: (i) preserve and maximize the overall group insolvency estate value and the estate value of the group entities; (ii) help safeguard key production assets and ensure continuous operational activity of the group and performance under existing contracts; (iii) bring down administration expenses, prevent unnecessary (intercompany) litigation and promote cost efficiency; (iv) facilitate reorganization of viable businesses or a uniform sale of all or a part of assets of the group as a going concern.

Recommendation 2: choice of law

2. In order to avoid complications and potential disputes around determining law applicable to an insolvency protocol (e.g. law governing its validity, interpretation, amendment and termination), insolvency practitioners and other contracting parties should be able to explicitly agree on such law in an insolvency protocol as *lex contractus*.

Recommendation 3: legal force

3. For the sake of clarity, insolvency practitioners and other contracting parties may divide an insolvency protocol into binding and non-binding sections or otherwise unambiguously state which provisions are meant to be binding and which provisions are mere statements of good faith or intent.

Recommendation 4: compliance with applicable law

4.1. When drafting an insolvency protocol, insolvency practitioners and other contracting parties shall ensure that the protocol complies with national laws of the proceedings concerned (*lex concursus*) and any applicable regional regulation (e.g. the EIR Recast).

4.2. Particular attention should be paid to provisions of insolvency protocols which restrict creditors' rights related to filing of claims (i.e. allocating creditors' claims to one proceeding or jurisdiction), introduce differentiated treatment of creditors or determine law applicable to claim resolution or validity of claims.

4.3. A protocol shall not interfere with independent exercise of jurisdiction by courts involved, including in their authority or supervision over insolvency practitioners, nor shall it interfere with national rules or ethical standards by which insolvency practitioners are bound pursuant to applicable law and professional rules.

Recommendation 5: use of soft law instruments

5. When negotiating and implementing an insolvency protocol, insolvency practitioners and other contracting parties should rely on or take into account best practices for cooperation in cross-border insolvency cases. Unless unfit for a group environment, such best practices should also include relevant guidelines drafted with respect to a single debtor insolvency.

Procedural fairness and participation rights

Recommendation 6: notification

6.1. To the extent that creditors and other stakeholders may have a legal or economic interest in the adoption of a protocol and its specific provisions, they should at least be informed about its negotiation and, ideally, have an opportunity for comment or objection.

6.2. The early involvement of and supervision by courts and their approval of an insolvency protocol in an open hearing with due notification should be sought to mitigate concerns over transparency.

Recommendation 7: procedural fairness

7.1. In order to guarantee procedural fairness, judicial impartiality and transparency of insolvency proceedings, court-to-court and court-to-IP communication under a protocol should be premised on timely notification and granting an opportunity for parties (e.g. creditors) to be present during such communication.

7.2. In exceptional circumstances, having regard to the demands of efficiency, economy and urgency, court-to-court and court-to-IP communication may take place on an *ex parte* basis, but only on matters of procedural or administrative nature.

Recommendation 8: participation rights

8.1. Insolvency protocols should authorize, confirm and promote cross-procedural participation by insolvency practitioners, allowing them to influence negotiations, to convey and test certain ideas, to communicate with creditors in various jurisdictions, to present and explain plans for group reorganization or liquidation to relevant persons or bodies.

8.2. If permitted by applicable law and if justified by the group's organizational and financial structure, participation rights should be extended to solvent group members, and may cover attendance of court hearings and creditors' meetings.

Information exchange

Recommendation 9: information exchange

9.1. Under a protocol, insolvency practitioners should agree to timely communicate to each other any information which may be relevant to the other proceedings and inform each other of any material developments.

9.2. To facilitate information exchange, a protocol may specify subjects on which information should be communicated. This might relate, inter alia, to the contemplated restructuring or liquidation plans, planned disposition of material assets and other transactions outside the ordinary course of business, termination of key contracts and resolution of certain claims.

9.3. Parties to an insolvency protocol may consider making a schedule (as a part of the protocol itself or as a standalone document) to prepare and exchange progress reports and to share regular updates and developments related to the respective proceedings.

9.4. Sharing of non-public information shall be subject to confidentiality arrangements and applicable privileges. Appropriate information security arrangements shall be established to prevent or at least reduce the probability of unauthorized or inappropriate access to such information.

Recommendation 10: conflicts of interest

10.1. Court-to-court, court-to-IP and IP-to-IP communication may be restricted in a situation where such communication entails a conflict of interest (e.g. enforcement of intra-group claims, challenging of intra-group and other related-party transactions).

10.2. Any limitation on communication and cooperation due to an actual or potential conflict of interest should be strictly and narrowly interpreted, well justified and rarely and cautiously used in practice. Communication and cooperation to the maximum extent possible is the rule, while restrictions based on the risk of conflicts of interest is an exception.

10.3. Presence of a conflict of interest should affect information exchange solely with respect to the specific matter at issue and should not bar or hinder communication on all other matters, not influenced by the conflict of interest.

Assets

Recommendation 11: preservation of material assets

11.1. To the extent justified by the integrated and interdependent operation of group members, and subject to applicable law of jurisdictions involved, an insolvency protocol should prescribe cooperation duties for insolvency practitioners and relief targeted at preservation of certain assets.

11.2. An insolvency protocol may direct insolvency practitioners to coordinate and cooperate expeditiously with each other regarding identification, preservation and realization of certain assets.

11.3. A protocol may establish or elaborate in detail additional duties (e.g. duty to notify other insolvency practitioners before disposing of certain assets or establishing security rights over them) and rights of insolvency practitioners (e.g. right to request a stay of execution against assets of another enterprise group member or an approval of intra-group financing to preserve such assets).

11.4. The application of this Recommendation and the proposed rights and duties may be restricted to 'material' assets to be defined in a protocol by way of reference to their market price and/or group-specific criteria (e.g. interest in such assets from one or more entities in the group).

Reorganization and liquidation plans

Recommendation 12: alignment and coordination of plans

12.1. If justified by the facts of the case, parties may agree in an insolvency protocol covering several group entities to (attempt or endeavour to) submit reorganization or liquidation plans that are principally aligned or are substantially similar to each other.

12.2. An insolvency protocol may request that courts, in addressing the issues related to a plan confirmation, should, as far as possible seek and take into account the views of other courts and participants. To that end, courts may coordinate the timing of such confirmation or engage in a joint hearing.

12.3. An insolvency protocol should establish rules ensuring that negotiations of reorganization or liquidation plans and their subsequent implementation are not disrupted by uncoordinated actions of insolvency practitioners or creditors. In this respect, a protocol should prescribe that, to the extent appropriate and permitted under applicable law, certain significant actions should be taken by insolvency practitioners or creditors with prior notice and consultation/approval. These actions may include: (i) commencement of insolvency or liquidation proceedings against other group members; (ii) significant borrowing; (iii) causing a group member to pledge material assets; (iv) causing a group member to dispose of shares in other group members outside the ordinary course of business; (v) initiating liability claims against directors of other members of the enterprise group; (vi) taking action regarding contracts (e.g. contract termination) that can substantially harm the operation of the group, or a part of the group.

Claims

Recommendation 13: resolution of intercompany claims

13.1. In order to deal with intercompany claims in an organized, expedient and cost-efficient way, an insolvency protocol may establish an agreement about a common set of financial accounting records to be relied on when calculating claims, a calculation methodology or the acceptance of certain rules of evidence with respect to such claims.

13.2. To facilitate resolution of intercompany claims, an insolvency protocol may provide for a special mediation- or arbitration-like mechanism (e.g. by installing a claims committee) aiding parties and courts in resolution of such claims. The establishment of this mechanism may be particularly desirable where intercompany claims are complex and numerous or where adjudication of such claims requires special knowledge and expertise. In addition to an insolvency protocol, stipulating the intention to create a special resolution mechanism, parties may decide to conclude a separate claims protocol at a later stage.

13.3. Creation of a special aiding mechanism or a special procedure for the resolution of intercompany claims should be organized in a way ensuring their compliance with applicable law of relevant jurisdictions and should not deprive courts of their competence or jurisdiction with respect to matters before them.

Recommendation 14: claim coordination

14.1. To promote legal certainty, avoid duplication of efforts, save time and encourage efficient and simplified coordination of parallel insolvency proceedings, an insolvency protocol may contain various agreements related to the treatment of claims and future transactions.

14.2. When claims concern a single debtor, parties may agree to pursue concentration of all or a set of claims in one jurisdiction, thus avoiding duplication of disputes around them and reducing the risk of conflicting judgments.

14.3. In a group scenario, an agreement about filing of claims should pursue the goal of facilitating a group solution. It can aid in setting common deadlines for filing of claims, making it easier to adopt aligned reorganization or liquidation plans.

14.4. Insolvency protocols should address problems arising from multiple filings under cross-liability arrangements (e.g. cross-guarantees, co-debtorship arrangements and intra-group provision of collateral). In this context, insolvency practitioners may agree that distributions to a creditor cannot exceed in the aggregate the amount under the main obligation and a related security arrangement. To do so, a sufficient level of communication should be established.

14.5. When drafting provisions on claim coordination, parties should keep in mind that the allocation of jurisdiction and applicable law for filing and resolution of claims, for transaction avoidance and approval of future transactions may depend upon (or be directly prescribed by) relevant rules of applicable law, including conflict of laws provisions.

Group governance

Recommendation 15: group-wide governance framework

15.1. To the extent permitted by applicable law and taking into account the needs, characteristics and structure of a group of companies, insolvency practitioners and other contracting parties may agree in an insolvency protocol to grant additional powers and a coordinating role to an insolvency practitioner appointed in one of the proceedings ('lead insolvency proceeding') or/and to allocate certain tasks amongst them.

15.2. An agreement on the allocation of tasks and roles in a group insolvency or/and on granting a leading coordinating role to one or several insolvency practitioner(s) shall not affect legal independence and equality of insolvency proceedings opened with respect to enterprise group members.

13

GROUP INSOLVENCY PROTOCOL DESIGN

13.01 The previous chapter offered a number of recommendations, which can be considered when drafting an insolvency protocol. The aim of this chapter is to further build upon these recommendations and to provide a design or a possible structure for an insolvency protocol addressing cooperation and communication in the context of insolvency within multinational enterprise groups (Group Insolvency Protocol Design, or GIP Design – see Table 13.1). The GIP Design may be used by insolvency practitioners and other parties having a task of drafting an insolvency protocol.

13.02 The GIP Design does not seek to present a one-size-fits-all model insolvency protocol or cover every element that can be introduced in an insolvency protocol. Some elements or sections might only be appropriate for a particular case, whereas others are of a more general nature, and therefore can be more widely and commonly seen in practice. We stress the need for an individual approach to an insolvency protocol, taking into account group specificity, rights and interests of different stakeholders, jurisdictions involved, as well as limitations and opportunities provided by applicable law.

13.03 The suggested GIP Design is based on our analysis of several sources.

13.04 The first source is the more than 40 existing insolvency protocols, concluded over the past 30 years and discussed throughout this book. These insolvency protocols represent the wealth of practical experience and knowledge in dealing with complex international insolvencies. They have proven instrumental in improving the administration of insolvency proceedings related to two or more members of a group of companies.

13.05 The second source is the so-called Checklist Protocol, found in the appendix to the European Communication and Cooperation Guidelines for Cross-border Insolvency (CoCo Guidelines, 2007). This Checklist Protocol was designed as a non-binding tool to apply within the EIR 2000, thus addressing insolvency of a single debtor and cooperation between main and secondary proceedings, rather than multiple debtors comprising a corporate group. Nevertheless, it puts forward a useful skeleton of an insolvency protocol with many structural components that can also be used in the context of group insolvency.

The third source is the UNCITRAL Practice Guide on Cross-Border Insolvency Cooperation (2009) which contains a valuable and detailed analysis of some of the most common and unique elements and provisions of insolvency protocols. It also includes the sample clauses, which provide examples of how the provisions of a cross-border insolvency agreement can address specific issues that arise in cross-border insolvency proceedings. **13.06**

Table 13.1 Group Insolvency Protocol Design

1. Background 1.1. Parties to the protocol 1.2. Structure of the corporate group 1.3. History of the insolvency proceedings 1.4. The need for the protocol	This section serves as an introduction to the insolvency protocol. It identifies participating debtors, their names, places of incorporations and, sometimes, respective insolvency practitioners. It may also explain the reasons for conclusion of a protocol, indicate the proceedings which have already been opened with respect to group members and describe the corporate group structure (e.g. with addition of a diagram in the annex to the protocol), including roles played by some of its key members. This should improve clarity and comprehensibility of the insolvency protocol.
2. General provisions 2.1. Terms used in the protocol 2.2. Legal force and effectiveness 2.3. Choice of applicable law 2.4. Application of soft law instruments	This section covers some important operational and legal issues, including the terms used throughout the protocol, entrance of the protocol into legal effect (commonly linked to a court approval), binding or non-binding character of provisions found in the protocol and law applicable to the protocol. It may also contain references to the existing soft law instruments and clarify whether, in case of a conflict or discrepancy, the protocol should take precedence over such instruments (or otherwise).

Table 13.1 (Continued)

3. Purpose and goals of the protocol 3.1. Coordination 3.2. Communication 3.3. Information and data exchange 3.4. Asset preservation and maximization of recoveries 3.5. Claims reconciliation 3.6. Alignment of reorganization or liquidation plans 3.7. Comity	This section clarifies the purpose of entering into a protocol and goals or aims pursued by it. It can serve as guidance to the application of the insolvency protocol, once it has been approved. The goals of the protocol may include promotion of coordination, cooperation and communication in group insolvency, preservation of material assets and maximization of recoveries for creditors, claims reconciliation, safeguarding of group synergies, synchronization and alignment of reorganization or liquidation plans and preservation of independent jurisdiction, sovereignty and authority of courts.
4. Comity and independence of courts	This section confirms the independence of courts involved in communication and cooperation. It also emphasizes that nothing in the protocol is intended to interfere with the exercise of jurisdiction by each of the courts in the proceedings, or to negate professional and ethical rules applicable to insolvency practitioners.
5. Participation rights 5.1. Right to appear and be heard 5.2. Notices 5.3. Participation in meetings of creditors	Participation rights are indispensable for facilitating coordinated resolution of group insolvencies. In this respect, a protocol may introduce, confirm and elaborate rights to appear and be heard in each state involved in the protocol. In certain cases, participation rights might also extend to solvent group members.

6. Communication and access to information 6.1. Communication between insolvency practitioners 6.2. Communication between courts 6.3. Communication between insolvency practitioners and courts 6.4. Coordination of hearings 6.5. Subjects and scope of communication 6.6. Methods of communication, including language, frequency and means 6.7. Preparation and sharing of progress reports 6.8. Information sharing protocol 6.9. Limitations on communication 6.9.1. Confidential information 6.9.2. Data protection 6.9.3. Conflicts of interest	This is one of the central sections of the insolvency protocol, as it sets the mechanics, procedures and scope of communication between relevant parties in insolvency proceedings. In a group insolvency context, it is crucial to ensure that information regarding debtors, their assets and liabilities, claims, (planned) disposition of material assets and other important matters, is shared, where permitted under applicable laws, and subject to necessary protections. Clear rules governing communication and cooperation should promote the adoption of efficient and effective group-wide solutions and coordinated crises responses.
7. Asset preservation 7.1. Definition of material assets 7.2. Agreements about location and ownership of assets 7.3. Notification obligations related to disposition of material assets 7.4. Coordination and approval of disposition of material assets 7.5. Provision of financing to preserve material assets	Cooperation is most needed in areas where uncoordinated actions may result in the loss of going-concern value and group synergies, and potentially lead to group disintegration. One of such areas concerns preservation of certain (material) assets. To safeguard them or to coordinate their use and disposal, parties may establish rules introducing special notification, consultation and approval requirements.

Table 13.1 (Continued)

8. Submission and treatment of claims 8.1. Claim coordination 8.1.1. Claims process 8.1.1.1. Jurisdiction 8.1.1.2. Submission of claims, including deadlines for filing of claims 8.1.1.3. Claim verification and admission 8.1.1.4. Distribution, including the issue of double payment 8.1.2. Applicable law, including to set-off and transaction avoidance 8.1.3. Cross-liability arrangements 8.2. Claims protocol 8.3. Resolution of intercompany claims 8.3.1. Agreements concerning financial accounting records 8.3.2. Claim resolution mechanism	Insolvency proceedings commonly lead to multiple filings of claims by creditors, both in insolvency proceedings concerning the same debtor, as well as in proceedings opened with respect to separate enterprise group members. The insolvency protocol could serve as a tool to bring clarity and structure to the otherwise complex and (potentially) discordant claims process and facilitate coordination of claims processing across different jurisdictions. It can also establish special rules dealing with intercompany claims or addressing cross-liability arrangements (e.g. cross-guarantees, co-debtorship arrangements and intra-group provision of collateral).
9. Reorganization and liquidation plans	This section seeks to promote consistency and alignment of reorganization or liquidation plans, adopted in separate proceedings. It may encourage insolvency practitioners to coordinate the procedures in connection with their plans, including all solicitation proceedings relating to their plans.

10. Administration of proceedings 10.1. Recognition of stays 10.2. Availability and coordination of relief 10.3. Retention and compensation of insolvency practitioners and professionals 10.4. Agreement to notify, coordinate or abstain from certain legal actions 10.5. Allocation of responsibilities between insolvency practitioners 10.6. Adoption of the group coordination plan 10.7. Post-commencement (intra-group) finance 10.8. Composition of governing bodies	This section deals with administration of parallel insolvency proceedings in a group insolvency context. It commonly provides for the mutual recognition of stays to protect the value of insolvency estates in the respective jurisdictions. It can also aim to introduce and maintain a level of group governance in insolvency. To do so parties may agree to grant additional powers to an insolvency practitioner appointed in one of the proceedings or to allocate certain tasks amongst them. In order to avoid disruptive or harmful behaviour by some of the insolvency practitioners or creditors, a protocol might also specify that certain material decisions or legal actions should be avoided or should be (preliminarily) notified, discussed or approved.
11. Miscellaneous 11.1. Amendment of the protocol 11.2. Adherence of new parties to the protocol 11.3. Interpretation of the protocol 11.4. Termination of the protocol 11.5. Costs 11.6. Dispute resolution under the protocol 11.7. Preservation of rights (safeguards) 11.8. Warranties 11.9. Signatures	This section covers issues related specifically to the insolvency protocol, including its amendment, interpretation and termination. It may also allocate costs between the proceedings and provide for a mechanism to resolve disputes arising from the application of the protocol. The safeguards might ensure no derogation from court authority and public policy, confirm that the protocol shall not lead to infringement of national law or the rights and obligations of parties in interest.

14

ANNEX*

A. MAXWELL PROTOCOL	200	F. PIONEER PROTOCOL	258
B. COMMODORE PROTOCOL	208	G. SENDO PROTOCOL	268
C. EVERFRESH PROTOCOL	217	H. LEHMAN BROTHERS PROTOCOL	278
D. LOEWEN PROTOCOL	228	I. MADOFF PROTOCOL	291
E. INVERWORLD PROTOCOL	241	J. JET AIRWAYS PROTOCOL	298

A. MAXWELL PROTOCOL

PROTOCOL

The Examiner and the Joint Administrators hereby agree, subject to entry by the Bankruptcy Court of the Final Supplemental Order Appointing Examiner and Approving Agreement Between Examiner and Joint Administrators (the "Proposed Order") to which this Protocol is an exhibit, as follows:

A. Annexed hereto as Schedule 1 is a list of entities that are integral parts of the businesses of Macmillan, Inc. ("Macmillan") and Official Airline Guides, Inc. ("OAG"), whether subsidiaries or affiliates thereof (as identified on Schedule 1 hereto, the "M&O Group" as may be varied from time to time by further agreement between the Examiner and the Joint Administrators subject to the approval, or further order, of the Bankruptcy Court).

B. With respect to those members of the M&O Group that are identified with an asterisk on Schedule 1 hereto (the "M&O Affiliates"), the Joint Administrators have expressed the need to analyze their duties and responsibilities under English or other applicable law concerning the potential rights of the shareholders and creditors of the M&O Affiliates and the Joint

* All protocols published in this book have been submitted to or approved by courts. Many of them have been published in the public domain, as part of a court's judgment or as research materials by institutions. We are indebted to all persons involved in these protocols' creation for enabling the inclusion of their texts in this book.

Administrators and the Examiner agree to work together in good faith to effectuate the current desire and intent for David Shaffer ("Shaffer") to continue overseeing the M&O Group, as provided in paragraph C hereof, without causing the Joint Administrators to be in breach of their duties and responsibilities under English or other applicable law, with the Joint Administrators and the Examiner reserving the right to seek relief from the Bankruptcy Court in the event the foregoing cannot be accomplished.

C. Subject to paragraph G.3(i) hereof, Shaffer shall (i) remain the Chairman, President and Chief Executive Officer of Macmillan, Inc., (ii) remain the Chairman of Official Airline Guides, Inc. ("OAG"), (iii) be paid by OAG and Macmillan, and (iv) be employed by the Debtor but without the Joint Administrators adopting or the Debtor assuming his contract of employment, it being the current desire and intent (subject to paragraph G.3(i) hereof) that his management role include overseeing management of the M&O Group.

D. The Joint Administrators and the Examiner shall consult and together agree as to the appropriate composition of the boards of directors of Macmillan and OAG. The Debtor under the direction of the Joint Administrators, in its capacity as the ultimate parent company of the M&O Group, shall procure the appointment of new boards of directors for Macmillan and OAG, provided that subject to paragraph G.3(i) hereof (i) Shaffer shall be a member of both boards, (ii) the Joint Administrators shall consult with Shaffer as to whether it may be appropriate to appoint one or more members of operating management of Macmillan or OAG to their respective boards, (iii) the remaining members of the respective boards shall be independent, outside directors of distinction, and (iv) the Joint Administrators and the Examiner shall have consented to each proposed appointment.

E. Should the Joint Administrators consider it appropriate to commence insolvency or other similar proceedings in respect of all or any of the intermediate holding companies between the Debtor and the M&O Group, they may commence such proceedings subject to giving such prior notice as is reasonable in all the circumstances of the commencement of such proceedings to the Examiner, and in that event they shall, or they shall cause the Debtor to subject to prior consultation with the Examiner, commence parallel proceedings under Chapter 11 in the United States with respect to such intermediate holding companies in which event the Joint Administrators and the Examiner shall apply to the Bankruptcy Court for an Order in relation to such companies appointing the Examiner to serve in such cases and otherwise in substantially the same terms as the terms of the Proposed Order insofar as they may be relevant.

F. The Debtor and the Examiner may retain on a joint basis (subject to approval by the Bankruptcy Court of the specific joint retention application) an investment banker of national and international reputation selected by the Joint Administrators and the Examiner.

G. The Joint Administrators and the Examiner shall exercise their powers and authority in accordance with the following:

1. With respect to the Debtor, the Joint Administrators and the Debtor at the direction of the Joint Administrators shall:

(a) except as provided in this Protocol and the Proposed Order, attempt, in good faith, to obtain the prior approval of the Examiner and shall obtain of the Bankruptcy Court to borrow funds or pledge or charge any assets of the Debtor;

(b) in good faith attempt to obtain the consent of the Examiner prior to seeking to convert the Debtor's case to a case under Chapter 7 of the Bankruptcy Code and shall obtain the approval of the Bankruptcy Court to any such conversion;

(c) obtain the prior consent of the Examiner or, having first attempted in good faith to obtain such consent, approval of this Court prior to filing a plan of reorganization for the Debtor during the period in which the Debtor has the exclusive right to file a plan of reorganization ("Plan") and seek acceptance of such a Plan as provided in Section 1121 of the Bankruptcy Code.

2. With respect to the M&O Group, and regardless of whether authorization to take such action is otherwise required from this Court or the English High Court, the Joint Administrators and the Debtor under the direction of the Joint Administrators shall, in good faith, attempt to obtain the consent of the Examiner and shall obtain the approval of the Bankruptcy Court prior to:

(a) commencing, or causing to be commenced or consented to, bankruptcy or insolvency proceedings (whether in the United States or elsewhere) with respect to any member of the M&O Group;

(b) in any Chapter 11 case involving any member of the M&O Group, acting to convert or seek to convert such case to a case under Chapter 7 of the Bankruptcy Code;

(c) causing any member of the M&O Group to borrow funds;

(d) causing any member of the M&O Group to pledge or charge any assigns;

(e) causing any member of the M&O Group to sell or dispose of any share or other assets outside the ordinary course of business.

3. The Joint Administrators and the Debtor under the direction of the Joint Administrators shall attempt in good faith to obtain the prior consent of the Examiner and, if such consent is not given, shall obtain the approval of the Bankruptcy Court prior to:

(a) replacing, firing, or materially reducing the operating responsibilities of Shaffer (without otherwise detracting from the Joint Administrators' powers and authority as corporate governance of the Debtor);

(b) exercising the voting rights of the Debtor or the M&O Group with respect to stock of any member of the M&O Group, except that such consent or approval shall not be required to exercise the voting rights of stock of M&O Affiliates to the extent:

(i) the Joint Administrators have first consulted with the Examiner concerning such exercise; and

(ii) such voting rights are not exercised in a manner inconsistent with the provisions, spirit or intent of this Order;

(c) filing a plan of reorganization under Chapter 11 for any member of the M&O Group (to the extent that any of them is the subject of a Chapter 11 case) during the period in which such member has the exclusive right to file a plan of reorganization and seek acceptance of such plan as provided in Section 1121 of the Bankruptcy Code;

(d) causing any member of the M&O Group to commence material legal proceedings;

(e) except as provided in paragraph D, procuring the appointment of any director of any member of the M&O Group;

(f) causing the Debtor or any of its subsidiaries to take any action which is intended to or the reasonably anticipated consequences of which would have a material adverse impact on any significant member of the M&O Group.

4. The Joint Administrators may, without the prior consent of the Examiner and without giving prior notice to him, carry out investigations into the financial dealings of the members of the M&O Group provided that the Joint Administrators shall report on the details of such matters to the

Examiner at weekly or such other intervals as may be agreed between the Joint Administrators and the Examiner.

5. With respect to the subsidiaries and affiliates of the Debtor that are not members of the M&O Group (the "Other Subsidiaries") or any other assets outside the M&O Group,

(a) The Joint Administrators and the Debtor under the direction of the Joint Administrators shall, in good faith, attempt to obtain the prior consent of the Examiner and shall obtain the approval of the Bankruptcy Court prior to:

(i) disposing of shares in any of the Other Subsidiaries or any other assets outside the M&O Group or cause any of the Other Subsidiaries to dispose of any assets, for a consideration, in any one case, in excess of £25,000,000;

(ii) causing any of the Other Subsidiaries to borrow funds or pledge or charge any of its assets to secure indebtedness (if the aggregate of all such borrowings, pledges and charges for any single Other Subsidiary is in an amount exceeding £5,000,000 at any one time) or lend money to Other Subsidiaries (if the aggregate amount so loaned by any single Other Subsidiary shall exceed £25,000,000 at any one time); or

(iii) causing any Other Subsidiary to commence a case under the Bankruptcy Code or file a petition for relief under section 304 of the Bankruptcy Code.

(b) The Joint Administrators and the Debtor under the direction of the Joint Administrators shall, in good faith attempt to obtain the prior consent of the Examiner and, if such consent is not given, shall obtain the approval of the Bankruptcy Court, prior to filing a plan of reorganization under Chapter 11 for any of the Other Subsidiaries (to the extent that any of them is the subject of a Chapter 11 case) during the period in which the relevant company has the exclusive right to file a plan of reorganization and to seek acceptance of such a plan as provided in section 1121 of the Bankruptcy Code.

(c) The Joint Administrators and the Debtor under the direction of the Joint Administrators may, subject to prior notification to the Examiner:

(i) exercise the voting rights of the relevant company with respect to stock of any of the Other Subsidiaries other than to effect matters covered by Clause (d) below;

(ii) dispose of shares in any of the Other Subsidiaries or any other assets outside the M&O Group, or cause any of the Other Subsidiaries to dispose of any assets, for a consideration, in any one case, in excess of £7,000,000 but not exceeding £25,000,000;

(iii) cause any of the Other Subsidiaries to borrow funds or pledge or charge any of its assets to secure indebtedness (if the aggregate of all such borrowings, pledges and charges for any single Other Subsidiary is in an amount exceeding £7,000,000 but not exceeding £25,000,000 at any one time) or lend money to Other Subsidiaries (if the aggregate amount so loaned by any single Other Subsidiary is in an amount exceeding £7,000,000 but not exceeding £25,000,000 at any one time);

(iv) cause any of the Other Subsidiaries to commence material legal proceedings;

(v) commence, cause to be commenced or consented to, bankruptcy or insolvency proceedings with regard to any of the Other Subsidiaries.

(d) The Joint Administrators and the Debtor under the direction of the Joint Administrators may without the prior consent of the Examiner and without giving prior notice to him:

(i) cause any of the Other Subsidiaries to borrow funds or pledge or charge any of its assets to secure indebtedness (if the aggregate of all such borrowings, pledges and charges for any single Other Subsidiary is in an amount not exceeding £7,000,000 at any one time) or lend money to Other Subsidiaries (if the aggregate amount so loaned by any single Other Subsidiary is in an amount not exceeding £7,000,000 at any one time);

(ii) dispose of shares in any of the Other Subsidiaries or any other assets outside the M&O Group, or cause any of the Other Subsidiaries to dispose of assets, for a consideration, in any one case, not exceeding £7,000,000;

(iii) cause any of the Other Subsidiaries to replace, fire or materially reduce the operating responsibilities of any executive officer; and

(iv) carry out investigations into the financial dealings of any of the Other Subsidiaries; provided that, with respect to each of the matters described in this paragraph G.5(d), the Joint Administrators shall report on the details of such matters to the Examiner at weekly or such other intervals as may be agreed between the Joint Administrators and the Examiner.

(e) For the purposes of this Clause G.5, "consideration" in relation to the sale of shares means the consideration for the shares plus the amount of intercompany debt repaid.

6. The Joint Administrators and the Examiner confirm that (i) the objective of the parties is for the Debtor's Chapter 11 plan and the Joint Administrators' proposals in the Administration to provide for essentially similar arrangements with respect to the M&O Group, (ii) during the period specified in paragraph G.1(iii), the Examiner will be consulted with respect to and be involved in the formulation and negotiation of any plan of reorganization in Chapter 11 that the Debtor under the direction of the Joint Administrators or the Joint Administrators propose to file at any time and after such period the Joint Administrators will keep the Examiner informed of any plan and will consult with the Examiner with respect to the formulation thereof, and (iii) Shaffer (subject to paragraph G.3(i) hereof) will also be consulted with, and his views will be considered, with respect to any such plan.

Dated:

15 January 1992

New York, New York

.... /s/ Richard Gitlin

Richard Gitlin, Examiner

.... /s/ Andrew Mark Homan

The Joint Administrators

by Andrew Mark Homan

SCHEDULE 1

THE M&O GROUP

Macmillan Inc

Official Airline Guides Inc

All subsidiaries or sub-subsidiaries of the above, except as noted below with respect to Berlitz International Inc.

- Molecular Design (UK) Limited
- Maxwell Macmillan Publishing Singapore
- Maxwell Macmillan Publishing Australia
- Maxwell Macmillan International Europe Limited
- OAG (Tonbridge)
- Ivory Crest
- Ivory Crest Holdings
- BRS Software Products Scandinavia A/S
- BRS Information Technologies
- BRS Europe
- Information on Demand
- Maxwell Dictionaries
- Caxton and English Education Programmes International
- MLL Holdings
- Macmillan McGraw-Hill School Publishing Company

The Examiner and the Joint Administrators have agreed to delete Berlitz International Inc. ("Berlitz") from this Schedule 1 for reasons of their own convenience. Such deletion is without prejudice to reinstatement of Berlitz on this Schedule 1 (after notice to Berlitz and an opportunity for a hearing) and without prejudice to any claim, assertion or position that Maxwell Communication Corporation plc or any of its subsidiaries and sub-subsidiaries, including Macmillan Inc (and its subsidiaries and sub-subsidiaries), may have or take regarding ownership of shares issued or to be issued by Berlitz and any other matter concerning Berlitz.

SCHEDULE 2

MEMBERS OF THE BANK COMMITTEE*

Bank of America N.T. & S.A.

Bank of Nova Scotia

Barclays Bank plc

- The Chase Manhattan Bank, N.A.
- Credit Lyonnais
- The Fuji Bank Ltd
- Mellon Bank, NA.
- Union Bank of Switzerland
- Westpac Banking Corporation

* Schedule 2 is subject to modification or supplementation from time to time on written notice filed with the Bankruptcy Court by counsel for the Bank Committee and served upon the Joint Administrators, the Examiner, the United States Trustee and any official committee formed in this case (as and when formed).

B. COMMODORE PROTOCOL

PROTOCOL

Commodore Electronics Limited ("CEL") and Commodore International Limited ("CIL") (CEL and CIL being collectively referred to as "Commodore") are both the subject of liquidations in the Supreme Court of the Commonwealth of the Bahamas ("Supreme Court"). The CEL liquidation has been continued under supervision by order of the Supreme Court, and CIL is being liquidated under order of the Supreme Court, with Franklyn R. Wilson and Macgregor N. Robertson having been appointed by the Supreme Court as the joint liquidators ("Liquidators") in both liquidations.

Certain creditors of CEL and CIL filed involuntary chapter 7 petitions against CEL and CIL in the United States Bankruptcy Court for the Southern District of New York ("Bankruptcy Court"), as to which the Liquidators filed motions for abstention and petitions for relief ancillary to foreign proceedings.

Thereafter, the petitioning creditors and other major creditors organized as an informal committee which was subsequently elected to be the Creditors' Committee for the purposes of the Bahamian bankruptcy proceedings (the "Committee").

The Bankruptcy Court has not yet acted upon the motions referenced above, but for the reasons set forth hereinafter, the Liquidators and the Committee desire to resolve the motions pending in the Bankruptcy Court on the basis hereafter set forth.

It is the intention of the parties to record herein their mutual agreement that the liquidation proceedings under Bahamian law shall continue unabated and that the Bankruptcy Court in the United States shall enter an Order for Relief in the involuntary chapter 7 proceeding of CIL and CEL (which the Liquidators shall convert to cases under chapter 11) for reason and good cause, more particularly set forth hereinafter.

It is the further purpose of the parties to memorialize and acknowledge that while dual proceedings are pending in The Bahamas and the United States, the parties will respect the independent non-delegable duties imposed by the laws of the respective countries, to wit: upon the Liquidators under Bahamian law; upon the debtor in possession under United States law; and upon the Committee under the legal systems of both countries.

Because it is the intention of the Liquidators to serve function customarily held by a debtor in possession under chapter 11 of the United States Bankruptcy Code and for, the same Committee to serve formally under Section 1103 of the United States Bankruptcy Code and applicable provisions of Bahamian law, it is necessary without altering the powers or duties of those parties to harmonize their work in order that they can fulfill their respective duties.

In the view of the Liquidators, facts previously unknown to the Liquidators have emerged in the nearly seven months since the commencement of the CEL and CIL liquidations, the following respects included:

(1) Over the last seven months, approximately 32 liquidations or insolvency proceedings involving Commodore subsidiaries have been initiated in 17 foreign jurisdictions involving the appointment of some liquidators not subject to the Liquidator's control and some of which are under the Liquidator's control.

(2) The Liquidators are now engaged in selling substantial assets of CEL and certain of its subsidiaries, involving approximately 10 corporate entities in different nations, not all of which are under the Liquidators' control.

(3) By virtue of the foregoing, the intervention of other courts in other jurisdictions is now avoidable.

(4) By virtue of the Liquidators' continuing investigation and other matters which have come to the attention of the Liquidators, they have had an opportunity to scrutinize the acts, conduct, property, and affairs of Commodore, its subsidiaries and their former officers, directors, and management and other insiders in the many jurisdictions in which Commodore carried on business. As a consequence, the Liquidators have determined that claims against officers, directors, and management, and other insiders ultimately may be available to the Liquidators, of which some may be pursued most effectively in courts of the United States. A factor which the Liquidators have taken into account is that the directors and officers liability insurance policy was issued by companies operating in the United States. Foreseeing such a possibility at the outset of the liquidations that litigation might ultimately be necessary in the United States, the Liquidators advised the parties in their papers filed in Bankruptcy Court that they would consent to the entry of an order for relief under chapter 11 if they were to determine that relief under chapter 11 were in the best interests of the Liquidators and creditors. It now appears to the Liquidators that their obtaining the powers of a debtor in possession through chapter 11 cases in the Bankruptcy Court will offer advantages to the estates of CIL and CEL, in view of the understanding reached with the Unofficial Committee of Unsecured Creditors ("Committee"), as described herein.

(5) Initially, the Liquidators were concerned that parallel proceedings in the United States would invite the possibility that two different fiduciaries (the Liquidators in The Bahamas and different ones in the United States) would be attempting to sell the same assets at the same time. The passage of time has afforded the Liquidators an opportunity to work with the Committee which has indicated a willingness to cooperate with the Liquidators in their efforts to sell assets and to coordinate its duties under Section 1103 of the Bankruptcy Code so as to maximize benefits to creditors.

(6) The Liquidators apprehend that Commodore's chief executive office was located in the United States prior to the commencement of the liquidation proceedings. Accordingly, the Liquidators apprehend the likelihood that their applications for ancillary relief and abstention in the United States may be denied, or overturned on appeal if initially granted in the Bankruptcy Court.

In such event, the possibility exists that fiduciaries other than the Liquidators could be appointed in the United States, thus presenting the potential of disrupting the efficient and effective liquidation of the estates of CEL and CIL. The advent of this Protocol obviates the possibility of adverse consequences to the estates of CEL and CIL resulting from the unfavorable outcome of litigation in the United States regarding ancillary relief and abstention.

In light of the foregoing changed circumstances, among others, and subject to approval by the Supreme Court and the Bankruptcy Court, the Liquidators and the Committee together have proposed this Protocol both to resolve the contemplated litigation and to provide a framework for the efficient and effective administration of the bankruptcy cases for CEL and CIL in both the United States and The Bahamas.

The Liquidators and each member of the Committee hereby agree, subject to entry of orders by the Bankruptcy Court and the Supreme Court approving this Protocol, as follows:

A. The Liquidators shall convert the involuntary chapter 7 cases of CEL and CIL to cases under chapter 11 of the Bankruptcy Code immediately following the courts' approval of this Protocol.

B. The Committee intends that proceedings in the United States be conducted under chapter 11 without the appointment of an examiner trustee and with the Liquidators' constituting the corporate governance and exercising the rights, powers, and duties of debtors in possession.

C. The Supreme Court alone shall govern the Liquidators' tenure in office, the conduct of the liquidation proceedings under Bahamian law, the retention and compensation of the Liquidators and their Bahamian professionals, and the hearing and determination of matters arising in the liquidation proceedings under Bahamian law. Subject to order of the Supreme Court, the liquidations in the Supreme Court shall be continued under court supervision and the Supreme Court, with Messrs. Wilson and Robertson continuing as Liquidators.

D. The Bankruptcy Court alone shall govern the conduct of the chapter 11 cases, the compensation of the Committee's professionals in the United States and the hearing and determination of matters arising in the chapter 11 cases. Should the Liquidators deem it appropriate that the estates of Commodore be substantively consolidated with one another or with those of some or all of their subsidiaries, the Liquidators may commence appropriate proceedings in the Bankruptcy Court, and creditors or parties in interest also may commence such proceedings regarding substantive consolidation in the Bankruptcy Court. Should the Liquidators deem it appropriate, the Liquidators may, at the request of foreign representatives such as those in Japan, the Netherlands, and New Zealand, bring actions in courts in the United States on behalf of such foreign representatives.

E. The Liquidators and the Committee recognize that the conduct of cases involving the same debtors in two courts simultaneously intertwines the two proceedings, presenting the possibility of prejudice to the interest of the Liquidators and creditors unless the proceeding, in the two courts are harmonized. Accordingly, it is the intention of the Liquidators and the Committee that the assets of the estate be liquidated and distributed and that the cases be administered in as economical and efficient, manner as may appear practicable under the circumstances, with one court deferring to the judgment of the other where feasible and the subject matter of a particular matter, action, proceeding, contested matter or adversary proceeding being determined in one court only, where feasible. Proceeding in accordance with the terms and intent of this Protocol shall be deemed consistent with the appropriate conduct of the chapter 11 cases of CEL and CIL and the liquidation proceedings under Bahamian law.

F. The cases of CEL and CIL in the United States shall proceed under chapter 11, with the Liquidators having the rights, powers, and duties of debtors in possession.

G. A proof of claim timely filed in either the Supreme Court or the Bankruptcy Court will be deemed timely filed in both courts. On consent of the Liquidators and the Committee, claims filed in either court may be finally allowed or compromised in either court under the procedures applicable in such court with the same force and effect as though such claim had been finally allowed or compromised in both courts. In the event that the Liquidators and a creditor do not agree on the disposition of such creditor's claim, the Liquidators may reject the claim under Bahamian law or may object to the allowance of such claim in the Bankruptcy Court, provided, however, that if the allowance of such claim is governed principally by the law of the United States or any of its states, then the Liquidators will bring the objection in the Bankruptcy Court. If the allowance of a disputed claim is governed principally by the laws of any nation other than the United States, the Liquidators may, but are not required to, bring such, objection in the Supreme Court. Nothing in Protocol shall be deemed to bind a creditor to the Liquidator's selection of a forum for an objection to claim. Nothing in this Protocol shall be deemed to bind a creditor to the Liquidator's selection of a forum for an objection to claim. Nothing herein shall limit the right of creditors or of the Committee to object to claims under 11 U.S.C. § 502(a).

H. Deloitte & Touche and Fullbright & Jaworski L.L.P. shall be retained as accountants and attorneys for the Liquidators in the United States. The retention by the Liquidators of any professionals resident in the United States, including Deloitte and Fulbright, will be approved by the Bankruptcy Court under 11 U.S.C. § 327. Except for the Liquidators' Bahamian professionals, the Liquidators may retain any professionals not resident in the United States with the approval of the Bankruptcy Court or with the consent of the Committee. The compensation of professionals for the Liquidators shall be determined and paid by order of the Supreme Court.

I. The Committee shall become the official committee of unsecured creditors of CEL and CIL under 11 U.S.C. 1103. Kaye, Fialkow, Richmond & Rothstein ("KFR&R") and Dupuch & Turnquest ("D&T") shall be retained as attorneys for the Committee in the United States and The Bahamas. The retention by the Committee of any professionals resident in the United States, including KFR&R will be approved by the Bankruptcy Court under 11 U.S.C. § 327, *nunc pro tunc* to July 8, 1994. The retention by the Committee of any professionals resident in The Bahamas will, if required, be approved by the Supreme Court, *nunc pro tunc* to July 15, 1994. The Committee may retain any professionals not resident either in the United States or The Bahamas with the approval of the Bankruptcy Court or with the consent of the Liquidators. The compensation of the professionals for the Committee shall be determined and paid pursuant to order of the Bankruptcy Court with respect to professionals resident in the United States and by order of the Supreme Court with respect to professionals resident in The Bahamas. The Liquidators may apply to the Supreme Court for compensation by the estates of CEL and CIL for the services and disbursements of D&T on behalf of the Committee rendered after July 8, 1994 but prior to the approval of this Protocol. KFR&R may apply to the Bankruptcy Court for compensation by the estates of CEL and CIL for the services and disbursements of KFR&R rendered after July 8, 1994 but prior to the approval of this Protocol. The Committee's professionals may apply thereafter for an order of interim compensation to be paid as often and in such manner as the Bankruptcy Court, or the Supreme Court in the case of the Bahamian professionals, may allow. On the approval of this Protocol, the Committee and the Liquidators shall agree upon guidelines for the conduct of the Committee in the liquidation proceedings under Bahamian law and the Liquidators will thereupon apply to the Supreme Court for recognition of the Committee in The Bahamas.

J. The time for the filing of the schedule of assets and liabilities, the statement of affairs, and the list of executory contracts shall be extended to forty-five days after the entry of the order for relief in chapter 11, without prejudice to such other applications for extensions as the Liquidators may determine to file.

K. The Liquidators shall file monthly operating reports with the United States Trustee, with the first report to be filed for both the months of December, 1994, if required, and January, 1995, by February 15, 1995. Operating reports shall be served on counsel for the Committee. The estates of CEL and CIL shall be subject to the payment of fees to the United States Trustee under 28 U.S.C. § 1930(a)(6) only on account of disbursements made from bank accounts maintained by the Liquidators in the United States.

L. Should the Liquidators consider it appropriate to commence insolvency or other similar proceedings in respect of the remaining subsidiaries of CEL or CIL not already in liquidation, they may commence such proceedings in such courts in such nations as they deem appropriate, provided, however, that the Liquidators shall, or they shall cause the debtor to, commence parallel proceedings for such debtor in the Bankruptcy Court under chapter 11 if it appears to the Liquidators that such debtor holds substantial assets, conducted substantial business, or is incorporated in the United States, in which event the Liquidators and the Committee shall apply to the Bankruptcy Court for an order in relation to such debtor appointing the Liquidators to serve in such cases and otherwise under substantially the same terms as the terms of this Protocol as they may be relevant. Absent circumstances requiring immediate action, the Liquidators shall give the Committee five (5) days' prior notice of the commencement of insolvency or other similar proceedings in respect of subsidiaries of CEL or CIL.

M. Without limiting the generality of paragraph "E" above but provided that such actions are taken in accordance with Bahamian law, including the making of such orders of the Supreme Court as may be required after any required notice to the Committee or hearing or opportunity for the Committee to be heard, the Liquidator shall be authorized, without specify approval of the Bankruptcy Court, to

1. deposit funds of the estates of CEL and CIL in accounts or investments outside of the United States;

2. with the consent of the Committee, borrow funds or pledge or charge any assets of CEL or CIL;

3. cause CEL or CIL without the approval of any court, to sell or dispose of any assets outside the ordinary course of business for a consideration in any one case, in the judgment of the Liquidators, of less than $250,000 or, with the consent of the Committee, of more than $250,000 but less than $1,000,000;

4. with the consent of the Committee, lend monies of the estates of CEL or CIL to any of their subsidiaries, with or without security.

5. with regard to subsidiaries which are not debtors in bankruptcy cases in the United States and are not the subject of bankruptcy or liquidation proceedings in any other nation, cause such subsidiaries without the consent of the Committee to take such actions as the Liquidators may deem appropriate, except for any transaction or settlement outside of the ordinary course of business involving, in any one case in the judgment of the Liquidators, greater than $500,000;

6. cause CEL or CIL to commence material legal proceedings, provided that any settlement be subject to approval as may be required by the Bankruptcy Court, in the case of litigation pending in the United States, or the Supreme Court in the case of litigations pending elsewhere. In the case of litigation pending other than in the United States or The Bahamas, any settlement shall be subject to approval as may be required by the Supreme Court. It is the express understanding of the parties that they will work together to maximize recoveries from the exercise of avoiding powers and other rights available under the Bankruptcy Code (including without limitation insider preference actions) the laws of The Bahamas, and the laws of such nations or states of the United States as may be applicable provided that no such avoiding powers, actions or other rights or claims available under the Bankruptcy Code or other applicable state law may be settled or otherwise compromised without the prior approval by the Bankruptcy Court and, if required, by the Supreme Court. The rights of the Liquidators and the Committee under the Bankruptcy Code and Bahamian law to investigate causes of action and claims belonging to the CIL and CEL estates will be exercised jointly in a manner designed to harmonize the administration of the cases.

Both the Committee and the Liquidators shall maintain confidentialities as the Liquidators may request or as may be appropriate under the circumstances. The exchange of opinions or information between the Liquidators and the Committee or their respective professionals shall not be deemed a waiver or any applicable privileges, including the attorney-client and work product privileges.

N. It is expected that upon reasonable request all books, records, reports and opinions of experts other than those of legal counsel will be exchanged by and between the Liquidators and the Committee in connection with the sale of assets and litigation unless the Bankruptcy Court or the Supreme Court orders otherwise, subject to appropriate confidentialities.

O. Neither this Protocol nor any actions taken pursuant hereto is intended to nor shall it have any effect on the rights of creditors, the Liquidators, or the estates of CEL and CIL under 11 U.S.C. § 508(a). Neither this Protocol nor any actions taken pursuant hereto are intended to nor shall they in any manner prejudice or affect the powers, rights, claims and defenses of (i) the Liquidators, CEL, CIL, their estates or any of their creditors under applicable law, including the law of The Bahamas and the Bankruptcy Code or (ii) the Committee in its capacity as a Creditors' Committee under Section 1103 of the Bankruptcy Code.

P. Property of the estates of CEL or CIL which is not administered in the Bankruptcy Court shall not be deemed abandoned under 11 U.S.C. § 554 if such property is administered by the Supreme Court.

Q. The Committee consists of The Prudential Insurance Company of America, Daewoo Telecome, Inc. Microsoft Corp., SCI Systems, Datatech Enterprises, Co., Acer, Inc., Seagate Technology, Inc., Anchor National Life Insurance Co., Credito Intaliano, and Speedy Tech.

R. The term "consent of the Committees" means that (a) the Committee has indicated its consent in writing or (b) the Liquidators have given the Committee not less than five (5) business days' written notice of a contemplated action and the Committee has not indicated its objection in writing within such five (5) day period. Notice to the Committee is sufficient if given to KFR&R. Notice to the Liquidators is sufficient if given to Fulbright & Jaworski L.L.P.

S. To the extent that they are referred to as Liquidators exercising powers granted to them hereunder as debtor in possession, the reference to Liquidators shall refer to the debtor in possession.

T. Nothing in this Protocol is intended to nor shall it affect, impair, limit, extend or enlarge the jurisdiction of the Supreme Court or the Bankruptcy Court.

U. Should questions arise as to the operations of the estates of CEL or CIL or as to the administration of their cases in The Bahamas or the United State pursuant to the terms or intent of this Protocol, the court to which the issue is addressed may hear and determine the matter after notice to the

Liquidators and the Committee and, if the issue is addressed to the Bankruptcy Court, to the United States Trustee.

.... Franklyn R. Wilson, as joint liquidator of CEL and CIL

.... Macgregor N. Robertson, as joint liquidator of CEL and CIL

UNOFFICIAL COMMITTEE OF UNSECURED CREDITORS

By: .... Chairman on behalf of its Members

Dated: Nassau, Bahamas and New York, New York

December 8, 1994

C. EVERFRESH PROTOCOL

STIPULATION REGARDING CROSS-BORDER INSOLVENCY PROTOCOL

Whereas, on November 17, 1995 (the "Filing Date"), Everfresh Beverages, Inc. ("Everfresh"), debtor and debtor-in-possession, and Sundance Beverages, Inc. ("Sundance"), debtor and debtor-in-possession (jointly, the "Debtors"), filed in the United States Bankruptcy Court for the Southern District of New York (together with any other court having jurisdiction over the bankruptcy cases, the "Bankruptcy Court") their respective voluntary petitions for reorganization (the "Chapter 11 cases") under Chapter 11 of Title 11, United States Code, 11 U.S.C. §§ 101 *et seq.* (the "Bankruptcy Code"); and

WHEREAS, no trustee has been appointed in the Chapter 11 cases and pursuant to Sections 1107 and 1108 of the Bankruptcy Code, the Debtors are continuing to operate their businesses and manage their properties as debtors-in-possession, and the Bankruptcy Court entered an order authorizing the joint administration of the Debtors' Chapter 11 cases for procedural purposes; and

WHEREAS, on December 1, 1995, the Bankruptcy Court appointed an official committee of unsecured creditors in these Chapter 11 cases (the "Creditors' Committee") and the Creditors' Committee has selected Obermayer, Rebmann, Maxwell & Hippel as its counsel (the "Committee's Counsel"); and

WHEREAS, Everfresh manufactures and distributes juices, juice drinks, lemonade, and related products throughout the United States and Canada under the brand names of Everfresh, Rich n' Ready and, only in the United States, Wagner (collectively, the "Product"), and maintains offices in Chicago, Illinois, and Mississauga, Ontario, and operates manufacturing plants in Warren, Michigan and Windsor, Ontario, Canada; and

WHEREAS, on the Filing Date, the Bankruptcy Court entered an order (the "Emergency Order") and thereafter on November 22, 1995, a preliminary order (the "Preliminary Order"), which orders, among other things, authorized the Debtors' use of cash collateral and the receipt of discretionary post-petition financing from The CIT Group/Business Credit, Inc. ("CITBC"), the Debtors' secured lender, pursuant to the terms and conditions of the Emergency Order and the Preliminary Order (together with any further orders concerning cash collateral and/or financing, the "Cash Collateral/ Financing Order") and pursuant to the terms of the stipulation and order (the "Stipulation") between the Debtors and CITBC, as approved by the Cash Collateral/Financing Order, of an aggregate amount of $750,000 (the "Advance") for the purposes set forth in a budget (the "Budget") annexed to the Stipulation, through December 12, 1995; and

WHEREAS, on the Filing Date, Everfresh filed a Notice of Intention to Make a Proposal (the "NOI") to its creditors under the Bankruptcy and Insolvency Act of Canada (the "Act") in which Ernst & Young Inc. was named as trustee under the proposal (the "Trustee"), and Everfresh filed a motion for an order in the Ontario Court (General Division), in Bankruptcy (together with any other court having jurisdiction over Everfresh's insolvency proceeding, the "Canadian Court") seeking the appointment of Ernst & Young Inc., as interim receiver (the "Interim Receiver") of the property, business, and assets of Everfresh situated in Canada, which order was entered simultaneously with the filing of the NOI (the "Interim Receiver Order"), a copy of which is annexed hereto as Exhibit "A" (the proceedings under the Act and pursuant to the Interim Receiver Order being referred to as the "Canadian Proceeding"); and

WHEREAS, pursuant to the Interim Receiver Order, the Interim Receiver has been authorized to borrow from time-to-time up to an amount not to exceed $400,000 from CITBC for the purposes of carrying out its responsibilities under the terms of the Interim Receiver Order; and

WHEREAS, on November 27, 1995, Everfresh filed with the Official Receiver, appointed under the Act, a cash flow statement (the "Cash Flow

Statement"), together with the Trustee's and Everfresh's reports on the Cash Flow Statement, in connection with the Canadian Proceeding; and

WHEREAS, it is presently contemplated that all (a) of the business and assets of every nature, tangible and intangible arising from or relating to the manufacture, distribution and sale of the Product in Canada as reflected on the books and records of Everfresh (the "Canadian Assets") and (b) of the business and assets of every nature, tangible and intangible arising from or relating to the manufacture, distribution and sale of the Product in the United Sates as reflected on the books and records of Everfresh (the "US Assets") will be liquidated through the sale thereof by the Debtors in accordance with the applicable provisions of the Bankruptcy Code and Act for the benefit of all secured, priority, and non-insider unsecured creditors of Everfresh, with the net proceeds of sale to be distributed in accordance with priorities established under the Bankruptcy Code and the Act; and

WHEREAS, as of the date hereof, the Debtors have been engaged in extensive negotiations with a number of potential buyers regarding the sale of Everfresh's assets in Canada, and have reviewed letters of intent, and accordingly, it is presently anticipated that a sale of Everfresh's assets in Canada will occur prior to sale of Everfresh's assets located in the United States; and

WHEREAS, pursuant to paragraph 29 of the Interim Receiver Order, the Interim Receiver is ordered to have regard to the Everfresh Chapter 11 case, to cooperate with actions taken in the Everfresh Chapter 11 case and to take such steps as are required to coordinate his administration under the Interim Receiver Order with the administration of the Everfresh Chapter 11 case, where so doing would enhance the value of the Canadian Assets and to review the appropriateness or advisability of a Cross-Border Insolvency Protocol to be submitted for the consideration of the Canadian Court and the Bankruptcy Court; and

WHEREAS, a framework of general principles should be agreed upon to address, among other things, issues that are likely to arise in connection with the cross-border insolvency proceedings of Everfresh, including, without limitation, (a) the sale of Everfresh's Canadian Assets; (b) the sale of Everfresh's US Assets; (c) the disposition of the proceeds of sale of the Canadian Assets and the U.S Assets (together, the "Assets"); (d) the determination of claims asserted against Everfresh, and the allowability and priority status of such claims; (e) the filing and implementation of a plan of reorganization under the Bankruptcy Code and a scheme or proposal under the Act (the "Proposal"); and (f) general administrative matters, similar to the principles proposed in the article of Committee J of the Section on Business Law of the International Bar Association entitled Cross-Border Insolvency Concordat (the "Concordat"), a copy of which is attached hereto as Exhibit "B", and that an agreement upon such matters is essential to the orderly and efficient administration of these cross-border cases; and

WHEREAS, the purpose of the protocol proposed in this Stipulation is to protect the interests of all creditors of Everfresh (in a situation where there is more than one plenary forum and no main forum as provided for in Principle 4 of the Concordat) wherever located and to protect the integrity of the process by which the Chapter 11 case and the Canadian Proceeding is administered.

NOW THEREFORE, the Debtors, CITBC, and the Creditors' Committee by their respective counsel, and Ernst & Young Inc., in its capacity as Interim Receiver and Trustee under the Proposal, hereby stipulate and agree, subject to Bankruptcy Court and Canadian Court approval, as follows:

1. The Debtors and the Interim Receiver will (i) have regard to the proceedings initiated by Everfresh under Chapter 11 of the Bankruptcy Code in the Bankruptcy Court and under the Act in the Canadian Court; (ii) co-operate with actions taken in both the Bankruptcy Court and the Canadian Court; and (iii) take steps to co-ordinate their respective administrations under the Bankruptcy Code and the Act in the Bankruptcy Court and the Canadian Court.

2. The Debtors, the Creditors' Committee and the Interim Receiver, and any other official representative that may be appointed by the Bankruptcy Court or the Canadian Court, shall receive notice of all proceedings in accordance with the practices of the respective Courts, and have the right to appear in all proceedings in any fora, whether in the Bankruptcy Court or the Canadian Court, subject to paragraph 7 hereof. The Debtors and the Interim Receiver shall be subject to jurisdiction in both fora for any matter related to the insolvency proceedings, but appearing in a forum shall not subject him/her to jurisdiction for any other purpose in the forum state, except to the extent otherwise set forth herein to the contrary.

3. The Interim Receiver shall be permitted to act in a manner consistent with the terms of the Interim Receiver Order under Canadian law, and Everfresh shall be permitted to act in a manner consistent with the terms of the Act, the Bankruptcy Code, the Interim Receiver Order, and the Cash Collateral/Financing Order, provided, that, (a) such prior advance notice as is reasonably practicable under the circumstances of any transaction and

hearing thereon concerning the use, sale or lease of Everfresh's Assets outside the ordinary course of business (the "Transactions") and (b) prior notice of those actions proposed to be taken in either the Chapter 11 cases or the Canadian Proceeding where notice of such action is required to be given under the applicable laws of procedures of the governing forum, shall be provided (the "Notice Procedures") by overnight mail, overnight delivery service or facsimile to counsel to the Debtors, Angel & Frankel, P.C., 460 Park Avenue, New York, New York 10022, Attn: Bruce Frankel, Esq., the Interim Receiver at Ernst & Young, Inc., P.O. Box 251, 21st Floor, Toronto Dominion Centre, Canada M5K 137, Attn: Alex Morrison, counsel to CITBC, Dewey Ballantine, 1301 Avenue of the Americas 10019, Attn: Stuart Hirshfield, Esq., special counsel to the Debtors, Lang Michener, BCE Place, Suite 2500, 181 Bay Street, Toronto, Ontario, Canada M5J 2T7, Attn: Joseph Marin, Esq., Canadian counsel to CITBC, Cassels, Brock & Blackwell, Scotia Plaza, Suite 2100, 40 King Street West, Toronto, Ontario, Canada M5H 3C2, Attn: Bruce Leonard, Esq., the Office of the United States Trustee, 80 Broad Street, Third Floor, New York, New York 10004, Attn: Catherine Lotrionte, Esq., the Committee's Counsel, Obermayer, Rebmann, Maxwell & Hippel, Packard Building, 111 South 15th Street, Philadelphia, PA 19102-2688, Attn: Lawrence J. Tabas, Esq., and the Committee's Canadian counsel, Stikeman, Elliott, Commerce Court West, P.O. Box 5300—Suite 5300, Toronto, Ontario, Canada M5L 1B9 Attn: David Byer, Esq., and all persons appearing on the notice of appearance list as reflected on the docket of the Chapter 11 cases and supplied by Everfresh to the Interim Receiver (the "Specified Parties"), which foregoing notice shall be in lieu of notice to all creditors of Everfresh.

4. All creditors of Everfresh shall have the right to appear in any forum to the same extent as creditors of the forum state, regardless of whether they have filed claims in that particular forum. All creditors shall have the opportunity to file a notice of appearance with the Clerk of the Bankruptcy Court, the Alexander Hamilton U.S. Custom House, One Bowling Green, 5th Floor, New York, New York 10004 or to participate in the proceedings in the Canadian Court; provided, however, that such filing or participation may subject such creditor to the jurisdiction in the Court in which the notice or appearance is filed or made.

5. Information publicly available in any forum state shall be publicly available in both fora. To the extent permitted, non-public information shall be made available to official representatives of the Debtors, including any official committee appointed in these cases and shall be shared with other official representatives, subject to appropriate confidentiality arrangements and all privileges under the applicable rules of evidence.

6. Transactions relating to the Canadian Assets will be subject to the sole approval of the Canadian Court. Transactions relating to the US Assets will be subject to the sole approval of the Bankruptcy Court. Any Transactions involving the Assets located both in Canada and the United States will be subject to the joint jurisdiction of the Bankruptcy Court and the Canadian Court. To the extent not otherwise provided for under the Act or the Bankruptcy Code, notice and requirements for approval and authorization of any Transactions shall be in accordance with the Notice Procedures and shall be provided by the Interim Receiver or the Debtors, as the case may be, to the Specified Parties.

7. All creditors of Sundance must file their proofs of claim with the Clerk of the Bankruptcy Court, the Alexander Hamilton U.S. Custom House, One Bowling Green, 5th Floor, New York, New York 10004. Any creditor of Everfresh may file a proof of claim in either the Bankruptcy Court or in the Canadian Proceeding. However, if a creditor files a claim in both the Bankruptcy Court and the Canadian Proceeding, then distribution to such creditor will be adjusted so that recovery is not greater than if the claim were filed in only one forum. A timely filed claim in either the Bankruptcy Court or the Canadian Proceeding will be deemed timely filed in both the Bankruptcy Court and the Canadian Proceeding. The Debtors and the Interim Receiver will endeavor to coordinate notice procedures and establish the same deadline for the filing of claims against the Debtors in both the Bankruptcy Court and the Canadian Proceeding, and all other matters regarding the filing, reviewing and objecting to claims.

8. The Bankruptcy Court shall have jurisdiction over all claims governed principally by the laws of the United States or any of its states. In the event that claims are governed principally by the laws of Canada, the objection to such claims may be brought in either the Canadian Proceeding or the Bankruptcy Court, as mutually agreed upon by the Interim Receiver and the Debtors, or if an agreement cannot be reached, by further order of the Canadian Court. Nothing in this Stipulation shall be deemed to bind a creditor to the foregoing forum selection for filing of objections to claims. The adjudicating forum shall decide the value, allowability and priority of claims filed using a choice of law analysis based upon the choice of law principles applicable in that forum. A creditor's rights to collateral and set-off will be determined under the choice of law principles applicable in that forum, except to the extent set forth in paragraph 12 hereof. No person will be subject to a forum's substantive rules unless under the choice of law principles applicable in that forum such persons would be subject to the forum's substantive laws in lawsuit on the same transaction in a non-insolvency proceeding, except to the extent set forth in paragraph 12 hereof.

Nothing herein shall limit the right of any party-in-interest to object to claims to the extent permitted under Section 502(a) of the Bankruptcy Code and the Bankruptcy Rules nor shall anything herein alter the substantive rights of any party filing a claim in any fora.

9. Neither this Stipulation nor any actions taken pursuant hereto is intended nor shall it have any effect on the rights of creditors, the Interim Receiver, or the estates of the Debtors with regard to the applicability of Section 508(a) of the Bankruptcy Code and any similar provisions under the Act or the Interim Receiver Order, it being intended that such Section 508(a) be, to the extent applicable, enforced in both fora. Neither this Stipulation nor any actions taken pursuant hereto are intended to nor shall they in any manner prejudice or affect the powers, rights, claims and defenses of (i) E&Y, the Debtors, their estates or any of their creditors under applicable law, including the Act and any other relevant Canadian law and the Bankruptcy Code, or (ii) the Creditors' Committee under Section 1103 of the Bankruptcy Code.

10. The proceeds of all Transactions shall be distributed in accordance with the laws of the jurisdiction approving such Transactions. The Bankruptcy Court and the Canadian Court shall apply their respective schemes for distribution to creditors, including, without limitation, the priority treatment respectively accorded to such claims under the Bankruptcy Code or the Act. Any proceeds available after the satisfaction in full of all valid allowed secured claims asserted against Everfresh, and the funding of the Budget, and the Cash Flow Statement as from time-to-time amended shall be maintained by Everfresh in the United States, in an account specifically designated for plan funding (the "Account"), which Account shall be maintained in accordance with Section 345 of the Bankruptcy Code. The distribution of all monies in the Account shall be pursuant to the terms of the Bankruptcy Code and the Act.

11. The classification and treatment of unsecured claims, meaning claims other than priority or secured claims, shall be determined by the Debtors, as to the Canadian Proceedings after consultation with the Trustee under the Proposal.

12. Except to the extent set forth in an order of the Canadian Court, all creditors subject to the jurisdiction of the Bankruptcy Court shall be subject to the avoiding laws set forth in the Bankruptcy Code, and other applicable laws of the United States which shall be the controlling law of each case to the extent permitted by applicable international law, notwithstanding anything to the contrary in paragraph 8. No avoiding actions will be taken

by the Interim Receiver in Canada without the express written consent of the Debtors or as may be directed by the Canadian Court.

13. To the extent permitted by the laws of the respective jurisdictions and to the extent practicable, the Interim Receiver and the Debtors shall endeavor to submit a proposal in Canada and a plan of reorganization in the United States substantially similar to each other and the Debtors, the Interim Receiver and the Trustee shall endeavor to coordinate all procedures in connection therewith, including, without limitation, all solicitation proceedings relating thereto, and all procedures regarding voting, the treatment of creditors, classification of claims, and the like, will either be established by the Debtors after consultation with the Trustee of the Proposal or be dealt with pursuant to a further order of the Bankruptcy Court or the Canadian Court. In order to coordinate the contemporaneous filing of the Proposal and the plan of reorganization, the Debtors shall take the actions necessary to seek extensions from time-to-time of the date for the filing of the Proposal, and the Debtors shall take the actions necessary from time-to-time to seek extensions of the exclusive time period during which only the Debtors may file a plan of reorganization pursuant to Section 1121 of the Bankruptcy Code.

14. Except with respect to matters where the Interim Receiver appears before the Bankruptcy Court pursuant to paragraph 2, hereof, the Canadian Court shall have sole jurisdiction and power over the Interim Receiver, including, without limitation, its tenure in office, the conduct of the liquidation proceedings under Canadian law, the retention and compensation of the Interim Receiver and other Canadian professionals, and the hearing and determination of matters arising in the liquidation proceedings under Canadian law. The Interim Receiver, and Lang Michener, shall be compensated for their services in accordance with Canadian principles under Canadian law, such that the Interim Receiver and Lang Michener are not required to file fee applications with the Bankruptcy Court, provided, that, they be paid as provided for in the Budget and the Cash Flow Statement to the extent contemplated by the Cash Collateral/Financing Order, the Interim Receiver be compensated under the provisions of the Interim Receiver Order to the extent consistent with the Cash Collateral/Financing Order, and notice of such payment is given pursuant to the Notice Procedures to the Specified Parties. The order entered by the Bankruptcy Court authorizing the retention of Lang Michener as Canadian counsel to the Debtors is hereby deemed to be modified to conform to the foregoing provisions.

15. The Bankruptcy Court shall have sole jurisdiction and power over the conduct of the Chapter 11 cases, the compensation of the professionals

rendering services to the Debtors and to the Creditors' Committee in the United States, and the hearing and determination of matters arising in the Chapter 11 cases. This Stipulation shall be without prejudice to the rights of the Debtors to seek the substantive consolidation of their estates in accordance with the Bankruptcy Code.

16. This Stipulation shall be binding on and inure to the benefit of the parties hereto and their respective successors, assigns, representatives, heirs, executors, administrators, trustees (including any trustees of the Debtors under Chapters 7 or 11 of the Bankruptcy Code), and receivers, receiver managers, or custodians appointed under Canadian law, as the case may be.

17. This Stipulation may not be waived, amended or modified orally or in any other way or manner (including, without limitation, pursuant to a plan of reorganization of the Debtors) except by a writing signed by the party to be bound, and such approval and authorization of the Bankruptcy Court or the Canadian Court as may be necessary and appropriate under the circumstances. Notice of any proposed amendment or modification of the Stipulation shall be provided by the party providing such to the Specified Parties in accordance with the Notice Procedures. This Stipulation may be supplemented from time-to-time by the parties hereto as circumstances require with any supplementing stipulations as approved by the Bankruptcy Court and the Canadian Court.

18. Any request for the entry of an order which is contrary to the provisions of this Stipulation must be made on notice by the proponent of the order to the Specified Parties in accordance with the Notice Procedures.

19. Each party represents and warrants to the other that its execution, delivery and performance of this Stipulation are within the power and authority of such party and have been duly authorized by such party except that, with respect to the Debtors and the Interim Receiver, Bankruptcy Court and Canadian Court approval is required.

20. This Stipulation may be signed in any number of counterparts, each of which shall be deemed an original and all of which together shall be deemed to be one and the same instrument, and may be signed by facsimile signature, which shall be deemed to constitute an original signature.

21. The Bankruptcy Court and the Canadian Court shall retain jurisdiction over the parties for the purpose of enforcing the terms and provisions of this Stipulation or approving any amendments or modifications thereto.

22. The parties hereto are hereby authorized to take such actions and execute such documents as may be necessary and appropriate to implement and effectuate this Stipulation.

23. This Stipulation shall be deemed effective upon its approval by the Bankruptcy Court and the Canadian Court.

IN WITNESS WHEREOF, the parties hereto have caused this stipulation to be executed either individually or by their respective attorneys or representatives hereunto authorized.

Dated: New York, New York, December 20, 1995

ANGEL & FRANKEL, P.C.
Counsel for Everfresh Beverages, Inc. and Sundance Beverages, Inc., debtors and debtors-in-possession
By: ....
Bruce Frankel (BF 9009)
460 Park Avenue
New York, New York 10022
(212) 752-8000

LANG MICHENER
Special Counsel for Everfresh Beverages Inc., debtor and debtor-in-possession
By ....
Joseph Marin
BCE Place
Suite 2500
181 Bay Street
Toronto, Ontario, Canada M5J 2T7

DEWEY BALLANTINE
Counsel for the CIT Group/Business Credit, Inc.
By: ....
Stuart Hirschfield (SH 0099)
Hugh M. McDonald (HM 2667)
1301 Avenue of the Americas
New York, New York 10019
(212) 259-8000

CASSELS, BROCK & BLACKWELL
Canadian Counsel for THE CIT Group/Business Credit, Inc.
By: ....
Bruce Leonard
Scotia Plaza
Suite 2100

40 King Street West
Toronto, Ontario, Canada M5H 3C2

ERNST & YOUNG INC.
As Interim Receiver of Everfresh Beverages, Inc., and Trustee of the Proposal
By: ....
Alex Morrison
P.O. Box 251
21st Floor
22 Bay Street
Toronto Dominion Center
Toronto, Ontario, Canada M5K 137

OBERMAYER, REBMANN, MAXWELL & HIPPEL
Counsel for the Creditors' Committee
By: ....
Lawrence J. Tabao
Packard Building
111 South 15th Street
Philadelphia, Pennsylvania 19102-2688

STIKEMAN, ELLIOT
Canadian Counsel for the Creditors' Committee
By: ....
Kenneth G. Ottenbrecht (KGO..........)
David Byer
126 East 56th Street
11th Floor, Tower 56
New York, New York 10022

D. LOEWEN PROTOCOL

CROSS-BORDER INSOLVENCY PROTOCOL

FOR THE LOEWEN GROUP INC. AND ITS AFFILIATES

Between the United States Bankruptcy Court for the District of Delaware (Case No. 99-1244)

and

the Ontario Superior Court of Justice at Toronto (Case No. 99-CL-3384)

This cross-border insolvency protocol (the "Protocol") shall govern the conduct of all parties in interest in the Insolvency Proceedings (as such term is defined herein):

A. Background

1. The Loewen Group Inc., a British Columbia corporation ("TLGI"), is the ultimate parent company of a multinational enterprise that operates, through its various subsidiaries and affiliates, in the United States, Canada and other countries.

2. TLGI and certain of its direct and indirect United States subsidiaries and affiliates (collectively, the "U.S. Debtors") have commenced reorganization cases (collectively, the "U.S. Cases") under chapter 11 of the United States Bankruptcy Code, 11 U.S.C. §§ 101-1330 (the "Bankruptcy Code"), in the United States Bankruptcy Court for the District of Delaware (the "U.S. Court"). The U.S. Debtors are continuing in possession of their respective properties and are operating and managing their businesses, as debtors in possession, pursuant to sections 1107 and 1108 of the Bankruptcy Code. On June 11, 1999, the office of the United States trustee (the "U.S. Trustee") appointed an official committee of unsecured creditors in the U.S. Cases (the "Committee").

3. TLGI and certain of its direct and indirect Canadian subsidiaries and affiliates (collectively, the "Canadian Debtors") have commenced insolvency proceedings (collectively, the "Canadian Cases") by filing an application under the applicable provisions of the Canadian Companies' Creditors Arrangement Act (the "CCAA") with the Ontario Superior Court of Justice (the "Canadian Court"). The Canadian Debtors have sought an order of the Canadian Court (as initially made under the CCAA

and as subsequently amended or modified, the "CCAA Order") under which (a) the Canadian Debtors will be determined to be entities to which the CCAA applies and (b) KPMG Inc. will be appointed as monitor of the Canadian Debtors (the "Monitor"), with the rights, powers, duties and limitations upon liabilities set forth in the CCAA Order.

4. For convenience, (a) the U.S. Debtors and the Canadian Debtors shall be referred to herein collectively as the "Debtors", (b) the U.S. Cases and the Canadian Cases shall be referred to herein collectively as the "Insolvency Proceedings" and (c) the U.S. Court and the Canadian Court shall be referred to herein collectively as the "Courts" (either one a "Court").

B. Purpose and Goals

5. While dual proceedings are pending in the United States and Canada for TLGI, the implementation of basic administrative procedures is necessary to coordinate certain activities in the Insolvency Proceedings, protect the rights of parties thereto and ensure the maintenance of the Courts' independent jurisdiction and comity. Accordingly, this Protocol has been developed to promote the following mutually desirable goals and objectives in both the U.S. Cases and the Canadian Cases:

- harmonize and coordinate activities in the Insolvency Proceedings before the U.S. Court and the Canadian Court;
- promote the orderly and efficient administration of the Insolvency Proceedings to, among other things, maximize the efficiency of the Insolvency Proceedings, reduce the costs associated therewith and avoid duplication of effort;
- honor the independence and integrity of the Courts and other courts and tribunals of the United States and Canada;
- promote international cooperation and respect for comity among the Courts, the Debtors, the Committee, the Estate Representatives (as such term is defined herein) and other creditors and interested parties in the Insolvency Proceedings;
- facilitate the fair, open and efficient administration of the Insolvency Proceedings for the benefit of all of the Debtors' creditors and other interested parties, wherever located; and
- implement a framework of general principles to address basic administrative issues arising out of the cross-border nature of the Insolvency Proceedings.

C. Comity and Independence of the Courts

6. The approval and implementation of this Protocol shall not divest or diminish the U.S. Court's and the Canadian Court's independent jurisdiction over the subject matter of the U.S. Cases and the Canadian Cases, respectively. By approving and implementing this Protocol, neither the U.S. Court, the Canadian Court, the Debtors nor any creditors or interested parties shall be deemed to have approved or engaged in any infringement on the sovereignty of the United States or Canada.

7. The U.S. Court shall have sole and exclusive jurisdiction and power over the conduct and hearing of the U.S. Cases. The Canadian Court shall have sole and exclusive jurisdiction and power over the conduct and hearing of the Canadian Cases.

8. In accordance with the principles of comity and independence established in paragraphs 6 and 7 above, nothing contained herein shall be construed to:

- increase, decrease or otherwise modify the independence, sovereignty or jurisdiction of the U.S. Court, the Canadian Court or any other court or tribunal in the United States or Canada, including the ability of any such court or tribunal to provide appropriate relief under applicable law on an ex parte or "limited notice" basis;
- require the Debtors, the Committee or the Estate Representatives to take any action or refrain from taking any action that would result in a breach of any duty imposed on them by any applicable law;
- authorize any action that requires the specific approval of one or both of the Courts under the Bankruptcy Code or the CCAA after appropriate notice and a hearing (except to the extent that such action is specifically described in this Protocol); or
- preclude any creditor or other interested party from asserting such party's substantive rights under the applicable laws of the United States, Canada or any other jurisdiction including, without limitation, the rights of interested parties or affected persons to appeal from the decisions taken by one or both of the Courts.

9. The Debtors, the Committee, the Estate Representatives and their respective employees, members, agents and professionals shall respect and comply with the independent, non-delegable duties imposed upon them by the Bankruptcy Code, the CCAA, the CCAA Order and other applicable laws.

D. Cooperation

10. To assist in the efficient administration of the Insolvency Proceedings, the Debtors, the Committee and the Estate Representatives shall (a) cooperate with each other in connection with actions taken in both the U.S. Court and the Canadian Court and (b) take any other appropriate steps to coordinate the administration of the U.S. Cases and the Canadian Cases for the benefit of the Debtors' respective estates and stakeholders.

11. To harmonize and coordinate the administration of the Insolvency Proceedings, the U.S. Court and the Canadian Court each shall use its best efforts to coordinate activities with and defer to the judgment of the other Court, where appropriate and feasible. The U.S. Court and the Canadian Court may communicate with one another with respect to any matter relating to the Insolvency Proceedings and may conduct joint hearings with respect to any matter relating to the conduct, administration, determination or disposition of any aspect of the U.S. Cases and the Canadian Cases, in circumstances where both Courts consider such joint hearings to be necessary or advisable and, in particular, to facilitate or coordinate with the proper and efficient conduct of the U.S. Cases and the Canadian Cases. With respect to any such hearings, unless otherwise ordered, the following procedures will be followed:

(i) a telephone or video link shall be established so that both the U.S. Court and the Canadian Court shall be able to simultaneously hear the proceedings in the other Court;

(ii) any party intending to rely on any written evidentiary materials in support of a submission to the U.S. Court or the Canadian Court in connection with any joint hearing or application shall file such materials, which shall be identical insofar as possible and shall be consistent with the procedural and evidentiary rules and requirements of each Court, in advance of the time of such hearing or the submission of such application. If a party has not previously appeared in or attorned or does not wish to attorn to the jurisdiction of either Court, it shall be entitled to file such materials without, by the act of filing, being deemed to have attorned to the jurisdiction of the Court in which such material is filed, so long as it does not request in its materials or submissions any affirmative relief from the Court to which it does not wish to attorn;

(iii) submissions or applications by any party shall be made only to the Court in which such party is appearing, unless specifically given leave by the other Court to make submissions or applications to it;

(iv) the Judge of the U.S. Court and the Justice of the Canadian Court who will hear any such application shall be entitled to communicate with each other in advance of the hearing on the application, with or without counsel being present, to establish guidelines for the orderly submission of pleadings, papers and other materials and the rendering of decisions by the U.S. Court and the Canadian Court, and to deal with any related procedural, administrative or preliminary matters; and

(v) the Judge of the U.S. Court and the Justice of the Canadian Court, having heard any such application, shall be entitled to communicate with each other after the hearing on such application, without counsel present, for the purpose of determining whether consistent rulings can be made by both Courts, and the terms upon which such rulings should be made, as well as to address any other procedural or non-substantive matter relating to such applications.

12. Notwithstanding the terms of paragraph 11 above, the Protocol recognizes that the U.S. Court and the Canadian Court are independent courts. Accordingly, although the Courts will seek to cooperate and coordinate with each other in good faith, each of the Courts shall be entitled at all times to exercise its independent jurisdiction and authority with respect to (a) matters presented to such Court and (b) the conduct of the parties appearing in such matters.

E. Retention and Compensation of Estate Representatives and Professionals

13. Except as provided in paragraphs 19 and 20 below, the Monitor Parties (as hereinafter defined) and any other estate representatives appointed in the Canadian Cases (collectively, the "Canadian Representatives") shall be subject to the sole and exclusive jurisdiction of the Canadian Court with respect to all matters, including: (a) the Canadian Representatives' tenure in office; (b) the retention and compensation of the Canadian Representatives; (c) the Canadian Representatives' liability, if any, to any person or entity, including the Canadian Debtors and any third parties, in connection with the Insolvency Proceedings; and (d) the hearing and determination of any other matters relating to the Canadian Representatives arising in the Canadian Cases under the CCAA or other applicable Canadian law. The Canadian Representatives and their Canadian counsel and any other Canadian professionals shall not be required to seek approval of their retention in the U.S. Court. Additionally, except to the extent that the Monitor is performing U.S. Services (as such term is defined below), the Canadian Representatives and their Canadian counsel and other Canadian

professionals (a) shall be compensated for their services solely in accordance with the CCAA and other applicable Canadian law or orders of the Canadian Court and (b) shall not be required to seek approval of their compensation in the U.S. Court.

14. The Monitor, its Affiliated Professionals (as hereinafter defined) and their officers, directors, employees, counsel and agents, wherever located (collectively, the "Monitor Parties"), shall be entitled to the same protections and immunities in the United States as those granted to them under the CCAA Order. In particular, except as otherwise provided in any subsequent order entered in the Canadian Cases, the Monitor Parties shall incur no liability or obligations as a result of the CCAA Order, the appointment of the Monitor or carrying out of the provisions of the CCAA Order by the Monitor Parties, except any such liability arising from actions of the Monitor Parties constituting gross negligence or willful misconduct.

15. Except as provided in paragraphs 19 and 20 below, any estate representatives appointed in the U.S. Cases, including any examiners or trustees appointed in accordance with section 1104 of the Bankruptcy Code but, for clarity, excluding Canadian professionals retained by the Committee (collectively, "U.S. Representatives" and, together with the Canadian Representatives, the "Estate Representatives"), shall be subject to the sole and exclusive jurisdiction of the U.S. Court with respect to all matters, including: (a) the U.S. Representatives' tenure in office; (b) the retention and compensation of the U.S. Representatives; (c) the U.S. Representatives' liability, if any, to any person or entity, including the U.S. Debtors and any third parties, in connection with the Insolvency Proceedings; and (d) the hearing and determination of any other matters relating to the U.S. Representatives arising in the U.S. Cases under the Bankruptcy Code or other applicable laws of the United States. The U.S. Representatives and their U.S. counsel and other U.S. professionals shall not be required to seek approval of their retention in the Canadian Court. Additionally, the U.S. Representatives and their U.S. counsel and other U.S. professionals (a) shall be compensated for their services solely in accordance with the Bankruptcy Code and other applicable laws of the United States or orders of the U.S. Court and (b) shall not be required to seek approval of their compensation in the Canadian Court.

16. Any Canadian professionals retained by or with the approval of the Canadian Debtors, including Canadian professionals retained by the Committee (collectively, the "Canadian Professionals"), shall be subject to the sole and exclusive jurisdiction of the Canadian Court. Accordingly, the Canadian Professionals (a) shall be subject to the procedures and standards

for retention and compensation applicable in Canada and (b) shall not be required to seek approval of their retention or compensation in the U.S. Court.

17. Any United States professionals retained by the U.S. Debtors and any United States professionals retained by the Committee (collectively, the "U.S. Professionals") shall be subject to the sole and exclusive jurisdiction of the U.S. Court. Accordingly, the U.S. Professionals (a) shall be subject to the procedures and standards for retention and compensation applicable in the U.S. Court under the Bankruptcy Code and any other applicable laws of the United States or orders of the U.S. Court and (b) shall not be required to seek approval of their retention or compensation in the Canadian Court.

18. Notwithstanding anything above to the contrary, the Debtors' independent auditors, KPMG LLP, a limited liability partnership organized under the laws of the Province of Ontario (the "Auditors"), and restructuring accountants, KPMG Inc. (in such capacity, the "Restructuring Accountants"): (a) shall be required to seek the approval of their retention in the U.S. Court; and (b) except to the extent that they are providing Canadian Services in accordance with paragraph 19 below, shall be subject to the procedures and standards for review and approval of compensation applicable in the U.S. Court under the Bankruptcy Code and any other applicable laws of the United States or orders of the U.S. Court. Save and except for the provisions of this paragraph, nothing in this Protocol shall be deemed to subject the Auditors and Restructuring Accountants to the jurisdiction of the U.S. Court or any court in the United States.

19. In performing their respective services in the U.S. Cases and the Canadian Cases, the Auditors, the Restructuring Accountants and the Monitor may from time to time utilize the services and expertise of individuals who are employed by, partners or members in or otherwise affiliated with certain related or affiliated entities (collectively, the "Affiliated Professionals"). The use of such Affiliated Professionals shall be subject to the following terms, conditions and procedures (collectively, the "Affiliate Fee Procedures"):

(a) The Auditors and the Restructuring Accountants may from time to time utilize the services and expertise of Affiliated Professionals in performing their services as independent auditors and restructuring accountants in the U.S. Cases. Among others, these Affiliated Professionals may include employees of, partners in or other individuals affiliated with the Monitor. All services provided by the Auditors, the

Monitor and the Restructuring Accountants in connection with the provision of services to the U.S. Debtors in the U.S. Cases, including services provided by the Affiliated Professionals (collectively, "U.S. Services"), shall be billed to the U.S. Debtors by and through the Auditors, the Monitor and Restructuring Accountants respectively and shall be subject to the procedures and standards for review and approval of compensation applicable in the U.S. Court under the Bankruptcy Code and any other applicable laws of the United States or orders of the U.S. Court. Accordingly, all of the Monitor's fees and expenses incurred in providing U.S. Services to the U.S. Debtors (e.g., through individuals acting as Affiliated Professionals) shall be subject to the review and approval solely by the U.S. Court; provided, however, that the Monitor shall not be subject to the jurisdiction of the U.S. Court for any other purposes, except as expressly provided herein. Notwithstanding the foregoing, services provided by the Monitor that are utilized by the U.S. Debtors in the U.S. Cases, but otherwise would be performed by the Monitor in the Canadian Cases even if the U.S. Cases were not pending, are excluded from the definition of "U.S. Services".

(b) The Monitor may from time to time utilize the services and expertise of Affiliated Professionals in performing its role as monitor in the Canadian Cases. Among others, these Affiliated Professionals may include employees of, partners in or other individuals affiliated with the Auditors or the Restructuring Accountants. All services provided by such Affiliated Professionals in connection with the provision of monitoring services to the Canadian Debtors in the Canadian Cases, including services provided by individuals affiliated with the Auditors or the Restructuring Accountants (collectively, "Canadian Services"), shall be billed to the Canadian Debtors by and through the Monitor and shall be subject to the procedures and standards for review and approval of compensation applicable in the Canadian Court under the CCAA, the CCAA Order and any other applicable Canadian law or orders of the Canadian Court. Accordingly, all of the Auditors' and the Restructuring Accountants' fees and expenses incurred in providing Canadian Services to the Monitor or the Canadian Debtors (i.e., through individuals acting as Affiliated Professionals to Monitor) shall be subject to review and approval solely by the Canadian Court.

(c) In implementing the foregoing procedures, the Auditors, Restructuring Accountants and the Monitor shall maintain separate and distinct billing functions. Therefore: (i) no fees or expenses incurred by the Auditors and the Restructuring Accountants or Affiliated Professionals for U.S. Services shall be charged by the Monitor, the Auditors or the

Restructuring Accountants in the Canadian Cases; and (ii) no fees or expenses incurred by the Monitor or its Affiliated Professionals for Canadian Services in connection with the Canadian Cases shall be charged by the Auditors or the Restructuring Accountants in the U.S. Cases.

(d) Notwithstanding the foregoing, the U.S. Trustee shall have the right, upon request, to review the invoices for fees submitted by the Monitor to the Canadian Debtors to ensure that the Affiliate Fee Procedures are being implemented properly.

F. Rights to Appear and Be Heard

20. The Debtors, their creditors and other interested parties in the Insolvency Proceedings, including the Committee, the Estate Representatives and the U.S. Trustee, shall have the right and standing to (a) appear and be heard in either the U.S. Court or the Canadian Court in the Insolvency Proceedings to the same extent as creditors and other interested parties domiciled in the forum country, subject to any local rules or regulations generally applicable to all parties appearing in the forum and (b) file notices of appearance or other papers with the Clerk of the U.S. Court or the Canadian Court in the Insolvency Proceedings; provided, however, that any appearance or filing may subject a creditor or interested party to the jurisdiction of the Court in which the appearance or filing occurs; provided further, that appearance by the Committee in the Canadian Cases shall not form a basis for personal jurisdiction in Canada over the members of the Committee. Notwithstanding the foregoing, and in accordance with the policies set forth in paragraphs 13 and 15 above: (a) the Canadian Court shall have jurisdiction over the U.S. Representatives and the U.S. Trustee solely with respect to the particular matters as to which the U.S. Representatives or the U.S. Trustee appear before the Canadian Court; and (b) the U.S. Court shall have jurisdiction over the Canadian Representatives solely with respect to the particular matters as to which the Canadian Representatives appear before the U.S. Court.

G. Notice

21. Notice of any motion, application or other pleading or paper filed in one or both of the Insolvency Proceedings and notice of any related hearings or other proceedings mandated by applicable law in connection with the Insolvency Proceedings or the Protocol shall be given by appropriate means (including, where circumstances warrant, by courier, telecopier or other

electronic forms of communication) to the following: (a) all creditors, including the Committee, and other interested parties in accordance with the practice of the jurisdiction where the papers are filed or the proceedings are to occur; and (b) to the extent not otherwise entitled to receive notice under subpart (a) of this sentence, the Monitor, to its counsel Geoffery B. Morawetz, Goodman Phillips & Vineberg, Suite 2400, 250 Yonge Street, Toronto, Ontario M5B 2M6, Fax: (416) 979-1234, the U.S. Trustee, John D. McLaughlin, Office of the United States Trustee, Curtis Center, Suite 950 West, 601 Walnut Street, Philadelphia, Pennsylvania 19106, Fax: (215) 597-5795, and such other parties as may be designated by either of the Courts from time to time. The Monitor shall provide the U.S. Court or the Canadian Court, as the case may be, with copies of the Orders and of any reasons or opinions of the other Court in the Insolvency Proceedings.

H. Joint Recognition of Stays of Proceedings Under the Bankruptcy Code and the CCAA

22. In recognition of the importance of the stay of proceedings and actions against the Canadian Debtors, their directors and their assets under section 11 of the CCAA and the CCAA Order (the "Canadian Stay") on the successful completion of the Insolvency Proceedings for the benefit of the Debtors and their respective estates and stakeholders, to the extent appropriate the U.S. Court shall extend and enforce the Canadian Stay in the United States (to the same extent such stay of proceedings and actions is applicable in Canada) to prevent adverse actions against the Canadian Debtors, their directors and the assets, rights and holdings of the Canadian Debtors in the United States. In implementing the terms of this paragraph, the U.S. Court may consult with the Canadian Court regarding (a) the interpretation and application of the Canadian Stay and any orders of the Canadian Court modifying or granting relief from the Canadian Stay; and (b) the enforcement in the United States of the Canadian Stay.

23. In recognition of the importance of the stay of proceedings and actions against the U.S. Debtors and their assets under section 362 of the Bankruptcy Code (the "U.S. Stay") to the successful completion of the Insolvency Proceedings for the benefit of the Debtors and their respective estates and stakeholders, to the extent appropriate the Canadian Court shall extend and enforce the U.S. Stay in Canada (to the same extent such stay of proceedings and action is applicable in the United States) to prevent adverse actions against the assets, rights and holdings of the U.S. Debtors in Canada. In implementing the terms of this paragraph, the Canadian Court may consult with the U.S. Court regarding (a) the interpretation and

application of the U.S. Stay and any orders of the U.S. Court modifying or granting relief from the U.S. Stay and (b) the enforcement in Canada of the U.S. Stay.

24. Nothing contained herein shall affect or limit the Debtors' or other parties' rights to assert the applicability or non-applicability of the U.S. Stay or the Canadian Stay to any particular proceeding, property, asset, activity or other matter, wherever pending or located.

I. Effectiveness; Modification

25. This Protocol shall become effective only upon its approval by both the U.S. Court and the Canadian Court.

26. This Protocol may not be supplemented, modified, terminated or replaced in any manner except by the U.S. Court and the Canadian Court. Notice of any legal proceeding to supplement, modify, terminate or replace this Protocol shall be given in accordance with paragraph 21 above.

J. Procedure for Resolving Disputes Under the Protocol

27. Disputes relating to the terms, intent or application of this Protocol may be addressed by interested parties to either the U.S. Court, the Canadian Court or both Courts upon notice in accordance with paragraph 21 above. Where an issue is addressed to only one Court, in rendering a determination in any such dispute, such Court: (a) shall consult with the other Court; and (b) may, in its sole and exclusive discretion, either (i) render a binding decision after such consultation, (ii) defer to the determination of the other Court by transferring the matter, in whole or in part, to the other Court or (iii) seek a joint hearing of both Courts. Notwithstanding the foregoing, each Court in making a determination shall have regard to the independence, comity or inherent jurisdiction of the other Court established under existing law.

K. Preservation of Rights

28. Neither the terms of this Protocol nor any actions taken under the terms of this Protocol shall prejudice or affect the powers, rights, claims and defenses of the Debtors and their estates, the Committee, the Estate Representatives, the U.S. Trustee or any of the Debtors' creditors under applicable law, including the Bankruptcy Code and the CCAA.

29. With respect to paragraphs 11, 22, 23 and 27 hereof and to the extent that the U.S. Court or the Canadian Court wish, during any consultations

between them, to provide advice or guidance to one another in relation to substantive or non-procedural issues:

(i) The U.S. Court or the Canadian Court, as the case may be, shall provide any such advice or guidance in respect of substantive or non-procedural issues to the other in writing;

(ii) Copies of such written advice or guidance shall be served in accordance with paragraph 21 hereof; and

(iii) Counsel shall be entitled to make submissions to the appropriate Court in connection with the written advice or guidance received by it.

L. The Claims Procedure

30. The determination of the amount, value, allowability, priority, classification and treatment of the claims of claimants of the Debtors, including issues with respect to a claimant's rights to collateral and set-off (the "Adjudication") shall be dealt with by the Courts in the Insolvency Proceedings as set out below:

(i) the Adjudication of claims against the Canadian Debtors, other than TLGI, shall be by the Canadian Court;

(ii) the Adjudication of claims against the U.S. Debtors, other than TLGI, shall be by the U.S. Court;

(iii) the Adjudication of claims against TLGI shall be by either the U.S. Court or the Canadian Court, whichever jurisdiction has the closest nexus to the claim. For greater certainty, the Adjudication of claims which are the subject of litigation shall be by the Canadian Court if the litigation was commenced in Canada and by the U.S. Court if the litigation was commenced in the United States, and the Adjudication of claims arising out of real property shall be by the Canadian Court if the real property is situated in Canada and by the U.S. Court if the real property is situated in the United States; and

(iv) the Adjudication of claims arising pursuant to or secured by the Collateral Trust Agreement shall be by the U.S. Court.

31. Notwithstanding paragraph 30, the Courts, acting jointly, may alter the jurisdiction in which a claim is to be adjudicated or may order that the claim be adjudicated in both jurisdictions by way of a joint hearing.

32. Where, as a part of the claims bar process to be established in each of the Insolvency Proceedings, a Debtor is required to send a notice of claim to its claimants (the "Notice to Claimants") such Notice to Claimants shall include the jurisdiction for the Adjudication of the claimant's claim in accordance with the principles set out in paragraph 30. Adjudication of any such claims shall be by the Court of the jurisdiction set out in the Notice to Claimants unless the claimant files a motion with such Court objecting to its jurisdiction within the period to be established in the claims bar process, failing which the claimant shall be conclusively deemed to have accepted the jurisdiction set out in the Notice to Claimants.

33. In the case of a claim filed by a claimant who had not been sent a Notice to Claimants in respect of such claim, the Debtors, shall upon receipt of the claimant's claim, send to such claimant a notice within the period to be established in the claims bar process which notice shall include the jurisdiction for Adjudication of the claimant's claim in accordance with the principles set out in paragraph 30. Any claimant wishing to object to such jurisdiction of Adjudication must file a motion objecting to the Court of such jurisdiction within the period set out in the claims bar process, failing which it shall be conclusively deemed to have accepted the jurisdiction.

34. The Adjudication of the claims by the U.S. Court shall be conducted pursuant to the substantive and procedural law of the United States. The Adjudication of claims by the Canadian Court shall be conducted pursuant to the substantive and procedural law of Canada. In each case, disallowance procedures and appeals therefrom shall be governed by the laws of the jurisdiction in which the claim is to be dealt with pursuant to this Protocol.

35. With respect to TLGI, where there has been a final Adjudication of a claim by a Court in one jurisdiction, such Adjudication shall be recognized as final and binding and as having the same effect in the other jurisdiction.

36. A claimant with two or more separate and distinct claims, which under this Protocol should be dealt with in different jurisdictions, shall prove each claim in the appropriate jurisdiction. Where a claimant files the same claim in both the Canadian Cases and the U.S. Cases, the duplicative claim which was not filed in the jurisdiction contemplated by virtue of the principles set out in paragraph 30 shall be deemed to be a nullity.

E. INVERWORLD PROTOCOL

STIPULATION REGARDING CROSS-BORDER INSOLVENCY PROTOCOL

Subject to authorization from the Cayman Court, Len B. Blackwell and Christopher D. Johnson of PricewaterhouseCoopers ("PWC"), as foreign representatives of IG Services Ltd. ("IGS"), and subject to authorization from the representatives of IWG Services Ltd. ("IWG"), and Len B. Blackwell and J. Robert Medlin of PWC as receivers for InverWorld, Inc. and InverWorld Securities Inc., enter into this Stipulation Regarding Cross-Border Insolvency Protocol, as follows:

PRELIMINARY STATEMENT

The purpose of this stipulation is to ensure the just, efficient, and speedy administration of pending insolvency proceedings involving IGS and IWG in three separate jurisdictions and, to the extent necessary, the SEC Receivership, referred to in paragraph 16 below. Thus, it is in the interests of all parties (including the liquidators of IGS, the provisional liquidators of IWG, and creditors of, and investors with claims against assets held by, IWG and IGS) to seek to cooperate in the conduct of the insolvency proceedings for IWG and IGS with a view to:

(i) minimize the total costs incurred by the liquidators of IGS ("Cayman Liquidators") and the liquidators of IWG ("English Provisional Liquidators") in protecting investors' and creditors' interests, in particular by avoiding unnecessary duplication between the tasks carried out by the Cayman Liquidators and the English Provisional Liquidators and unnecessary litigation or court applications;

(ii) avoiding any potential conflict between the insolvency proceedings in different jurisdictions;

(iii) ensuring transparency and accountability in the conduct of the proceedings in the United States, the Cayman Islands, and England and receiving input from, and involvement of, investors in a forum which is convenient for them; and

(iv) providing a framework for protecting the interests of and maximizing returns to investors.

With these goals in mind, the parties enter into this stipulation.

BACKGROUND

I. The Parties.

A. IWG Services, Ltd.

1. IWG is an English-registered subsidiary of IWG Holdings, Ltd. ("IWG Holdings"), also an English-registered corporation. IWG was created to provide investment management and financial services and act as a financial intermediary for investors outside of the United States, particularly for investors based in Mexico and Latin America.

B. IG Services, Ltd.

2. IGS is a Cayman Islands-registered corporation providing investment management and financial services and acting as a financial intermediary for investors outside of the United States, particularly for investors based in Mexico and Latin America. IGS is also owned by IWG Holdings.

C. The United States Companies.

3. InverWorld Holding, Inc. ("Holding") is a United States-registered company which owned certain operating United States-registered companies (the "InverWorld Companies"), including InverWorld Securities, Inc. ("InverWorld Securities") and InverWorld, Inc. The InverWorld Companies are all based in San Antonio, Texas, and comprise companies incorporated and operating in the United States and Latin America. The InverWorld Companies provided services to IGS, which include investment consulting, trade execution, data processing. and client and accounting support. Though providing services both to IWG and IGS, the InverWorld Companies are not directly owned or operated by either IWG or IGS. Ultimate beneficial ownership of the InverWorld Companies, IWG and IGS, however, is the same.

4. InverWorld Securities is a registered broker/dealer operating as custodian of funds for various United States and Mexican investors. InverWorld Securities maintains counterparty accounts bearing IGS's name. InverWorld, Inc. operates a computer that generates the customer account data for IWG and IGS.

II. Relationship Between the Foreign Companies and the United States Companies.

A. Services Agreement Between IWG and IGS.

5. IWG and IGS entered into the Administrative Services and Assistance Agreement dated December 31, 1996 ("Services Agreement"), which authorized IGS to furnish IWG assistance with respect to general management and accounting, financial, legal, reporting, general management communications with customers, and computer technology related to the management of accounts of customers relating to the securities and investment business. The stated purpose of the Services Agreement is to have IGS assist IWG in general administration and management of accounts of customers relating to the securities and investment business of IWG. The Services Agreement provides that IGS is the investment manager for IWG and is to perform all functions relative to IWG's relationships with clients and account brokerages.

B. Consulting Agreement Between IGS and InverWorld, Inc.

6. To facilitate management of IGS's and subsequently IWG's operations, IGS retained InverWorld, Inc. to perform consulting services pursuant to an agreement dated July 1, 1993 ("Consulting Agreement"). The Consulting Agreement provided that IGS engage InverWorld, Inc. to provide technical support services to IGS. These services included (a) maintaining all records with respect to the purchase, sale, and settlement of portfolio securities, (b) monitoring, expediting, and recording the collection of all income due IGS or its client, (c) summarizing, posting, recording, and reconciling all items of cash receipts and disbursements, (d) recording all transactions to the account of IGS for its clients, (e) preparing and issuing monthly reports to IGS and providing all necessary information for the preparation and filing of any and all tax returns and reports to governmental agencies by IGS, (f) preparing information for monthly statements for clients of IGS, and (g) such other statistical, record keeping, or administrative services as may have been agreed upon from time to time between InverWorld, Inc. and IGS.

7. In consideration for those consulting services, InverWorld, Inc. was to receive a monthly fee of the percentage of assets managed by InverWorld, Inc. As a result of the Consulting Agreement, InverWorld, Inc. has accumulated data and records relating to IWG's and IGS's clients that are valuable to the liquidation of IWG and IGS.

III. Foreign Proceedings.

A. Commencement of IGS's Insolvency Proceedings in the Grand Court of the Cayman Islands.

8. The directors of IGS met on July 1, 1999, and concluded that IGS was unable to continue as a going concern. The sole shareholder of IGS (namely IWG Holdings) passed a resolution on July 2, 1999, for the voluntary winding up of IGS ("Cayman Proceedings"). On the same day, an Order ("Cayman Court Order") was entered by the Grand Court of the Cayman Islands ("Cayman Court") for court supervision of the liquidation of IGS. Len B. Blackwell, of PwC Dallas, and Christopher D. Johnson, of PwC Cayman Islands, were appointed as liquidators. At the time of the initiation of the Cayman Proceedings, IGS had seven employees in the Cayman Islands.

B. Commencement of IWG's Insolvency Proceedings in the High Court of Justice Chancery Division Companies Court.

9. On July 6, 1999, by written resolution of IWG Holdings, as sole shareholder of IWG, Mark Novak, as sole director of IWG, was authorized to present a petition in the name of IWG for compulsory winding up under the Insolvency Act of 1986 ("English Proceedings"). On July 7, 1999, through counsel, Mr. Novak presented to the High Court of Justice, Chancery Division Companies Court, in England ("English Court") a Winding Up Petition and an application for the appointment of provisional liquidators of IWG. On that same day, the English Court ordered the appointment of Christopher John Hughes and Andrew Mark Homan, both of PwC, Plumtree Court, London EC4A 4HT, as Joint Provisional Liquidators of IWG until the final determination of the Winding Up Petition or further order of the English Court. The English Court initially set a date for the hearing of IWG's winding up petition for August 11, 1999, which hearing has been adjourned until November 11, 1999. At the time of the commencement of the English Proceedings, IWG had no employees in England, was believed to have no assets in England, and no place of business in the United Kingdom, aside from a registered office (Baker Street address).

IV. United States Proceedings.

A. State Court Actions.

10. IGS has assets in a number of jurisdictions, including assets that are currently being held in the United States, which include, among other things, books and records related to customer accounts and cash and securities being held by United States-registered banks and brokerages.

11. Two actions were filed in Bexar County, Texas, styled Cesar Garcia Mendez v. IWG, Ltd., et al., No. 1999-CI-09400, and Nocando Mem Holdings Limited, et al. v. IWG Services Ltd., et al., No. 1999-Cl-09738 ("State Court Actions"). These State Court Actions could have resulted in judgments against the IGS and/or IWG or companies related to IGS and/or IWG.

B. The Section 304 Proceedings.

12. To facilitate the foreign court supervised liquidation and provisional liquidation proceedings and to prevent entry of judgments against IWG and/or IGS, on July 13, 1999, Len B. Blackwell on behalf of IGS filed a petition for relief under section 304 of the Bankruptcy Code with the United States Bankruptcy Court for the Western District of Texas, San Antonio Division ("US Bankruptcy Court").

13. On July 14, 1999, Christopher J. Hughes on behalf of IWG filed a petition for relief under section 304 of the Bankruptcy Code with the US Bankruptcy Court. The two section 304 proceedings are collectively referred to as the "304 Proceedings". In the 304 Proceedings, the US Bankruptcy Court entered orders staying all proceedings against IWG and IGS.

C. Involuntary Chapter 7 Petitions Against IGS and IWG.

14. On July 13, 1999, involuntary petitions ("Involuntary Proceedings") were filed under chapter 7 of the Bankruptcy Code against IGS and IWG in the US Bankruptcy Court. The 304 Proceedings and the Involuntary Proceedings are referred to as the "US Proceedings".

15. The State Court Actions were removed to the US Bankruptcy Court.

D. The SEC Enforcement Action.

16. On Wednesday, August 4, 1999, the United States Securities & Exchange Commission ("SEC") commenced an action ("SEC Proceedings") against InverWorld, Inc., InverWorld Securities, Inc., IGS, IWG, George H. Fahey, and Jose P. Zollino in the United States District Court for the Western District of Texas, San Antonio Division ("US District Court"). J. Robert Medlin and Len B. Blackwell of PwC have been appointed as receivers of InverWorld, Inc. and InverWorld Securities Inc. ("SEC Receivers"). They were also appointed receivers for the "Relief Defendant LHH Partnership, Ltd". Although IGS and IWG are named as defendants, they are not currently under an SEC receivership. The US District Court has entered orders freezing the assets of the defendants and requiring a repatriation of funds to the US. An order has been obtained modifying the freezing order so as not to prevent the foreign liquidators of IWG and IGS from performing their duties and obligations.

PURPOSE OF STIPULATION

17. The English Provisional Liquidators and the Cayman Liquidators (collectively referred to as the "Liquidators") contemplate that all (a) of the business and assets of every nature, tangible and intangible, arising from or relating to IGS ("IGS Assets") and (b) of the business and assets of every nature, tangible and intangible, arising from or relating to IWG ("IWG Assets"), will be protected and, to the extent considered necessary, liquidated [and/or distributed in specie] as appropriate in accordance with the applicable law.

18. A framework of general principles should be agreed upon to address, among other things, issues that are likely to arise in connection with the cross-border insolvency proceedings of IGS and IWG, including, without limitation, (a) the recovery and/or securing and the potential liquidation and/or disposition of IGS Assets; (b) the recovery and/or securing and the potential liquidation and/or disposition of IWG Assets; (c) the holding and/or disposition of the proceeds of the IGS Assets and the IWG Assets (together, the "Assets"); (d) the determination of claims asserted against IGS and IWG, and the allowance and priority status of such claims; and (e) general administrative matters. An agreement upon such matters is essential to the orderly and efficient administration of these cross-border cases.

19. The purpose of the protocol proposed in this Stipulation is to protect the interests of all creditors of IGS and IWG wherever located and to

protect the integrity of the process by which the SEC Proceedings, US Bankruptcy Proceedings, Cayman Proceedings, and English Proceedings are administered. There is a need for such a protocol to provide a framework for cooperation between the various jurisdictions and provide input by counsel representing a significant portion of the creditors of IGS and IWG and to further promote a cost-effective mechanism to minimize duplication.

NOW THEREFORE the SEC Receivers, Cayman Liquidators, and English Provisional Liquidators, hereby stipulate and agree, subject to US District Court, US Bankruptcy Court, Cayman Court, and English Court approval, as follows:

1. The SEC Receivers, the Cayman Liquidators, and the English Provisional Liquidators will (i) cooperate in good faith with each other to the extent permitted by the applicable law when taking action in the US District Court, US Bankruptcy Court, Cayman Court, and the English Court, subject to the restrictions of their respective appointing courts and (ii) take steps to coordinate their respective administrations in the Cayman Islands, the US and England and shall coordinate any court action brought in the context of those administrations where possible and subject to any applicable law.

2. One Ad Hoc Committee consisting of counsel who represent investors shall be formed to participate in the US District Court, US Bankruptcy Proceedings, Cayman Proceedings and the English Proceedings ("Committee"). Initially, the Committee will be composed of Cox & Smith Incorporated, Hughes & Luce, L.LP., Jackson Walker, L.L.P., Jenkens & Gilchrist, P.C., Pope Shoemake Kerr & Hendershot, P.C., and Piper & Marbury LLP. Following approval of this protocol by the respective Courts, the SEC Receivers, the Cayman Liquidators and the English Provisional Liquidators will discuss with a view to agreeing the most practicable and effective method for giving all other investors or creditors of IWG and IGS notice of the existence and current membership of the Ad Hoc Committee and the opportunity to be represented on the Committee as additional members if this is considered appropriate by either the English Court, Cayman Court or US Bankruptcy Court, giving due regard to the value of the claim of such investor or creditor against IWG or IGS. Without submitting to the jurisdiction of any Court, the members of the Committee shall file contemporaneously with each Court a statement of Counsel informing the Courts of the investors (by account number) which they represent. The members of the Committee (a) reserve the right to seek

official status in any Court and (b) shall have the right to seek reimbursement for fees and expenses, including, without limitation, under §503 of the Bankruptcy Code and similar provisions in the English and Cayman Proceedings. Any action and/or position taken by the Committee shall be authorized if approved by a majority of the members of the Committee. The US District Court, US Bankruptcy Court, Cayman Court and English Court shall each have jurisdiction to alter the composition of the Committee upon request of a third party other than the Liquidators.

3. This stipulation will govern "Phase I" of the insolvency proceedings. Phase I shall consist of two discrete subparts. Subpart A of Phase I will govern the investigation, freezing, protection, collection, recovery, and possible liquidation and/or disposition of assets other than causes of action against related and/or third parties. Subpart B of Phase I shall be the investigation, analysis, and prosecution of causes of action against related and/or third parties to the extent possible and appropriate. All parties, including the Liquidators, agree that both subparts of Phase I should proceed simultaneously, provided that this agreement is subject to the entry of any orders staying, freezing, or abating any of the proceedings.

4. Phase II shall consist of the process of filing claims, the assessment, investigation, allowance and disallowance of claims, including any proprietary claims, and the distribution of assets. All parties have agreed that Phase II will not be addressed in this stipulation. All parties agree to work in good faith to present a stipulation governing Phase II. The parties agree to request the respective courts to suspend to the extent necessary or permissible the application of any rules, statutes, procedures, or orders relating to the filing of claims, the allowance end disallowance of claims, and the distribution of assets.

5. Assets will be categorized for purposes of reference as Counterparty Accounts, Material Assets and Non-Material Assets.

(i) Counterparty Accounts are the custodian accounts that contain fixed-income and equity securities from issuers other than IWG, IGS or InverWorld-related entities. These securities are sometimes referred to as External Products.

(ii) Material Assets are those assets outside of Counterparty Accounts that have a gross estimated market value of $1,000,000.00 (US) or more.

(iii) The Non-Material Assets are those assets outside of Counterparty Accounts that have a gross estimated market value of less than $1,000,000.00 (US).

6. In regard to Non-Material Assets, the Liquidators may seek entry of orders from the applicable courts authorizing the disposition of Non-Material Assets in a fashion that would not require obtaining court approval for each and every disposition.

7. With respect to Material Assets located in the Caymans, the Liquidators shall be entitled to seek all necessary instructions from the Cayman Court and shall not be required to seek any approvals from the US Bankruptcy Court. With respect to Material Assets located in the US, Liquidators shall be entitled to seek all necessary instructions from the US Bankruptcy Court and shall not be required to seek approval from the Cayman Court. With respect to Material Assets located in neither the Caymans nor the United States other than Counterparty Accounts appropriate approvals from the US Bankruptcy Court and the Cayman Court (in addition to such other approvals or directions of such other courts as the Liquidators consider to be necessary or convenient) and will not move forward with respect to such assets unless the necessary approvals are received from both courts.

8. With respect to Counterparty Accounts located in the Caymans, the Liquidators shall be entitled to seek all necessary instructions from the Cayman Court and shall not be required to seek any approvals from the US Bankruptcy Court. With respect to Counterparty Accounts located in the United States, Liquidators shall be entitled to seek all necessary instructions from the US Bankruptcy Court and shall not be required to seek approval from the Cayman Court. With respect to Counterparty Accounts located in neither the Caymans nor the United States, the Liquidators shall seek appropriate approvals from the US Bankruptcy Court and the Cayman Court (in addition to such other approvals or directions of such other courts as the Liquidators consider to be necessary or convenient) and will not move forward with respect to such assets unless the necessary approvals are received from the appropriate courts, provided that, if the Investment Advisor referred to in paragraph 9 below advises that there is a threat of immediate dissipation of value, the Liquidators shall not be required to seek such approvals. With respect to any required hearing relating to the liquidation and/or disposition of assets, there will be at least five business days' notice to the members of the Committee absent an emergency.

9. With respect to the Counterparty Accounts, the Liquidators shall seek the appointment of an investment advisor (the "Investment Advisor") whose appointment will be approved jointly by the Cayman Court and US Bankruptcy Court, subject to the Joint Protocol and the Orders authorizing retention and defining the scope of the authority of the Investment Advisor

(the "Investment Advisor's Retention Order"). Subsequently, the Liquidators will initiate the liquidation and/or disposition in specie of the Counterparty Accounts to the extent they have obtained authorization from the appropriate court(s).

10. The disposition of any asset governed by this Joint Protocol shall not prejudice an investor's or any other third party's right or ability to assert a claim against such specific asset or the proceeds from the disposition of such asset. The Liquidators shall be required to maintain books and records which will individually account for the disposition of assets from the inception of the proceedings.

11. The Liquidators shall use their best efforts, on or before the 25th day of each month, to file monthly status reports with the US Bankruptcy Court, the Cayman, and the English Court setting forth the status of their efforts for the prior month. A copy of such report shall be served on the members of the Committee. The Liquidators shall use their best efforts to ensure that a representative of the Liquidators shall also be available for weekly conference calls with the Committee at which time the Liquidators or their representatives will fully apprise and inform the Committee of the status of their efforts, subject to appropriate confidentiality arrangements, the dictates of governmental agencies, and all privileges under the applicable rules of evidence.

12. Subject to the provisions herein and the prior orders of the appropriate courts, the SEC Receivers and the Liquidators are hereby authorized to coordinate with the Committee:

(i) the identification, preservation, collection, and realization of, if necessary, the relevant assets of IGS and IWG, including evaluation of causes of action for recovery of avoidable transfers and damages;

(ii) all investigation and analysis necessary to establish the financial position of IWG and IGS;

(iii) analysis of the type, nature and amount of investor claims (and the Committee agrees to work cooperatively with the Liquidators to develop a methodology for claims assessment and, ultimately, the claims adjudication process);

(iv) the investigation of the extent and cause of any shortfall to investors;

(v) the review of whether investors have any proprietary rights (and whether they are advantaged by maintaining them);

(vi) the making of proposals regarding the next steps or further action to be taken in order to realize or distribute assets, including an asset realization strategy, suggestions for the procedure to be used to effect a distribution of assets to investors (e.g., schemes of arrangement or plans of liquidation);

(vii) the taking of any action necessary for the Cayman Liquidators to fulfill their duties and obligations as Liquidators under Cayman law;

(viii) the taking of any action necessary for the English Liquidators to fulfill their duties and obligations under English law;

(ix) the taking of any action necessary for the SEC Receivers to fulfill their duties and obligations in administering and overseeing the SEC Receivership;

(x) the allocation of particular tasks to the Cayman Liquidators, the SEC Receivers, or the English Provisional Liquidators so as to efficiently, effectively and economically promote the objectives set forth herein, and specifically considering which individual(s) are best placed to carry out the tasks on a cost effective basis. It is currently anticipated that the Cayman Liquidators will take the lead in locating and seizing assets and the Liquidators and the SEC Receivers, in close cooperation and in full consultation with the Committee and having sought its view in this matter, and any official representative that may be appointed by the US Bankruptcy Court or the US District Court, will take the lead in the investigation, analysis, and prosecution of causes of action against related and/or third parties and shall have authority to conduct discovery in all jurisdictions, including without limitation pursuant to § 304 of the Bankruptcy Code; and

(xi) providing for cooperation with, and assistance to, governmental agencies.

13. Pursuant to the order dated August 23, 1999 ("Order") of the US District Court, the SEC Receivers and Liquidators recognize their responsibilities to be observant for and to preserve third party causes of action belonging to the SEC Receivers or Liquidators which ultimately might benefit investors of the entities referred to in the Order. To this end, the SEC Receivers and the Liquidators will use their best efforts to work with the Department of Justice or other governmental authorities to assist the Committee in obtaining access to documents (as defined in Fed. R. Civ. P. 34(a)) and other forms of discovery, so long as such assistance does not threaten the integrity of any criminal investigation.

14. The Cayman Liquidators, the English Provisional Liquidators, and the SEC Receivers and any other official representative that may be appointed by the US District Court, the US Bankruptcy Court, Cayman Court, or the English Court, shall receive and give notice of all proceedings in accordance with the practices of the respective Courts and have the right to appear in all proceedings in any forum.

15. For the avoidance of doubt, the Cayman Liquidators shall be permitted to act in a manner consistent with the terms of the Cayman Court Orders and shall be permitted to act in a manner consistent with the laws governing the US Proceedings and the Cayman Proceedings, provided that, (a) prior notice of any transaction concerning the use, sale, or lease of Material Assets not located in the United States and (b) prior notice of those actions proposed to be taken in either the US Proceedings and the Cayman Proceedings, where notice of such action is required to be given under the applicable laws of procedures of the governing forum, shall be provided ("IGS Notice Procedures") by overnight mail, overnight delivery service, or facsimile to the members of the Committee and all persons appearing on the request for service list as reflected on the docket in the US Proceedings and the Cayman Proceedings (the "IGS Specified Parties"). Nothing in this stipulation requires the Cayman Liquidators to take any action that violates any provision of Cayman Law or any order of any Cayman Court or any other applicable law.

16. For the avoidance of doubt, the English Provisional Liquidators shall be permitted to act in a manner consistent with the terms of the English Court Orders and shall be permitted to act in a manner consistent with the laws governing the English Proceedings, provided that, prior notice of those actions proposed to be taken in either the U.S. Proceedings and the English Proceedings where notice of such action is required to be given under the applicable laws of procedures of the governing forum, shall be provided (the "IWG Notice Procedures") by overnight mail, overnight delivery service, or facsimile to members of the Committee and all persons appearing on the request for service list as reflected on the docket in the US Proceedings and the English Proceedings (the "IWG Specified Parties"). Nothing in this stipulation shall require the English Provisional Liquidators to take any action that violates any provision of English Law or any order of any English Court or any other applicable law.

17. All creditors of IGS and IWG shall have the right to appear in any forum to the same extent as creditors of the forum state, regardless of whether they have filed claims in that particular forum. All creditors shall have the opportunity to file a request for service with the Clerk of the US Bankruptcy Court, or to participate in the case or proceedings in the

Cayman Court or the English Court, provided, however, absent the filing of a claim, filing of a request for service or participation shall not subject such creditor to personal jurisdiction in the Court in which the notice or appearance is filed or made.

18. Notice and requirements for approval and authorization of any transactions regarding disposition, liquidation or distribution in specie of assets shall be in accordance with applicable law and the Notice Procedures and shall be provided by the SEC Receivers, any chapter 7 or chapter 11 trustee ("Bankruptcy Representative"), Cayman Liquidators and the English Provisional Liquidators, as the case may be, to the Specified Parties.

19. Where considered necessary or appropriate, the Liquidators will seek orders from the US Court, the Cayman Court and the English Court authorizing and directing that all cash in the possession of the Liquidators and proceeds from the liquidation of assets shall be maintained by IGS and IWG in a fiduciary account(s) in an appropriate banking institution(s) located in any jurisdiction the Liquidators, with the consent of the Committee, shall agree upon, and all three courts shall approve. Such account(s) shall be specifically designated for deposit of the proceeds from the disposition of assets and the funding of court approved expenses (the "Account"). In the absence of the obtaining of such orders from all three courts, the proceeds from the sale or disposition of assets shall remain in the jurisdiction in which those assets were situated.

20. Except as specifically provided herein, the Cayman Court shall have sole jurisdiction and power over the Cayman Liquidators, as to their tenure in office, the conduct of the liquidation proceedings under Cayman law, the retention of the Cayman Liquidators and other Cayman professionals, and the hearing and determination of matters arising in the liquidation proceedings under Cayman law. Subject to the budget process described below, the Cayman Liquidators shall be compensated for their services in accordance with Cayman principles under Cayman law.

21. Except as specifically provided herein, the English Court shall have sole jurisdiction and power over the English Provisional Liquidators as to their tenure in office, the conduct of the provisional liquidation under English law, the retention of the English Provisional Liquidators and other English professionals, and the hearing and determination of matters arising in the provisional liquidation proceedings under English law. Subject to the budget process described below, the English Provisional Liquidators shall be compensated for their services in accordance with English principles under English law.

22. Except as specifically provided herein, the US District Court shall have sole jurisdiction and power over the conduct of the SEC Proceedings, the compensation of the professionals rendering services in the SEC Proceedings, and the hearing and determination of matters arising in the SEC Proceedings in accordance with principles under United States law.

23. The US Bankruptcy Court shall have sole jurisdiction and power over the conduct of the US Proceedings, the compensation of the professionals rendering services in the US Proceedings, and the hearing and determination of matters arising in the US Proceedings. The Cayman Liquidators, the English Provisional Liquidators, the SEC Receivers, and any trustee to be appointed under the Bankruptcy Code shall individually and jointly propose a quarterly budget to the Committee for anticipated fees and expenses. The initial fees and expense budget shall be submitted to the Committee on or before October 15, 1999, for the period October 1, 1999, to December 31, 1999. Subsequent quarterly budgets shall be submitted 30 days prior to the expiration of the preceding budget. The Committee shall have seven (7) business days to approve or object to the budget. If the Committee objects and an agreement on the budget cannot be reached, the matter will be submitted to Judge Leif Clark as a special master appointed by the US District Court for determination. The Liquidators will provide the Committee with monthly reports on fees and expenses incurred in the administration of the estates. If in any budget period, an individual Liquidators' budget exceeds anticipated fees and expenses by 20% or the collective budget of the Liquidators is exceeded by 15%, and the fees are to be paid out of assets located in the US, a fee application hearing will be held upon a request from the Committee before the US Bankruptcy Court in addition to any approvals which are considered necessary from the English and Cayman Courts. Upon approval of a budget, the Liquidators can be paid on a monthly basis the lesser of the fees and expenses incurred in that month or the amount budgeted for that respective month. Within twenty days of the end of each budgetary quarter, so long as the fees and expenses are within the margins set forth above and a fee application hearing is not implicated, the Liquidators shall be paid any additional fees and expenses. If a fee application hearing is requested under the procedures set forth above, additional payments shall be subject to orders of the US Bankruptcy Court and, to the extent necessary, the English Court and the Cayman Court. In the event of a conflict between the different courts, the party applying for such fees shall receive the lowest amount allowed by the different courts and all parties shall work in good faith to resolve any such conflict.

24. Payment of fees and expenses by an estate under the process outlined above shall not be a final determination of liability of such costs to that estate. Such allocation efforts will be reviewed and approved by the Courts pursuant to Phase II.

25. The US Bankruptcy Court will be requested to hold monthly status conferences.

26. The US District Court, US Bankruptcy Court, the Cayman Court, and/or the English Courts may, to the extent permitted by practice and procedure, and with the prior consent (if available) of each court, conduct joint hearings or conferences with respect to any matter related to the conduct, administration, determination or disposition of any aspect of the SEC Proceedings, Cayman Proceedings, English Proceedings, or US Bankruptcy Proceedings where considered by any two or more Courts to be necessary or advisable and in particular, without limiting the generality of the foregoing, to facilitate or coordinate the proper and efficient conduct of the SEC Proceedings, US Bankruptcy Proceedings, Cayman Proceedings, and English Proceedings. With respect to any such hearings or conferences, unless otherwise ordered, the following may be considered to be appropriate:

(i) A telephone link may be established such that all participating Courts may be able to simultaneously hear the proceedings in the other Courts.

(ii) Any party intending to rely upon any written evidentiary material in support of a submission shall file identical materials in advance of such hearing or conference with each Court, as reasonably possible and consistent with the procedural and evidentiary rules and requirements of each participating Court. Any party which does not wish to attorn or consent to the jurisdiction of a particular Court, shall be entitled to file such materials without, by the sole act of filing anything other than a proof of claim, being deemed to have attorned or consented to the jurisdiction of the Court in which such material is filed.

(iii) The Judge of the Cayman Court, the Judge of the English Court, the Judge of the US District Court, and the Judge of the US Bankruptcy Court may, but are not required to, communicate with one another, without advance notice to counsel or counsel being present, for any purpose, including, without limitation, to establish guidelines for the orderly making of submissions and rendering of decisions to deal with any other procedural, administrative, or preliminary matters or for the purpose of determining whether consistent rulings can be made by the Cayman Court, the English Court, the US District Court, and/or the US Bankruptcy Court, and the terms upon which such rulings should be made, and to deal with any other procedural or non-substantive matter in relation to such applications.

27. Due to the complicated nature of this cross-border insolvency, however, the Liquidators have requested that the Committee (and the petitioning creditors) temporarily suspend the pending Involuntary Petitions until such time as the parties can decide on the optimal approach to coordinate the proceedings. As such, subject to further orders of the US Bankruptcy Court, the Involuntary Proceedings against IGS and IWG shall be temporarily suspended under 11 USC § 305, until January 7, 2000. Any party in interest may request the US Bankruptcy Court to enter an order for relief in the involuntary proceedings upon applicable notice to the Liquidators, their counsel, the Committee, and other parties who have filed a request for service with the US Bankruptcy Court. All of the parties reserve the right to seek entry of orders for relief in the Involuntary Proceedings prior to January 7, 2000, in the event an emergency arises after entry of this stipulation.

28. The parties agree to request the Cayman, English, and US District Court enter a Confidentiality Order similar in substance to the order entered by the US Bankruptcy Court providing for the confidentiality of the identities of investors. The Liquidators shall use their best efforts to keep confidential the identities of the investors. Parties in interest recognize that the Liquidators may be requested to comply with the demands of governmental agencies for disclosures.

29. This Stipulation shall be binding on and inure to the benefit of the parties hereto and their respective successors, assigns, representatives, heirs, executors, administrators, trustees (including any trustees under chapters 7 or 11 of the Bankruptcy Code), and receivers, receiver managers, or custodians appointed under US law, Cayman law, or English law, as the case may be.

30. This Stipulation may not be waived, amended, or modified orally or in any other way or manner except by a writing signed by the party to be bound, and such approval and authorization of the US District Court, US Bankruptcy Court, Cayman Court, or the English Court as may be necessary and appropriate in the circumstances. Notice of any proposed amendment or modification of the Stipulation shall be provided by the party providing such to the Specified Parties in accordance with the Notice Procedures. This Stipulation may be supplemented from time to time by the parties hereto as circumstances require with any supplementing stipulations as approved by the US District Court, US Bankruptcy Court, Cayman Court, and the English Court.

31. Any request for the entry of an order which is contrary to the provisions of this Stipulation must be made on notice by the proponent of the order to the Specified Parties in accordance with the Notice Procedures.

32. Each party represents and warrants to the other that its execution, delivery, and performance of this Stipulation are within the power and authority of such party and have been duly authorized by such party, except that, with respect to the Cayman Liquidators and the English Liquidators, US District Court, US Bankruptcy Court, Cayman Court, and English Court approval is required.

33. This Stipulation may be signed in any number of counterparts, each of which shall be deemed an original and all of which together shall be deemed to be one and the same instrument, and may be signed by facsimile signature, which shall be deemed to constitute an original signature.

34. The US District Court, US Bankruptcy Court, Cayman Court, and the English Court shall retain Jurisdiction over the parties for the purpose of enforcing the terms and provisions of this Stipulation or approving any amendments or modifications thereto.

35. The parties hereto are hereby authorized to take such actions and execute such documents as may be necessary and appropriate to implement and effectuate this Stipulation.

36. The Stipulation is not intended to otherwise circumvent, alter, or otherwise affect the rights, obligations, or laws of any jurisdiction and accordingly, if a party to the Stipulation is directed by its Court to act (or not act) with respect to a particular issue whether on his own application or otherwise, that party's obligation to follow its Court's direction should not be impaired or abridged by the Stipulation. To the extent any party's obligation to follow its Court's order conflicts with its obligations under the Stipulation, that party shall be relieved from its obligation under the Stipulation, but such party must notify in writing all other parties of the conflict between its Court's direction or order and the Stipulation. In all other material respects, the affected party will remain bound to the terms of the Stipulation.

37. This Stipulation shall be deemed effective upon its approval by the US District Court, US Bankruptcy Court, Cayman Court, and the English Court. This Stipulation shall have no binding or enforceable legal effect until approved by the US District Court, the US Bankruptcy Court, the Cayman Court, and the English Court.

IN WITNESS WHEREOF the parties hereto have caused this stipulation to be executed either individually or by their respective attorneys or representatives hereunto authorized.

Dated: October 1999

San Antonio, Texas

F. PIONEER PROTOCOL

CROSS-BORDER INSOLVENCY PROTOCOL

FOR PIONEER COMPANIES INC. AND ITS AFFILIATES

This cross-border insolvency protocol (the "Protocol") shall govern the conduct of all parties in interest in the Insolvency Proceedings (as such term is defined below):

A. Background

1. Pioneer Companies, Inc., a United States corporation ("PCI") the ultimate parent company of a multinational enterprise that operates, through its various subsidiaries and affiliates, in the United States and Canada.

2. PCI and certain of its direct and indirect subsidiaries and affiliates (collectively, the "U.S. Debtors") have commenced reorganization cases (collectively, the "U.S. Cases") under chapter 1 of the United States Bankruptcy Code, 11 U.S.C. §§ 101-1330 (the "Bankruptcy Code"), in the United States Bankruptcy Court for the Southern District of Texas, Houston Division (the "U.S. Court"). The U.S. Debtors are continuing in possession of their respective properties and are operating and managing their businesses, as debtors in possession, pursuant to sections 1107 and 1108 of the Bankruptcy Code. In the coming weeks it is anticipated that the office of the United States trustee (the "U.S. Trustee") will appoint an official unsecured creditors' committee in the U.S. Cases (the "Committee").

3. PCI Chemicals Canada Inc., a Debtor in the U.S. cases (but referred to herein as the "Canadian Debtor") has also commenced insolvency proceedings (the "Canadian Case"") by filing an application under the Canadian Companies' Creditors Arrangement Act (the "CCAA") with the Quebec Superior Court in Montreal, Quebec (the "Canadian Court") and

an Order (the "CCAA Order") has been made under which, among other things: (i) the Canadian Debtor has been determined to be entity to which the CCAA applies; and (ii) a claims process has been established in respect of the filing of claims against the Canadian Debtor in the Canadian Case.

4. For convenience, (a) the U.S. Debtors and the Canadian Debtor shall be referred to herein collectively as the "Debtors"; (b) the U.S. Cases and the Canadian Case shall be referred to herein collectively as the "Insolvency Proceedings"; (c) the U.S. Court and the Canadian Court shall be referred to herein collectively as the "Courts"; and (d) the business carried on by the Debtors (wherever such business may be carried on) shall be referred to as the "PCI Business".

B. Purpose and Goals

5. While proceedings are pending in the United States and Canada, the implementation of basic administrative procedures is necessary to coordinate certain activities in the Insolvency Proceedings, protect the rights of parties thereto and ensure the maintenance of the Courts' independent jurisdiction and to give due effect to the doctrine of comity and collateral estoppel, while at the same time recognizing that the PCI Business is carried on in an integrated manner on a transnational basis and further that it is in the interest of the Debtors and their stakeholders for the U.S. Court to take charge of the principal administration of the reorganization of the PCI Business. Accordingly, this Protocol has been developed to promote the following mutually desirable goals and objectives in both the U.S. Cases and the Canadian Case:

- harmonize, coordinate and minimize and avoid duplication of activities in the Insolvency Proceedings before the U.S. Court and the Canadian Court;
- promote the orderly and efficient administration of the Insolvency Proceedings to, among other things, maximize the efficiency of the Insolvency Proceedings, reduce the costs associated therewith and avoid duplication of effort;
- set forth general principles for the manner in which claims made against the Debtors in the Insolvency Proceedings are to be adjudicated;
- honor the independence and integrity of the Courts and other courts and tribunals of the United States and Canada;
- promote international cooperation and respect for comity among the Courts, the Debtors, the Committee and other creditors and interested parties in the Insolvency Proceedings;

- facilitate the fair, open and efficient administration of the Insolvency Proceedings for the benefit of all of the Debtors' creditors and other interested parties, wherever located; and
- implement a framework of general principles to address basic administrative issues arising out of the cross-border nature of the Insolvency Proceedings all in order to allow the PCI Business to be reorganized on a coordinated basis.

C. Comity and Independence of the Courts

6. The approval and implementation of this Protocol shall not divest or diminish the U.S. Court's and the Canadian Court's independent jurisdiction over the subject matter of the U.S. Cases and the Canadian Case, respectively. By approving and implementing this Protocol, neither the U.S. Court, the Canadian Court, the Debtors nor any creditors or interested parties shall be deemed to have approved or engaged in any infringement on the sovereignty of the United States or Canada.

7. The U.S. Court shall have sole and exclusive jurisdiction and power over the conduct of the U.S. Cases and the hearing and determination of matters arising in the U.S. Cases. The Canadian Court shall have sole and exclusive jurisdiction and power over the conduct of the Canadian Case and the hearing and determination of matters arising in the Canadian Case.

8. In accordance with the principles of comity and independence established in paragraphs 6 and 7 above, nothing contained herein shall be construed to:

- increase, decrease or otherwise modify the independence, sovereignty or jurisdiction of the U.S. Court, the Canadian Court or any other court or tribunal in the United States or Canada, including the ability of any such court or tribunal to provide appropriate relief under applicable law on an *ex parte* or "limited notice" basis;
- require the Debtors or the Committee to take any action or refrain from taking any action that would result in a breach of any duty imposed on them by any applicable law; or
- authorize any action that requires the specific approval of one or both of the Courts under the Bankruptcy Code or the CCAA after appropriate notice and a hearing (except to the extent that such action is specifically described in this Protocol).

9. The Debtors, the Committee and their respective employees, members, agents and professionals shall respect and comply with the independent, nondelegable duties imposed upon them by the Bankruptcy Code, the

CCAA Order and other applicable laws, regulation or orders of tribunals of competent jurisdiction.

D. Matters relating to the Proving of Claims against the Debtors

10. In order to co-ordinate the restructuring of the PCI Business and avoid any unnecessary duplication of effort and expense or inconsistent rulings by the Courts, the following principles are applicable in connection with establishing the validity, amount and treatment of any claims against the Debtors:

(a) any claims against any of the Debtors arising under or in connection with:

(i) the 9 1/4% notes in the original principal amount of US $175,000,000 issued by the Canadian Debtor pursuant to an indenture dated as of October 30, 1997 among the Canadian Debtor (as issuer), the United States Trust Company of New York (as Trustee and Collateral Agent) and others (the "Canadian Indenture");

(ii) the guarantee of the U.S. Debtors of the obligations of the Canadian Debtor under the Canadian Indenture;

(iii) the Term Loan Agreement dated as of October 30, 1997 in the original principal amount of US $83,000,000 among Pioneer Americas, Inc, DLJ Capital Funding Inc, (as syndication agent), Bank of America National Trust and Savings Association (as administrative agent), and others (the "Canadian TLA");

(iv) the guarantee of the Canadian Debtor dated as of October 30, 1997 of the obligations of the U.S. Debtors under the Canadian TLA;

(v) the 9 1/4% notes in the original principal amount of US $200,000,000 issued by the Pioneer Corporation of America pursuant to an indenture dated as of June 17, 1997 among Pioneer Corporation of America (as issuer), the Subsidiary Guarantors (as defined therein) and the United States Trust Company of New York (as Trustee and Collateral Agent) (the "US Indenture");

(vi) the guarantee of the Canadian Debtor dated October 31, 1997 of the obligations of the U.S. Debtors under the U.S. Indenture;

(vii) the Term Loan Agreement dated as of June 17, 1997 in the original principal amount of US $100,000,000 among Pioneer Americas, Inc, DLJ Capital Funding Inc. (as syndication agent), Bank of

America National Trust and Savings Association (as administrative agent), and others (the "U.S. TLA"); and

(viii) the guarantee of the Canadian Debtor dated October 30, 1997 of the obligations of the U.S. Debtors under the U.S. TLA,

shall be determined by the U.S. Court in the U.S. Cases;

(b) all claims against any of the U.S. Debtors (other than the Canadian Debtor) shall be determined by the U.S. Court in the U.S. Cases;

(c) all claims against the Canadian Debtor (with the exception of the claims described in paragraph 10(a) hereof shall be determined in accordance with the following principles:

(i) any person filing a proof of claim against the Canadian Debtor in the U.S. Cases shall be deemed to have elected to have the validity, amount and treatment of such claim determined by the U.S. Court;

(ii) any person filing a proof of claim against the Canadian Debtor in the Canadian Case shall be deemed to have elected to have the validity, amount and treatment of such claim determined by the Canadian Court; and

(iii) any person filing a proof of claim against the Canadian Debtor in both the U.S. Cases and the Canadian Case shall be deemed to have elected to have the validity, amount and treatment of such claim determined by the U.S. Court.

E. Cooperation

11. To assist in the efficient administration of the Insolvency Proceedings, the Debtors and the Committee shall (a) cooperate with each other in connection with actions taken in both the U.S. Court and the Canadian Court and (b) take any other appropriate steps to coordinate the administration of the U.S. Cases and the Canadian Case for the benefit of the Debtors' respective estates and stakeholders.

12. To harmonize and coordinate the administration of the Insolvency Proceedings, the U.S. Court and the Canadian Court each shall use its best efforts to coordinate activities with and defer to the judgment of the other Court, where appropriate and feasible.

(a) The Courts shall use their best efforts to coordinate activities in the Insolvency Proceedings so that the subject matter of any particular action, suit, request, application, contested matter or other proceeding may be determined in one Court only.

(b) The U.S. Court and the Canadian Court may communicate with one another with respect to any matter relating to the Insolvency Proceedings.

(c) The U.S. Court and the Canadian Court may conduct joint hearings with respect to any matter relating to the conduct, administration, determination or disposition of any aspect of the U.S. Cases or the Canadian Case if both Courts determine and agree that such joint hearings are necessary or advisable to facilitate the proper and efficient conduct of the Insolvency Proceedings. With respect to any such joint hearings, unless otherwise ordered by both Courts, the following procedures shall be followed:

- A telephone or video link shall be established so that both the U.S. Court and the Canadian Court shall be able to simultaneously hear the proceedings in the other Court.
- Submissions or applications by any party that are or become the subject of a joint hearing of the Courts (collectively, "Pleadings") shall be made or filed initially only with the Court in which such party is appearing and seeking relief. Promptly after the scheduling of any joint hearing, the party submitting such pleadings to one Court shall file courtesy copies with the other Court. In any event, Pleadings seeking relief from both Courts must be filed with both Courts.
- Any party intending to rely on written evidentiary materials in support of a submission to the U.S. Court or the Canadian Court in connection with any joint hearing (collectively, "Evidentiary Materials") shall file such Evidentiary Materials in advance of the joint hearing. To the fullest extent possible, the Evidentiary Materials filed in each Court shall be substantially identical and shall be consistent with the procedural and evidentiary rules and requirements of each Court.
- If a party has not previously appeared in or otherwise attorned to the jurisdiction of a Court, it shall be entitled to file Pleadings or Evidentiary Materials in connection with the joint hearing without being deemed to have attorned to the jurisdiction of the Court by virtue of filing such Pleadings or Evidentiary Materials, provided that the party does not request any affirmative relief from such Court.
- The Judge of the U.S. Court and the Justice of the Canadian Court shall be entitled to communicate with each other in advance of any

joint hearing, with or without counsel being present, to (i) establish guidelines for the orderly submission of pleadings, Evidentiary Materials and other papers and the rendering of decisions by the U.S. Court and the Canadian Court and (ii) address any related procedural or administrative matters.

- The Judge of the U.S. Court and the Justice of the Canadian Court shall be entitled to communicate with each other after any joint hearing, without counsel present, for the purposes of (i) determining whether consistent rulings can be made by both Courts, (ii) coordinating the terms of the Courts' respective rulings and (iii) addressing any other procedural or administrative matter.

13. Notwithstanding the terms of paragraph 12 above, the Protocol recognizes that the U.S. Court and the Canadian Court are independent courts. Accordingly, although the Courts will seek to cooperate and coordinate with each other in good faith, each of the Courts shall be entitled at all times to exercise its independent jurisdiction and authority with respect to (a) matters presented to such Court and (b) the conduct of the parties appearing in such matters.

F. Retention and Compensation of Professionals

14. Any professionals retained by the Canadian Debtor or the Committee for activities performed in Canada or in connection with the Canadian Case (collectively, the "Canadian Professionals") shall be subject to the sole and exclusive jurisdiction of the Canadian Court. Accordingly, the Canadian Professionals (a) shall be subject to the procedures and standards for retention and compensation applicable in the Canadian Court under the CCAA, the CCAA Order and any other applicable Canadian law or orders of the Canadian Court and (b) shall not be required to seek approval of their retention or compensation in the U.S. Court.

15. Any professionals retained by the U.S. Debtors or the Committee for activities performed in the United States or in connection with the U.S. Cases (collectively, the "U.S. Professionals") shall be subject to the sole and exclusive jurisdiction of the U.S. Court. Accordingly, the U.S. Professionals (a) shall be subject to the procedures and standards for retention and compensation applicable in the U.S. Court under the Bankruptcy Code and any other applicable laws of the United States or orders of the U.S. Court and (b) shall not be required to seek approval of their retention or compensation in the Canadian Court.

G. Rights to Appear and Be Heard

16. The Debtors, their creditors and other interested parties in the Insolvency Proceedings, including the Committee, and the U.S. Trustee, shall have the right and standing to: (a) appear and be heard in either the U.S. Court or the Canadian Court in the Insolvency Proceedings to the same extent as creditors and other interested parties domiciled in the forum country, subject to any local rules or regulations generally applicable to all parties appearing in the forum; and (b) file notices of appearance or other papers with the Clerk of the U.S. Court or the Canadian Court in the Insolvency Proceedings; provided, however, that any appearance or filing may subject a creditor or interested party to the jurisdiction of the Court in which the appearance or filing occurs, except that any appearance by the Committee in the Canadian Case shall not form a basis for personal jurisdiction in Canada over the individual members of the Committee. Notwithstanding the foregoing the Canadian Court shall have jurisdiction over the U.S. Trustee solely with respect to the particular matters as to which the U.S. Trustee appears before the Canadian Court.

H. Notice

17. Notice of any motion, application or other pleading or paper filed in one or both of the Insolvency Proceedings and notice of any related hearings or other proceedings mandated by applicable law in connection with the Insolvency Proceedings or the Protocol shall be given by appropriate means (including, where circumstances warrant, by courier, telecopier or other electronic forms of communication) to the following: (a) all creditors and other interested parties in accordance with the practice of the jurisdiction where the papers are filed or the proceedings are to occur; and (b) to the extent such entities are not otherwise entitled to receive notice under subpart (a) of this sentence, counsel to the Committee, the U.S. Trustee and such other parties as may be designated by either of the Courts from time to time. Notice in accordance with this paragraph shall be given by the party otherwise responsible for effecting notice in the jurisdiction where the underlying papers are filed or the proceedings are to occur. In addition to the foregoing, upon request, the Debtors shall provide the U.S. Court or the Canadian Court, as the case may be, with copies of all orders, decision, opinions or similar papers issued by the other Court in the Insolvency Proceedings.

I. Recognition of Stays of Proceedings

18. The Canadian Court hereby recognizes the validity of the stay of proceedings and actions against the U.S. Debtors and their assets under section 362 of the Bankruptcy Code (the "U.S. Stay"). In recognition of the importance of the U.S. Stay to the successful completion of the Insolvency Proceedings for the benefit of the Debtors and their respective estates and stakeholders, the Canadian Court shall extend and enforce the U.S. Stay in Canada (to the same extent that such stay of proceedings and actions is applicable in the United States) to prevent adverse actions against the assets, rights and holdings of the U.S. Debtors in Canada. In implementing the terms of this paragraph, the Canadian Court may consult with the U.S. Court regarding (a) the interpretation and application of the U.S. Stay and any orders of the U.S. Court modifying or granting relief from the U.S. Stay and (b) the enforcement of the U.S. Stay in Canada.

19. The U.S. Court hereby recognizes the validity of the stay of proceedings and actions against the Canadian Debtor, and its assets under the CCAA Order (the "Canadian Stay"). In recognition of the importance of the Canadian Stay to the successful completion of the Insolvency Proceedings for the benefit of the Debtors and their respective estates and stakeholders, the U.S. Court shall extend and enforce the Canadian Stay in the United States (to the same extent that such stay of proceedings and actions is applicable in Canada) to prevent adverse actions against the assets, rights and holdings of the Canadian Debtor in the United States. In implementing the terms of this paragraph, the U.S. Court may consult with the Canadian Court regarding (a) the interpretation and application of the Canadian Stay and any orders of the Canadian Court modifying or granting relief from the Canadian Stay and (b) the enforcement of the Canadian Stay in the United States.

20. Nothing contained herein shall affect or limit the Debtors' or other parties' rights to assert the applicability or non-applicability of the U.S. Stay or the Canadian Stay to any particular proceeding, property, asset, activity or other matter, wherever pending or located.

J. Effectiveness; Modification

21. This Protocol shall become effective only upon its approval by both the U.S. Court and the Canadian Court.

22. This Protocol may not be supplemented, modified, terminated or replaced in any manner except upon the approval of both the U.S. Court and the Canadian Court. Notice of any legal proceeding to supplement,

modify, terminate or replace this Protocol shall be given in accordance with paragraph 17 above.

K. Procedure for Resolving Disputes Under the Protocol

23. Disputes relating to the terms, intent or application of this Protocol may be addressed by interested parties to either the U.S. Court, the Canadian Court or both Courts upon notice in accordance with paragraph 17 above. In rendering a determination in any such dispute, the Court to which the issue is addressed: (a) shall consult with the other Court; and (b) may, in its sole and exclusive discretion, either (i) render a binding decision after such consultation, (ii) defer to the determination of the other Court by transferring the matter, in whole or in part, to the other Court or (iii) seek a joint hearing of both Courts in accordance with paragraph 12(c) above. Notwithstanding the foregoing, in making a determination under this paragraph, each Court shall give due consideration to the independence, comity and inherent jurisdiction of the other Court established under existing law.

24. In implementing the terms of paragraphs 12, 18, 19 and 23 above and the other provisions of the Protocol, the U.S. Court and the Canadian Court may, in their sole discretion, provide advice or guidance to each other with respect to substantive legal issues in accordance with the following procedures:

- The U.S. Court or the Canadian Court, as applicable, shall provide any such advice or guidance to the other Court in writing.
- Copies of such written advice or guidance shall be served by the applicable Court in accordance with paragraph 16 hereof.
- The Debtors, the Committee, the U.S. Trustee and any other affected or interested party shall be entitled to make submissions to the appropriate Court in response to or in connection with any written advice or guidance received from the other Court.

L. Preservation of Rights

25. Neither the terms of this Protocol nor any actions taken under the terms of this Protocol shall prejudice or affect the powers, rights, claims and defenses of the Debtors and their estates, the Committee, the U.S. Trustee or any of the Debtors' creditors under applicable law, including the Bankruptcy Code and the CCAA.

G. SENDO PROTOCOL

PROTOCOL AGREEMENT FOR THE COORDINATION OF A MAIN INSOLVENCY PROCEEDING WITH A SECONDARY INSOLVENCY PROCEEDING

FILED IN CONFORMITY WITH EUROPEAN REGULATION NO. 1346-2000 OF 29 MAY 2000

BETWEEN

SCP BECHERET-THIERRY-SENECHAL, a professional society of judicial liquidators registered with the national service, having their offices at 3-5-7 avenue Paul Doumer, Rueil-Malmaison (92500), France,

Acting in its capacity as judicial liquidator of the French main office of SENDO INTERNATIONAL LIMITED, located at 100 avenue Charles de Gaulle, Neuilly-sur-Seine (92200), France, a company established under foreign law

Appointed to this office by order of the Commercial Court of Nanterre, on 3 August 2005,

Represented by Marc SENECHAL, Esq., judicial liquidator,

hereafter referred to as the "**French liquidators**"

AND

Alastair P. Beveridge and Simon J. Appell (the "Joint Administrators") of KROLL, Corporate Advisory & Restructuring Group, having its offices at 10 Fleet Place, London EC4M 7RB, England, acting in their capacity as Joint Administrators of the Cayman Islands company SENDO INTERNATIONAL LIMITED, having its offices at Filling Centre, BP 613 George Town Grand Cayman (Cayman Islands) and is registered as a foreign company in the United Kingdom

Appointed to this office by order of the High Court of Justice, Chancery Division of London on 29 June 2005, such order has subsequently been amended by Court order dated 20 December 2005,

Represented by Reinhard DAMMANN, Esq., Member of the Paris Bar, Cabinet White & Case, having his offices at 11 boulevard de la Madeleine, Paris (75001),

hereafter referred to as the "**Joint Administrators**"

WITNESSETH THE PARTIES HERETO:

That, by a motion on 29 June 2005, the directors of SENDO INTERNATIONAL LIMITED filed before the High Court of Justice in London an insolvency proceeding under Article 3 of the European Regulation on Insolvency Proceedings 2000 (No. 1346/2000) of May 29, 2000 (hereinafter the "**(EC) Regulation**") against SENDO INTERNATIONAL LIMITED,

That by order of 29 June 2005, the High Court of Justice, Chancery Division of London, ruled in favor of the application of a proceeding of judicial administration (*Administration*) to SENDO INTERNATIONAL LIMITED and appointed Alastair P. Beveridge and Simon J. Appell as Joint Administrators. The appointment of the Joint Administrators was extended to 28 December 2006 by order of the High Court of Justice, Chancery Division, on 20 December 2005.

In a motion filed on 6 July 2005 with the Examining Magistrate of the Commercial Court of Nanterre, the Joint Administrators requested the opening of a secondary proceeding of insolvency against the French establishment of SENDO INTERNATIONAL LIMITED in conformity with Article 29(a) of the (EC) Regulation,

That under a decision dated 3 August 2005, the Commercial Court of Nanterre ruled in favor of the application of a secondary proceeding of judicial liquidation (*liquidation judiciaire*) to the French establishment of SENDO INTERNATIONAL LIMITED and appointed SCP BECHERET-THIERRY-SENECHAL in its capacity as liquidator and Mr. Jérôme MANDRILLON in his capacity as judge in charge of the proceedings,

That this insolvency proceeding is a secondary proceeding under Articles 3.2. and 3.3. of the (EC) Regulation,

WHEREAS:

The Joint Administrators and French Liquidators have come to understand that the (EC) Regulation establishes only very general operating principles,

Consequently, the Joint Administrators and the French Liquidators have concluded that they wish to enter into an informal agreement for the purpose of defining a practical means of functioning which would allow for the efficient coordination of the two insolvency proceedings and would respect the general operating principles established by the (EC) Regulation,

This protocol is established in respect of the insolvency of SENDO INTERNATIONAL LIMITED only, and the particular circumstances of this company. It is not intended to create a binding precedent and should not be considered appropriate for all other secondary proceedings in France pursuant to the EC Regulation, however may be regarded indicative of achieving good practice. It is established for the purposes of implementing such operating means by the Joint Administrators and the French Liquidators agreeing to act in conformity with the following principles:

- Mutual trust,
- Adherence to the duty to communicate information and to cooperate as defined by Article 32 of the (EC) Regulation,
- Precedence of the main insolvency proceeding over the secondary proceeding.

That there is a genuine need to establish a practical means of treating the liabilities (I) and the assets (II) of the French branch of SENDO INTERNATIONAL LIMITED.

I. PRACTICAL MEANS OF TREATING THE LIABILITIES OF SENDO INTERNATIONAL LIMITED

I-1. Practical means of treating notification sent to the creditors of SENDO INTERNATIONAL LIMITED

The obligation to notify the creditors is regulated by Article 40 of the (EC) Regulation, which holds that "*As soon as insolvency proceedings are opened in one Member State, the court having jurisdiction in such State or the liquidator appointed by such [court] shall immediately inform known creditors who have their habitual residences, domiciles or registered offices in other Member States*". This article further specifies the content of such notification.

Consequently, given the relative lack of precision of Article 40 of the (EC) Regulation, the parties consider that this protocol must specify the means of implementation of this article. The practical means agreed upon by the parties are as follows:

▶ The Joint Administrators in the main proceeding, having a direct contact with the manager and the accounting departments of SENDO INTERNATIONAL LIMITED, as well as direct access to the entirety of the accounting documents of this company, will notify by regular mail and in conformity with the terms and conditions of Article 40.2 of the (EC) Regulation all of the debtor's creditors based in France, without exception. Such notice shall be in the form of an individual notice and shall set forth the required formalities and penalties provided by English law and applicable to the main proceedings. It has been agreed in this instance, following the appointment of the French Liquidators, that all French claims are to be notified to the French Liquidators following which the French Liquidators will then make one overall claim in the Administration.

▶ The French Liquidators shall send a notice:

- To the Joint Administrators in order for them to be able to implement, under Article 32.2 of the (EC) Regulation, the overall claims lodged under the main proceedings;
- To any possible liquidators appointed in the context of secondary proceedings filed against SENDO INTERNATIONAL LIMITED in other Member States of the European Union;
- abroad, and a list of such creditors shall be provided to the French Liquidators by the head of such establishment. The creditors thus notified shall be qualified as "local" in this protocol agreement. The creditors not known to the secondary establishment shall not be notified by the French Liquidators.

This notice shall respect both Article 40.2 of the (EC) Regulation and the terms and conditions of French law, applicable only to the secondary proceedings. Such notice shall specify all of the time periods and formulae to be observed as well as any penalties that may be incurred by creditors and/or foreign liquidators appointed in other secondary proceedings under French law in the case of failure to lodge a claim or the tardy lodging of claims with the liquidator.

The Joint Administrators and the French Liquidators shall exchange their lists of creditors in France that have been notified in order to identify those who have been so notified by both the Joint Administrators and the French Liquidators.

I-2. Practical means of treating the claims lodged by the creditors of SENDO INTERNATIONAL LIMITED

- Under Article 32.1 of the (EC) Regulation, any creditor may lodge on its own behalf its claims in the main proceedings and in the secondary proceedings.
- Under Article 32.2 of the (EC) Regulation, the Joint Administrators and the French Liquidator must in principle produce the global amount of liabilities claimed with such Joint Administrators or the French Liquidators to the other proceedings. The Joint Administrators and the French Liquidators are nonetheless exempted from such production when such production is not in the interest of the creditors it represents. In the case of SENDO INTERNATIONAL LIMITED, the assets previously situated in France were of minimal value.

Accordingly, the Joint Administrators, given regular notification by the French Liquidators in conformity with I-1 hereinabove, are exonerated from production to the secondary insolvency proceeding of the liabilities for the proceeding for which it was appointed given the poor assets included in the scope of the secondary proceeding. Redistribution among creditors is not possible in the secondary proceeding; therefore the lodgment of claims by the Joint Administrators in the secondary proceedings holds no interest for the creditors they represent.

The French Liquidators must however and given the interest that such represents for the "local" creditors, produce to the Joint Administrators appointed under the main proceeding, the amount of claims lodged with it.

In conformity with the same rules and regulations, the French Liquidators will produce this amount to all secondary proceedings filed or to be filed against SENDO INTERNATIONAL LIMITED within European territory.

Each of these such productions shall be accompanied by a list providing the names of the creditors with claims which make up this debt. As per Article 41 of the (EC) Regulation, in addition to the names of each of these such creditors, the list must also state the creditor's address, the amount and nature of the claim lodged and any possible security interests, or other encumbrances attached thereto.

I-3. Practical means of verification of claims made against SENDO INTERNATIONAL LIMITED

I-3.1. Independence of the proceedings of verification of the liabilities

Whilst it is preferred that each party shall verify the amount and the form of the claims made directly to each such party in conformity with the applicable national legislation, in the case of SENDO INTERNATIONAL LIMITED, it was agreed that the French Liquidators would collect details of claims and subsequent to verifying same, would provide a listing of proved debts to the Joint Administrators,

In conformity with Articles 4.2(h) and 28 of the (EC) Regulation, such verification shall be made independently in conformity with the national legislation applicable to each of the two insolvency proceedings.

I-3.2. Dual-Verification Obligation

Given the European dimension of the insolvency proceedings in question, each of the Joint Administrators and the French Liquidators must check and double check, for each of the claims accepted by each of them if such claim has not been filed twice under I-2 hereof in conformity with Article 32 of the (EC) Regulation.

Such verification shall be made by each of the Joint Administrators and French Liquidators by using the list of creditors which is to be annexed to the production made to the other Joint Administrator or French Liquidators in conformity with Article I-2 hereof.

Each claim lodged twice by the foreign liquidator in conformity with Article 32.2 of the (EC) Regulation on the one hand and by the creditor itself in conformity with Article 32.1 of the (EC) Regulation on the other hand, may be counted only once in the liabilities total for each of the insolvency proceedings.

Each Joint Administrator or French Liquidators shall thus ensure that it does not make multiple distributions to the same creditor in the insolvency proceeding to which it has been appointed.

I-4. Treatment of Legal costs

Article 30 of the (EC) Regulation foresees only the theoretical instance of the opening of secondary insolvency proceedings if the debtor's assets are sufficient to cover in whole or in part the costs and expenses of such proceedings.

Internal French law does not require such financial coverage in the context of French insolvency proceedings prior to the opening of such proceedings.

Nevertheless, to the extent where the opening of the secondary proceeding was requested by the Joint Administrators in conformity with Article 29 of the (EC) Regulation, it is hereby stipulated and agreed by the parties that Article 30 of the (EC) Regulation shall be applicable.

The financial burden of all legal costs in connection with the opening of the secondary insolvency proceeding filed on French territory, and specifically the fees due to the French Liquidators for the actions and rates for such established by Decree No. 85-1390 of 27December 1985 setting the remuneration and rates for judicial liquidators in the context of judicial liquidation and bankruptcy proceedings for companies shall be borne from the assets of SENDO INTERNATIONAL LIMITED as an expense of the administration in England. It has been agreed that in the case of the secondary proceedings of SENDO INTERNATIONAL LIMITED, the fees payable as expenses of the administration in England shall be subject to a limit of € 3604,05, to be determined by the judge.

The actions and tarification for such under Decree No. 85-1390 of 27 December 1985 for the practice of the mission of judicial liquidator are as follows:

- verification of claims lodged (art. 13)
- establishment of statements of wages due (art. 14)
- recovery of the assets created by actions initiated or pursued by the judicial liquidator (art. 18)

Furthermore, the French Liquidators will receive, under Article 12-1 of the Decree No. 85-1390 of 27 December 1985, a fixed fee in the pre-tax amount of 2,287.00 € to be paid from the assets of SENDO INTERNATIONAL LIMITED as an expense of the administration in England.

The amount of the fees that the French Liquidators will receive for its actions, the rates for which are established under Decree No. 85-1390 of 27 December 1985, is set by the judge having jurisdiction in conformity with Articles 16 and 22 of Decree No. 85-1390 of 27 December 1985.

Coverage of the fees of the French Liquidators under the secondary proceedings defined by the application of the Decree No. 85-1390 of 27 December 1985 are subsidiary in the event where the recovery of assets included in the scope of the secondary proceeding would allow for all or part of such coverage.

II. PRACTICAL MEANS OF TREATING THE ASSETS OF THE FRENCH BRANCH OF SENDO INTERNATIONAL LIMITED

II-1. Treatment of the recovery of assets in time

II-1.1. Preparation of the transfer by coordination between and among the various proceedings

In conformity with the principles defined by the (EC) Regulation:

► The sections of Article 31 of the (EC) Regulation relating to the obligation to cooperate and inform, provide that:

- Each Joint Administrator and French Liquidators establishes individually, prior to any disposition of such, a list of assets, limited to those assets in France, entering into the scope of the proceeding for which such Joint Administrator or French Liquidators has been appointed. Once established, this list is produced to the other Joint Administrator or French Liquidators.
- The Joint Administrators shall provide to the French Liquidators in the secondary proceedings, at the earliest opportunity and in any case after receipt of the list cited above, proposals concerning the assets of the debtor in France in conformity with Article 31.3 of the (EC) Regulation.

► Article 33.1 of the (EC) Regulation provides that the Joint Administrators may request of the court where the secondary proceeding was filed to stay for a three-month period, which period shall be renewable, all judicial liquidation proceedings carried out in the context of the secondary proceeding.

▶ Article 28 of the (EC) Regulation provides that the law applicable to the secondary proceeding is the law of the Member State within whose territory the proceedings was opened.

The parties hereto accept and agree to apply harmoniously the following principles: –

- In order to privilege the best means of recovery of the assets of SENDO INTERNATIONAL LIMITED in France or to enable their use in support of adoption of a winding-up arrangement or any comparable measures, the Joint Administrators undertake not to request, for a three-month period from the date of the pronouncement of the filing of the secondary proceeding, the stay of liquidation proceedings within French territory by the French Liquidators.

  An extension of such delay may be made upon agreement by both of the parties hereto.

- In compensation for and, again, to allow a possible transfer of all of the assets, or a winding-up arrangement, the French Liquidators undertake not to proceed, for the same (renewable) three-month period, with the forced recovery of assets entering into the scope of the secondary insolvency proceeding.

  If the recovery of such assets is required of the French Liquidator prior to the expiration of this (renewable) three-month period, the French Liquidator shall notify Joint Administrators that this latter may request the Commercial Court of Nanterre to stay liquidation proceedings in conformity with Article 33 of the (EC) Regulation.

- As soon as it has established the list of inventoried assets, and no later than two months from the pronouncement of the opening of the secondary proceeding, the French Liquidators shall produce such list to the Joint Administrators.

- Within one month from the receipt of such list, the Joint Administrators shall submit to the French Liquidators its recovery proposals, and will request the French Liquidators' opinion as to such. If the proposals include all or part of the assets falling under the scope of the secondary proceeding, it must in any case respect, with regard to the recovery of such assets, the provisions of French law, in conformity with Article 28 of the (EC) Regulation.

  In the absence of agreement, and subject to a stay of the secondary proceeding upon the Joint Administrators' request in conformity with Article 33 of the (EC) Regulation, the French Liquidators will recover the assets in the scope of the secondary proceeding in conformity with applicable French law.

II-1.2. Operating proceedings for the disposal of the assets

Article 20.2 of the (EC) Regulation aims to protect equal treatment for each category of creditors by excluding any creditor who has obtained a dividend in one of the insolvency proceedings from distributions made in the context of another proceeding when creditors of the same rank or category as that creditor have not received, in the other proceeding, an equivalent dividend.

Articles 4.2 (i) and 28 of the (EC) Regulation provide that operations concerning distribution of the income from the recovery of assets included in the scope of the secondary proceedings are governed by French law.

The parties hereby stipulate that the income from the recovery of assets included in the scope of the secondary proceedings shall be paid, including in the event of a total transfer of the assets as defined in II-1 hereof, to the French Liquidators to be deposited with the *Caisse des dépôts et consignations* for later distributions to those creditors whose claims were entered as a liability in the accounts in the secondary proceedings.

In order to avoid the risk, incurred by the plurality of insolvency proceedings, of granting a creditor an amount that is greater than his or her receivable, each Joint Administrator or French Liquidator is required to send to the other Joint Administrators or French Liquidators of the other proceedings, main or secondary:

- after the payment of sums, the list providing the names of the creditors who have received a dividend. This list shall provide the name and address of each of the creditors paid, the amount and nature of the claim and the amount of the dividend paid.
- prior to any payment, the draft distribution plan based on which the payment of dividends will be made. The Joint Administrators or the French Liquidators to whom this draft is sent shall respond to such within fifteen days from the date of receipt of such draft. Failure to respond within this time period shall be considered as acceptance of the draft plan.

The Joint Administrator or the French Liquidator who carries out the distribution shall enter such amount as having been paid and notified to him by his foreign colleagues.

In Paris, on June 1, 2006

In 5 original counterparts,

SCP BECHERET-THIERRY-SENECHAL

_________________________ Represented by Mr. Marc Sénéchal, Esq.

Alastair P. Beveridge and Simon J. Appell of KROLL

_________________________ Represented by Maître Reinhard Dammann

_________________________ Before Mr. Jérôme Mandrillon, Bankruptcy Judge with the Commercial Court of Nanterre

H. LEHMAN BROTHERS PROTOCOL

CROSS-BORDER INSOLVENCY PROTOCOL

FOR THE LEHMAN BROTHERS GROUP OF COMPANIES

This cross-border insolvency protocol (the "Protocol") establishes a framework for the conduct of the Proceedings (as such term is defined herein) concerning Lehman Brothers Holdings Inc. ("LBHI") and its affiliated debtors worldwide that are parties hereto (collectively, the "Debtors" and, collectively with their non-debtor affiliates, "Lehman") and the management of the estates of the Debtors pursuant to those Proceedings.

Background*

A. The Proceedings

Commencing on September 15, 2008 and periodically thereafter (as applicable, the "Commencement Dates"), the Debtors commenced (or in some cases, had initiated against them) plenary insolvency, administration, liquidation, rehabilitation, receivership, or like proceedings ("Plenary Proceedings") in different jurisdictions (the "Plenary Fora") and before different courts and governmental, regulatory, or administrative bodies (the "Tribunals"), as well as

* Factual statements contained in this Background are for informational purposes only and shall not be deemed admissions by, or binding on, any party hereto.

proceedings that are secondary or ancillary to a Plenary Proceeding ("Limited Proceedings," and together with the Plenary Proceedings, the "Proceedings") in jurisdictions other than the Plenary Fora (together with the Plenary Fora, the "Fora" and each a "Forum").

In certain of these Proceedings, the Debtors remain authorized to operate their businesses and manage their properties as "Debtors in Possession," while in others, liquidators, administrators, trustees, custodians, supervisors or curators have been appointed to manage the Debtors' affairs and represent their insolvency estates (collectively, with Debtors in Possession, the "Official Representatives"). Furthermore, in certain of these Proceedings, one or more statutory committee of creditors or equity holders has or have been appointed (the "Committees").

B. Lehman's Global Business

Lehman was a truly global group of companies. Prior to the events leading up to these Proceedings, Lehman was the fourth largest investment bank in the United States, and one of the largest financial services firms in the world. For more than 150 years, Lehman was a leader in the global financial markets by serving the financial needs of corporations, governmental units, institutional clients and individuals worldwide. Its headquarters in New York and regional headquarters in London and Tokyo were complemented by a network of offices in North America, Europe, the Middle East, Latin America and the Asia Pacific region.

To manage their businesses efficiently, Lehman utilized a centralized cash management system to collect and transfer the funds generated by its operations and disburse those funds to satisfy the obligations required to operate their businesses. The cash management system facilitated Lehman's cash monitoring, forecasting, and reporting, subject to the regulatory requirements of various jurisdictions. Furthermore, prior to the commencement of the Proceedings, LBHI and its direct and indirect subsidiaries continuously worked together and shared information in unison. This information was spread across 2,700 different software applications and dispersed throughout ledger accounts in its subsidiaries across the globe.

C. The Need for a Protocol

Given the integrated and global nature of Lehman's businesses, many of the Debtors' assets and activities are spread across different jurisdictions, and require administration in and are subject to the laws of more than one Forum.

The efficient administration of each of the Debtors' individual Proceedings would benefit from cooperation among the Official Representatives. In addition, cooperation and communication among Tribunals, where possible, would enable effective case management and consistency of judgments.

Accordingly, this Protocol is designed to facilitate the coordination of the Proceedings, and to enable the Tribunals and Official Representatives to co-operate in the administration of their respective Debtors' estates in the interest of all of the Debtors' creditors.

Terms

1. Purpose and Aims

1.1. The parties acknowledge that this Protocol represents a statement of intentions and guidelines designed to minimize the costs and maximize recoveries for all creditors of the Proceedings, by promoting the sharing of relevant information among the parties and the international coordination of related activities in the Proceedings, while respecting the separate interests of creditors and other interested parties to each Proceeding (which shall be subject at all times to the local laws of the jurisdiction applicable to each Official Representative), and the independence, sovereignty, and authority of each Tribunal.

1.2. In recognition of the substantive differences among the Proceedings in each jurisdiction, this Protocol shall not be legally enforceable nor impose on Official Representatives any duties or obligations, including (but not limited to) any obligations (i) that may be inconsistent with or that may conflict with the duties or obligations to which the Official Representative is subject under applicable law, or (ii) that are not in the interests of the Debtor's estate represented by the Official Representative and/or its creditors. Furthermore, nothing in this Protocol should be interpreted in any way so as to interfere with (i) the proper discharge of any duty, obligation or function of an Official Representative, or (ii) the exercise of statutory or other powers otherwise available to an Official Representative under applicable law.

1.3. Official Representatives should coordinate with each other and co-operate in all aspects of the Proceedings, subject in appropriate cases to bilateral protocols and protocols for communication among Official Representatives, Tribunals and Committees, that may be executed in furtherance of this Protocol. In doing so, the Official Representatives acknowledge and agree that the parties shall deal in good faith with each other in the interests of maximizing recovery for all of the Debtors' creditors.

1.4. The aims of this Protocol are:

1.4.1. **Coordination** – To promote international cooperation and the coordination of activities in the Proceedings; and to provide for the orderly, effective, efficient, and timely administration of the various Proceedings in order to reduce their cost and maximize recovery for creditors.

1.4.2. **Communication** – To promote communication among Official Representatives and Committees; and to provide, wherever possible, for direct communication among Tribunals.

1.4.3. **Information and Data Sharing** – To provide for the sharing of relevant information and data among Official Representatives in order to promote effective, efficient, and fair administrations, and to avoid duplication of effort and activities by the parties.

1.4.4. **Asset Preservation** – To identify, preserve, and maximize the value of the Debtors' worldwide assets for the collective benefit of all creditors and other interested parties.

1.4.5. **Claims Reconciliation** – To coordinate an efficient and transparent claims process; and in particular, to provide for a consistent and measured approach to the calculation and adjudication of intercompany claims that avoids unnecessary intercompany litigation.

1.4.6. **Maximize Recoveries** – To cooperate in marshalling the assets of the Debtors in order to maximize recovery for all of the Debtors' creditors.

1.4.7. **Comity** – To maintain the independent jurisdiction, sovereignty, and authority of all Tribunals.

1.5. Notwithstanding the multilateral nature of this Protocol, nothing herein shall restrict Official Representatives from dealing with other Official Representatives on a bilateral basis on matters that concern only their respective Debtors, provided that Official Representatives should keep each other generally informed of any bilateral protocols with other parties hereto, to the extent that such bilateral protocols address similar aims as this Protocol.

2. Notice

2.1. Official Representatives should provide adequate notice by email to the parties hereto, as well as to any Committees established in the Proceedings, of relevant matters in which those parties have an interest.

2.2. Where appropriate, each Official Representative should provide adequate notice by email as far in advance as possible of any matters in which other Official Representatives have a material interest and that may require preparation and/or travel by such Official Representatives, such as any creditors' or shareholders' meetings, statutory deadlines, administrative deadlines, or hearings before a Tribunal.

3. Rights of Official Representatives and Creditors to Appear

3.1. Subject to the laws of each Forum, Official Representatives shall have the right to appear in all of the Proceedings, whether before a Tribunal or in statutory meetings convened pursuant to applicable law. If required and available in a particular Forum, an exequatur or similar proceeding may be utilized to implement recognition of the Official Representative.

3.2. Official Representatives shall not, by virtue of their being a party to this Protocol, be deemed to have submitted to jurisdiction in any Forum, nor shall appearing in a Forum, whether in person or pursuant to Section 3.3, subject an Official Representative to jurisdiction for any purpose other than the matter with respect to which the appearance is made, except, (i) to the extent otherwise set forth herein to the contrary, and (ii) to the extent that an Official Representative otherwise submits to the jurisdiction of a Forum.

3.3. To the extent that an Official Representative is entitled to appear in the Proceedings under applicable law but cannot be present before the Tribunal or Committee(s) (or similar body, as the case may be) either in person or through counsel, the parties hereto shall consent to the Official Representative's communication of any observations to such Tribunal or Committee(s) prior to any order (or similar action) being made, provided that such communication is made in writing and copies of such communication are non-confidential and delivered to all interested parties or filed on the Tribunal's public records.

4. Communication and Access to Data and Information Among Official Representatives

4.1. Official Representatives should keep each other generally informed when appropriate of any relevant information and material developments in matters involving the Debtors and their Proceedings, and should consent wherever possible to the sharing of information among Official Representatives, which consent should not be unreasonably withheld.

4.2. Official Representatives should share information regarding the Debtors, and their assets and liabilities, which each may lawfully share with the other; provided, however, that with respect to work product or other privileged information, Official Representatives may, but are not obliged, to share such information with each other, subject to all privileges under the applicable rules of evidence or applicable law, and provided that sharing work product or privileged information shall not be deemed a waiver of any attorney-client privilege or work product protections under the applicable rules of evidence or applicable law.

4.3. To facilitate access to information, Official Representatives should make available to each other, upon request, any information that is publicly available in their respective Fora; and may, where permitted under applicable laws, share non-public information with other Official Representatives, subject to appropriate confidentiality arrangements and all privileges under the applicable rules of evidence.

4.4. Official Representatives agree that each shall not (and shall direct their respective agents and representatives not to) provide any non-public information received from the other to any third party, unless such information is (i) agreed to by the other party, (ii) required by applicable law, or (iii) required by order of any Tribunal.

4.5. The approval of this Protocol by a Tribunal (by entry of an order or otherwise) shall constitute the recognition by such Tribunal and the Official Representative in that Tribunal's Proceeding that communications among Official Representatives and their respective professionals, employees, agents, and representatives are subject to, and do not waive any attorney-client, work-product, legal, professional, or other privileges recognized under any applicable law; provided, however, that approval of this Protocol by a Tribunal shall not result in the parties hereto, other than the Official Representative in that Proceeding, becoming subject to the jurisdiction and laws of that Tribunal and Forum.

4.6. Each Official Representative should cooperate in the gathering and sharing of certain data and share analysis of certain transactions by:

4.6.1. sharing, via free, read-only access, all relevant information and data that it has the right to disclose and for which it is not required to make payment relating to (i) material interest holders of an asset, (ii) restitution of assets, and (iii) relevant information that assists such other

Official Representative to fulfill its duties, except where (x) litigation has commenced (or is contemplated), or (y) statutory or regulatory requirements prohibit disclosure;

4.6.2. if an Official Representative is in possession of the books, records, correspondence and other materials or documents that belong to another Debtor, providing the Official Representative of such other Debtor's estate such books, records, correspondence and other materials or documents;

4.6.3. coordinating in good faith the investigations of pre-filing activities with any other Official Representative with an interest in such activities, so long as the interests of the Official Representatives coordinating such investigations do not diverge; and

4.6.4. liaising with any other Official Representatives on matters (i) in which such other Official Representatives have a significant mutual interest, so long as their interests do not diverge and (ii) relating to a significant strategy to exit from a Proceeding in which such other Official Representatives have an interest.

4.7. Any sharing of information and data shall not include or give an Official Representative a right of automatic access to (i) documents relating to a Debtor's post-filing transactions, or (ii) working papers, summaries, or other work product drafted by an Official Representative, and any professionals retained in the course of a Proceeding.

5. Communication Among Tribunals

5.1. The Guidelines Applicable to Court-to-Court Communication in CrossBorder Cases (the "Guidelines") attached as Schedule "A" hereto, shall, where applicable to the relevant Proceeding and where recognized by the Tribunal of the relevant Proceeding, be incorporated by reference and form part of this Protocol subject to formal adoption of the Guidelines in whatever form by each Tribunal, in whole or in part and with or without modifications (if any). Where there is any discrepancy between the Protocol and the Guidelines, this Protocol shall prevail.

6. Communication Among Committees

6.1. To the extent permitted and approved by the respective Committee, nonpublic information available to the Committee in any Forum may, if relevant to a matter in which another Debtor has an interest, be shared with the Committees of such Debtor, subject to appropriate confidentiality arrangements and all privileges under the applicable rules of evidence or applicable law.

7. Asset Preservation

7.1. Each Tribunal should administer the assets subject to its jurisdiction.

7.2. If, in the course of a Proceeding, an Official Representative learns or believes that another Debtor could have a material interest in a particular asset whose value and/or recovery is at risk, such Official Representative may notify the Official Representative of the Debtor whose estate includes such asset and, where practicable and consistent with the duties of such Official Representative under applicable laws, the Official Representative of the Debtor whose estate includes such asset should consult with the Official Representative of the Debtor that may have such material interest prior to: (i) the sale, abandonment, or any disposition of such asset; (ii) the termination, suspension, or other transition of any employees managing such asset; or (iii) the commencement of any judicial, or non-judicial, proceeding affecting such asset.

7.3. In the event that (a) an Official Representative claims to have a legal or beneficial interest in property which is transferred to, or received by another Debtor, or (b) an Official Representative determines that the estate for which it is responsible has improperly received or is improperly holding property transferred from or owned by another estate, such Official Representatives should cooperate in:

7.3.1. Assessing the ownership of such transferred property and provide all relevant information, to the extent not otherwise restricted, allowing each Official Representative to ascertain ownership of the property; and

7.3.2. Where ownership of the property has been established and subject to applicable laws: (i) returning the property to the Official Representative of the Debtor establishing its right to such property; and (ii) refraining (to the extent an Official Representative may do so and subject to applicable laws) from transferring or co-mingling property once another Official Representative establishes ownership of such transferred property.

7.4. Official Representatives should, to the extent permitted under applicable law and where appropriate, cooperate to maximize the realizable value of assets for which multiple Debtors have an interest. Official Representatives also recognize that in certain cases such as where a Debtor (the "Funding Estate") has an existing interest in an asset which forms part of another Debtor's estate (the "Funded Estate"), the Official Representative of the Funding Estate may wish to provide funding towards the asset held by the Funded Estate in order to preserve and maximize its realizable value. In such event, the Official Representative of the Funded Estate may, subject to applicable laws, allow such funding to be provided on mutually acceptable bilateral terms.

7.5. Should the Funded Estate, after appropriate consultation with the Funding Estate and after obtaining any necessary approval in an applicable Proceeding, (i) dispose of the asset after receiving funds from the Funding Estate, and (ii) receive proceeds in respect of such disposition, then the Funding Estate shall receive a fair allocation of share of such proceeds.

7.6. Where applicable, compliance with sections 7.2 through 7.5 by Official Representatives is subject to approval from their respective Tribunals or Committees, as the case may be under local law.

8. Claims

8.1. Where there are two or more Proceedings pending as to the same Debtor, those being one or more Plenary Proceedings and/or one or more Limited Proceedings, a claim should be filed only in the Proceeding(s) designated by the Official Representative of such Debtor (provided that certain Official Representatives may be required to make such designation in accordance with applicable law).

8.2. Without prejudice to secured claims or rights in rem, and subject to applicable law, Official Representatives should adjust distributions so that a creditor who has received payment with respect to its claim in one Proceeding may not receive a payment for the same claim in any other Proceeding as to the same Debtor, so long as the payment to the other creditors of the same class is proportionately less than the payment the creditor has already received in respect of that claim.

8.3. Consistent with section 8.2 above, if any claim against one or more Debtors (a "Direct Claim") is subject to a guarantee issued by another Debtor (a "Guarantee"), the Official Representatives shall seek to adjust distributions on the allowed Direct Claim and allowed Guarantee claim so that distributions on the Direct Claim and distributions on the Guarantee do not exceed in the aggregate the amount of the Direct Claim or the Guarantee, whichever is highest. Subject to the preceding sentence, distributions on a Direct Claim shall not reduce the amount of any claim asserted under a corresponding Guarantee, and distributions under a Guarantee shall not reduce the amount of any corresponding Direct Claim.

8.4. Official Representatives should, where possible and subject to the applicable laws of the relevant forum, endeavor to coordinate notice procedures and establish the same deadlines for the filing of claims in their respective Proceedings, and in all other matters regarding the filing, reviewing and objecting to claims.

9. Special Procedures for Intercompany Claims

9.1. The Official Representatives agree that in order to provide for the efficient and timely administration of these Proceedings, and to reduce their cost and maximize recovery for creditors, resources and time should not be spent reviewing historical intercompany accounting records to resolve claims asserted in their respective Proceedings by other Official Representatives on the basis of (i) the allocation of overhead or expense from one Debtor to another Debtor, (ii) the flow of funds from one Debtor to another Debtor, (iii) the incurrence of a liability by one Debtor on behalf of another Debtor, or (iv) a transaction between Debtors (collectively, "Intercompany Claims"); but that rather, it is in the best interests of the Debtors' creditors for Official Representatives to agree to a common set of financial accounting records that form the basis of Intercompany Claims, and that those financial records shall be prima facie valid unless there are elements of proof suggesting that a transaction was recorded in error, or that no such transaction ever occurred or is inconsistent with the intercompany accounting records of the relevant Debtor(s).

9.2. Subject to the other provisions of this section 9, the Official Representatives shall endeavor to negotiate in good faith to attempt to reach a consensual resolution of any differences in their accounting of Intercompany Claims. Only to the extent that Official Representatives certify that they are unable to consensually resolve in good faith any differences in their accounting of Intercompany Claims, the Official Representatives shall resort to adjudication by the Tribunal holding jurisdiction over such claims.

9.3. The Official Representatives shall establish a committee (the "Procedures Committee"), whose members shall be jointly appointed by the Official Representatives and, where required, the Committees, and confirmed by the Tribunals (where applicable) overseeing each Proceeding, to consensually resolve, in accordance with section 9.1 above and in good faith, any differences in the accounting of Intercompany Claims.

9.4. The Procedures Committee shall propose the (i) procedures, (ii) accounting methodologies, and (iii) elements of proof that it intends to use in its calculation and consensual resolution of Intercompany Claims (the "Accounting Procedures"). Furthermore, if two or more Debtors were counterparties to a derivative contract in which the contractual obligations are referenced to one or more underlying assets or indices of asset values and subject to movements in the financial markets (such as contracts for the purchase, sale, or loan of securities; forward contracts; repurchase agreements; or swap agreements; and in some cases, multiple such agreements governed by a master agreement) (the "Intercompany Derivative Contracts"), and if an Intercompany Derivative Contract has been rejected, terminated, liquidated, or accelerated by any of the Debtor counterparties thereto, any damages (the "Intercompany Derivatives Claims") that arise shall be measured and fixed by the Procedures Committee, pursuant to a methodology to be agreed upon by the members of the Procedures Committee (the "Derivatives Methodology").

9.5. As soon as is practicable after the Procedures Committee has agreed upon its Accounting Procedures and Derivatives Methodology, the Official Representatives shall, to the extent required under applicable law, seek approval from their respective Tribunals or Committees (where required) for the use of the Accounting Procedures and Derivatives Methodology in their respective Proceedings in the resolution of Intercompany Claims either as a general rule or on a case by case basis.

9.6. The Official Representatives should cooperate to submit the findings of the Procedures Committee (the "Procedures Committee Findings"), in a form substantially similar to each other, for approval by their respective Tribunals or Committees to the extent required by applicable law.

9.7. To the extent that creditors, Committees, or other interested parties object to (i) the application of the Accounting Methodology, or (ii) the application of the Derivatives Methodology, or (iii) any of the Procedures Committee Findings, all Official Representatives should coordinate a response to such objections.

10. Submission of Winding-Up Plan, Plan of Reorganization or Liquidation, or Deed of Company Arrangement

10.1. Where applicable and permitted under the law of the Forum in a Proceeding, Official Representatives should endeavor to submit a winding-up plan, plan of reorganization or liquidation, or deed of company arrangement (a "Plan") in their respective Proceedings, or to amend a Plan once submitted (to the extent permitted by applicable law) so that each Official Representative's Plan is consistent with Plans filed by other Official Representatives, provided that nothing herein shall require an Official Representative to agree (or shall be deemed to be an agreement), and shall not constitute a waiver of such Official Representative's right to object, to the Plan of another Official Representative.

10.2. Official Representatives should endeavor to coordinate all procedures in connection with their Plans to the extent permitted by applicable law, including, without limitation, all solicitation proceedings relating to their plans.

10.3. No provision of this Protocol contemplates that any Official Representative is required to delay filing, prosecuting or consummating a Plan with respect to the estate administered by such Official Representative.

11. Comity

11.1. The parties hereto agree that each Tribunal is an independent, sovereign Tribunal, entitled to preserve its independent jurisdiction and authority with respect to matters before it and the conduct of the Official Representatives.

11.2. Each Tribunal shall have sole jurisdiction and power over the conduct of the Proceeding in that forum; the appointment of the Official Representatives and their professionals, their retention, tenure in office, and compensation; and the hearing and determination of matters arising in that forum.

11.3. Nothing in this Protocol is intended to interfere with the exercise of jurisdiction by each of the Tribunals in the Proceedings, or to interfere with the natural rules or ethical principles by which an Official Representative is bound according to applicable national law and professional rules.

12. Amendment

12.1. This Protocol may not be waived, amended, or modified orally or in any other way or manner (including, without limitation, pursuant to a Plan) except by a writing signed by a party to be bound and, where applicable, approved by the Tribunal with jurisdiction over that party. Notice of any proposed amendment to this Protocol shall be provided via email by the party or parties hereto proposing such to all Official Representatives, and their respective Committees.

12.2. Additional parties may be added to this Protocol at any time after the effective date of this Protocol by means of an amendment pursuant to section 12.1.

13. Adherence

13.1. Notwithstanding the provisions of section 12, nothing in this Protocol shall preclude Official Representatives who are not parties hereto from adhering to the terms of this Protocol.

14. Execution and Application

14.1. This Protocol shall inure to the benefit of the parties hereto and their respective successors, assigns, representatives, heirs, executors, administrators, trustee, receivers, custodians, or curators, as the case may be, to the extent permitted under applicable law. Nothing herein shall create a right for any entity that is not a party to the Protocol, and a party hereto shall not be bound by this Protocol in its dealings with any entity that is not a party hereto.

14.2. Any request for the entry of an order which is contrary to the provisions of this Protocol must be made on notice to all Official Representatives and their respective Committees by the proponent of the order.

14.3. This Protocol may be signed in any number of counterparts, each of which shall be deemed an original and all of which together shall be deemed to be one and the same instrument, and may be signed by facsimile signature, which shall be deemed to constitute an original signature.

14.4. A Tribunal having jurisdiction over an Official Representative shall retain jurisdiction over such Official Representative for the purpose of approving any amendments or modifications thereto in accordance with applicable laws; provided, however, in no event shall this or any other provision in this Protocol be deemed to create any liability on the part of an Official Representative for any reason.

14.5. Each Official Representative shall exercise good faith efforts to take such actions and execute such documents as may be necessary and appropriate to implement and effectuate this Protocol.

14.6. This Protocol shall be deemed effective with respect to each Official Representative and the estate administered thereby upon execution by all Official Representatives whose signature blocks appear below, and its approval by the Tribunal with jurisdiction over such estates or the relevant Committee (or similar body), where such approval is required under applicable law.

14.7. This Protocol shall remain in effect with respect to any Official Representative who is a party hereto and the estate administered thereby until the earlier of (i) the conclusion of that Official Representative's Proceeding as respectively defined by applicable law; or (ii) where applicable, and after providing notice to the parties hereto, entry of an order (or similar action) terminating this Protocol by the Tribunal having jurisdiction over such Proceeding, or approval of such termination by the relevant Committee(s) (or similar body) where such approval is required under applicable law, upon a determination by such Tribunal or Committee(s) that the Protocol has achieved all of its objectives as to that Official Representative's Proceeding.

[*signature pages follow*]

I. MADOFF PROTOCOL

CROSS-BORDER INSOLVENCY PROTOCOL

FOR THE BERNARD MADOFF GROUP OF COMPANIES

This cross-border insolvency protocol (the "**Protocol**") establishes a framework for cooperation between, and coordination of, the liquidation proceedings of Bernard L. Madoff Investments Securities LLC ("**BLMIS**") and Madoff Securities International Limited ("**MSIL**") (collectively, the "**Debtors**").

Background

A. The Proceedings

On 15 December 2008, Irving H. Picard was appointed as trustee for the liquidation of the business of BLMIS (the "**Trustee**") following an application to the United States District Court for the Southern District of New York by the Securities Investor Protection Corporation ("**SIPC**").

On 19 December 2008, Mark Richard Byers, Andrew Lawrence Hosking and Stephen John Akers were appointed joint provisional liquidators of MSIL (the "**JPLs**"), following the presentation of a winding up petition by the directors of MSIL.

In their respective proceedings, the JPLs and the Trustee have been appointed, *inter alia*, to manage and/or liquidate the relevant Debtor's affairs, to collect and realise its assets, and as the representative of its estate (collectively the "**Representatives**").

The provisional liquidation of MSIL before the High Court of Justice, Chancery Division in England (the "**English Court**") and the BLMIS liquidation proceeding in the United States Bankruptcy Court for the Southern District of New York (collectively the "**Tribunals**" and the "**Proceedings**") may in due course be supplemented by proceedings in other jurisdictions.

The Trustee has already, on 27 February 2009, been recognised by the English Court as the "*foreign representative*" of BLMIS pursuant to the Cross-Border Insolvency Regulations 2006.

The JPLs were granted full administration and realisation of all of the assets of MSIL in the United States as provided in 11 U.S.C. § 1509 upon the recognition of the Provisional Liquidation as a foreign main proceeding by the United States Bankruptcy Court for the Southern District of Florida on 14 April 2009 which proceeding was transferred to the United States Bankruptcy Court for the Southern District of New York pursuant to Bankruptcy Rule 1014.

B. The Debtors

BLMIS was a securities broker-dealer and investment adviser established in New York, with its office at 885 Third Avenue. It is registered with the US Securities and Exchange Commission and is a member of both the Financial Industry Regulatory Authority and SIPC. The sole member of BLMIS is Bernard L. Madoff.

MSIL is a company incorporated in England and Wales. It was authorised and regulated by the FSA. Mr Madoff is the principal shareholder in MSIL.

On 11 December 2008, Mr Madoff reportedly confessed to an agent of the US Federal Bureau of Investigation that BLMIS' investment advisory business in fact amounted, in his own words, to "*a giant Ponzi scheme*".

This is a fraud of potentially unprecedented scale and breadth. Mr Madoff has himself estimated the losses from this fraud to be in the region of US$50 billion.

C. The Need for a Protocol

The nature of the business and the fraud conducted by Mr Madoff is such that each of the Debtors is likely to have assets and/or liabilities in both England and the United States (as well as many other jurisdictions). Furthermore, whilst the precise nature of the relationships between BLMIS and MSIL requires further investigation, the affairs of the two companies are closely intertwined. As a result, evidence relating to the assets and liabilities of each Debtor is held by the other Debtor.

Both the Trustee and the JPLs therefore consider the proper administration of each of the Proceedings to be dependent upon cooperation between the Representatives, and that it is in their common interest to share information with each other expeditiously relating to the affairs of the two companies.

The need to share information has been recognised by the English Court. The Order appointing the JPLs on 19 December 2009 expressly provides that the JPLs shall cooperate as shall be appropriate with the Trustee. On 27 February 2009, a further Order was made by the English Court which provides that the JPLs be at liberty, subject to their being satisfied that the provision of the information is in the interests of the provisional liquidation of MSIL, to disclose to the Trustee broad categories of information. The English Court held that the provision of such information is necessary, *inter alia*, for the proper conduct of the provisional liquidation of MSIL and in connection with the liquidation of BLMIS.

As part of the information sharing process, the Representatives have entered into an Information Sharing Protocol, of even date which sets out specific guidance with respect to the sharing and transfer of information by and between the Representatives and their respective agents.

In addition to information sharing between the Representatives, effective and consistent management of the Proceedings may also require cooperation and communication between the Tribunals.

This Protocol is therefore designed to set a framework for the coordination of the Proceedings, and to enable the Tribunals and Representatives to operate efficiently, expeditiously and effectively in the interest of all of the Debtors' creditors and other stakeholders, including the victims of the underlying fraud.

Terms

1. Purpose and Aims

1.1. The Representatives shall, to the extent appropriate having regard to their respective duties under applicable law, coordinate with each other and cooperate in all aspects of the Proceedings in order to meet the aims of this Protocol.

1.2. The aims of this Protocol are:

1.2.1. Coordination – To promote international cooperation and the coordination of activities in the Proceedings.

1.2.2. Efficiency – To provide for the orderly, effective, expeditious and efficient administration of the Proceedings in order to reduce their cost and to maximize recovery for creditors.

1.2.3. Communication – To promote communication among Representatives; and to provide, to the extent desirable, for direct communication between the Tribunals.

1.2.4. Information and Data Sharing – To provide for the expeditious sharing of information and data between the Representatives in order to promote effective, efficient and fair administrations and to avoid duplication of effort and activities by the parties.

1.2.5. Assets – To promote coordination and cooperation between the Representatives in relation to the identification, preservation and realisation of assets and their fair distribution among all classes of creditors.

1.2.6. Comity – To maintain the independent jurisdiction, sovereignty, and authority of all Tribunals.

2. Notice

2.1. Notice of any meetings, applications and any relevant court hearings or statutory deadlines, and any other matters, in which the relevant Representative has an interest, shall be provided by each Representative to the other Representative by email as far in advance as possible.

3. Right of Representatives to Appear

3.1. The Representatives where possible shall have the right to appear in all of the Proceedings, whether before a Tribunal or in statutory meetings convened pursuant to applicable law, provided however that appearing before a Tribunal shall not in itself subject a Representative to jurisdiction for any purpose other than any relief that Representative may be seeking from the relevant Tribunal.

3.2. If a Representative cannot be present before a Tribunal, he shall be entitled, to the extent permitted by applicable law, to communicate in writing any observations to that Tribunal in advance of any order being made.

4. Communication and Information Sharing

4.1. To the extent appropriate having regard to their respective duties under applicable law, each Representative shall:

4.1.1. keep the other Representative apprised of its activities and of all relevant information and material developments in matters involving the Debtors and the Proceedings; and

4.1.2. share with the other Representative non-public information available to it regarding the Debtors, their pre-appointment activities and transactions, and their assets and liabilities.

4.2. The Representatives agree that each shall not (and shall direct that its respective agents and representatives shall not) provide any non-public information received from the other to any third party, unless the provision of such information is (i) agreed to by the other Representative; (ii) required by applicable law; or (iii) required by order of any Tribunal.

4.3. All communications between the Representatives (and their respective professionals, employees, agents, and representatives) are subject to, and do not waive, any applicable attorney-client, work-product, legal, professional, common interest or other privilege recognised under any applicable law. In that connection, the Representatives shall be entering into an agreement concerning confidential and/or privileged information of common interest.

5. Communication Between Tribunals

5.1. It is intended that the Guidelines Applicable to Court-to-Court Communication in Cross-Border Cases (the "**Guidelines**") attached as Schedule "A" hereto, shall be formally adopted by each Tribunal, whether in whole or in part and with or without modifications. Where there is any discrepancy between the Protocol and any guidelines which may eventually be adopted by the Tribunals, those guidelines shall prevail.

6. Assets

6.1. To the extent appropriate having regard to their respective duties under applicable law, and to the extent that a Representative learns or believes that the other Representative may have a material interest in a particular asset, the Representatives shall coordinate and cooperate expeditiously with each other regarding the identification, preservation and realisation of that asset.

6.2. The Representatives shall endeavour to reach agreement expeditiously, on a case by case basis, as to which Representative is best placed to deal with any particular asset.

6.3. The Representatives shall provide assistance in respect of recovery of the identified assets, which may include enabling and/or confirmatory acts and instruments such as comfort letter, assignments and powers of attorney in favour of the Representative who is pursuing recovery of such assets.

7. Intercompany Claims

7.1. The Representatives shall cooperate and negotiate in good faith regarding any potential claims by either Debtor against the other Debtor. At the appropriate stage, the Representatives shall consider whether it is sensible to implement, subject to the approval of the Tribunals, a mechanism for the resolution of intercompany claims.

8. Law Enforcement Agencies

8.1. The Representatives recognise that there is a substantial public interest in the investigation of fraud and the effective prosecution of those responsible.

8.2. To the extent appropriate having regard to their respective duties under applicable law, the Representatives:

8.2.1. shall endeavour to coordinate with each other regarding the cooperation provided to law enforcement or other agencies (including, without limitation, the Department of Justice, the Securities and Exchange Commission, and SIPC in the United States, and the Serious Fraud Office, the Metropolitan Police Fraud Squad, the City of London Police and the Financial Services Authority in England); and

8.2.2. take steps to ensure that evidence provided to law enforcement agencies is in a manner and form which assists those agencies and, in the case of agencies in the United States, does not include testimony obtained under powers of compulsion save where appropriate safeguards (which shall be mutually agreed) are put in place regarding such evidence.

9. Costs

9.1. Subject to any further agreement between the Representatives, each Representative's costs of performing its obligations under this Protocol (including the costs of its agents and representatives) shall be borne in the same manner as its other costs incurred in the relevant Proceeding.

10. Comity

10.1. The Representatives agree that each Tribunal is an independent, sovereign Tribunal, entitled to preserve its independent jurisdiction and authority with respect to matters before it.

10.2. Nothing in this Protocol is intended to interfere with the rules or ethical principles by which a Representative (including, in each case, a Representative's legal advisor) is bound, according to applicable national law and professional rules.

11. Amendment

11.1. The Protocol may be supplemented from time to time by the Representatives as circumstances require, for example detailing specific procedures for the exchange of information and data. Such supplements shall not require the approval of either Tribunal.

11.2. Subject to the agreement of the Representatives, and the entry of an order by each of the Tribunals, additional parties may be added to this Protocol.

12. Execution and Application

12.1. This Protocol shall be binding on, and inure to the benefit of, the Representatives' respective successors and assigns, including any liquidator subsequently appointed over MSIL.

12.2. This Protocol shall not create any right for any person or entity that is not a party hereto.

12.3. Each Representative represents and warrants to the other that its execution, delivery, and performance of this Protocol is within its power and authority, except to the extent that Tribunal approval is required.

12.4. This Protocol may be signed in any number of counterparts, each of which shall be deemed an original and all of which together shall be deemed to be one and the same instrument.

12.5. This Protocol shall be deemed effective upon its approval by both Tribunals.

IN WITNESS WHEREOF the Representatives have caused this Protocol to be executed either individually or by their respective attorneys or representatives hereunto authorised.

Dated 21st May 2009

[Signatures]

J. JET AIRWAYS PROTOCOL

CROSS-BORDER INSOLVENCY PROTOCOL

THIS PROTOCOL IS DATED [•] AND ENTERED INTO BETWEEN:

(1) Ashish Chhawchharia, in his capacity as the Resolution Professional of **Jet Airways (India) Limited**, a company incorporated under the provisions of the Companies Act, 1956, and an existing company under the Companies Act, 2013, and having its registered office at Siroya Centre Sahar Airport Road, Andheri (East) Mumbai 400099, India (the "**Company**"), appointed by the order of the National Company Law Tribunal, Mumbai Bench, India, ("**NCLT**") dated 20 June 2019 (the "**RP**");

and

(2) Rocco Mulder, in his capacity as the administrator in bankruptcy of the Company appointed by Noord-Holland District Court, Trade, Sub-district and Insolvency in the Netherlands ("**Dutch Bankruptcy Court**") by its order dated 21 May 2019 (the "**Dutch Trustee**"),

each a "**Party**" and together the "**Parties**".

BACKGROUND:

(A) The Company is subject to parallel insolvency proceedings in India and in the Netherlands.

(B) In India, the Company has been admitted into a corporate insolvency resolution process under the Insolvency and Bankruptcy Code, 2016 (the "**Indian Proceedings**"). Pursuant to the order of the NCLT and resolutions duly passed at the meeting of the committee of creditors of the Company ("**CoC**") dated 16 July 2019, the RP has been appointed, resulting in the powers of the board of directors of the Company being vested with the RP.

(C) In the Netherlands, the Company has been declared bankrupt and the Dutch Trustee has been appointed to manage the estate of the Company (the "**Dutch Proceedings**"). The Dutch Proceedings together with the "**Indian Proceedings**": the "**Proceedings**".

(D) On an application made by the Dutch Trustee, appealing the 20 June 2019 order of the NCLT before the Hon'ble National Company Law Appellate Tribunal, New Delhi ("**NCLAT**"), the NCLAT, by its orders dated 12 July 2019 and 21 August 2019 ("**NCLAT Order**"), inter alia, directed the RP, in consultation with the CoC, to consider the prospect of cooperating with the Dutch Trustee so as to have joint "corporate insolvency resolution process of the Company" and further vide its order dated 04 September 2019 directed the RP under the Indian Proceedings to reach an arrangement/ agreement with the Dutch Trustee to extend such cooperation to each other, further allowing the CoC to guide the RP to enable him to prepare an agreement in reaching the terms of arrangement of cooperation with the Dutch Trustee in the best interest of the Company and all its stakeholders ("**Proposed Cooperation**").

(E) The Parties wish to facilitate and formulate the Proposed Cooperation with this Protocol.

THE PARTIES AGREE AS FOLLOWS:

1. CONSTRUCTION

1.1.1. In this Protocol, unless a contrary indication appears:

(a) any reference to this "**Protocol**" or any other document also refers to any amendment or supplement to it and any restatement or novation of it;

(b) any reference to a "**Party**" also refers to its successors in title, permitted assigns and permitted transferees;

(c) "**the Netherlands**" refers to the part of the Kingdom of the Netherlands located in Europe (and all derivate terms, including "**Dutch**", are to be construed accordingly).

1.1.2. Headings do not affect the interpretation of this Protocol.

PURPOSE

2.1.1. The Parties acknowledge that while the Indian Proceedings is one that is focused on the revival/resolution of insolvency of the Company and the maximization of the value of its assets for the benefit of all its stakeholders, the main objective of the Dutch Proceedings is to deal with the liquidation of the assets of the Company located in the Netherlands and therefore, agree:

(a) this Protocol represents a statement of intentions and guidelines designed to minimize the costs and maximize value of assets/recoveries for all creditors of the Proceedings, by promoting the sharing of relevant information among the Parties and the international coordination of related activities in the Proceedings, while respecting the separate interests of creditors and other interested parties to the Proceeding, and the independence, sovereignty, and authority of the NCLT/NCLAT and Dutch Bankruptcy Court.

(c) in recognition of the substantive differences among the Proceedings in both jurisdictions, this Protocol shall not impose on the RP or the Dutch Trustee any duties or obligations (i) that may be inconsistent with or that may conflict with the duties or obligations to which the Parties are subject under applicable law, or (ii) that are not in the interests of the Company's estate represented by the Parties and/or its creditors. Furthermore, nothing in this Protocol should be interpreted in any way so as to interfere with (i) the proper discharge of any duty, obligation or function of the Parties, or (ii) the exercise of statutory or other powers otherwise available to a Party under applicable law.

(d) the Parties should coordinate with each other and cooperate in all aspects of the Proceedings in terms of this Protocol. In doing so, the Parties acknowledge and agree that the Parties shall deal in good faith with each other in the interests of maximizing value of assets/recovery for all of the Company's creditors.

3. AIM OF THE PROTOCOL

The Parties recognize that the Company being an Indian company with its centre of main interest in India, the Indian Proceedings are the main insolvency proceedings and the Dutch Proceedings are the non-main insolvency proceedings:

(a) *Coordination* – To promote international cooperation and the coordination of activities in the Proceedings; and to provide for the orderly, effective, efficient, and timely administration of the Proceedings in order to reduce their cost and maximize recovery for creditors.

(e) *Communication* – To promote communication among the Parties and the CoC; and to provide, wherever possible, for direct communication among NCLT, NCLAT and Dutch Bankruptcy Court.

(f) *Information and Data Sharing* – To provide for the sharing of relevant information and data among the Parties in order to promote effective, efficient, and fair Proceedings, and to avoid duplication of effort and activities by the parties.

(g) *Preservation* – To identify, preserve, and maximize the value of the Company's worldwide assets for the collective benefit of all creditors and other interested parties.

(h) *Claims Reconciliation* – To coordinate an efficient and transparent claims process.

(i) *Maximize value of assets/recoveries* – To cooperate in marshalling the assets of the Company in order to maximize value of assets/recovery for all of the Company's creditors.

(j) *Comity* – To maintain the independent jurisdiction, sovereignty, and authority of NCLT, NCLAT and Dutch Bankruptcy Court.

4. EFFECTIVENESS

4.1.1. The terms of this Protocol shall come into effect upon receiving an approval on its terms from (i) NCLT/NCLAT; and (ii) the Dutch Bankruptcy Court or other appropriate adjudicating authority in the Netherlands responsible for overseeing the Dutch Proceedings.

5. COMMUNICATION AND INFORMATION

5.1.1. The Parties undertake to liaise with each other on matters related to the Company in which they have a material interest.

5.1.2. Each Party shall keep the other Party adequately informed as far in advance as possible of any relevant information and material developments in matters in which the other Party has a material interest (and may require preparation and/or travel by the Parties or the authorized representative of the CoC) including but not limited to any creditors' or shareholders' meetings, statutory or administrative deadlines or court hearings. The Dutch Trustee acknowledges that the RP may be required to and may disclose all information received by it from the Dutch Trustee to the CoC, under and in accordance with the Insolvency and Bankruptcy Code 2016.

5.1.3. Each Party shall share such information and data regarding the Company and its assets and liabilities, that is publicly available, and may, where permitted under applicable laws, share non-public information with the other Party, as reasonably requested by the other Party, and subject at any time to applicable law and the Non-disclosure Agreement dated [•] entered into between the Parties (the "**NDA**"). In this regard, the Parties agree that each shall not (and shall direct their respective agents and representatives not to) provide any non-public information received from each other to any third party, unless such information is (i) agreed to be disseminated/shared by the other Party, (ii) required by applicable law, or (iii) required by order of any Court.

5.1.4. Further, each Party shall co-ordinate in good faith the investigations of any avoidance transactions with the other Party so as to maximise recoveries to the estate of the Company.

5.1.5. No Party shall have or obtain a right of automatic access to any information from the other Party.

6. RIGHTS TO APPEAR AND ATTEND

6.1.1. Subject to the applicable laws of each jurisdiction and Clause 7 (Indian Proceedings), the Parties shall have the right to appear, either in person or duly represented, in the Proceedings.

6.1.2. xxx

6.1.3. No Party shall be deemed to have submitted to any other than his own jurisdiction by virtue of being Party to this Protocol or having appeared in any Proceeding.

7. INDIAN PROCEEDINGS

7.1.1. The Dutch Trustee in the Indian Proceedings:

(a) In the spirit of cooperation, the Dutch Trustee aims to not take any decision under the Dutch Proceedings that would adversely impact the interests of the Company or the creditors. In the event it becomes necessary for the Dutch Trustee in compliance of the Dutch Bankruptcy Court or any other court, or under any applicable law, to take any decision that might adversely impact the interests of the Company or the creditors, the Dutch Trustee shall give advance intimation of such decision to the RP.

(k) In the event a resolution plan for the Company is submitted to the NCLT, the Dutch Trustee shall facilitate the submission (by the Company) of a consistent reorganization plan in the Dutch Proceedings ('*schuldeisersakkoord*') in order to implement the resolution plan in the Dutch jurisdiction incorporating the payout mechanism that is included in such resolution plan so submitted to the NCLT for distribution of various amounts to various stakeholders including the creditors of the Company, in accordance with applicable Dutch laws.

7.1.2. The Dutch Trustee shall seek inputs, notify the RP and consult the RP, and will be mindful of the Indian Proceedings prior to any material decision being taken in the Dutch Proceedings, which may, inter alia, include:

(a) matters relating to any proposal or approval of a plan of reorganization or a resolution plan or plan of compromise or any other similar arrangement in the Dutch Proceedings;

(l) matters relating to assuming, ratifying, rejecting, repudiating, modifying or assigning executory contracts having a material impact on the assets, operations, obligations, rights, property or business of the Company; and

(m) matters which are otherwise prohibited under Section 14 of the Indian Insolvency and Bankruptcy Code, 2016, as further specified in Clause 11 below, if it were to apply in the Netherlands.

8. Assets

8.1.1. Each Party shall do everything reasonable in its power and capacity, and the Parties shall cooperate, to maintain and preserve the value of the assets of the Company which are located in the Netherlands including, without limitation:

(a) the economic interest in the aircraft situated on the date of this Protocol at Schiphol International Airport (BOEING 777-35RER, VT-JEW, S/N 35164) (the "**Aircraft**") or its residual value after enforcement by or on behalf of US Exim Bank ("**US Exim Bank**");

(n) the spare parts situated on the date of this Protocol being stored on the premises of Koninklijke Luchtvaart Maatschappij N.V. or any of its (in)direct subsidiaries or otherwise related entities (collectively "**KLM**") at Schiphol International Airport;

(o) the office inventory, at the date of this Protocol being stored on the premises of KLM at Schiphol International Airport; and

(p) the value of the flight slots at Schiphol International Airport which the Company was entitled to use immediately prior to 21 May 2019 in connection with all activities required to maintain such value,

collectively referred to as the "**Dutch Assets**".

8.1.2. In the interest of having a joint insolvency Proceeding for the administration, preservation and enhancement of the estate of the Company, and in the spirit of Clause 2 and 3, and the Proposed Cooperation, the Dutch Trustee and the RP shall cooperate to preserve and enhance the value of assets of the Company wherever located in the Netherlands, subject to Dutch Law.

8.1.3. In the spirit of Clause 2 and 3, and the Proposed Cooperation, the Dutch Trustee shall not, without consulting the RP:

(a) sell, transfer, encumber, alienate, abandon or dispose of any asset of the Company in or outside the Netherlands or any legal right or beneficial interest therein and make all reasonable attempts and efforts, at all times, in preventing any third party/creditor from undertaking any such action anywhere during the course of the Proceedings; or

(q) commence any judicial or non-judicial proceedings affecting any asset of the Company in or outside the Netherlands.

8.1.4. In the event, the Dutch Trustee conducts a sale of any of the assets of the Company, subject to Dutch Law, the Dutch Trustee shall hold the sale proceeds of the sale of any assets of the Company in a Bankruptcy Account: IBAN NL76KASA0222622202 "Ten name van Mr R Mulder qq curator in het faillissement van Jet Airways (India) Limited". The distribution of such sale proceeds shall be made in consultation with the RP.

8.1.5. If in the course of the Proceedings, the Dutch Trustee learns or believes that a creditor or a third party having material interest in a particular asset whose value and/or recovery is at risk, is intending to sell, dispose off or foreclose a particular asset of or belonging to the Company or its beneficial interest therein in the Netherlands, then the Dutch Trustee shall immediately make all reasonable attempts to gather information relating to the purported transaction and soon after shall provide/convey any and all such information relating to the transaction in question to the RP. Where practicable and consistent with his duties under applicable laws, the Dutch Trustee shall consult with the RP about possible steps and measures, including obtaining appropriate direction(s)/a prohibitory injunction from the appropriate court of law, if required, for preventing/prohibiting any such other third party from (i) selling, abandoning, or disposing of such asset; (ii) terminating, suspending, or other transitioning of any employees managing such asset; or (iii) the commencing of any judicial, or non-judicial, proceeding affecting such asset.

9. CLAIMS

9.1.1. In order to ensure a complete and effective overview of claims and to enable each Party to fulfil his obligations, creditor claims should be submitted by the respective creditors in each Proceeding in accordance with the relevant applicable law.

9.1.2. The Dutch Trustee shall collate all claims received by him and shall forward these claims to the RP, who shall then verify and admit such claims in accordance with the Indian law.

9.1.3. Also on behalf of the creditors involved, the RP shall forward the list of creditors and details of all admitted claims under the Indian Proceedings to the Dutch Trustee, which claims shall be provisionally recognized and admitted by the Dutch Trustee in accordance with Dutch Law.

9.1.4. The Parties agree that the RP might be best placed to investigate the admissibility of claims that were first submitted in the Indian Proceedings and the Dutch Trustee might be best placed to investigate the admissibility of claims that were first submitted in the Dutch Proceedings. Each Party is authorized to randomly or otherwise, but not unreasonably, verify claims that were admitted by the other Party.

9.1.5. With regard to each Claim that were first submitted in the Indian Proceedings, the RP shall represent to the Dutch Trustee whether and on which basis, he has admitted or denied the Claim in the Indian Proceedings.

Similarly, with regard to each Claim that were first submitted in the Dutch Proceedings, the Dutch Trustee shall represent to the RP whether and on which basis, he has admitted or denied the Claim in the Dutch Proceedings. In this respect, the Dutch Trustee and RP shall verify such claims in accordance with applicable laws.

10. COSTS

10.1.1. On behalf of the CoC, the RP represents vis-à-vis the Dutch Trustee that it is the intention of the CoC to include the fees and costs incurred by the Dutch Trustee and any advisor/professional engaged by him for the purposes of the Dutch Proceedings as part of the insolvency resolution process costs (as defined under Section 5(13) of the Indian Insolvency and Bankruptcy Code, 2016) for the same to be paid in accordance with the Indian law, subject to verification by the RP and approval by the CoC, provided that:

(a) such fees and costs have not already been recovered by the Dutch Trustee from proceeds of the sale of any assets of the Company in the Netherlands;

(r) the claims of the members of the CoC filed in accordance with Clause 9 and admitted by the RP will be provisionally recognized by the Dutch Trustee as being submitted in the Dutch Proceedings.

(s) the amount of any legal and professional fees incurred by the Dutch Trustee has been approved by the Dutch Court;

10.1.2. In the spirit of cooperation, the Dutch Trustee and the RP shall be treated equally.

11. STAYS OF PROCEEDINGS

11.1.1. The Dutch Trustee takes note of the order passed by the NCLT on 20 June 2019 as detailed out in the Background above, which imposes a moratorium on, inter alia, the following actions under Section 14 of the Indian and Bankruptcy Code, 2016:

(a) the institution of suits or continuation of pending suits or proceedings against the Company, including execution of any judgment, decree or order in any court of law, tribunal, arbitration panel or other authority;

(t) transferring, encumbering, alienating or disposing off by the Company of any of its assets, including the Dutch Assets, or any legal right or beneficial interest therein;

(u) any action to foreclose, recover or enforce any security interest created by the Company in respect of its property; and

(v) the recovery of any property by an owner or lessor where such property is occupied by or in the possession of the Company.

11.1.2. The Dutch Trustee agrees to make reasonable endeavour to implement the terms of the moratorium imposed by the said order in respect of the Dutch Assets, and to take all reasonable action under applicable Dutch laws to ensure that the order is complied with in this respect, including, without limitation, actions that the Dutch Trustee is bound to undertake under Clause 8.1.5 of this Protocol.

11.1.3. The provisions of Clause 11.1.2 shall not preclude the Dutch Trustee from taking such steps as may be required to protect and preserve the value of the assets of the Company in his possession or control to maximize the value of such assets of the Company for the benefit of its creditors, in accordance with Clause 8.1.5.

12. MISCELLANEOUS

12.1. Signing

12.1.1. Subject to Clause 4 of this Protocol, this Protocol does not have any legal effect until each Party has validly signed this Protocol.

12.1.2. If this Protocol is signed in counterparts, these counterparts will count as one Protocol.

12.2. Validity

12.2.1. Unless otherwise agreed this Protocol shall remain valid until:

(a) approval of the resolution plan in accordance with the Insolvency and Bankruptcy Code, 2016 in respect of the Company which has become final or approval of the reorganization plan under Dutch law (*'schuldeisersakkoord'*), which has become final, whichever is later, unless agreed otherwise before such date; or

(b) the passing of a liquidation order against the Company by the NCLT.

12.2.2. In this respect, it should be noted that in the event of the liquidation of the Company, the liquidators appointed for the Company both in India and in the Netherlands may enter into a similar arrangement as this Protocol, for purposes of coordinating the liquidation of the Company in both jurisdictions.

12.3. Rights cumulative

12.3.1. The rights and remedies of each Party provided in this Protocol are cumulative and not exclusive of any rights or remedies provided by law.

12.4. Amendments and waivers

12.4.1. The terms of this Protocol shall not be waived, amended, terminated orally or in any other manner (including, without limitation, pursuant to a resolution plan) except by a written agreement signed by each Party, and such waiver, amendment or termination shall not come into effect unless approved, where applicable, by both the NCLT/NCLAT and the Dutch Courts after notice and a hearing.

12.5. No deemed waivers

12.5.1. No failure to exercise, nor any delay in exercising, by a Party, any right or remedy under this Protocol will operate as a waiver. No single or partial exercise of any right or remedy will prevent any further or other exercise or the exercise of any other right or remedy.

12.6. Third party rights

12.6.1. Except where this Protocol expressly provides otherwise:

(a) it contains no stipulations for the benefit of a third party (*derdenbedingen*) which may be invoked by a third party against a Party; and

(w) where this Protocol contains a stipulation for the benefit of a third party, this Protocol (including the relevant third party's rights under this Protocol) may be terminated, amended, supplemented or waived (in each case either in its entirety or in part) without that third party's consent.

12.7. No rescission; errors

12.7.1. No Party may fully or partly rescind (*ontbinden*) this Protocol.

12.7.2. If a Party has made an error (*heeft gedwaald*) in relation to this Protocol, it shall bear the risk of that error.

12.8. No suspension

12.8.1. No Party may suspend (*opschorten*) performance of its obligations under or in connection with this Protocol on any ground whatsoever.

12.9. No assignment

12.9.1. No Party may fully or partly assign or encumber rights and obligations under this Protocol without the other Party's prior written consent. Without this consent, no assignment or encumbrance is effected.

12.10. Communications in writing

12.10.1. Any communication to be made under or in connection with this Protocol must be made in writing and sent by regular mail or e-mail.

12.11. Addresses

12.11.1. The address and e-mail addresses of each Party for any communication to be made under or in connection with this Protocol are:

(a) those identified with its name in Schedule 1; or

(x) any substitute address or officer as the Party may notify to the other Party by not less than five days' notice.

13. COMITY

13.1.1. The parties hereto agree that each Court is an independent, sovereign Court, entitled to preserve its independent jurisdiction and authority with respect to matters before it and the conduct of the RP and the Dutch Trustee.

13.1.2. Each Court shall have sole jurisdiction and power over the conduct of the Proceeding in that forum; the appointment of the RP and the Dutch Trustee and their professionals, their retention, tenure in office, and compensation; and the hearing and determination of matters arising in that forum.

13.1.3. Nothing in this Protocol is intended to interfere with the exercise of jurisdiction by each of the Courts in the Proceedings, or to interfere with the natural rules or ethical principles by which the RP of the Dutch Trustee is bound according to applicable national law and professional rules.

The NCLAT directed to insert Clause 6.1.2., as suggested by the 'Dutch Trustees', which reads as follows:

6.1.2. The Dutch Trustee shall be invited to participate in the meetings of the CoC as an observer but shall not have a right to vote in such meetings.

BIBLIOGRAPHY

Al-Attar, Adam, 'Using and Losing Secondary Proceedings', (2009) 22(5) *Insolvency Intelligence* 76.

Anderson, Gary, McCormick, Robert and Tollison, Robert, 'The Economic Organization of the English East India Company', (1983) 4(2–3) *J. Econ. Behav. Organ.* 221.

Apeldoorn, Jan van, *Human Rights in Insolvency Proceedings* (Kluwer Legal Publishers 2012).

Arner, Douglas, et al. (eds), *Research Handbook on Asian Financial Law* (Edward Elgar Publishing 2020).

Avgouleas, Emilios, *Governance of Global Financial Markets. The Law, the Economics, the Politics* (CUP 2012).

Baird, Douglas, 'The New Face of Chapter 11', (2004) 12(1) *Am. Bankruptcy Inst. Law Rev.* 69.

Balz, Manfred, 'The European Union Convention on Insolvency Proceedings', (1996) 70 *Am. Bankr. Law J.* 485.

Baudino, Patrizia, Richardson, Tracy and Walters, Ruth, 'Cross-Border Resolution Cooperation and Information-sharing: An Overview of Home and Host Authority Experience', FSI Insights on policy implementation No. 22 (January 2020) <https://www.bis.org/fsi/publ/insights22.htm>.

Baumert, Andreas and Schmitt, Frank, 'Phoenix Kapitaldienst – ein Verfahren schreibt BGH-Rechtsprechung', (2012) *NZI* 394.

Bebchuk, Lucian, Kraakman, Reinier and Triantis, George, 'Stock Pyramids, Cross-Ownership, and Dual Class Equity: The Creation and Agency Costs of Separating Control from Cash Flow Rights' in R Morck (ed.), *Concentrated Corporate Ownership* (University of Chicago Press 2000).

Beckering, Kevin, 'United States Cross-Border Corporate Insolvency: The Impact of Chapter 15 on Comity and the New Legal Environment', (2008) 14(2) *Law & Bus. Rev. Am* 281.

Belohlávek, Alexander, *Rome Convention – Rome I Regulation* (Juris Publishing Inc 2010).

Benedetti, Lorenzo, 'Information Flows in the Insolvency of Enterprise Groups', (2019) 30(3) *Eur. Bus. Law Rev.* 417.

Black's Law Dictionary (8th edn, Thomson Reuters 2004).

Blumberg, Phillip, 'Limited Liability and Corporate Groups', (1986) 11 *J. Corp. L.* 573.

Bogdan, Michael and Pertegás Sender, Marta, *Concise Introduction to EU Private International Law* (4th edn, Europa Law Publishing 2019).

Bork, Reinhard, *Principles of Cross-Border Insolvency Law* (Intersentia 2017).

Bork, Reinhard, 'The European Insolvency Regulation and the UNCITRAL Model Law on Cross-Border Insolvency', (2017) 26(3) *Int. Ins. Rev.* 246.

Bork, Reinhard and Van Zwieten, Kristin (eds), *Commentary on the European Insolvency Regulation* (OUP 2016).

Braun, *Insolvenzordnung (InsO)* (8th edn, C.H. Beck 2020).

Braun, Eberhard and Tashiro, Annerose, 'Cross-border Insolvency Protocol Agreements between Insolvency Practitioners and their Effects on the Rights of Creditors', <https://www.iiiglobal.org/sites/default/files/BraunTashiroandBraunCBProtocols.pdf> accessed 2 September 2020.

Brinkmann, Moritz (ed.), *European Insolvency Regulation. Article-by-Article Commentary* (C.H. Beck/Hart/Nomos 2019).

Buckingham, Sophie, Atanasova, Svetlana, Frazzani, Simona and Véron, Nicolas, 'Study on the differences between bank insolvency laws and on their potential harmonisation, Final Report', (November 2019) <https://ec.europa.eu/info/publications/191106-study-bank-insolvency_en> accessed 2 September 2020.

Bufford, Samuel, 'Coordination of Insolvency Cases for International Enterprise Groups: A Proposal', (2012) 86(4) *Am. Bankr. L. J.* 685.

Bufford, Samuel, 'Center of Main Interests, International Insolvency Case Venue, and Equality of Arms: The Eurofood Decision of the European Court of Justice', (2007) 27(2) *Nw. J. Int'l. L. & Bus.* 351.

Busch, Danny, Van Rijn, Mirik and Louisse, Marije, 'How Single is the Single Resolution Mechanism?', (2019) 30 EBI Working Paper Series <https://papers.ssrn.com/sol3/papers.cfm?abstract_id=3309189#> accessed 2 September 2020.

Busch, Peter, Remmert, Andreas, Rüntz, Stefanie, Vallender, Heinz, 'Kommunikation zwischen Gerichten in grenzüberschreitenden Insolvenzen – Was geht und was nicht geht', (2010) *NZI* 417.

Capri, Alex, 'Coronavirus Accelerates Techno-Nationalism and Puts Multinationals in Spotlight', (*Forbes*, 25 March 2020) <https://www.forbes.com/sites/alexcapri/2020/03/25/coronavirus-accelerates-techno-nationalism-and-piles-new-constraints-on-multinationals/#30cc47d85af8> accessed 2 September 2020.

Carlos, Ann and Nicholas, Stephen, '"Giants of an Earlier Capitalism": The Chartered Trading Companies as Modern Multinationals', (1988) 62(3) *Bus. Hist. Rev.* 398.

Carson, Thomas, 'Conflicts of Interest and Self-Dealing in the Professions: A Review Essay', (2004) 14(1) *Bus. Ethics Q.* 161.

Chapman, Robert, 'Judicial Abstention in Cross-border Insolvency Proceedings: Recent Protocols in Simultaneous Plenary Cases', (1998) 7(1) *Int. Ins. Rev.* 1.

Chen, Vivien, Godwin, Andrew and Ramsay, Ian, 'Cross-Border Cooperation in Bank Resolution: A Framework for Asia', (2016) *SJLS* 1.

Conac, Pierre-Henri, 'Director's Duties in Groups of Companies – Legalizing the Interest of the Group at the European Level', (2013) 10(2) *ECFR* 195.

Cooper, Neil, 'Insolvency Proceedings in Case of Groups of Companies: Prospects of Harmonisation at EU Level', (2011) Note to European Parliament <https://www.europarl.europa.eu/thinktank/en/document.html?reference=IPOL-JURI_NT%282011%29432762> accessed 2 September 2020.

Cooper, Richard, Cestero, Francisco and Mosier, Jesse, 'Oi S.A.: The Saga of Latin America's Largest Private Sector In-Court Restructuring', (2018) 14(5) *Pratt's Journal of Bankruptcy Law* 209.

'Corporate Group Law for Europe', (2000) 1 *EBOR* 165.

Dammann, Jens, 'Related Party Transactions and Intragroup Transactions' in Luca Enriques and Tobias Tröger (eds), *The Law and Finance of Related Party Transactions* (CUP 2019).

Dargan, Sean, 'The Emergence of Mechanisms for Cross-border Insolvencies in Canadian Law', (2001) 17(1) *Conn. J. Int. Law* 107.

Davies, Paul, 'Resolution of Cross border Groups' in Matthias Haentjens and Bob Wessels (eds), *Research Handbook on Crisis Management in the Banking Sector* (Edward Elgar Publishing 2015).

Dengler, Jente, 'Debt Restructuring in the UK and Spain: Is the Grass Still Greener on the Other Side?', III Prize submission (2019), <https://www.iiiglobal.org/iiiprizehistory> accessed 2 September 2020.

Djuric, Djuro and Jovanovic, Vladimir, '"Too big to fail"? The Agrokor Case and its Impact on West Balkan Economies', (2019) 28(1) *Int. Ins. Rev.* 22.

Eidenmüller, Horst, 'What is an Insolvency Proceeding?', (2016) 335 ECGI Working Paper Series in Law, <https://ecgi.global/sites/default/files/working_papers/documents/SSRN-id2712628.pdf> accessed 2 September 2020.

Erikson, Emily, *Between Monopoly and Free Trade: The English East India Company* (Princeton University Press 2014).

Esher, Jack, 'Recent Use of Mediation for Resolution and Effective Management of Large Case Insolvencies', (2015) 12(6) *International Corporate Rescue* 349.

Fabok, Zoltan, 'Jurisdiction Concerning Annex Actions in the Context of the Insolvency and Brussels Ibis Regulations', (2020) 29(2) *Int. Ins. Rev.* 204.

Fabok, Zoltan, 'Vis Attractiva Concursus Throughout the EU? New Ruling of the Hungarian Curia on the Jurisdiction for Post-opening Actions Against an Insolvent Debtor', Oxford Business Law Blog (31 October 2017),

<https://www.law.ox.ac.uk/business-law-blog/blog/2017/10/vis-attractiva-concursus-throughout-eu-new-ruling-hungarian-curia> accessed 2 September 2020.

Farley, James, 'A Judicial Perspective on International Cooperation in Insolvency Cases', (1998) 17 *Am. Bankruptcy Inst. J.* 6.

Farley, James, Leonard, Bruce and Birch, John, 'Cooperation and Coordination in Cross-Border Insolvency Cases', INSOL International Annual Regional Conference (2006) <https://www.iiiglobal.org/sites/default/files/JMFarley.pdf> accessed 2 September 2020.

Feder, Benjamin and Hahn, Devin, 'Mediation in Large Chapter 11 Cases', (2015) 2(3) ABI Committee Newsletter, <http://promo.abi.org/committees/newsletters/Mediation/vol2num3/feder.html> accessed 2 September 2020.

Finch, Vanessa and Milman, David, *Corporate Insolvency Law: Perspectives and Principles* (3rd edn, CUP 2017).

Flaschen, Evan and Silverman, Ronald, 'Cross-border Insolvency Cooperation Protocols', (1998) 33(3) *Tex. Int. Law J.* 587.

Flaschen, Evan, Smits, Antony and Plank, Leo, 'Foreign Representatives in US Chapter 11 Cases: Filling the Void in the Law of Multinational Insolvencies', (2001) 17(1) *Conn. J. Int'l L.* 3.

Fletcher, Ian, 'The European Union Convention on Insolvency Proceedings: An Overview and Comment, with U.S. Interest in Mind', (1997) 23 *Brook. J. Int'l L.* 25.

Fontaine, Marcel and De Ly, Filip, *Drafting International Contracts: An Analysis of Contract Clauses* (2nd edn, Transnational Publishers 2009).

Franko, Lawrence, *The European Multinationals: A Renewed Challenge to American and British Big Business* (Harper and Row 1976).

Galen, Robert van, 'Insolvent Groups of Companies in Cross Border Cases and Rescue Plans', (2012) Report to the Netherlands Association for Comparative and International Insolvency Law.

Godwin, Andrew, Howse, Timothy and Ramsay, Ian, 'The Inherent Power of Common Law Courts to Provide Assistance in Cross-Border Insolvencies: From Comity to Complexity', (2017) 26(1) *Int. Ins. Rev.* 5.

Göretzlehner, Erik, *Maritime Cross-Border Insolvency: An Analysis for Germany, England & Wales and the USA* (Springer 2019).

Guo, Shuai, 'Cross-border Resolution of Financial Institutions: Perspectives from International Insolvency Law', III Prize submission (2018), <https://www.iiiglobal.org/iiiprizehistory> accessed 2 September 2020.

Hadfield, Gillian, 'Legal Infrastructure and the New Economy', (2012) 8(1) *ISJLP* 1.

Haentjens, Matthias, 'National Insolvency Law in International Bank Insolvencies' in Bernard Santen and Dick van Offeren (eds), *Perspectives on International Insolvency Law: A Tribute to Bob Wessels* (Kluwer: Deventer 2014).

Haentjens, Matthias, Wessels, Bob and Guo Shuai, *New Bank Insolvency Law for China and Europe, Volume 3: A Comparative Analysis* (The Hague: Eleven International Publishing, forthcoming).

Hansmann, Henry, Kraakman, Reinier and Squire, Richard, 'Law and the Rise of the Firm', (2006) 119(5) *Harv. L. Rev.* 1333.

Herring, Richard and Carmassi, Jacopo, 'The Corporate Structure of International Financial Conglomerates: Complexity and its Implications for Safety and Soundness' in Allen Berger, Phillip Molyneux, and John Wilson (eds), *The Oxford Handbook on Banking* (1st edn, OUP 2012).

Hess, Burkhard et al., *The Implementation of the New Insolvency Regulation: Improving Cooperation and Mutual Trust* (Nomos/Hart 2018).

Ho, Look Chan (ed.), *Cross-Border Insolvency: A Commentary on the UNCITRAL Model Law* (4th edn, Global Law and Business 2017).

Hopt, Klaus, 'Groups of Companies. A Comparative Study on the Economics, Law and Regulation of Corporate Groups', (2015) Law Working Paper No. 286/2015, ECGI Working Paper Series in Law.

Jackson, Thomas, *The Logic and Limits of Bankruptcy Law* (HUP 1986).

Kamalnath, Akshaya, 'Cross-Border Insolvency Protocols: A Success Story?', (2013) 2(2) *IJLSR* 172.

Kirshner, Jodie Adams, *International Bankruptcy: The Challenge of Insolvency in a Global Economy* (The University of Chicago Press 2018).

Kokorin, Ilya, 'Conflicts of Interest, Intra-group Financing and Procedural Coordination of Group Insolvencies', (2020) 29(1) *Int. Ins. Rev.* 32.

Kokorin, Ilya, 'Contracting Around Insolvency Jurisdiction: Private Ordering in European Insolvency Jurisdiction Rules and Practices' in Vesna Lazić and Steven Stuij (eds), *Recasting the Insolvency Regulation: Improvements and Missed Opportunities. Short Studies in Private International Law* (Asser Press 2020).

Kokorin, Ilya and Wessels, Bob, 'Recognition of Foreign Insolvency Judgments: The Case of Yukos', (2017) 14(6) *Eur. Co. Law* 226.

Lehavi, Amnon, *Property Law in a Globalized World* (CUP 2019).

Lehmann, Matthias, 'Bail-in and Private International Law: How to Make Bank Resolution Measures Effective Across Borders', (2017) 66(1) *Int'l & Comp. L.Q.* 107.

Leonard, Bruce, 'The Development of Court-to-Court Communications in Cross-Border Cases', (2008) 17 *Norton Journal of Bankruptcy Law and Practice* 619.

Leonard, Bruce, 'The Everfresh Reorganisation: Advancing Co-operation in Cross-Border Insolvencies' in Jacob Ziegel and David Baird (eds), *Case Studies in Recent Canadian Insolvency Reorganisations (In Honour of the Honourable Lloyd William Houlden)* (Carswell 1997).

LoPucki, Lynn, 'The Case of Cooperative Territoriality in International Bankruptcy', (2000) 98(7) *Mich. L. Rev.* 2216.

Madaus, Stephan, 'Insolvency Proceedings for Corporate Groups under the New Insolvency Regulation', (2015) *Int. Ins. L. Rev.* 235.

Madaus, Stephan, 'Abuse of Companies in Insolvency Law' in Hanne Birkmose, Mette Neville et al. (eds), *Abuse of Companies* (Wolters Kluwer 2019).

Mankowski, Peter (ed.), *Research Handbook on the Brussels Ibis Regulation* (Edward Elgar Publishing 2020).

Mannan, Morshed, 'Are Bangladesh, India and Pakistan Ready to Adopt the UNCITRAL Model Law on Cross-Border Insolvency?' (2016) 25(3) *Int. Ins. Rev.* 195.

Manóvil, Rafael (ed.), *Groups of Companies: A Comparative Law Overview* (Springer 2020).

Mason, Rosalind and Martin, John, 'Conflict and Consistency in Cross border Insolvency Judgments' (2017), http://www.uncitral.org/pdf/english/congress/Papers_for_Programme/46-MASON_and_MARTIN-Conflict_and_Consistency_in_Cross_border_Insolvency_Judgments.pdf.

Maltese, Michele, 'Court-To-Court Protocols In Cross-Border Bankruptcy Proceedings: Differing Approaches Between Civil Law And Common Law Legal Systems', III Prize submission (2019), <https://www.iiiglobal.org/iiiprizehistory> accessed 2 September 2020.

Mayes, David, Bank Resolution in New Zealand and its Implications for Europe, in Charles Goodhart, Daniela Gabor, Jakob Vestegaard and Ismail Ertürk (eds), *Central Banking at a Crossroads: Europe and Beyond* (Anthem Press 2014).

McCormack, Gerard, Keay, Andrew and Brown, Sarah, *European Insolvency Law: Reform and Harmonization* (Edward Elgar Publishing 2017).

McCormack, Gerard, Keay, Andrew, Brown, Sarah, Dahlgreen, Judith, Study on a New Approach to Business Failure and Insolvency (2016) <https://ec.europa.eu/info/sites/info/files/insolvency_study_2016_final_en.pdf> accessed 2 September 2020.

Mevorach, Irit, 'A Fresh View on the Hard/Soft Law Divide: Implications for International Insolvency of Enterprise Groups', (2019) 40(3) *Mich J Int'l L* 505.

Mevorach, Irit, 'Cross-Border Insolvency of Enterprise Groups: The Choice of Law Challenge', (2014) 9(1) *Brook J. Corp. Fin. & Com. L.* 226.

Mevorach, Irit, *Insolvency within Multinational Enterprise Groups* (OUP 2009).

Mevorach, Irit, 'Modified Universalism as Customary International Law', (2018) 96(7) *Tex. Law Rev.* 1403.

Mevorach, Irit, 'On the Road to Universalism: A Comparative and Empirical Study of the UNCITRAL Model Law on Cross-Border Insolvency', (2011) 12(4) *EBOR* 517.

Mevorach, Irit, *The Future of Cross-Border Insolvency: Overcoming Biases and Closing Gaps* (OUP 2018).

Mevorach, Irit, 'Towards a Consensus on the Treatment of Multinational Enterprise Groups in Insolvency', (2010) 18(2) *Cardozo J. Intl. & Comp. L.* 359.

Mevorach, Irit, 'Transaction Avoidance in Bankruptcy of Corporate Groups', (2011) 8(2) *ECFR* 235.

Mevorach, Irit and Walters, Adrian, 'The Characterization of Pre-insolvency Proceedings in Private International Law', (2020) *EBOR* <https://doi.org/10.1007/s40804-020-00176-x> accessed 2 September 2020.

Miller, D.J. and Shakra, Michael, 'Nortel: The Long and Winding Road' in Janis Sarra and Barbara Romaine (eds), *Annual Review of Insolvency Law* (Carswell 2015).

Miller, Harvey, Fife, Lori and Horwitz, Maurice, 'In re Lehman Brothers Holdings Inc. From Chaos to Consensus', (22 June 2012) <https://www.iiiglobal.org/sites/default/files/media/Miller_Fife_Horwitz_Lehmen_Bros_Holdings_From_Chaos_to_Consensus_0.pdf> accessed 2 September 2020.

Millett, Peter, 'Cross-Border Insolvency: The Judicial Approach', (1997) 6(2) *Int. Ins. Rev.* 99.

Millqvist, Göran, 'Cross-border Insolvency Agreements – Protocols from a Swedish Perspective' in *Essays in Honour of Michael Bogdan* (Juristförlaget, Lund 2013).

Mohan, S. Chandra, 'Cross-Border Insolvency Problems: Is the UNCITRAL Model Law the Answer?', (2012) 21(3) *Int. Ins. Rev.* 199.

Moss, Gabriel, 'Are JIN Guidelines a Tonic for Cross-border Insolvencies?', (2017) 30(7) *Insolvency Intelligence* 102.

Moss, Gabriel and Smith, Tom, 'Commentary on Council Regulation 1346/2000 on Insolvency Proceedings and Regulation (EU) 2015/848 of the European Parliament and of the Council of 20 May 2015 on Insolvency Proceedings (Recast)' in Gabriel Moss, Ian Fletcher and Stuart Isaacs (eds), *Moss, Fletcher and Isaacs on the EU Regulation on Insolvency Proceedings* (OUP 2016).

Moustaira, Elina, *International Insolvency Law: National Laws and International Texts* (Springer 2019).

Muchlinski, Peter, *Multinational Enterprises and the Law* (2nd edn, OUP 2007).

Münchener Kommentar InsO (4th edn, C.H. Beck 2020).

Omar, Paul, 'The Landscape of International Insolvency Law', (2002) 11 *Int. Ins. Rev.* 173.

Orr, Kevyn, Moss, Dan and Wetzel, Anna, 'Courts, Cooperation, and More: Incorporating U.S. Case-Specific Provisions in Insolvency Protocols', (July 2017) Jones Day <https://www.jonesday.com/en/insights/2017/07/courts-cooperation-and-more-a-review-of-us-crossborder-insolvency-protocols–part-1> accessed 2 September 2020.

Overduin, J.H. and Pool, J.M.W., 'De curator in de spagaat: tussen Nederlandse taakuitoefening en het belang van een internationale herstructurering', (2020) 9 *TvI* 58.

Paulus, Christoph, 'Judicial Cooperation in Cross-Border Insolvencies: An outline of some relevant issues and literature', (2006) <https://www.iiiglobal.org/sites/default/files/paulus_judicial_cooperation_in_cross-border_insolvencies_0.pdf> accessed 2 September 2020.

Paulus, Cristoph, '"Protokolle" – ein anderer Zugang zur Abwicklung grenzüberschreitender Insolvenzen', (1998) Zeitschrift für Wirtschaftsrecht (ZIP) 977.

Payne, Jennifer, *Schemes of Arrangement: Theory, Structure and Operation* (CUP 2014).

Peacock, Lauren, 'A Tale of Two Courts: The Nortel Cross-Border Bankruptcy Trial', (2015) 23 *Am. Bankr. Inst. Law Rev.* 543.

Peck, James, 'Introduction' in Howard Morris, James M. Peck and Sonya van de Graaff, *The Art of the Ad Hoc* (GRR 2017).

Pistor, Katharina, 'The Standardization of Law and Its Effects on Developing Economies', (2002) 50(1) *Am. J. Comp. L.* 97.

Pottow, John, 'Two Cheers for Universalism: Nortel's Nifty Novelty' in Janis Sarra and Barbara Romaine (eds), *Annual Review of Insolvency Law* (Toronto: Carswell 2015).

Pottow, John, 'The Dialogic Aspect of Soft Law in International Insolvency: Discord, Digression, and Development', (2019) 40(3) *Mich. J. Int'l L.* 479.

Pottow, John, 'The Maxwell Case' in Robert Rasmussen (ed.), *Bankruptcy Law Stories* (New York: Foundation Press 2007).

Qiang, Christine Zhenwei et al., 'Foreign Direct Investment and Global Value Chains in the Wake of COVID-19' (*World Bank Blogs*, 1 May 2020) <https://blogs.worldbank.org/psd/foreign-direct-investment-and-global-value-chains-wake-covid-19> accessed 2 September 2020.

Queirolo, Ilaria and Dominelli, Stefano, 'Cooperation and Communication Between Parties in the Management of Cross-Border Parallel Proceedings Under the European Insolvency Regulation Recast' in Vesna Lazić and Steven Stuij (eds), *Recasting the Insolvency Regulation: Improvements and Missed Opportunities. Short Studies in Private International Law* (The Hague: Asser Press 2020).

Resnick, Alan and Sommer, Henry (eds), *Collier Guide to Chapter 11: Key Topics and Selected Industries* (Lexis Nexis 2016).

Richter, Tomáš and Thery, Adrian, 'INSOL Europe Guidance Note on the Implementation of Preventive Restructuring Frameworks under EU Directive 2019/1023: Claims, Classes, Voting, Confirmation and the Cross-Class Cram-Down', (April 2020) <https://www.insol-europe.org/download/documents/1705> accessed 2 September 2020

Ringe, Wolf-Georg, 'Insolvency Forum Shopping, Revisited' in Vesna Lazić and Steven Stuij (eds), *Recasting the Insolvency Regulation: Improvements and Missed Opportunities. Short Studies in Private International Law* (Asser Press 2020).

Roe, Mark, 'Three Ages of Bankruptcy', (2017) 7 *Harvard Business Law Review* 217.

Sexton, Anthony, 'Current Problems and Trends in the Administration of Transnational Insolvencies Involving Enterprise Groups: The Mixed Transnational Insolvencies Involving Enterprise Groups: The Mixed Record of Protocols, the UNCITRAL Model Insolvency Law, and the EU Insolvency Regulation', (2012) 12(2) *Chic. J. Int. Law* 811.

Scheuch, Alexander, 'Konzernrecht: An Overview of the German Regulation of Corporate Groups and Resulting Liability Issues', (2016) 13(5) *Eur. Co. Law* 191.

Schlosser, Peter, 'Jurisdiction and International Judicial and Administrative Cooperation', (2000) 284 Recueil des Cours de l'Académie de droit international.

Schmidt, Jessica, 'General Duty of Cooperation and Communication (Article 56(1))', in Reinhard Bork and Kristin Van Zwieten (eds), *Commentary on the European Insolvency Regulation* (OUP 2016).

Schoenmaker, Dirk, *Governance of International Banking: The Financial Trilemma* (OUP 2013).

Shah, Devi and Snead, Jeremy, 'The UNCITRAL Practice Guide on Cross-border Insolvency Cooperation: A Good Practice Guide to Cross-border Insolvency Agreements', (2010) 7(5) *Int. Corp. Rescue* 325.

Singh, Dalvinder, *European Cross-Border Banking and Banking Supervision* (OUP 2020).

Skeel, David, *Icarus in the Boardroom: The Fundamental Flaws in Corporate America and Where They Came From* (OUP 2005).

Slaughter, Anne-Marie, 'A Global Community of Courts', (2003) 44(1) *Harv. Int. Law J.* 191.

Stanghellini, Lorenzo, Mokal, Riz, Paulus, Christoph and Tirado, Ignacio (eds), *Best Practices in European Restructuring: Contractualised Distress Resolution in the Shadow of the Law* (Wolters Kluwer, CEDAM 2018).

Sussman, Edna and Gorskie, Jennifer, 'Capturing the Benefits of Arbitration for Cross Border Insolvency Disputes' in Arthur Rovine (ed.), *Contemporary Issues in International Arbitration and Mediation* (Martinus Nijhoff Publishers 2013).

Teichmann, Christoph, 'Towards a European Framework for Cross-Border Group Management', (2016) 13(5) *Eur. Co. Law* 150.

Thole, Christoph and Dueñas, Manuel, 'Some Observations on the New Group Coordination Procedure of the Reformed European Insolvency Regulation' (2015) 24(3) *Int. Ins. Rev.* 214.

Troiano, Vincenzo, 'Cross-border Cooperation Between Resolution Authorities in the BRRD' in Matthias Haentjens and Bob Wessels (eds), *Research Handbook on Crisis Management in the Bankruptcy Sector* (Edward Elgar Publishing 2015).

Uhlenbruck, *Insolvenzordnung: InsO* (15th edn, C.H. Beck 2019).

Umfreville, Chris, et al., 'Recognition of UK Insolvency Proceedings Post-Brexit: The Impact of a "No Deal" Scenario', (2018) 27(3) *Int. Ins. Rev.* 422.

Vallar, Giulia, 'Protocols as Means of Coordination of Insolvency Proceedings of Cross-Border Banking Groups' in Loïc Cadiet, Burkhard Hess and Marta Requejo Isidro (eds), *Procedural Science at the Crossroads of Different Generations* (Nomos 2015).

Vallar, Giulia, 'Use of Cross-Border Insolvency Protocols in Banking and Financial Sector' in Rebecca Parry and Paul Omar (eds), *Banking and Financial Insolvencies: The European Regulatory Framework* (INSOL Europe 2016).

Van de Ven, Fabian, 'The Cross-Border Insolvency Protocol: what it is and what is in it?', (2015) Leiden University Master Thesis.

Virgos, Miguel and Schmit, Etienne, 'Report on the Convention on Insolvency Proceedings' (1996) [EU Council of the EU Document].

Viswanathan, L. and Kumar, Dhananjay, 'Cross-border Insolvency Protocols: A New Beginning in India', (2020) 17(2) *International Corporate Rescue* 95.

Wessels, Bob, 'Contracting Out of Secondary Insolvency Proceedings: The Main Liquidator's Undertaking in the Meaning of Article 18 in the Proposal to Amend the EU Insolvency Regulation', (2014) 9(1) *Brook. J. Corp. Fin. & Com. L.* 63.

Wessels, Bob, *International Insolvency Law Part I. Global Perspectives on Cross-Border Insolvency Law* (4th edn, Wolters Kluwer 2015).

Wessels, Bob, 'Mediation in Restructuring and Insolvency', (2016) Spring *Eurofenix* 24.

Wessels, Bob, 'Secondary Insolvency Proceedings', in Reinhard Bork and Kristin van Zwieten (eds), *Commentary on the European Insolvency Regulation* (OUP 2016).

Wessels, Bob, 'Should the EU Adopt UNCITRAL Model Law on Cross-Border Insolvency?' Blog of Bob Wessels, 28 October 2016.

Wessels, Bob, *International Insolvency Law Part II. European Insolvency Law* (4th edn, Wolters Kluwer 2017).

Wessels, Bob, 'International Insolvency Law and EU Bank Resolution Rules' in Matthias Haentjens and Bob Wessels (eds), *Research Handbook on Cross-border Bank Resolution* (Edward Elgar Publishing 2019).

Wessels, Bob and Boon, Gert-Jan, 'Soft Law Instruments in Restructuring and Insolvency Law: Exploring its Rise and Impact', (2019) 2 *TvOB* 53.

Wessels, Bob and Kokorin, Ilya, *European Union Regulation on Insolvency Proceedings: An Introductory Analysis* (Alexandria: American Bankruptcy Institute 2018).

Wessels, Bob and Madaus, Stephan, 'Rescue of Business in Insolvency Law, Instrument of the European Law Institute' (2017) <http://www.europeanlawinstitute.eu/fileadmin/user_upload/p_eli/Publications/Instrument_INSOLVENCY.pdf> accessed 2 September 2020.

Wessels, Bob, Markell, Bruce and Kilborn, Jason, *International Cooperation in Bankruptcy and Insolvency Matters* (OUP 2009).

Wessels, Bob, 'Judicial Co-operation in Cross-Border Insolvency Cases (short version inaugural lecture Leiden 2008)' in Bob Wessels and Paul Omar (eds), *Crossing (Dutch) Borders in Insolvency. Papers from the INSOL Europe Academic Forum and Meijers Institute of the Leiden Law School Joint Insolvency Conference* (INSOL Europe 2009).

Wessels, Bob, 'The Ongoing Struggle of Multinational Groups of Companies under the EC Insolvency Regulation', (2009) 6(4) *Eur. Co. Law* 169.

Westbrook, Jay, 'Comment: A More Optimistic View of Cross-Border Insolvency', (1994) 72(3) *Wash. U. L. Rev.* 947.

Westbrook, Jay, 'Corporate Formalism in a Global Economy' in Janis Sarra and Barbara Romaine (eds), *Annual Review of Insolvency Law* (Carswell 2015).

Westbrook, Jay, 'The Globalisation of Insolvency Reform', (1999) 3 *N.Z. L. Rev.* 401.

Wetzer, Thom, 'In Two Minds: The Governance of Ring-Fenced Banks', (2019) 19 *J. Corp. Law Stud.* 197.

Wilkins, Mira, *The Emergence of Multinational Enterprise: American Business Abroad from the Colonial Era to 1914* (HUP 1970).

Wilkins, Mira, 'The History of Multinational Enterprise' in Alan Rugman (ed.), *The Oxford Handbook of International Business* (2nd edn, OUP 2009).

Williamson, Óliver, 'The Modern Corporation: Origins, Evolution, Attributes', (1981) 19(4) *J. Econ. Lit.* 1537.

Winner, Martin, 'Group Interest in European Company Law: An Overview', (2016) 5(1) *Acta Universitatis Sapientiae: Legal Studies* 85.

Witting, Christian, *Liability of Corporate Groups and Networks* (CUP 2018).

Wood, Philip, *Principles of International Insolvency* (Sweet & Maxwell 1995).

Wouters, Nora and Raykin, Alla, 'Corporate Group Cross-Border Insolvencies Between the United States and European Union: Legal and Economic Developments', (2013) 29 *Emory Bankruptcy Developments Journal* 387.

Yamamoto, Kazuhiko, 'New Japanese Legislation on Cross-border Insolvency as Compared with the UNCITRAL Model Law', (2002) 11(2) *Int. Ins. Rev.* 67.

Yamauchi, Keith, 'Should Reciprocity Be a Part of the UNCITRAL Model Cross-Border Insolvency Law?', (2007) 16(3) *Int. Ins. Rev.* 145.

Yandreski, Andrea and Empey, Brian, 'Officer of the Court: Exploring the Role of the Information Officer' in Janis Sarra (ed.), *Annual Review of Insolvency Law* (Carswell 2016).

Zhang, Daoning, *Insolvency Law and Multinational Groups: Theories, Solutions and Recommendations for Business Failure* (Routledge 2020).

Zwieten, Kristin van, 'Related Party Transactions in Insolvency' in Luca Enriques and Tobias Tröger (eds), *The Law and Finance of Related Party Transactions* (CUP 2019).

INDEX

Note: Page locators in italics denote page references where no paragraph numbers are present.

access to information 3.17, 4.27, 8.16–8.29, *283*
accounting procedures 10.32, *287–8*
administration of insolvency proceedings 1.01, 3.11, 4.01, 4.38, 6.07–6.08, 6.13, 6.16, 7.31, 8.14, 8.20, 10.01, 10.17, 10.30, 13.04
  Practice Guide on 5.13
Affaire Cipolletta v. Italy 8.09
Affiliated Professionals *233–5*
affiliate fee procedures *234*, *236*
AgriBioTech Canada protocol (2000) 7.25, 8.32, 8.41, 10.43
AIOC protocol (1998) 4.34–4.35, 7.26, 10.22, 10.43, 10.67
akkoord 9.09
ALI-III
  Global Guidelines for Court-to-Court Communications in International Insolvency Cases 10.72, 10.74
  Global Principles for Cooperation in International Insolvency Cases (2012) 4.28, 9.07
  Guidelines Applicable to Court-to-Court Communications in Cross-Border Cases (2001) 4.45, 8.24, 8.25, 8.46
American Law Institute (ALI) 1.08, 4.06
appear and be heard, rights to
  Loewen Protocol (1999) *236*
  Pioneer Protocol (2001) *265*
appear, right to 4.31, 5.13, 8.11, 10.13–10.16, *220*, *221*, *252*, *282*, *294*, *302*
asserted guarantee claims, enforceability of 10.28
asset preservation 4.07, 10.08, 10.67, *281*, *285–6*
attorney-client privilege 8.21, *283*
auditors *234*, *236*
Australian Council of Financial Regulators 11.19
Australian Cross-Border Insolvency Act (2008) 9.06
Australian Prudential Regulation Authority 11.19
Australian Securities and Investments Commission 11.19
Australian Treasury 11.19

Bahamian bankruptcy proceedings *209*
Banco Central do Brasil (Brazil) 11.20
Bank Indonesia 11.17
banking industry 11.11, 11.25
Banking Union 11.03
bank insolvencies 1.02
  cooperation agreements
    cross-border 11.11
    between resolution authorities 11.10–11.26
  cooperation within
    resolution colleges and crisis management groups 11.05–11.09
  cross-border effects 11.01
  implementation of resolution measures 11.11
  resolution of 11.02
  rules for transnational bank resolution 11.10
  from self-interest to close cooperation 11.01–11.04

standards for credit institutions 11.02
Bank of Albania (Albania) 11.20
Bank of England 1.02, 11.18
Bank of Japan 11.17
Bank Recovery and Resolution Directive (BRRD) 2.10, 11.07
implementation of 11.06
bank resolution
cooperation arrangements in 11.25
characteristics of 11.25
cross-border 1.18, 11.25
ex ante format of 11.24
bankruptcy 6.01, 7.26, 10.35, *205*
Federal Rules of Bankruptcy Procedure 9.03
Bankruptcy Act 1987 (Sweden) 9.20
Bankruptcy and Insolvency Act of Canada *218*
Bankruptcy Code (US) 4.14–4.15, 7.25, 8.41, 9.02, 10.43, *201*, *204*, *209–11*, *219*, *223*, *225*, *228*, *230*, *233*, *258*, *267*, *302*, *307*
against IGS and IWG *245*
joint recognition of stays of proceedings under *237–8*
provisions of 9.03
section 345 of *223*
section 1121 of *224*
Bankruptcy Court *200*, *211*, *213*, *215*, *217–18*, *249*, *256*
jurisdiction of *222–3*
Bankruptcy Rules *223*, *292*
Basel Committee on Banking Supervision (BCBS) 1.08, 11.01
Berlitz International Inc. *207*
Bernard L. Madoff Investments Securities LLC (BLMIS) 4.08, 4.46, *291*
bilateral settlements, of intercompany claims 10.33
blockchain 2.15
Bochan v. Ukraine 8.09
British Columbia corporation *228*
Brussels Convention (1968) 6.01
Brussels I Recast 7.12, 7.14
applicability of 7.15
choice-of-court clauses 7.16
insolvency protocol 7.15
prorogation agreements 7.16
Brussels Regulation 7.14, 7.18
burden of proof 7.11

Calpine case 4.08
Calpine protocol (2007) 4.08
Canada Deposit Insurance Corporation (CDIC) 11.20
Canadian Companies' Creditors Arrangement Act (CCAA) 4.24, 5.06, 9.04, *228*, *230*, *238*, *258*
CCAA Order *230*, *259*, *261*
joint recognition of stays of proceedings under *237–8*
'Pre-Model-Law' CCAA 9.04
capital gains tax (CGT) 10.24
capital markets 2.05, 3.07, 10.11
Caribbean Group of Banking Supervisors (CGBS) 11.17
Cash Flow Statement *218–19*, *223–4*
cash pooling system 3.16, 5.12, 6.18, 10.02, 10.11, 12.01–12.02
Cayman Court Order *244*, *252*
Cayman law 7.33, *251–3*, *256*
Cayman Liquidators 10.16, *241*, *246*, *246–7*, *251–4*, *257*
Cayman Proceedings *244*, *247–8*, *252*, *255*
Central American College of Banking Supervisors (CCSBSO) 11.17
centralized cash management 3.15, 10.64, *279*
centralized crisis resolution, idea of 10.58
Checklist Protocol 13.05
choice-of-court clauses 7.16
civil-law jurisdictions 1.06, 4.06
in Germany 9.13–9.18
insolvency protocols and 9.09–9.22
in the Netherlands 9.09–9.12
other jurisdictions 9.19–9.22
civil rights and obligations, concept of 8.08
claimant's claim, adjudication of *240*
claim coordination 10.53
claims
adjudication against
Canadian Debtors *239*
TLGI *239*
U.S. Debtors *239*

admissibility of 10.51
agreements addressing coordination of 10.36–10.53
filing of claims 10.49–10.53
allowance disputes 10.35
asserted guarantee claims 10.28
direct *286*
Dutch Proceedings 10.51
filing of
agreements addressing coordination of 10.36–10.53
against guarantor 10.53
hotchpot rule for 10.51
multi-cross-border filings 10.52
against principal debtor 10.53
process of *248*
Sendo protocol for 10.52
intercompany *see* intercompany claims
intercompany derivatives claims *288*
intra-group 10.35
under Jet Airways protocol *305–6*
jurisdictional agreements for
certain (future) transactions 10.45–10.48
claims against debtor(s) 10.37–10.44
lodged by creditors in parallel proceedings 10.52
reconciliation process 7.26, 10.43, *281*
Sendo protocol 10.52
treatment of 1.05
agreements addressing coordination of claims and transactions 10.36–10.53
financial accounting records 10.28–10.29
resolution of intra-group claims 10.23–10.27
special intercompany claim resolution mechanism 10.30–10.35
UNCITRAL Practice Guide 10.38
unsecured *223*
value-destroying litigation 10.27
verification of 10.51
Collateral Trust Agreement *239*
comity, concept of 4.24, 4.38, 4.43, 6.22, 7.26, 9.05, 10.43
under Jet Airways Protocol *301*, *309–10*
under Lehman Brothers Protocol *281*, *289*
under Loewen Protocol *230*, *238*, *259*
under Madoff Protocol *297*
under Pioneer Protocol *260–61*, *267*
Committees
committee of creditors (CoC) *299*, *302*
communication among *284–5*
Procedures Committee 10.32, *287–8*
Commodore Protocol (1994)
Commodore Electronics Limited (CEL) *208*
Commodore International Limited (CIL) *208*
consent of the Committees *216*
in insolvency proceedings 4.18–4.22, 4.28, 10.67, *208–217*
Unofficial Committee of Unsecured Creditors *210*
common-law jurisdictions 4.04, 4.06
common law systems 6.22
common pool problem 5.28
common working language, determination of 11.21
communication
among Committees *284–5*
among Official Representatives *281*, *282–4*
among Tribunals *281*, *284*, *295*
confidentiality of 5.13
between courts *see* court-to-court communication
e-communication 8.25
EU JudgeCo Guidelines 8.25
ex parte 8.29
of information 6.12
and information sharing *295*
transnational 9.11
Community law, principles of 8.07
Companies Act (1862), UK 2.02
company arrangement, deed of 10.19, *288–289*
company law 1.03, 2.04, 3.04–3.05, 7.30, 8.12
Company Law Action Plan 3.05
compensation
in accordance with the CCAA *233*

under Bankruptcy Code (US) *233*, *235*
of estate representatives and professionals 4.38
of professionals rendering services *254*
Conference on European Restructuring and Insolvency (CERIL) 6.22
confidential information, protection of 5.23, 9.21, 11.09
confidentiality and privilege, issues of 10.31
conflicting judgments, risk of 10.53
conflict of interest 3.22, 5.23, 5.39, 6.11, 6.14, 8.45–8.48, 10.01
definition of 6.13
obligations to avoid 6.13
requirement to avoid 3.23
risks of 8.48
conflict-of-laws 5.04, 10.30, 10.53
harmonization of 6.01
conflicts of interest 3.21–3.22, 4.29, 4.32, 5.23, 5.39, 6.13, 8.05, 10.01, 12.01
information exchange and 8.45–8.48
consent of the Committees *213–16*, *253*
consulting agreement, between IGS and InverWorld, Inc. *243*
contract documentation 10.24
contract law 7.10, 7.12
contractual obligation, definition of 7.11, 7.23, *288*
cooperation agreements
characteristics of 11.25
in cross-border bank resolution 11.11, 11.25
framework arrangement in 11.18
for information sharing 11.21
institution-specific 11.11–11.12
Memorandum of Understanding (MOU) 11.18, 11.22
negotiation of 11.12
between resolution authorities 11.10–11.26
cooperation between courts 3.09, 3.19, 4.04, 5.02, 5.27, 9.07, 9.13
coordination of activities, in the Proceedings 4.12, *281*, *294*, *301*
coordination procedure, mechanism of 9.14
corporate governance 4.24, 10.45, *203*, *211*
corporate group
centralized 2.13
decentralized 2.13
definition of 2.08–2.11
economic interconnectedness of companies in 3.08
economic reality of 3.05
insolvency of 3.01, 5.10
administration of 3.11
coordinated treatment of 6.19
cross-border insolvency protocols 4.47
cross-border recognition and implementation 5.27
in Germany 3.11
proceedings of 6.17
recognition of 3.08–3.13
regulation of 3.11
types of 3.08
insolvency plans of the individual group members 6.18
rise of 'group insolvency solution' 3.14–3.23
treatment in insolvency proceedings 5.19, 6.01–6.06
types of insolvency regulation applicable to
separate entity approach 3.08
single enterprise approach 3.08
corporate laws 3.04
liberalization of 2.01
in USA 2.01
corporate nets 2.04, 2.13
corporate ownership 2.15
of shares 2.01–2.02
court-appointed examiners 10.75
court-created treaty 7.07
court hearings 3.20, 4.06, 8.26, 10.16, *294*, *302*
Court of Justice of the European Union (CJEU) 7.14
Eurofood IFSC Ltd. case 8.07, 8.13
jurisprudence of 6.03
non-insolvency 'civil and commercial' regulation 7.14
Nortel Networks SA and Others 7.12, 7.18–7.19
Rastelli case 6.05
courts
comity and independence of 4.38, *230*

ex parte 230
on "limited notice" basis *230*
principles of *230*
jurisdiction of *231*
court-to-court communication 4.38, 5.13, 6.22, 8.24, 8.29, 9.06
ALI-III Guidelines Applicable to 8.24–8.25, 10.72, 10.74
conflicts of interest 12.01
in cross-border cases 8.24
direct communication 8.27
e-communication 8.25–8.26
ex parte 8.27
guidelines applicable to *284*
Law 29/2015 of 30 July 2015 (Spain) 9.22
modalities of 9.07, 10.79
open court hearing 8.26
in procedural matters 8.28
procedure for joint hearings 8.27
process of 8.27
structuring of 10.71–10.79
telephone or video conference 9.07
value of 10.72
COVID-19 pandemic, outbreak of 1.04
creditors
claims, resolution of 4.07, 4.10, 7.27, 8.36, 10.26
committee of creditors (CoC) *299*, *302*
insolvency protocols on
limitations imposed by 8.36
obligation of 4.38
obligation to notify *270*
rights of 4.25, 6.22, 8.30, 9.17, 10.44, *223*
to appear *282*
violation of 8.36
treating the claims lodged by *272*
crisis management 4.15
crisis-management groups (CMGs) 1.18, 11.05, 11.08
membership in 11.17
objective of 11.08
crisis prevention and response, *ex ante* tools of 11.24
cross-border bank resolution 1.18, 11.12, 11.17, 11.22, 11.25
cross-border civil cooperation 4.12
cross-border communication 3.20, 4.46, 5.01
Cross-Border Companies 10.67
cross-border cooperation
arrangement of 4.03
effectiveness of 7.22
in multiple insolvency proceedings 6.21
promotion of 5.20
purposes of facilitating 6.21
transnational cooperation in 9.22
cross-border crisis management 11.18
cross-border financial crisis 11.08
cross-border group resolution 11.06
cross-border insolvency agreements 5.21, 9.01
adoption of 5.22
group-wide protocols for 5.22
cross-border insolvency cases 1.08, 5.05, 6.21, 7.07, 7.24, 9.11, 12.01
Cross-Border Insolvency Concordat (Concordat) 4.22, 4.25
application of 4.30–4.35
and early harmonization process 4.23–4.35
as framework for harmonizing cross-border insolvency proceedings 4.26
Glossary of Terms 4.27
IBA Cross-Border Insolvency Concordat (1996) 4.45
objective of compensating 4.26
Principle 4C of 4.34
principles of 4.23–4.29
scope of 4.28
cross-border insolvency cooperation 1.08, 1.12, 1.20, 4.49, 5.01, 5.08, 9.06, 9.12, 10.78, 13.06
cross-border insolvency proceedings *229*
administration of 3.09, 4.34, 5.02, 10.01
allocation of responsibilities 5.13, 5.16
communication and cooperation 8.48
cooperation between courts 4.04
of enterprise groups 12.01
in EU involved groups of companies 6.02
evolution of 4.42–4.49
framework for harmonizing 4.26
national law reform concerning 9.10

Practice Guide for 7.24
principles governing 8.02
protocols for 1.05, 1.07, 1.11–1.12, 3.06, 4.03
Commodore protocol 4.18–4.22
corporate group insolvency 4.47
early cases of 4.09–4.22
under EIR Recast 6.21–6.22
Everfresh protocol 4.30, 4.32, 4.39, 4.48
evolution of 4.42–4.49
instrument of 4.04
in *Jet Airways* case 4.12
Loewen model of 4.36–4.41, 4.48
Macfadyen protocol 4.09–4.12
Madoff protocol 4.08
Maxwell protocol 4.13–4.17
Olympia & York protocol 4.24
purpose of 4.05
standardization of 4.46
sui generis protocols 4.08
use of 5.41
purpose and goals of 4.01–4.08
use of 5.20
cross-border insolvency protocols 11.10, 12.01, *219*
approval of 9.08
circumstances supporting conclusion of 10.01–10.04
negotiation of 10.01
stipulation regarding *217–27*
Cross-Border Insolvency Regulations (2006), UK 5.06, *292*
cross-border intra-group transactions 10.24
cross-border liquidation protocol 4.03
cross-border liquidations and restructurings 4.42
Cross-Border Management 10.67
Cross-Border Matters 10.48
cross-guarantees 12.01
enforcement of 10.26
cross-liability arrangements 10.26, 12.01

data protection 10.73, 10.79
debt instruments 3.15
debtor-in-possession 7.03, *217*
financing documents 10.46
debtors *224–5*
Canadian Debtors *228–229*, *235*, *258–259*, *261*
adjudication of claims against *239*
proof of claim against *262*
claims and defences of 4.38, *261*
insolvency estates 4.38
jurisdictional agreements for claims against 10.37–10.44
obligation of 4.38
powers of *210*
subsidiaries 10.47, 10.67
U.S. Debtors *237*
rights and holdings in Canada *266*
debt restructuring 10.26
decision-making 5.28, 11.06
centralized 10.64
corporate 2.15
deed of company arrangement 10.19, *288–289*
deferred severance payments, disbursement of 7.13
depositors and clients, rights of 3.10
depositors, rights of 1.18
Directive on the reorganisation and winding up of credit institutions (CIWUD) 3.01
distributed ledger technologies (DLT) 2.15
domestic groups 5.35
domestic systemically important banks (D-SIBs) 11.16
Dutch Bankruptcy Act (*Faillissementswet*) 9.09
Dutch Civil Code (*Burgerlijk Wetboek*) 2.08
Dutch East India company 2.01
Dutch Proceedings 3.16, 8.38, 10.51, *300–301*, *303*, *305–6*
Dutch Trustee, in the Indian Proceedings 7.38, 8.12, 10.70, *299–307*

e-communication 8.25–8.26
economic inefficiency 1.10
economic interconnectedness, of companies 3.08
EC Regulation
Article 20.2 of *277*
Article 28 of *276*

Article 31.3 of *275*
Article 31 of *275*
Article 33.1 of *275–6*
Article 33 of *276*
electronic forms of communication 8.14, *237*, *265*
English East India company 2.01
English High Court 10.59, *202*
English Proceedings 8.40, *244*, *247*, *252*, *255*
English Provisional Liquidators *241*, *246*, *251–2*, *254*
enterprise centre of main interests (ECOMI) 10.58
enterprise group insolvency 1.10, 1.12–1.13, 1.19, 2.10, 3.01, 3.10, 3.14, 3.23, 4.29, 4.49, 5.15, 5.22, 5.25, 5.35, 7.29, 8.11–8.12, 10.04, 10.64
enterprise groups
characteristics of 5.30
cross border insolvency of 12.01
insolvency of 3.09, 5.25–5.26, 5.35
legal distinction of debtors in 6.03
enterprise law 3.08
entity-by-entity asset liquidation value 10.03
entity law 3.08
entity separateness, principle of 1.10, 2.05, 3.03, 3.05, 3.23, 4.48
equity capital 6.17
Ernst & Young Inc. *218*, *220–21*, *223*
estate representatives and professionals
Affiliated Professionals *233*
Monitor Parties *232–3*
retention and compensation of 4.38, *232–6*
in accordance with the CCAA *233*
under Bankruptcy Code (US) *233*
rights to appear and be heard *236*
EU Charter of Fundamental Rights 8.07
EU civil law jurisdictions 6.22
EU Cross-Border Insolvency Court-to-Court Communications Guidelines 8.25
EU JudgeCo Principles and Guidelines 8.25, 9.11, 10.72
Eurodis Electron plc. 9.11
Eurofood IFSC Ltd 6.03, 8.07, 8.13
European Banking Authority (EBA) 11.06
European banking sector, financial distress in 11.04
European colonial trading companies 2.01
European Commission (EC) 2.04, 6.06
Consultation on the Future of European Company Law 3.05
European Communication and Cooperation Guidelines for Cross-border Insolvency (CoCo Guidelines, 2007) 4.06, 4.28, 6.21, 13.05
European company law
EC Consultation on the Future of 3.05
'group interest' in 3.05
European Convention for the Protection of Human Rights and Fundamental Freedom 8.07
European Convention on Human Rights (ECHR) 8.02
civil rights and obligations 8.08
European Court of Human Rights (ECtHR) 8.08, 8.26
European Economic Area (EEA) 11.03
European Insolvency Regulation (EIR 2000) 1.13, 3.01, 3.10, 6.06, 7.13, 9.10
application of 6.06, 7.14
Article 40 of 8.15
on duty to inform creditors 8.15
insolvency regulation 7.22
European Insolvency Regulation (EIR Recast, 2015) 1.06, 1.10, 2.10, 3.12, 3.21, 4.02, 4.48, 5.04, 6.15, 7.12, 7.21, 7.37, 8.03, 8.07, 8.11, 8.30, 8.36, 8.43, 9.10, 9.12, 10.01, 10.03, 10.13, 10.54, 10.63, 10.72, 10.75, 12.01
on appointment of insolvency practitioner 10.05
Article 7(2)(f) of 8.35
Article 23(2) of 4.10
Article 56 of 3.22
background of 6.01–6.06
Brussels I Recast 6.01
coordinated solution to group insolvencies 6.07–6.20
cooperation and communication 6.09–6.15

group coordination proceeding 6.16–6.20
cross-border insolvency protocols under 6.02, 6.21–6.22
CoCo Guidelines for 6.21, 6.22
differences in legal systems and cultures 6.22
differences in substantive insolvency law 6.22
EU JudgeCo Principles and Guidelines for 6.21, 6.22
JIN Guidelines for 6.21
lack of knowledge and experience with 6.22
language barriers and 6.22
legal nature of 6.22
roles played by courts 6.22
rules on international insolvency jurisdiction 6.22
goals of 6.08
group coordination proceeding under 6.07, 6.16–6.20, 11.05
insolvency protocols 7.19–7.20
insolvency regulation 6.06
on insolvency-related actions 8.39
on non-Member State proceedings 6.20
notion of separate legal personalities 6.08
procedural rules on coordination of insolvency proceedings 6.16
scope of 9.22
uniform rules on asset localization 7.20
European Union (EU) 1.06, 6.03, 11.03, 12.01
Europe mediation and arbitration 10.31
eurozone 11.03, 11.22
Everfresh case 4.30, 4.45, 8.41
Everfresh Protocol (1995) 9.05, 10.08, 10.47
Cash Flow Statement *218–219*, *223*
Creditors' Committee *217*
Emergency Order *218*
Interim Receiver Order *218*
Preliminary Order *218*
stipulation regarding cross-border insolvency protocol *217–27*
Evidentiary Materials *231*, *255*, *263–4*
ex ante (preparatory) agreement 11.21, 11.24, 11.25
Executives' Meeting of East Asia-Pacific Central Banks (EMEAP) 11.17
ex parte communication 4.38, 8.29
between courts 8.29

fair trial 8.07–8.15
breach of 8.09
organization and conduct of 8.13
principles of 8.16
violation of the right to 8.09–8.10
Federal Deposit Insurance Corporation (FDIC), US 11.18, 11.20
Federal Mogul group 2.07
Federal-Mogul protocol (2001) 10.67
fees and expenses, payment of *235*, *248*, *254–5*
file claims, rights to 8.36, 10.44
financial accounting 7.15, 10.27, 10.35, 12.01, *287*
records of agreement concerning 10.28–10.29
financial distress 1.04, 2.16, 4.33, 5.28, 10.02, 11.04, 11.19
financial obligations, restructuring of 10.26
Financial Services Agency (Japan) 11.20
Financial Stability Board (FSB) 1.08, 11.02, 11.08
institution-specific agreements 11.11
Principles for Cross-border Effectiveness of Resolution Actions 11.12
Financial Stability Institute (FSI) 11.16
financial stability, preservation of 11.22
force majeure 7.10
foreign direct investment, proliferation of 1.04
foreign insolvencies 9.10–9.11, 10.03
transnational cooperation and recognition of 10.03
foreign insolvency judgment 9.11
foreign insolvency proceedings 4.38, 9.11
forum concursus 5.09, 8.35, 8.39, 8.44
jurisdiction of 8.40
framework protocols 1.11, 4.46
France 9.19

Funding Estate *285–6*
  Official Representative of *286*

German Stock Corporation Act (*Aktiengesetz*) 2.09
Germany
  civil law jurisdictions in 9.13–9.18
  Insolvency Code (InsO) 9.13–9.14
  insolvency plan 9.17
  insolvency protocols in 9.09–9.12
  reform in
    group insolvency 9.14
    insolvency law 9.13
  rules on group insolvencies 9.13
Global Close Balance Sheet 10.29
global financial crisis of 2008–2009 1.18, 11.01, 11.26
globalization, process of 1.04
Global Principles for Cooperation in International Insolvency Cases (2012) 4.06, 9.07
Global Rules on Conflict-of-Laws Matters in International Insolvency Cases 9.07
global supply chains 1.04, 10.24
Global Systemically Important Financial Institutions (G-SIFIs) 11.08
good faith, notion of 4.15–4.16, 7.20, 7.39, 10.21, 10.34, 10.67, *202–4*, *232*, *247–8*, *254*, *264*, *287*, *296*
Group Center Court 10.61
group centralization
  and group governance in insolvency 10.57–10.70
group-COMI, concept of a 10.58
group coordination proceeding 3.11, 6.07, 6.16–6.20, 9.14, 10.55, 11.05
group coordinator, role of 6.19
group distress resolution 10.49
group entities, legal personality of 5.30
group financial support agreements 11.02
group governance
  elements of 10.66
  group-wide governance framework 12.01
  in insolvency 10.57–10.70
group insolvencies 8.45, 9.10, 9.13
  alignment and coordination of plans 12.01
  choice of law for 12.01
  circumstances justifying conclusion of protocols 10.01–10.04, 12.01
  claim coordination 12.01
  claims 12.01
  conflicts of interest 12.01
  enterprise 12.01
  estate value 10.03
  German reform on 9.14
  legal complications 10.17
  legal force 12.01
  notification of 12.01
  participation rights 10.13–10.22, 12.01
  protection of valuable assets 10.05–10.12
  recommendations for protocols in 12.01
    claims 12.01
    general recommendations 12.01
    group governance 12.01
    information exchange 12.01
    preamble 12.01
    procedural fairness and participation rights 12.01
  reorganization and liquidation plans 12.01
  resolution of intercompany claims 12.01
  right to appear and be heard in 10.13–10.16
  rules on 4.29
  solution for *see* group insolvency solution
  supplementing existing cooperation frameworks 10.54–10.79
  treatment of claims 10.23–10.53
  use of soft law instruments 12.01
Group Insolvency Protocol Design (GIP) 1.19, 13.01–13.06
group insolvency solution
  adoption of 5.30, 5.32
  concept of 5.30
  cooperation and communication in 6.09–6.15
  defined 3.14, 5.30
  development of 10.14
  EIR Recast and 6.07–6.20
  intra-EU group 6.09
  limits of 3.19–3.23
  planning proceeding 5.31
  rise of 3.14–3.23
group interest, concept of 3.05

group of companies 6.07, 10.47, 12.01
 centralized crisis resolution in 10.58
 concept of 3.04
 definition of 1.09, 2.10
 insolvency proceedings
  administration of 10.17
  commencement of 5.18
 insolvency-specific rules 2.10
 Lehman Brothers 10.28
 recognition of 1.10
group proceedings, centralisations of 5.09
group recovery and resolution plans 11.02
 adoption of 11.02
group reorganization plans
 adoption of 10.18
 group-related coordinated-driven clauses 10.20
 insolvency court-led restructuring 10.26
 insolvency practitioners 10.20
 insolvency protocols 10.22
 negotiation and implementation of 10.17–10.22
 participation rights and facilitation of 10.13–10.22
 pre-insolvency contractual 10.26
 restructuring of financial obligations 10.26
 right to appear and be heard in group insolvency 10.13–10.16
group representative, appointment of 5.29, 5.31, 10.06, 10.63
group resolution plans, development of 11.06
group resolvability 11.02
 assessment of 11.06
group restructuring 3.19, 6.08, 6.11, 6.16, 10.12
group structure, reorganization of 6.18
group-wide
 governance framework 1.05, 10.64, 12.01
 reorganization strategy 10.17
 resolution scheme 11.07
Guidelines for Coordination of Multinational Enterprise Group Insolvencies 4.06

hard law 1.06, 5.04, 7.40
homologatie 9.09
Hong Kong Monetary Authority 11.17
'hotchpot' rule 4.10
Hudson's Bay Company 2.01

IBA Cross-Border Insolvency Concordat 1.11, 4.45
Icelandic insolvency law 8.35
IG Services, Ltd. *242*
 assets of *246*
 Bankruptcy Code against *245*
 consulting agreement with InverWorld, Inc. *243*
 cross-border insolvency proceedings of *246*, *256*
 insolvency proceedings in
  Grand Court of the Cayman Islands *244*
  High Court of Justice Chancery Division Companies Court *244*
 notice procedures *252*
 services agreement with IWG *243*
industrial manufacturing 10.03
industrial technologies, development of 2.01
information exchange 1.05, 4.05, 5.23, 8.45–8.48, 9.17, 11.02, 11.06, 11.07, 11.11, 11.18, 11.21, 12.01, *297*
information security 12.01
information-sharing 4.07, 11.17, *281*
 among Official Representatives *282–4*
 commitment to 11.23
 communication and *295*
 limitations to 11.21
 regulation of 1.06
INSOL Europe 1.08
INSOL International 1.08, 2.07
insolvency 1.01
 effects on rights based on reservation (retention) of title 7.20
 of enterprise groups 3.09, 5.25–5.26
 group centralization and group governance in 10.57–10.70
 of KPN Qwest 3.06
 of multinational enterprise groups 1.07, 1.19, 2.17, 6.02
 of non-financial enterprises 1.18

of Nortel Networks 3.06
recognition of a corporate group in 3.08–3.13
regulation of
types of 3.08
UNCITRAL Legislative Guide 2010 on 3.08
Sendo International Limited 7.22
single-debtor 8.12
transnational 4.03
treatment of enterprise groups in 5.20
types of
separate entity approach 3.08
single enterprise approach 3.08
Insolvency Act of 1986 (English Proceedings) *244*
insolvency administration, mechanics of 5.16
insolvency disputes, involving property and assets 4.24
insolvency estates 4.01, 9.17–9.18
administration of 4.37
of group entities 10.25
insolvency estate value 3.06, 3.15, 9.20, 10.03
insolvency law
conflict-of-laws aspects of 6.01
differences in 6.22
entity-by-entity approach in 3.01–3.07
goals of 5.28
harmonization of 6.22
in India 4.12
modernization of 3.12
reformation of 4.12
Insolvency Law Committee 4.12
insolvency practitioners 8.18, 10.13, 10.53, 10.64, 11.25, 12.01
allocation of responsibilities between 10.66
appointment of 5.23, 6.12, 6.22, 10.05
communication between 8.24
compliance with applicable law 12.01
cooperation and communication between 6.02
cross-procedural participation by 10.16
data and information exchange between 8.21
division of insolvency protocol 12.01
EIR Recast 6.20
equal treatment of 7.28
foreign insolvency practitioners 5.05, 10.15
of group companies 9.13
independence and impartiality of 8.48
information exchange 12.01
initiation of insolvency proceedings against group members 5.16
in insolvency proceedings 5.21
Lehman Brothers protocol 8.22
in non-EU countries 6.09
obligation of 4.38
powers of 6.22, 8.30
rights of 10.12
on tools developed in cross-border insolvency 9.09
transnational cooperation in insolvency cases 9.22
insolvency proceedings
administration of 1.05, 3.09, 3.11, 4.01, 4.31, 6.07, 6.13, 8.14, 8.37, 10.01, 13.05, *231*, *262*
efficiency in 6.16
commencement of 5.18, 7.03
conduct of 5.22
cross-border *see* cross-border insolvency proceedings
Cross-Border Insolvency Regulations (2006), UK 5.06
effects of winding-up 8.35
efficiency and effectiveness of 6.01
EU civil law jurisdictions over 6.22
lex concursus 7.20
main *versus* secondary 6.22
in Member State 6.05
opening of 8.35
plurality of *277*
procedural rules on coordination of 6.16
protocols for *see* insolvency protocols
separateness of 3.17
substantive matter relating to 8.29
transparency of 8.27, 8.29, 12.01
values of 1.03
World Bank Principles (2015) on 3.09
insolvency protocols 1.06, 10.10, 10.27, 10.69, 11.24–11.25, 12.01

adoption of 1.08, 1.17, 1.19, 6.22, 8.10, 10.01
applicability of rules of 7.15
contract law 7.10
private international law 7.10
assessment of evidence 7.11
Brussels I Recast 7.15
burden of proof 7.11
circumstances justifying conclusion of 12.01
classification of 7.12, 7.38
cross-border 1.05, 1.07, 1.11–1.12, 3.06, 7.06
debtors' obligations and 7.17
dual nature of 7.19
EIR Recast 7.19–7.20
enforcement of duties and rights under 7.40
evidence agreement 7.11
French law on 9.21
groups of
binding effect 7.35
non-binding effect 7.35
no special indication 7.35
issue of applicable law 7.19–7.30
and issue of jurisdiction 7.12–7.18
lack of knowledge and experience with 6.22
legal certainty and predictability 7.10
legal characterization of 1.14
legal effect of 7.31–7.40
limitations of 10.43
meaning of 7.01–7.11
nature of 7.05
participation rights 10.16
Practice Guide on 5.13, 7.32
practice of entering into 4.13
procedural agreement 7.11
procedural principles of *see* procedural principles, of insolvency protocols
rights and obligations for different parties 7.02
Sendo protocol 7.22
unpopularity of 6.22
in USA 9.01
use for efficient group resolution 4.06
insolvency-related judgment 1.14, 7.08, 7.12
defined 7.08
insolvency stakeholders, rights and obligations of 8.26
insolvency standards, for credit institutions 11.02
insolvent debtors
claims against
agreement stipulating 8.36
competence to decide 8.35
jurisdiction for 8.32–8.36, 8.37
monetary 8.35
resolution of 8.31
Recast EIR in respect of 9.21
Institute for the Protection of Bank Savings (Mexico) 11.20
intellectual property 3.15, 9.06, 10.12
retention and compensation of 8.01
intellectual property rights 3.06, 5.37
intercompany claims 1.05, 10.28
accounting of 10.32
bilateral settlements 10.33
calculation of 10.32, *287*
consensual resolution of 10.32, *287*
nature and validity of 10.28
Procedures Committee 10.32
resolution of 7.15, 9.17, 11.25, 12.01
Madoff protocol for 10.34, *296*
mechanism for 10.30–10.35
special procedures for *287–8*
transaction between Debtors *287*
treatment of 10.28
intercompany derivatives claims *288*
inter-company disputes, resolution of 10.31
inter-company financial relations 10.27
intercompany stock ownership, power of 2.02
Interim Funding and Settlement Agreement (IFSA) 7.13–7.14
Interim Receiver 10.18, *218*, *219*, *220*, *222*, *224*
Interim Receiver Order *219*, *223*
International Association of Restructuring, Insolvency and Bankruptcy Professionals (INSOL) 5.19
International Bar Association (IBA) 4.23, 4.25
international comity, principles of 9.05

international group of companies 2.04
international insolvencies 10.68
  administration of cases 7.01, 12.01
  resolution of 6.22
International Insolvency Institute (III) 1.08, 4.06, 5.11
international insolvency law 1.01
  principle of 4.02
  rules of 1.03
international insolvency rules 5.03, 9.12
intra-EU banking groups 11.10
intra-EU group insolvencies 6.09
intra-group cash pooling system 3.16, 6.18
intra-group claims 10.35
  enforcement of 6.13, 12.01
  resolution of 4.32, 5.23, 10.23–10.27
intra-group debts, treatment of 5.18
intra-group disputes, settlement of 3.17, 6.18
intra-group dividends, tax exemptions for 2.05
intra-group financial arrangements 10.02
intra-group financing 5.23, 5.30, 10.11, 12.01
  approval of 5.31
intra-group interdependence 3.17
intra-group loans 3.07, 10.02, 12.01
intra-group support transactions 10.11, 10.25
  documentation of 10.24
InverWorld protocol 8.40, 10.09, 10.16
  background of
    foreign proceedings *244*
    parties *242*
    relationship between the foreign companies and the United States companies *243*
    United States proceedings *245–6*
  IG Services, Ltd. *242*
  IWG Services, Ltd. *242*
  preliminary statement *241*
  purpose of stipulation *246–58*
  stipulation regarding cross-border insolvency protocol *241*
investment advisors
  appointment of *249*
  authority of *249–50*
  Retention Order *250*
Involuntary Petitions *256*
IWG Services, Ltd. *242*
  assets of *246*
    disposition of *250*
  Bankruptcy Code against *245*
  cross-border insolvency proceedings of *246*, *256*
  liquidation of *243*
  notice procedures *252*
  relationships with clients and account brokerages *243*
  services agreement with IGS *243*
  winding up petition *244*

Jet Airways case 4.12, 4.46, 7.38, 8.12, 8.38, 9.11, *298*
Jet Airways protocol 8.38, 10.51, *298–310*
  aim of *301*
  amendments and waivers under *308*
  assets *303–5*
  background of *299*
  claims, overview of *305–6*
  comity *309–10*
  communication and information *301–2*
  construction *299–300*
  for coordinating the liquidation of the Company *308*
  and Dutch Trustee in the Indian Proceedings *303*
  effectiveness of *301*
  non-main insolvency proceedings
    claims reconciliation *301*
    comity *301*
    communication *301*
    coordination *301*
    information and data sharing *301*
    maximize value of assets/recoveries *301*
    preservation *301*
  purpose of *300*
  rights and remedies under *308*
  on rights to appear and attend *302*
  signing of *307*
  stays of proceedings *306–7*
  third party rights under *308*
  validity of *307–8*
JIN Guidelines 9.07, 9.11, 10.72, 10.79

joint hearings 4.38, 9.08, 10.22, 10.48, *231, 238, 239, 263*
cross-border coordination in 6.22
procedure for 8.27
Joint Protocol *249–50*
joint ventures 2.06
judicial impartiality 8.29, 12.01
judicial innovation 1.06
Judicial Insolvency Network 10.79
juge commissaire 9.21
jurisdictional agreements 7.17, 10.27
for certain (future) transactions 10.45–10.48
for claims against debtor(s) 10.37–10.44
jurisdiction, rules on 6.01
for adjudication of the claimant's claim *240*
Bankruptcy Court *223*
civil law *see* civil law jurisdictions
for claims against debtors 8.32–8.36
common law jurisdictions 9.01–9.08
of courts in main and secondary proceedings 7.13, *238*
of *forum concursus* 8.40
insolvency protocols and 7.12–7.18
for insolvency-related actions 8.37, 8.39
Model Law 1997 and 9.01–9.08

Key Attributes of Effective Resolution Regimes 11.02, 11.09
King, Mervyn 1.02
knowledge-sharing 1.07, 11.17
KPN Qwest, insolvency of 3.06

language barriers 6.22, 10.72
law applicable to claims, agreement on 8.41–8.44, 12.01
law enforcement agencies *296–7*
laws and legislations
Canadian Companies' Creditors Arrangement Act (CCAA) 4.24, 5.06, *228*
Companies Act (1862), UK 2.02
Company Law Action Plan 3.05
Cross-Border Insolvency Regulations (2006), UK 5.06
enterprise law 3.08
entity law 3.08
German Stock Corporation Act (*Aktiengesetz*) 2.09
Insolvency Act (1986), UK *244*
lead insolvency proceeding 10.65, 12.01
legally binding obligations 11.18
legal personality, of group entities 5.30
legal separability, principle of 3.08, 3.22, 8.45
legal systems and cultures, differences in 6.22
Legislative Guide on Insolvency Law, Part III (2010) 1.08, 3.08, 3.21, 4.49, 5.17–5.24, 7.09
in context of single-debtor insolvency 5.20
first draft of 5.18
on practice of cross-border insolvency 5.19
principles of cooperation and communication 5.22
on reducing the cost of litigation 5.22
on risk of piecemeal insolvency proceedings 5.21
on sharing of commercially sensitive or confidential information 5.23
treatment of
corporate groups in insolvency 5.18
intra-group debts 5.18
use of cross-border insolvency protocols 5.19
Working Group V 5.18, 5.20
Lehman Brothers Holdings Inc. (LBHI) 1.05, 2.07, 3.16, 4.08, 4.46, 8.11, 9.11
books and records of 10.29
cash pooling system 5.12
group of companies 10.28
Lehman Brothers International (Europe) (LBIE) 3.16
Lehman Brothers protocol (2009) 8.21, 8.47, 9.17, 10.08, 10.10–10.11, 10.15, 10.19, 10.32, 10.41, 10.53, 10.67
adherence *290*
aims of *281*
amendment *289*
approval of 10.28
background of
Lehman's Global business *279*
proceedings *278–279*

claims *286–7*
comity *289*
communication among
Committees *284–5*
Official Representatives *282–4*
Tribunals *284*
cross-border insolvency protocol *278–91*
deed of company arrangement *288–9*
execution and application *290–91*
for Lehman Brothers group of companies *278–91*
need for *279–80*
notice *282*
Official Representatives *280*, *282*
communication and access to data and information among *282–4*
recognition of *282*
rights of *282*
plan of reorganization *288–9*
saving clause 10.12
special procedures for intercompany claims *287–8*
submission of winding-up plan *288–9*
terms of
notice *282*
purpose and aims *280–81*
lex concursus 6.13, 7.20, 8.42–8.43, 8.44, 12.01
application of 8.35
lex concursus secondarii 8.43
lex contractus 12.01
lex generalis 9.22
lex societatis 7.30
lex specialis 9.22
liability claims, against directors 2.07, 12.01
liability insurance policy *210*
limited liability
concept of 1.04
limited liability partnership (LLP) *234*
liquidation of the Company *307*
proceedings for 8.09, 12.01
lis pendens 7.15
litigants' rights, protection of 8.26
Livent protocol (1999) 10.40
Loewen Group Inc. 4.36–4.37, *228*
Loewen model, of insolvency proceedings 4.36–4.41, 4.45, 7.16, 8.10, 8.14
background of *228–9*
claims procedure *239–40*
comity and independence of the courts *230*
cooperation *231–2*
cross-border insolvency protocol 4.37, 4.48, *228–240*
dual proceedings *229*
effectiveness of *238*
estate representatives and professionals retention and compensation of *232–6*
modification of *238*
notice *236–7*
operations of 4.36
preservation of rights under *238–239*
procedure for resolving disputes under *238*
purpose and goals of *229*
rights to appear and be heard *236*
sections of
background of 4.38
comity and independence of the courts 4.38
cooperation 4.38
effectiveness and modification 4.38
joint recognition of stays of proceedings 4.38
notice 4.38
preservation of rights 4.38
procedure for resolving disputes under the protocol 4.38
purpose and goals 4.38
retention and compensation of estate representatives and professionals 4.38
rights to appear and be heard 4.38
standardization of 4.36

MacFadyen case 4.05, 4.09–4.10, 4.12, 4.18
Macfadyen protocol (1908) 4.09–4.12
Macmillan, Inc. *200–201*, *207*
Madoff Investment Securities 4.08, 4.46, 10.12
Madoff protocol 7.32, 8.11, 8.46, 10.34, 10.67
background of debtors *292*

need for a protocol *293*
proceedings *291–2*
cross-border insolvency protocol *291–8*
terms of
amendment *297*
assets *296*
comity *297*
communication and information sharing *295*
communication between Tribunals *295*
costs *297*
execution and application *297–8*
intercompany claims *296*
law enforcement agencies *296–7*
notice *294*
purpose and aims *294*
right of representatives to appear *294–5*
Madoff Securities International Limited (MSIL) 1.05, *291*
Manhattan Investment Fund Limited 10.67
material assets, preservation of 12.01
Matlack case 10.76
Matlack protocol (2001) 7.36
Maxwell case 4.13, 4.23
Maxwell Communication Corporation plc 4.05, 4.13, 4.16, *207*
Maxwell protocol (1992) 4.13–4.17, 7.01, 10.21, 10.47, 10.67, *200–206*
Bankruptcy Code *202*
Joint Administrators *200–204*, *206*
Macmillan Inc *207*
members of the bank committee
Bank of America N.T. & S.A. *208*
Bank of Nova Scotia *208*
Barclays Bank plc *208*
M&O Group *202*, *206*, *207*
Official Airline Guides Inc *207*
plan of reorganization *202*
Proposed Order *200–201*
Schedule 1 *207*
Schedule 2 *208*
voting rights of the Debtor *203*
Maxwell, Robert 4.14
Member States of EU 1.06, 3.04, 3.21, 7.12, 8.07, 8.35, 8.42, 10.55, 11.03
insolvency proceedings in 6.05
national resolution authorities in 11.06
memorandum of association 2.02
Memorandum of Cooperation (MOC) 11.19
Memorandum of Understanding (MOU) 4.03, 11.17–11.18
cross-border crisis management 11.18, 11.22
mergers and acquisitions 2.06
Millett, Peter 1.03
M&O Affiliates *200*, *203*
Modalities of Court-to-Court Communication 10.79
Model Law on Cross-Border Insolvency (1997) 1.06, 1.12, 3.01, 3.10, 4.02–4.03, 4.49, 5.01–5.10, 6.02, 7.28, 9.10, 10.03, 10.72
for administration of cross-border insolvencies 5.02
adoption of 4.12, 5.03
Article 20 of 4.38
Article 25 of 5.06
Article 26 of 5.06
Article 27 of 5.07
Article 32 of 4.10
in Canadian law 9.04
and common law jurisdictions 9.01–9.08
concepts of 5.05
contribution of 5.04
effect on administration of group insolvencies 5.08
Guide to Enactment of Model Law 1997 (2013) 5.05
implementation of 6.22
incorporation of 9.04
legislation based on 5.03
principles of cooperation and communication 5.22
for promotion of cross-border cooperation 5.04
soft law nature of 3.01, 5.04
Model Law on Enterprise Group Insolvency (2019) 1.10, 1.12, 2.10, 3.12, 4.48–4.49, 10.03, 10.14, 10.30, 10.54, 10.58, 10.75, 11.05
adoption of 5.33
group insolvency solution 5.30
Draft Guide to Enactment of 3.14

and insolvency agreements 5.34–5.41
objectives of 5.27
purpose and goals of 5.25–5.28
scope and tools of 5.29–5.33
UNCITRAL approval of 5.26
modified universalism, principle of 5.04
M&O Group *200–202, 206, 207*
Monitor's fees and expenses *235*
Mosaic protocol (2003) 8.46
MPOE resolution strategy 11.14
Muchlinski, P. 2.03
multi-cross-border filings 10.52
multilateral resolution forum 11.17
multinational enterprise groups (MEG)
definition of 2.08–2.11
European colonial trading companies 2.01
formation of 1.04
growth of 4.43
insolvency of 1.07, 1.19, 2.17
problems related to 2.17
memoranda of association 2.02
in mid- to late 19th century 2.01
proliferation of 2.08
rise of 2.01–2.07
rules dealing with insolvency of 6.02
typology of 2.12–2.17
in USA 2.01
multinational enterprises (MNEs)
American dominance 2.03
characteristics of 2.08
competition from European MNEs 2.03
emergence of 2.03
evolution of
first period (1850–1914) 2.03
second period (1918–1939) 2.03
third period (1945–1990) 2.03
expansion of 2.03
growth of 2.03
Muscovy Company 2.01

National Bank of Serbia (Serbia) 11.20
National Company Law Appellate Tribunal, New Delhi (NCLAT) 8.12, *299*
NCLAT Order *299*
national corporate insolvency regimes 5.17
national economic policy 1.03
national insolvency laws 1.01, 1.05, 1.12, 4.02, 4.14, 4.29, 4.43, 5.01, 5.04, 6.22, 8.11, 8.35, 8.45
national security 11.21, 11.25
The Netherlands
civil law jurisdictions in 9.09–9.12
Dutch Bankruptcy Act (*Faillissementswet*) 9.09
insolvency protocols in 9.09–9.12
national insolvency law 9.09
national law reform concerning cross-border insolvency 9.10
Yukos case 9.11
New Zealand Treasury 11.19
non-bank groups, cross-border restructuring of 11.07
nonbanking corporate groups 11.05
non-bank insolvency protocols 11.25
non-binding soft law instrument 11.23
Non-disclosure Agreement (NDA) *302*
Non-Filing Subsidiaries 10.46
non-judicial proceedings *285, 304–5*
non-public information 8.02, 8.46, 11.13, *221, 283, 302*
Nordic-Baltic countries 11.17
Nordic-Baltic Stability Group (NBSG) 11.17
Nortel Networks 1.05, 10.35
insolvency of 3.06
Nortel Networks SA and Others 7.12, 7.18–7.19
notice *236–7, 265, 294*
to claimants *240*
of legal proceeding *266*
limited notice *260*
by Official Representatives *282*
Notice of Intention to Make a Proposal (NOI) *218*
Notice Procedures *221, 222*

Official Airline Guides Inc (OAG) 4.16, *200–201, 207*
Official Representatives *282, 285, 290*
appointment of *289*
communication and access to data and information among *282–4*

Debtors' creditors for *287*
of Funded Estate *286*
legal advisor *297*
recognition of *282*
rights of *282*
special procedures for intercompany claims *287–8*
Olympia & York protocol, in insolvency proceedings 4.24, 4.28
Ontario Superior Court of Justice 4.37, *228*
Organisation for Economic Co-operation and Development (OECD) 1.04, 2.08

parallel insolvency proceedings, administration of 1.05, 3.18, 4.31, 7.21, 8.19, 8.37, 9.01, 9.14, 10.35, 10.71
parallel proceedings, claims lodged by creditors in 10.52
parent undertaking 2.09–2.10
pari passu, process of 4.10, 4.29, 6.01
participation rights 1.17, 8.01, 8.10–8.11, 8.16, 10.13, 10.15–10.16, 12.01
PCI Business *259–60*
restructuring of *261*
PCI Chemicals Canada Inc. *258*
People's Bank of China 11.17
Pioneer Companies, Inc. (PCI) *258*
Pioneer protocol (2001) 8.41, 8.43
approval of *260*
background of *258–9*
comity and independence of the courts *260–61*
cooperation *262–4*
cross-border insolvency protocol *258–67*
effectiveness of *266–7*
implementation of *260*
insolvency proceedings *259*
modification of *266–7*
notice *265*
preservation of rights under *267*
procedure for resolving disputes under *267*
proving of claims against the debtors matters relating to *261–2*
purpose and goals of *259–60*
recognition of stays of proceedings *266*
retention and compensation of professionals *264*
rights to appear and be heard *265*
planning proceeding
defined 5.31
mode of operation of 5.31
recognition of 5.31
platform-based businesses, operation of 2.15
plurality of insolvency proceedings *277*
Practice Guide on Cross-Border Insolvency Cooperation (2009) 1.08, 4.04, 5.08, 5.11–5.16, 7.09, 7.24, 10.30, 10.68, 13.06
aims of 5.12
clauses offered by 5.14
cross-border agreements 5.12
on insolvency protocols 5.13, 7.32
on single-debtor insolvency 5.12
Working Group V 5.11
principal debtor 3.11, 10.26, 10.28
claim filed against 10.53
Principles for Cross-border Effectiveness of Resolution Actions 11.12
private international law, unification of 6.22, 7.10, 7.19
privately owned manufacturing firms 2.03
procedural efficiency, principle of 8.03–8.06, 8.13
procedural fairness 8.29, 9.07, 12.01
procedural justice 8.07–8.15
principles of 8.16
procedural principles, of insolvency protocols
agreement on
COMI and jurisdiction for related actions 8.37–8.40
jurisdiction for claims against debtors 8.32–8.36
law applicable to claims 8.41–8.44
background of 8.01
compatibility with national law and EIR recast framework 8.30–8.44
fair trial and procedural justice 8.07–8.15
information exchange and conflicts of interest 8.45–8.48
procedural efficiency 8.03–8.06
resolution of disputes arising from the protocol 8.01

rights of parties 8.02
rules of national law and 8.30
on transparency and access to information 8.16–8.29
Procedures Committee 10.32, *287–8*
professional secrecy and confidentiality 11.07
professionals rendering services *254*
professionals, retention and compensation of *264*
Protocol Agreement 4.03, 10.67, *271*
public funds, protection of 3.10
public scrutiny 8.26

Quebecor protocol (2008) 10.46

Rastelli case 6.05
recitals 5.13, 5.15, 6.09
Reflection Group on the Future of EU Company Law 2.04
Reserve Bank of Australia 11.17, 11.19
Reserve Bank of New Zealand (RBNZ) 11.19
resolution colleges
cooperation within 11.05–11.09
creation of 11.02, 11.06
functions of 11.07
'Resolution Professional' of India 7.38, 8.12, 10.51, *298*
resolving disputes, procedure for 4.38, 7.09, *238*, *267*
restructuring accountants *234–6*
Restructuring Directive 6.22
restructuring plan, implementation of 6.11, 6.22, 8.39, 10.05, 10.13
rights to appear and be heard 4.38, 8.10, *236*, *265*
right to a fair trial 8.08–8.10, 8.19
right to be heard 1.15, 4.27, 4.34, 8.07, 8.11
right to transfer 5.31, 10.06
Rome I Regulation (Rome I) 7.23, 7.30
Article 3(1) of 7.27
on equal treatment of insolvency practitioners 7.28
Russian insolvency proceedings 9.11

schuldeisersakkoord 303, *307*
SEC Proceedings *246–7*, *254–5*
SEC Receivers 10.16, *246*, *247*, *250–52*
Selling Debtors 7.13
Sendo International Limited 4.46, *270*
forced recovery of assets of *276*
insolvency of 7.22
means of treating
assets of French branch *275–8*
liabilities *270–75*
notification sent to the creditors of *270–72*
recovery of the assets of *276*
treatment of
claims lodged by creditors *272*
legal costs *274–5*
recovery of assets in time *275–8*
verification of claims made against
dual-verification obligation *273*
independence of the proceedings of *273*
Sendo protocol (2006) 7.22, 8.15, 10.52, *268–78*
on coordination between
and among the various proceedings *275–7*
main and secondary insolvency proceeding *268–9*
notice provisions 8.15
operating proceedings for the disposal of the assets *277–8*
separate legal personality, doctrine of 1.03–1.04, 5.18, 5.24, 5.30, 6.08, 6.16
service-oriented economy 2.15
services agreement, between IWG and IGS *243*
shares, corporate ownership of 2.01–2.02
single-debtor insolvency 4.28–4.29, 5.09, 5.41, 8.12, 10.64
single debtor insolvency 12.01
Legislative Guide on 5.20
Practice Guide on 5.12
Single Resolution Board (SRB) 11.03, 11.20
Single Resolution Mechanism Regulation (SRMR) 2.10, 11.03
soft law 1.06, 1.08, 3.01, 3.09, 3.21, 4.28, 4.49, 5.04, 6.22, 7.05, 7.40, 8.07, 9.12, 9.14, 10.72, 11.10
Solv-Ex protocol (1998) 10.09, 10.42
sovereign power 1.02
Spain 5.03, 9.19, 10.59

statement of intent 7.34, 10.07, 11.21, *280*, *300*
status of insolvent proceedings, determination of 8.37
stay of proceedings
  under Bankruptcy Code and the CCAA *237–8*
  against Canadian Debtors *237*
  Loewen Protocol *237–8*
  Pioneer Protocol *266*
  recognition of *237–8*, *266*
Subsidiary Guarantors *261*
sui generis protocols 4.08, 4.46, 5.15, 5.31
supply chains 10.02
  creation of 1.04
  global 1.04
Sweden 9.19
Syncreon Group BV 3.11
synthetic insolvency proceedings 5.29, 10.55

tax allowances 2.05
taxes
  capital gains tax (CGT) 10.24
  value-added tax (VAT) 10.24
taxpayer interests, protection of 11.19
Term Loan Agreement *261*
Tramiel, Jack 4.19
trans-border resolution, of insolvency disputes 4.24
transferred property, ownership of *285*
transnational bank resolution, rules for 11.10
transnational communication 6.22, 9.11
transnational cooperation, in insolvency cases 9.22
  obligations of 9.22
  Spanish law on 9.22
transnational insolvencies
  administration of 8.04, 9.09
  communication 9.21
  coordination and cooperation in 4.49
  management of 4.03
  regulation of 6.01
transparency
  of insolvency proceedings 12.01
  of public proceedings 8.16–8.29
trans-Tasman bank distress 11.19
Trans-Tasman Council on Banking Supervision (TTBC) 11.19
Trans-Tasman crisis resolution 11.19
Tribunals, communication among *281*, *284*, *295*
Trustee of the Proposal *224*

Uber (ride-hailing service) 2.15
ultra vires of a company 2.02
United Nations Commission on International Trade Law (UNCITRAL) 2.04
  cross-border insolvency cases 1.08
  Legislative Guide on Insolvency Law, Part III (2010) 1.08, 3.08, 3.21, 4.49, 5.17–5.24, 7.09
  Model Law on Cross-Border Insolvency (1997) *see* Model Law on Cross-Border Insolvency (1997)
  Model Law on Enterprise Group Insolvency (2019) 1.10, 1.12, 2.10, 3.12, 4.48–4.49
    Draft Guide to Enactment of 3.14
  Model Law on Insolvency-Related Judgments 7.08
  Practice Guide on Cross-Border Insolvency Cooperation (2009) 1.08, 4.04, 5.08, 5.11–5.16, 7.09, 7.24, 7.32, 9.07, 10.30, 13.06
  vision of international insolvencies 5.33
  Working Group V 3.01, 5.31
United States companies *242*, *243*
United States proceedings
  involuntary chapter 7 petitions against IGS and IWG *245*
  SEC enforcement action *246*
  section 304 proceedings *245*
  state court actions *245*
United States Securities & Exchange Commission (SEC) *246*
United States Trustee *214*, *236*, *237*, *258*, *265*
unsecured claims, classification and treatment of *223*
US Bankruptcy Proceedings *247*, *255*
US Exim Bank *304*

valuable assets
  protection of 10.05–10.12
    rights and duties related to 10.12
  value-destroying litigation 10.27
value-added tax (VAT) 10.24
Valukas Report 3.16
video conference communications 9.07
Videology Limited case 8.38
vis attractiva concursus, doctrine of 8.34–8.35, 10.44
voting rights 8.12, *310*
  of Debtor *203*

winding-up 6.01, 10.19
  arrangement, adoption of *276*
  plan, submission of *288–9*
  proceedings, effects of 8.35
World Bank 1.08
  World Bank Principles (2015) 3.09
World Trade Organization (WTO)
  establishment of 2.03

Yukos case 9.11

Zavodnik v. Slovenia 8.09